ONE MAN'S JUSTICE

ONE MAN'S JUSTICE

A Life in the Law

THOMAS R. BERGER

Douglas & McIntyre
VANCOUVER/TORONTO

University of Washington Press
SEATTLE

Douglas & McIntyre
2323 Quebec Street, Suite 201
Vancouver, British Columbia
V5T 4S7
www.douglas-mcintyre.com

NATIONAL LIBRARY OF CANADA CATALOGUING IN PUBLICATION DATA

Berger, Thomas R.
One man's justice
ISBN 1-55054-919-7

   1. Berger, Thomas R. 2. Judges–British Columbia–Biography.
3. Actions and defenses–Canada–Cases. I. Title.
KE416.B37A3 2002   340'.092   C2002-910876-4
KF373.B37A3 2002

Published in the United States of America
by the University of Washington Press,
PO Box 50096, Seattle, WA 98145-5096

LIBRARY OF CONGRESS CATALOGING-IN-PUBLICATION DATA

Berger, Thomas R.
One man's justice / by Thomas R. Berger.
   p. cm.
   Includes bibliographical references and index.
   ISBN 0-295-98276-4
   1. Berger, Thomas R. 2. Judges–British Columbia–Biography.
I. Title.
   KE416.B47 A36 2002
347.711'014'092–DC21

                          2002011942

Editing by Brian Scrivener
Cover and text design by Val Speidel
Cover photograph by Chick Rice
Printed and bound in Canada by Friesens on acid-free paper

The publisher gratefully acknowledges the financial support of the Canada Council for the Arts, the British Columbia Ministry of Tourism, Small Business and Culture, and the Government of Canada through the Book Publishing Industry Development Program (BPIDP) for its publishing activities.

Contents

Preface

I HOPE that this book is more than just one darned case after another; I prefer to think of it as the adventures of a lawyer.

The chapters in this book do lead more or less from one case to another, from one subject to another. Thus a lawyer's life, even his career, may seem well organized. But life is not like that. You may be working on one case when another erupts in crisis. You may be tearing from one courtroom to another. Tactical decisions, even strategic decisions, are made on the run, sometimes in the middle of a case because you are suddenly convinced there is only one way to win. Learning to trust your judgement is perhaps a lawyer's greatest asset.

I was called to the British Columbia bar in 1957. I've been practising law ever since, but not continuously. My career as a lawyer has been interrupted: I went briefly into politics in the 1960s; I became a judge of the Supreme Court of B.C. in 1971, where I remained for twelve years; and from time to time I've been away on commissions in the Mackenzie Valley, Alaska and even India. But always I made my way back into law practice.

When I was in high school I decided I wanted to be a teacher, a lawyer or a journalist. By the time I had spent a year or two at university, I had chosen law. All of these professions have one thing in common—they involve using language; they involve communicating ideas, speaking and writing. I've tried other things, but I've always returned to law.

In 1998, when my wife, Bev, and I moved out of our home of twenty-three years, I found the manuscript of a book I had started to write about my first fourteen years as a lawyer, before going on the bench. So I decided to write the second half of the book, about my second career as a lawyer, which began in earnest in 1985, on my return from Alaska.

Some of my early cases are as vivid in memory as the cases I have argued in recent years, even cases I did last month. I've never become jaded—weary, dispirited, furious, frustrated perhaps, but I've never lost my faith in the law. After every disappointment, I was soon eager to see the next client who might walk through the door. I've always believed in the cases and the causes I've served. Of course, I represented actual men and women, and sometimes children. You will meet some of them in this book.

Starting out, I worked for a small law firm for five years. The firm gave me a multitude of opportunities. I appeared in the Small Claims Court, the old Magistrate's Court, the County Court, the Supreme Court of B.C., the Court of Appeal for British Columbia, even the Supreme Court of Canada.

I also turned up at administrative tribunals. In my first year as a lawyer, I represented the Ding-Ho Drive-In before Vancouver's Board of Variance in an application to enlarge its Chinese food drive-in on 41st Avenue in Kerrisdale. The drive-in was the scene of a lot of noise and clatter as teenagers gathered every night, disturbing if not sometimes alarming the elderly residents who lived nearby. After a dozen of these folks had tottered to the witness stand, I said to the board, whose members were as venerable as the complainers—in fact, they included the legendary "Cyclone" Taylor, an old-time hockey great—"This has all the earmarks of a conspiracy against youth!"

Well, it could not have been my advocacy, but we won the case anyway.

In 1963 I opened my own law practice. When my first client, a man charged with impaired driving, came in, I had a desk but only one chair. How to handle the problem of the one chair? Where was the client to sit? Where was I to sit? I couldn't ask him to stand while I remained seated. On the other hand, it would seem peculiar if I remained on my feet throughout. I decided to move the chair to the other side of the desk, then I invited my client to sit down while I sat companionably on the corner of the desk, my hands folded in my lap, in an attitude of confidentiality. Perhaps he didn't notice the absence of furniture.

I started out in the criminal courts, defending drug addicts, traffickers, thieves, burglars and prostitutes. I represented miners who had contracted silicosis; after that, trade unions and their members in their battles with employers in B.C.'s tumultuous labour relations scene.

In the mid-1960s, I argued early cases dealing with Aboriginal rights, which led my career, unexpectedly, down a lengthy road. I had a small walk-up law office. I practised by myself and the rent was $120 a month. I had a secretary and my mother, Perle, acted as my bookkeeper. From that pocket-sized office, the land claims industry developed. It helped that I was young and tireless and not fully aware of all the obstacles that had to be surmounted. In 1971, on behalf of the Nisga'a Tribal Council, I argued *Calder v. British Columbia* before the

Supreme Court of Canada, asserting that Aboriginal rights had a distinct place in Canadian law. By the time the Supreme Court's judgement was handed down, I had been appointed to the bench. My years at the bar had come to an end. Or so I thought.

I served as a trial judge on the Supreme Court of British Columbia for twelve years. During that time, I headed three royal commissions. One of them, the Mackenzie Valley Pipeline Inquiry, made me famous in Canada for a time. My recommendations regarding the need to settle Native claims in the Mackenzie Valley and the Western Arctic confirmed my public persona as a champion of Aboriginal rights. But this notoriety was to lead in 1983 to my departure from the bench. When Canada's new Constitution and Charter of Rights was adopted, I publicly protested the abandonment of those provisions that recognized the rights of the Indians, the Inuit and the Metis. Those same provisions were restored, but I was chastised by Prime Minister Pierre Trudeau and by Bora Laskin, then chief justice of Canada. I left the bench and returned to law practice in Vancouver. That's where I am today.

I find my law practice as fascinating as ever. It has taken me often to the Supreme Court of Canada to argue what I think are some of the major cases of recent times.

I never truly made a specialty of any branch of the law except, perhaps, Aboriginal rights. But I always took on cases in many other areas of the law. The law is not a series of watertight compartments. What you learn in one field may turn out to be useful in an unrelated field; it can provide a new angle of vision. I started out in criminal law, then moved into labour law, defamation, personal injury, medical malpractice, Aboriginal rights, constitutional law and Charter cases. I didn't do these cases by myself. I had colleagues who worked with me, and I have thought it right to refer to them, because their contribution was indispensable.

This is not a legal tome. The cases I discuss here highlight the struggles of clients, many of them brave and determined individuals; of progress sometimes made in the cause of human rights and human dignity. When these cases were won or lost, many of them were of real legal significance, but the law has since moved forward or, in some cases, backward. The cases may still be milestones, but the path of the law rolls on.

The account I give is not complete. There were missteps along the way. Sometimes fortuitous accidents, lucky finds, enabled us to remain in the contest. Usually the cases described here involved a four- or five-year grind, often coming out right in the end, sometimes not. Compressed as they are in this book, they have a dramatic quality they may only have possessed for an instant.

Yet that instant can be electrifying—a series of questions to a witness; an argument that, as you utter it, takes on the tangible shape of success; the impossibly intense moment when a jury is about to render its verdict; or the vigil by the fax machine in Vancouver at 7:00 A.M. to find out what the Supreme Court of Canada, in the latest case you have argued before that court, has decided the same day. How will the years of work turn out? Will your client be vindicated, or will the cause you have urged be repudiated? The victories offer immense satisfaction. The defeats can be discouraging, disheartening, enervating, especially when you have to tell your client you've lost.

Like most lawyers, I've been retained by hundreds of clients; had hundreds of cases. So why write about the cases I've chosen to include in this book? Some of them may once have been important legal precedents; others had a demonstrable influence on public policy; still others possess a compelling human dimension. In sitting down to write about thirty years or more as an advocate, I realize that these cases loom large in my memory. They were cases that, through their planning, preparation as well as presentation, occupied my mind. They entailed a consideration of—indeed might perhaps move—public attitudes and the policies of governments. Or they may have vindicated the rights of an individual. They may also have been cases where I failed.

Throughout I was engaged in a search for justice. The law is the means by which we struggle towards an end—the achievement of justice. I didn't set out, at age twenty-four when I was called to the bar, to do these kinds of cases. But I was animated by a belief—and now it is a profound belief—that the law as enforced in the courts can move us incrementally towards a just society.

Sometimes that advance comes in the form of a case that materially alters the legal landscape.

Calder in 1973—in which the Supreme Court of Canada upheld the place of Aboriginal rights in Canadian law—was instrumental in bringing about a change in federal policy. That case led to treaty-making for more than twenty-five years, culminating in the Nisga'a treaty.

For Linda Macdonald, who was subjected to hideous brainwashing experiments at the Allan Memorial Institute in Montreal, the lawsuit we brought on her behalf resulted in the federal government adoption of a program to compensate many other victims of that institution. The outcome of a suit on behalf of a Guatemalan refugee was a court ruling requiring the province's Legal Services Society to pay for legal representation for thousands of refugees entering Canada through British Columbia.

It may be a case that affects the fortunes of one person only. For George

Jones, a public servant, I engaged in legal combat against the premier of B.C. The premier was held liable to pay damages for slander, demonstrating that ordinary citizens can obtain legal remedies against heads of government.

I have argued before the Supreme Court of Canada some of the abstrac questions beloved of law professors, which permeate the law of torts and determine whether a client is compensated. Sometimes I have represented the disabled and the vulnerable: a brain-damaged baby who had been aborted and abandoned; paraplegics; quadriplegics; mentally disabled women who had been unlawfully sterilized. But I did not always succeed.

I could provide a list of causes that failed. In the case of Dr. Jerilynn Prior, a Quaker, the Federal Court of Appeal rejected my argument that the use of any of her taxes for military purposes was a violation of her freedom of conscience. In the case of Trinity Western University, I failed to persuade the Supreme Court that homosexuals should receive the same measure of protection under the Charter of Rights as racial and religious minorities.

In some ways the greatest satisfaction may have come from saving a young man's career, or preserving an older man's chance for a new start, or travelling a legal labyrinth to obtain compensation for a little girl.

In all of these cases we were engaged in the pursuit of justice. But justice is an ever-receding objective on the legal horizon; lawyers struggle to reach that objective in any given case. I concede that in a great many instances I may have won or I may have lost, and the cause of justice wasn't advanced or retarded. In some cases, however, I feel that the cause of justice was measurably advanced.

Why have I spent my professional life doing the kind of cases I do? It is an impossible question to answer. I do remember something my father said when I was a boy. My father, Theodore (Ted), had emigrated from Sweden at twenty-two and joined the RCMP; he was not a man who espoused any particular political views. During the early years of the Second World War, Japanese Canadians were interned by the government of Canada solely on the grounds that they were of Japanese descent. Most of them were Canadian citizens, but they were taken from their homes, their property was seized, and they were interned in camps until long after the war was over. There was only one member of parliament— Angus MacInnis, a Vancouver MP who represented the CCF—who protested in the House of Commons against the treatment of the Japanese Canadians. At the time, this position did not make you popular in Vancouver, or in British Columbia, or even in Canada. I couldn't have been more than nine or ten years old but I remember my father saying that Mr. MacInnis was a courageous man. That stuck with me over the years.

We are all of us animated by a mixture of motives. I acknowledge that ambition has played its part in my career. And I have often been captivated by the professional challenge that these causes represented. But I hope it can be said about my work as a lawyer that the overriding impulse has been one of service; to help the people who believed they needed my help. And I think I've been able to live by that credo, in a bumpy sort of way.

1 "The Bitch"

Aᴀᴛᴇʀ ɪ ɢʀᴀᴅᴜᴀᴛᴇᴅ from law school at the University of
British Columbia, I articled with Shulman, Tupper, Southin and Gray, a small
Vancouver firm of five lawyers. My first day on the job I arrived at the office much
too early and waited in the corridor until the members of the staff arrived. It was
an ordinary office, but it was to me a place infused with glamour.

On that first day the lawyers in the firm took me for coffee. Isaac ("Ike")
Shulman was the dynamic head of the firm; Harold Tupper was its quiet conscience; Mary Southin, a first-class scholar and advocate, would go on to become a
judge of the Court of Appeal; Les Gray specialized in commercial law. Bill Worrall,
a recently called gold medallist at UBC law school, had just joined the firm.

We were seated around a table in the coffee shop when Tom Hurley joined
us. Tom was in his seventies. Born in Ireland, he had made his way to Canada,
and by 1957 he was the dean of Vancouver's criminal bar. He always wore a suit
and vest, even if they could have used a visit to the dry cleaner's. *Coffin*, a famous
Quebec murder case, had just been decided by the Supreme Court of Canada.
Everyone was talking at once, offering opinions. When Tom joined us, Ike
Shulman introduced me as the new kid on the block, and then asked Tom what
he thought of the decision in *Coffin*. Tom had a slight air of reserve but was
always courteous. He expressed a cautious opinion, and then, to my astonish-
ment, he turned to me and said, "What do you think, Mr. Berger?" I can't remember what my answer was, but what struck me was his genuine interest in my
opinion, even though it was my first day as an articled student.

As an articled student or clerk I earned $100 a month. When I was called to
the bar I earned $300 a month. But the firm of Shulman, Tupper, Southin and
Gray offered me an abundance of opportunities. Ike Shulman, only forty, had a
burgeoning criminal law practice. For his clients I conducted preliminary hearings in the Magistrate's Court (now the Provincial Court). Even before I was
called to the bar, I started to do criminal trials in the Magistrate's Court.

In my first jury trial I represented a young taxi driver charged with stealing $200 from an elderly tourist who had hired him for the day to show him Vancouver. I had been less than a year at the bar, so Harold Tupper, who had been almost a decade at the bar, volunteered to be my junior. This offer was— even in those days—generous. But it was typical of Harold. With Harold at my side, helping me to navigate the shoals of cross-examination, I brought my client safely into harbour.

Ike Shulman arranged for me to act in his stead as junior counsel for the prosecution at the Vancouver Assizes, a two-month assignment. In those days senior lawyers would take two months off to prosecute at the Assizes. The prosecution work is now done by full-time salaried prosecutors. Arthur Harper, a litigator of great experience, was senior counsel for the prosecution. He allowed me to conduct many of the trials. Together we conducted sixteen jury trials. It was invaluable experience for someone little more than a year at the bar.

In my second year at the bar, Ike was asked by a client named Ronnie Fontaine to defend him on a murder charge. Ike and I went down to the Vancouver City Jail to see Fontaine after his arrest. Ike persuaded him that I should conduct his defence. Fontaine, a veteran thug, was charged with hiring his co-accused to burn down a hotel to do away with one of the tenants living there. Fontaine was not by any means likely to attract sympathy, but he was entitled to the presumption of innocence. The main witnesses against him were a young man and woman in their twenties, who already had lengthy criminal records. I recall that, doing my best to discredit them, I told the jury, "They are young, but their lives are steeped in crime." Fontaine was acquitted.

Defence of a murder case in those days was uncommonly stressful because your client could be hanged if convicted. Most death sentences were commuted to life imprisonment by Prime Minister John Diefenbaker's government, but the last execution in Canada took place in 1962 and capital punishment in Canada was not abolished until 1976. The verdict in Ronnie Fontaine's case was an intense relief. I took the next day off and spent it roaming the bookstores in downtown Vancouver.

Early on I went to the Court of Appeal for a teenager, Margaret Hall, convicted of possession of drugs. Seventeen-year-old Margaret was in a hotel room with a nineteen-year-old girl, who was about to shoot up. When "the door came down" and the police entered, the other girl tossed her needle and eyedropper into Margaret's lap. Margaret immediately threw the paraphernalia out the window. The case came down to a law school question: Was Margaret in possession of heroin? The magistrate found Margaret guilty on the ground that she had knowledge and possession—that she knew it was heroin was obvious because

she had chucked the needle and eyedropper out the window; she had possession, if only briefly.

In the Court of Appeal, I argued that Margaret was not in possession. The
court, in overturning her conviction, held that for there to be possession there
had to be control, and control did not include "a casual or hasty manual han-
dling, not consistent with one's own purposes or use for a 'fix.' "

But my earliest appearances in the courts were also accompanied by missteps.
The first time I cross-examined an RCMP officer in a drug case, I was so nervous
that my knees rattled as I sat at the counsel table; if they had bounced any closer
to the bottom of the table I might have appeared to be conducting a seance.

My opponent in most of the drug cases was Wilfred Heffernan, a senior
member of the bar appointed by the federal government to prosecute all cases
under the Narcotic Control Act. He seemed nettled whenever I was successful.
He seemed to think it was a failure of justice whenever an accused person was
acquitted.

The crime of possession had a number of variants. There was, under the
Narcotic Control Act, which came into force in 1961, the crime known as possession; there was also a crime known as possession for the purpose of trafficking.
In the latter type of case, a hearing would determine whether the accused was
guilty of possession; if the court found him guilty of possession, there would be
a further hearing to determine whether he had possession of drugs for his own
use or for the purpose of trafficking. I appeared in one case for a client who was
plainly in possession of heroin; the only issue would be whether he intended to
sell any of the drugs—that would be trafficking. I wanted to get to the main issue,
so I had my client plead guilty to what I thought was merely the charge of possession. I didn't appreciate that once he had done so, he would be treated as having plead guilty to possession for the purpose of trafficking as well as simple
possession. Almost as soon as my client had made his plea, I realized my mistake. Oscar Orr, Vancouver's senior magistrate, was presiding. I at once told him
I wanted the court to allow my client to withdraw his plea of guilty and to substi-
tute a plea of not guilty. I told him I had made a mistake. My client shouldn't face
the consequences of my inadvertence.

The magistrate turned to Wilfred Heffernan, merely as a formality. There
could be no question but the court would allow a change of plea. Ordinarily,
Heffernan would be expected to say "No objection." Instead, he said, "Mr. Berger
should know we're not running a law school here." (I suppose I was no more than
a year at the bar.) Magistrate Orr said, "Mr. Heffernan, counsel has said he made a
mistake. I am going to allow a change of plea. But I think you should apologize for
your remark. You have no right to insult counsel." Heffernan mumbled inaudibly.

Orr said, "You will apologize." More mumbling. Orr said, "Very well, I can't make you apologize. Let's get on with the case."

I don't recall how the case turned out. Wilf Heffernan did phone me at home that evening and offered an apology. But it was a useful lesson. If you're in the wrong, take your medicine at once; you'll feel the better for it.

I had a run of success in jury cases. In one, I was able to use my developing expertise in the law of possession to good effect. My client, Bruce Abbey, a pre-med student at UBC, had been charged with possession of marijuana. A matter, you may say, of little consequence. But in the 1960s, the use of marijuana was new in Canada, and judges, determined to prevent its use from becoming widespread, were imposing sentences of six months' imprisonment for mere possession. For Bruce to enter his chosen profession of medicine, we had to obtain an acquittal.

Bruce had unwisely agreed to permit a friend named Hawkins to mail him envelopes containing marijuana at his address at Robson Hall, a student residence at UBC. Bruce was to hold the letters for Hawkins. Bruce passed on to him the first three letters that arrived. More had arrived by the time of Bruce's arrest. The police found envelopes, ten in all, in Bruce's mailbox and, what was worse, more of them in his briefcase.

The police claimed that the envelopes were bulging with sufficient marijuana to make 450 joints. Bruce had never opened the envelopes. But he admitted to the police he had been told that the envelopes contained marijuana.

The consequences of a guilty finding were so appalling we had to obtain an acquittal. I advised Bruce to choose trial by jury. It was in truth a case of possession. Nevertheless, I relied on Margaret Hall's case. Hadn't the Court of Appeal in that case said that there was no possession or control unless you had it for "[your] own purposes or use for a 'fix' "? I told the judge in advance that I wanted to argue before the jury members that they could find there had been no possession. Justice Angelo Branca, who had been an outstanding criminal lawyer, understood the nuances of the law of possession. He allowed me to make the argument and did not, in his charge to jury members, tell them that they could not acquit on the basis of my argument. This was essential. After the closing speeches of counsel, the judge gives the jury his "charge," a summing up of the law and the evidence. In a jury trial, the jury is bound to apply the law as given by the judge.

I told jury members that to find Bruce guilty of possession, they had to find that Bruce had not only control of the drugs but also the intention to keep the drugs for his own purposes, for his own use. I pointed out that Bruce had received no money for allowing Hawkins to use the mail drop. He had never smoked marijuana; never even (as the police conceded) opened the envelopes.

True, he had received the envelopes in the mail and kept them for Hawkins, but that was for Hawkins's purposes, not Bruce's.

We called character witnesses who told the jury that Bruce had an unblemished record of achievement and community service. In a criminal case you can call witnesses as to character, which allows you to argue before the jury that your client is not the kind of person who would commit the crime in question. I did a great many jury cases, and I always used character evidence whenever I had a client with no previous criminal record. In such cases, I found that juries are often willing to give an accused a second chance.

The jury was out a long time. Bruce's mother, Irene, devoted to her son, told me that if Bruce were sent to prison, she was going with him. But the jury members were not willing to destroy a young man's life and career. They brought in a verdict of not guilty. Bruce was able to go to medical school and become a doctor.

Wilf Heffernan was the prosecutor in Bruce Abbey's case. After the trial was over, I received a letter from Bruce. On the second day of the trial, after court had adjourned, he had run into Heffernan on the street. According to Bruce, Heffernan said to him, "Between you and me and the gatepost, it would have been better if you had just pleaded guilty. Then we wouldn't have to go through this ordeal." When Bruce wrote to tell me of the encounter, I wrote back, saying about Wilf: "It is his firm belief that everybody who is charged with anything anytime, anywhere, should plead guilty. Otherwise, how can law and order be preserved?"

Very early on I went to the Supreme Court of Canada. It was in 1958, my second year at the bar, on an application for leave to appeal in an arson case. Three of the nine judges of the court would sit to hear applications for leave. I appeared before Chief Justice Patrick Kerwin and two of his colleagues. I had arrived in Ottawa two days before to review the law. In those days before photocopying, you had to get the volumes of the law reports containing the cases you intended to rely on out of the library, bring them to the courtroom on a trolley, and line them up on the counsel table. I must have had twenty or thirty volumes lined up, stretching from the lectern into the middle distance. W.R. ("Bill") Burke-Robertson, a prominent Ottawa lawyer, who appeared for the attorney general of B.C. in opposition to my motion, brought only one volume, the Criminal Code. An austere rebuke.

Chief Justice Patrick Kerwin said, "Mr. Berger, you're not going to read all those cases to us, are you?" I don't remember my reply. But it was not a good start. Nor a good finish. I did not get leave to appeal.

After I began to take on my share of criminal cases, Tom Hurley became my mentor in criminal law. We didn't look up any law, because his law library was in the same condition as his clothing—not altogether tidy. Instead, at his suggestion, we would adjourn to a beer parlour. Tom was a man who liked a drink. At the beer parlour, we talked about my cases. He would listen, then say, "Be sure to ask such and such a question" or "The key to the case may well be such and such." No one could interrupt us with messages or telephone calls, though one of the other patrons might turn out to be an old client of Tom's and would send beer over to our table.

Tom shared office space with his wife, Maisie. She had become a champion of the Indian people of the province; she started the *Native Voice,* a publication of the Native Brotherhood of B.C. devoted to their cause. Maisie would go to band meetings to offer her husband's services for those in trouble with the law. Between Tom's office and Maisie's, a secretary sat at a desk, behind a counter that stood near the door. Tom and I were making a quiet departure from his office for the beer parlour one day when Maisie emerged from her office. She was tall, dressed in black, wearing black beads and black horn-rimmed glasses, hair dyed black, a majestic, forbidding figure. In her right hand she held a black cane. She said, "Tom Hurley, where do you think you're going?"

"Just off for a conference with Mr. Berger."

"No, you're not! I know you're headed to the beer parlour."

"How can you say such a thing, my love?" Tom looked at me, as if I ought to say something useful, but I kept retreating towards the door. As we reached the door, Maisie brought her stick down against the counter with a crack. She cried, "Come back, you dreadful man." Tom murmured, "Be back in a moment, my love." When we had scuttled down the hallway, into the elevator and the doors had closed behind us, Tom took out his handkerchief and touched his forehead with it. Then he turned to me, "Didn't I tell her?"

In 1963 Tom and I took on a case in which we invoked John Diefenbaker's Canadian Bill of Rights, passed in 1960. The Bill was a precursor of Pierre Trudeau's Charter of Rights, enacted twenty-two years later. There was a direct line of descent. If Trudeau was the father of the Charter of Rights, Diefenbaker was its grandfather. His Bill of Rights applied only to federal legislation and was not constitutionally entrenched, so the courts were not inclined to treat it as anything more than a guide to interpretation of statutes. But it did get the legal profession used to the idea of cataloguing human rights and fundamental freedoms. In this it laid the groundwork for the Charter.

Our client was an Indian named Gonzales. He had been convicted of possession of liquor off the reserve, which for Indians was at that time prohibited by the Indian Act. We relied on section 1(b) of the Canadian Bill of Rights, which declared "the right of the individual to equality before the law . . . without discrimination by reason of race, national origin, colour, religion or sex . . ." Our argument would be that section 94(a) of the Indian Act, because it applied to Indians and no one else (for example, a white person in possession of liquor off a reserve committed no crime), constituted discrimination by reason of race.

On the morning of the Court of Appeal hearing, before we went into court, Tom met me in the barristers' room, and he said he was ill and could not argue the case himself. Would I be able to do it on my own? It was a poignant moment. I think Tom realized his career was over. I did argue the case on my own, and I lost it. The Court of Appeal held that equality before the law meant no more than that all persons to whom section 94(a) applied should be treated equally; that is, if the law applied to Indians and no one else, all you had to do was make sure it applied to every Indian. This stunted definition of equality was rejected by the Supreme Court of Canada in 1970 in a Northwest Territories case called *Drybones*, the only case in which the Canadian Bill of Rights was used to strike down a provision of a statute. Maisie was furious with me, not for losing the case but for giving in—she thought too easily—to Tom's urging that I carry on in his stead. She didn't want him to give up his place at the bar, even if it was a diminished place. He died within a few months.

I USED TO GO to Oakalla Prison Farm in Burnaby each Saturday to see clients. Oakalla Prison Farm was not really a farm but a provincial institution (now the Lower Mainland Regional Correctional Centre) where accused persons on remand and convicted persons serving sentences of less than two years were held. Keys turned, doors clanged, and clients were brought to an interview room. For the most part, they had been in prison often. In the criminal courts, you become used to the fact that often the same people are convicted, go to prison, are released, and then commit further crimes. Isn't there a better approach? Why can't we simply put these people away for good?

We tried that once.

Prosecutions against habitual criminals began in 1947 in Canada. In that year Parliament passed legislation that gave the courts, in any case where a person had been convicted of an indictable offence, the power to declare him to be a habitual criminal if he had already been convicted since turning eighteen, on three seperate occasions, of an offence for which he could be sentenced to at least five years in prison (covering a list of crimes from theft to murder) and if he had been leading persistently a criminal life. In effect, on a fourth conviction, such a person could be proceeded against as a habitual criminal. It wasn't three strikes and you're out, but four strikes and you're out. Anyone found to be a habitual criminal could be sentenced to preventive detention, which meant imprisonment for life.

Until the 1960s, there were not many prosecutions against habitual criminals in Canada. In 1963, however, Stewart McMorran, Vancouver's city prosecutor, launched a series of prosecutions against alleged habitual criminals. The net was cast wide, and anyone who had been before the courts many times was in danger. If you were charged and prosecuted to conviction, and had the requisite three previous convictions, you might well be proceeded against as a habitual criminal. Those who were liable to find themselves targeted called it "The Bitch." Stewart McMorran was using "The Bitch" to clean up the city of offenders who were regularly caught and sentenced but then, having served their sentences, were on the street again. The idea was to catch persistent offenders and send them to prison for the rest of their lives.

These provisions of the Criminal Code were a startling departure from established concepts of criminal justice. We had never before in Canada allowed a man to be charged except for a specific crime such as fraud or theft or murder. But where a man was found to be a habitual criminal, he could be sentenced, not because he had committed a specific crime, but because he had committed certain crimes in the past—crimes for which he had already served his time—and because he was "leading persistently a criminal life."

Well, what's wrong with that? If you're persisting in a criminal life, you must be committing crimes all along the way. Ordinarily, the only way of punishing you for such crimes would be to lay a charge and prove each of them. But with "The Bitch" you didn't have to do that. No crimes, except the four crimes that had brought you before the courts, needed to be proved. As for "leading persistently a criminal life," the concept was elastic.

Normally the proof that a person was leading persistently a criminal life consisted of evidence relating to the manner in which the fourth offence was committed. The offence might have entailed planning, organizing, collaborating with others; that is, some indication a person was deeply involved in crime. At other times, however, proof that someone was leading persistently a criminal life might take the form of evidence that he had been seen in company with drug addicts or other persons involved in criminal activity. In other words, a person could be convicted by the company that he was keeping—guilt by association.

Then there was the matter of sentencing. Not all habitual criminals would be sentenced to life imprisonment. There was a further test. Even if he was a habitual criminal, was it "expedient for the protection of the public" to sentence him to preventive detention? If the sentence was passed, it was not five years or ten years or fifteen years. It was "preventive detention": anyone found to be a habitual criminal would spend the rest of life in prison—a lifer—unless released by the National Parole Board.

Even on parole, such a person remained branded as a habitual criminal and could be deprived of liberty at the discretion of the board. The habitual criminal legislation was repealed in 1977. We now have a dangerous offender law on the books; "dangerous offenders" can be sentenced to the penitentiary for an indeterminate period, but it must be shown they have a demonstrated capacity for violence.

Throughout the 1960s, I represented many of those proceeded against as habitual criminals.

At the request of the John Howard Society, a prisoners' aid organization, I used to go once a month to the B.C. Penitentiary in New Westminster to conduct a clinic. On one of these Saturday clinics I saw George Paton, who had been found to be a habitual criminal in 1956.

Paton had been convicted in 1946 of breaking and entering and sentenced to five years' imprisonment. In 1953, he was convicted of breaking and entering and stealing $1000, for which he was again sentenced to five years' imprisonment. In 1956 he was convicted twice, once at Vancouver and later at Kelowna. Both were cases of breaking and entering. In Vancouver he stole some cash and share certificates. While out on bail he went to Kelowna and stole $14,000 from a safe. By the time he was tried in Kelowna on the charge of breaking and entering, he had already been convicted and sentenced in Vancouver to five years' imprisonment for stealing the cash and share certificates. That meant that he had three previous convictions. When he was again convicted in Kelowna, he could be proceeded against as a habitual criminal, for that was a fourth conviction.

In Kelowna the judge held that Paton was a habitual criminal and sentenced him to eight years' imprisonment for safecracking and to preventive detention as a habitual criminal.

Paton appealed to the Court of Appeal for British Columbia. The court decided that the judge's decision should stand.

On the face of it, Paton was a perfect candidate for "The Bitch." He was a burglar whose crimes required planning and a certain steadfastness or single-mindedness. It is not surprising that the court found that he was leading persistently a criminal life, and that it was expedient for the protection of the public to put him away.

Once the Court of Appeal had decided against him, the Supreme Court of Canada was the only court to which Paton could appeal. But to do so, he had to obtain leave from the Supreme Court. On October 28, 1957, Paton applied to the Supreme Court for leave, but the application was denied.

Paton spent ten years trying to get his case before the courts again. Like hundreds of inmates in our penitentiaries, he devoted much of his time to drawing up petitions, motions and appeals. He sent these off in all directions: to members of parliament, to lawyers, to judges. None of these applications advanced his case; all were rejected.

Paton's applications were usually written by hand, difficult to read and often unintelligible. Even if he did obtain access to a typewriter and manage to type out his application or had another inmate at the penitentiary type it for him, his line of argument was difficult to follow. He cited precedent upon precedent, he invented numerous legal propositions, and he made all kinds of assertions about his case that had never been proved. But no court would consider reopening his case. He could not bring another appeal, because the Court of Appeal had already dismissed his appeal and the Supreme Court of Canada had refused to grant leave to appeal.

Paton's appeal to the Court of Appeal and his motion to the Supreme Court for leave had been dismissed in 1957. Yet, in 1967, a decade afterward, I argued Paton's case in the Supreme Court of Canada. He may have been leading persistently a criminal life, but he showed the same persistence in getting his case before the courts again.

Paton had filed innumerable motions for habeas corpus. These were futile, because in Canada the courts will not grant habeas corpus to a man who has been sentenced to prison by a court with jurisdiction to try and sentence him (that is, a court of competent jurisdiction) and where the warrant under which he is held is valid. When a judge sentences a man to prison, the judge signs a warrant of committal, which is the warden's authority for holding the prisoner when he is brought from the courtroom to the prison gates. If there has been a mistake in drawing up the warrant, a man can apply for habeas corpus, and it may be granted, because it can be argued that the warden has no legal authority to keep him in prison. But if there has been no mistake in drawing up the warrant of committal, you cannot go behind the warrant of committal.

So when judges hear an application for habeas corpus, they simply look at the warrant of committal, and if it is a warrant authorized by a court with jurisdiction to try the accused, the judges will go no further. They will not hold a new hearing and go into the evidence. They will not even consider points of law. There is no machinery in our legal system for getting a case back into court once the trial is over and the appeals have been heard. In the United States, a man convicted in a state court who has exhausted his appeals may still go before a federal judge to seek habeas corpus. Nothing like that exists in Canada. Here you can spend months, even years, examining the evidence and looking up the law, but if the warrant is not defective, you will not be able to find a judge who will be prepared to listen to your argument.

I saw Paton at the B.C. Penitentiary in New Westminster. Anyone sentenced to two years or more was liable to imprisonment in the "Pen," a federal institution. There were guards with rifles on the exterior walls of the institution, and iron gates had to be locked and unlocked as you passed into the visiting area. An office was made available for our interview. Paton, a man in his forties and, not surprisingly, inclined to view the world with a suspicious eye, was nevertheless businesslike in the manner of many inmates. His papers were voluminous. He gave me copies of the applications he had filed with the courts since 1957. He gave me innumerable legal citations. I took the papers away to see if there was anything that could be done. While I considered the matter, Paton sent me long letters from the penitentiary about his case. He continued filing motions in the courts, and the courts kept turning him down.

But I did find something. Or, I should say, Paton had found something. It should have been obvious from the beginning, but it had not occurred to anyone except Paton. His point, almost lost in the jumble of words that he had written, was this: True, he had been convicted three times before his fourth offence at Kelowna, but he had never served his sentence on the third conviction. He had been sentenced in Vancouver on October 23, 1956, to five years' imprisonment for stealing cash and share certificates. That was the sentence he received on his third conviction. On December 11, 1956, he was tried and convicted on the charge of breaking and entering at Kelowna, and the hearing to determine whether he was a habitual criminal was held the day after, on December 12, 1956.

Paton's point was that he should have been given a chance to serve his five-year sentence for the third conviction; he should only have been proceeded against as a habitual criminal if he had actually served his sentence and then been convicted *after that* of a fourth offence. But, he claimed, the hearing at Kelowna to determine whether he was a habitual criminal had been held before he had served his sentence on the third count. It may be that if he'd served his five-year sentence on the third conviction at Vancouver, he would have learned his lesson. Perhaps not. The point is that the legislation was intended to apply to those who *persisted* in crime, those for whom the ordinary sanctions of the criminal law were no deterrent to crime. But the sanctions of the criminal law had to be given a chance to work. In Paton's case, he was certainly persisting in crime, but would he have continued to persist even after serving the five years imposed at Vancouver on his third conviction? The law should have adopted a "wait and see" approach instead of rushing in, following Paton's fourth conviction, to find him to be a habitual criminal before he had served his sentence on his third conviction.

The argument had to be this: For Paton to be deemed a habitual criminal, it had to be shown that his previous sentences had not deterred him. How could he have been deterred or not deterred by a sentence—his third—he still hadn't served? The proceeding was premature.

One obstacle remained: How could Paton's case be got before the courts? I considered habeas corpus. But how could we get a judge to listen to an application for habeas corpus? Paton had been tried many years before. The judge at Kelowna had issued a warrant of committal, authorizing the warden at the B.C. Penitentiary to hold him in custody as a habitual criminal. The Court of Appeal had rejected his appeal. The Supreme Court of Canada had refused to consider the case.

I decided to go to the minister of justice. Under Canada's Criminal Code, the minister of justice has the power to send a case back to the Court of Appeal of any province for a rehearing. This was the obvious thing to do in Paton's case. We had raised a point of law of great importance to the case. We had no means of getting the case back into the courts. We asked Lucien Cardin, then minister of justice, to make an order for a rehearing. Only in this way could Paton's case be reopened.

In my submission to Mr. Cardin I argued that preventive detention should only be imposed when a man had shown that the sentences imposed on him had not altered his pattern of criminal behaviour. In Paton's case, we had no way of knowing whether the cumulative weight of the sentences imposed on him would have had any effect on him. The first time he was sentenced, it had no effect. The second time he was sentenced, it had no effect. But we had no way of telling whether the sentence imposed on him for the third conviction had done any good, because he had never had an opportunity to serve that sentence. It was not as if Paton had served the five years, been released, and then committed the fourth offence. At a time when he had only begun to serve his third sentence of five years, he was, before two months were out, convicted a fourth time and sentenced as a habitual criminal.

Cardin referred my submission to the National Parole Board. The chairman of the board, Frank Miller, replied on behalf of the minister. Miller conceded that a "strong argument can be put forward to show that it was never intended by Parliament that a man should be sentenced to preventive detention when the sentences imposed on him in connection with his previous convictions had not yet been served." But, he said, even though the Crown had brought forward only three previous convictions at the hearing in Kelowna, there were four other previous convictions against Paton, for which a sentence of five years' imprisonment could be imposed, and Paton had served these sentences. Because, Miller said, any of these could have been used against him, there was no justification for referring the case back to the Court of Appeal.

I objected strenuously to these convictions being brought up. They had never been raised at the hearing in Kelowna; it amounted to moving the goalposts after the contest was over. I wrote to Miller:

The Board has gone completely outside the charges against Paton, completely outside the evidence against him, and has brought up for the first time four prior convictions and sentences. This is quite extraordinary . . .

The Crown adduced evidence of three previous convictions—it may be it could have adduced proof of the convictions referred to in your letter, but it elected not to do so—and the case must be judged on the basis of the proof brought forward by the Crown at the time. There is absolutely no warrant for the National Parole Board seeking at this late date to change the whole footing on which this case was conducted.

When you are tried, the Crown puts all its evidence before the court. That's the case you have to meet. The Crown can't come along after the trial is over and say, "Well, there was other evidence we could have called, but it didn't seem necessary at the time so we didn't use it." If the Crown had used it, the accused might have been able to answer it.

Frank Miller wrote from a bureaucratic point of view: the evidence of these other previous convictions, for which Paton had served in each case the complete sentence, was there. What could it possibly matter that they hadn't been laid before the court?

It was, however, more than a technicality. Had Paton been found to be a habitual criminal according to law? That was the question; not, if the Crown had called evidence it didn't call, would that evidence have supported a finding that Paton was a habitual criminal?

I believe it is a mistake to take the expedient approach in such matters. If you do, you can easily move to the next stage: "Oh, we had a witness we didn't call, but if we had it would have filled the gaps in the Crown's case." Or: "It may now be apparent that a Crown witness misled the court, but we all know your client is guilty." The minister of justice and the Parole Board remained unmoved.

I felt we had reached the end of the road. But not Paton. Undaunted, he kept filing motions in the courts. One of these, an application for habeas corpus, he sent to the Supreme Court of Canada early in 1967.

An application to the Supreme Court for habeas corpus is heard by a single judge of the court. On April 4, 1967, Paton's papers came before Justice Wilfred Judson. Justice Judson dismissed Paton's application, because the warrant of committal was valid and had been issued by a court of competent jurisdiction. The Supreme Court of Canada Act at the time provided that in the case of such a ruling an appeal could be taken to the court itself. The registrar of the Supreme Court of Canada sent a telegram to Paton, advising him that he could appeal Justice Judson's decision to the court if he wanted to. This advice was, of course, a routine courtesy extended by the court to prisoners who might not know they had a right of appeal.

Paton, however, was ecstatic when he received his telegram. He telephoned and asked me to make a submission to the Supreme Court. He felt that the gates of justice had opened for him. I was not as sure. I felt that the Supreme Court of Canada would have no choice except to uphold Justice Judson. We had no grounds on which to appeal the refusal to grant habeas corpus. We were still confronted by a warrant that was perfectly valid and issued by a court of competent jurisdiction.

Nevertheless I sent a telegram to the Supreme Court of Canada saying that Paton had retained me to make representations on his behalf. Then I sent a written submission to the court. I had no basis for saying that habeas corpus should be granted, but I felt that I might as well urge upon the court the argument that Paton should never have been sentenced to preventive detention, because he had never been given an opportunity to serve the five-year sentence imposed on him for his third conviction.

On June 17, 1967, Paton's appeal from the refusal of habeas corpus came before a panel of five members of the Supreme Court. I could not be there. My client had no funds to get me there. I confess I thought it would be a pro forma hearing. The court had my written submission before it. Bill Burke-Robertson appeared for the Crown. He asked the court to dismiss the appeal, because there was no basis for granting habeas corpus. Burke-Robertson phoned me to tell me what had happened.

When the hearing began, Chief Justice John Cartwright told Burke-Robertson the court agreed that habeas corpus could not be granted. But, said the chief justice, what about the argument I had raised in my written submission? Burke-Robertson agreed that it was an interesting argument, and an important one, but the court could not consider it on an application for habeas corpus. The chief justice then suggested that the court should treat the appeal from Justice Judson's decision as if it were an application for leave to appeal from the judgement of the Court of Appeal handed down in 1957. Such appeals had to be brought within thirty days. Burke-Robertson pointed out that this appeal would require an unprecedented extension of time, ten years in fact. Moreover, he pointed out, the court had refused ten years earlier to consider the appeal. How could it do so now? Chief Justice Cartwright pointed out that the argument I had raised had not been considered by the court when Paton applied for leave to appeal in 1957.

Therefore, the chief justice said, the Supreme Court had decided to grant leave to appeal to Paton. He added that the court was of the view that the attorney general of British Columbia should pay my fees and expenses to enable me to come to Ottawa to argue Paton's appeal.

This was the first time that the Supreme Court of Canada had ever agreed to hear an appeal ten years after the decision had been handed down in the lower court. It was also the first time that the Supreme Court of Canada had ever agreed to hear an appeal in a criminal case after it had already once before refused leave to appeal in the same case.

In those days the judges of the Supreme Court of Canada were unknown, or barely known, to the public. If in recent years we have established a judicial pantheon, Chief Justice Cartwright belongs there. He spoke softly and had an ascetic appearance, but in his quiet way he expressed his firm belief in fairness for accused persons in criminal cases.

On October 10, 1967, all nine judges of the court assembled to hear Paton's case. At the outset, Justice Gerald Fauteux asked, "How did this case get here?" He had not been on the panel that had granted leave. I told him. He seemed skeptical. I went through the argument again: Parliament intended that the legislation should apply to the case of a man who had been convicted on three occasions and then, after serving his sentence on the third occasion and being released from imprisonment, persisted in a life of crime. A man had to be given an opportunity to respond to the punishment imposed for the three previous convictions before he could be proceeded against as a habitual criminal. He didn't have to serve his sentence on the fourth conviction; that conviction only served as a trigger. But he did have to serve his sentence on the first, second and third convictions. If he relapsed into crime after that, he was fair game. But until it could be determined whether incarceration had worked, how could it be said that he was persisting in a criminal life?

During my argument, Justice Fauteux asked me a question. Before I could answer, Justice Emmett Hall said, "I suppose, Mr. Berger, your answer would be such and such." Justice Fauteux at once spoke: "I do not want to be interrupted when I am asking questions." Justice Hall responded, "I'm entitled to ask questions too." I looked at Chief Justice Cartwright. He simply raised one eyebrow; I took it as an indication that I should proceed. It was apparent the judges were already choosing sides.

On March 13, 1968, the Supreme Court of Canada handed down its decision in Paton's case. Chief Justice Cartwright agreed with the argument that we had put forward. He said, "Parliament intended the extraordinary sentence of preventive detention to be imposed only after it appeared that convictions on three separate and independent occasions had failed to deter the accused from committing the substantive offence." He pointed out that if the legislation were given a literal interpretation, it would mean that a man on separate days during the same month might break into four different houses. If he were apprehended on the fourth occasion, and then was separately indicted and convicted for each of the first three offences, he could be sentenced to preventive detention once he had been convicted the fourth time.

The chief justice went on to say:

The number of previous convictions chosen by Parliament as a condition precedent to the holding of an enquiry as to whether a person is an habitual criminal is three. Those convictions bring home to the convicted person on three separate occasions the knowledge of guilt *and the punishment* which it entails. It is the fact that he, thereafter, with such knowledge, commits yet another indictable offence that Parliament has declared shall be a condition precedent to the enquiry as to whether he shall be sentenced to preventive detention. [emphasis added]

The chief justice was looking beyond the letter of the law to the spirit of the law. Parliament had not actually said anything about waiting to see if deterrence worked, but that must have been the intention.

Three other judges agreed with the chief justice. The majority did not. We lost, five to four.

Justice Judson, writing for the five judges in the majority, said: "The habitual criminal is not imprisoned for doing something, but rather for being something." He held that three previous convictions meant three previous convictions, and nothing more. If a man had three previous convictions, it did not matter whether he had served the sentences imposed by the courts. The fact that he had been convicted was enough. Justice Judson concluded: "The serving of the sentence is not one of the conditions that must be met in order to establish that a person is an habitual criminal." This was a literal reading of the statute. Chief Justice Cartwright interpreted the statute on the basis of what he understood to be the intention of Parliament. Justice Judson confined himself to the bare words of the statute itself. Did the statute say anything about deterrence? No. That was as far as he had to go to uphold the finding against Paton.

Paton had come near to securing his freedom, falling only one judge short.

In 1977 Parliament repealed the habitual criminal legislation and substituted the provision relating to dangerous offenders. This change raised the question: What about the men who were still serving life sentences under legislation now repealed? There were 102 of them, forty-seven from B.C. Thirty-two of the 102 were still in prison, the remainder on parole. Over time all of them were released. Paton was one of the last to be released. He continued to dispatch letters, motions, appeals to the courts, none of them successful, until he finally gained release in 1984.

George Paton was a burglar and a safecracker. But the net that Stewart McMorran cast had also caught petty criminals. One such was Johnny Hadden, who in 1963 was found guilty of stealing a $2.99 can opener. But he was prosecuted, found to be a habitual criminal and sentenced to preventive detention.

Johnny Hadden was a heroin addict and a petty thief. When heroin wasn't available, Hadden would use alcohol to find his way to nirvana or oblivion. He used to beg, borrow or steal to buy a capsule of heroin. Often, he was caught. His crime was shoplifting just about every time. Once he was stopped trying to get out of a department store with a pipe wrench under his sweater. Another time he had a package of coffee. Then he stole a spinning reel for a fishing rod. The police used to stop him just about every time they saw him on the street. Usually, he was on welfare. He might have a few cents in his pocket. He would be staying at some ramshackle rooming house or hotel on Vancouver's skid row.

Hadden could scarcely be described as a menace to society. In fact, he barely made the grade as a nuisance. Vancouver's Downtown Eastside has for many years been inhabited by hundreds of drug addicts whose lives are just as futile as Hadden's. But the depredations of many of them are not serious. This is not to say that the area is not inhabited by dangerous characters. But the Johnny Haddens do not fall into this category. If you own a store on skid row, the activities of Hadden and other addicts might make it costlier to insure your merchandise against theft, but that is about all. Besides, Hadden and other addicts are usually caught when they try to steal.

On July 30, 1963, Hadden was arrested. A police constable was called to the manager's office at Woolworth's store at about 5:00 P.M. He found Hadden in the manager's office. The manager said Hadden had stolen a can opener worth $2.99. The next day Hadden appeared in court and pleaded guilty to the charge, and he was sentenced to seven months' imprisonment.

The Crown then notified Hadden that he would be proceeded against as a habitual criminal. The Crown's case was based on Hadden's many convictions for possession of drugs. His only friends were drug addicts. He had never been known to work for a living.

But to have a man adjudged a habitual criminal, it was necessary to go beyond merely proving that he had been convicted many times of possession of drugs. The Crown had to prove that he was leading persistently a criminal life.

As proof of this, the Crown relied on Hadden's most recent series of convictions for theft:

July 1961	Shoplifting	two months
September 1961	Shoplifting	two months
December 1961	Shoplifting	four months
May 1962	Shoplifting	six months
December 1962	Shoplifting	six months
July 1963	Shoplifting	seven months

This record hardly qualified Johnny Hadden for Vancouver's list of public enemies. The convictions were pathetic markers in a life of petty crime.

The Crown's argument was that Hadden would not give up his life of crime. No matter how often he was caught, no matter how often he was convicted, no matter how often he was sentenced, he would keep on stealing whatever he could whenever he could. What else, asked the Crown, was there to do, except to declare him to be a habitual criminal and sentence him to preventive detention, putting him away indefinitely?

The magistrate found Hadden to be a habitual criminal and sentenced him to preventive detention. Hadden appealed to the Court of Appeal, but he was unsuccessful there. He then filed an application to the Supreme Court of Canada for leave to appeal, and asked me to represent him. The Supreme Court granted leave to appeal.

On the appeal the first thing to consider was whether the evidence established that Hadden had persisted in crime. The Crown had to show that a man was persisting in crime during the period immediately preceding his last conviction. Hadden's conviction for stealing the can opener had been on July 31, 1963. What had the Crown been able to prove about his way of life during the period immediately preceding that date? In May 1963, Hadden had been released after serving his sentence on his last conviction for shoplifting. There was no evidence regarding Hadden's way of life from the time he was released from prison early in May to the time he was found stealing the can opener at Woolworth's, except the evidence of Police Constable Needham of the Vancouver City Police Department. PC Needham had stopped Hadden on the street on May 12. Hadden told Needham he was on social assistance and that he had been released from prison one week earlier after serving a six-month sentence. He had fifty cents in his pocket.

It was PC Needham who arrested Hadden, almost three months later, for stealing the can opener. Needham said Hadden appeared to be mildly intoxicated.

But did this mean that Hadden was persisting in crime? During the vital period, from early May until July 30, there was no evidence that Hadden had been engaged in any crime at all.

Before the Supreme Court, I argued that a drug addict who engaged in shoplifting could not be said to be persisting in crime. Hadden's was not the case of a man determined to live by crime. When Hadden stole the can opener, he was simply lapsing into his old ways. Although the previous convictions for shoplifting might reveal a pattern, it was not a pattern of persistence. There was not a wilful, stubborn determination to stay with crime, but rather a drifting back into crime and nothing more. Hadden was hardly capable of persisting at anything.

Moreover, Hadden's crime had obviously not been planned or premeditated. Where a man had yielded to a sudden impulse, he could not be said to be guilty of persisting in crime. Even if Hadden was persisting in crime, I urged, was there any justification for putting him away for life? Hadden had never been involved in any crime of violence. Was he a threat to members of the public? His use of drugs, no doubt deplorable, was not something that placed anyone but himself in danger. His shoplifting activities could not be regarded as serious crime. Anything he stole was of little value, and he was usually caught.

I argued that merchants in the Downtown Eastside had a right to be protected from people like Hadden, but that the right could not be absolute. I urged the court that to sentence Hadden to preventive detention would not serve any legitimate public interest, but would only serve to extend the protection already afforded in sufficient measure to the merchants on skid row. They had the police to protect them. They had insurance against theft. Were they entitled to more? Hadden had been sentenced to seven months' imprisonment for stealing the can opener. There was no justification for imposing an additional sentence, tantamount to life imprisonment.

Finally, I argued that there was a public interest in the paramountcy of personal freedom. How could it be said that a sentence of preventive detention was justified because a drug addict stole a can opener? What overriding public interest required such protection? The fact that Hadden was anti-social and a nuisance, or that it would be convenient to the police to get him out of their way forever, was not sufficient justification for sentencing him to preventive detention. That would constitute punishment out of all proportion in its severity to the nature of the offences that he had committed.

Johnny Hadden's case was heard in November 1967, a month after George Paton's case. When I had flown to Ottawa to argue Paton's case, Bev had accompanied me; we were travelling onward on our first trip to Europe. On the flight to Ottawa I was working on both cases. I told her about them and asked her what she thought. She said she believed I would lose Paton's case and win Hadden's. She thought Paton a hardened criminal; as for Hadden, how could a man be sentenced to life imprisonment for stealing a can opener? So far she was on the money: we had lost Paton's appeal. Would she be right about Hadden?

Just as in Paton's case, the court was badly divided. One judge made the difference. The court had gone five to four against Paton. That majority of five included Justice Wilfred Judson. In Hadden's case, five judges were in favour of allowing his appeal; four judges were against it. The difference was Justice Judson. This time he voted for the accused.

Chief Justice Cartwright, for the five judges in the majority, ruled that the Crown had failed to show that Hadden was leading persistently a criminal life when he stole the can opener.

There is no evidence that since his release early in May, 1963, the appellant was leading a criminal life, persistently or otherwise, except the commission of the [fourth] offence on July 31st, 1963. In some circumstances the commission of the substantive offence may in itself furnish sufficient evidence that the accused is leading persistently a criminal life, but this is not one of such cases.

All that the Crown's case amounted to, according to the chief justice, was this:

The picture is of a man . . . stealing a can opener worth $2.99 rather than one persisting in leading a criminal life. The facts are . . . consistent with the yielding to a sudden impulse . . . No doubt the record shows that the appellant has for years been addicted to the use of drugs and from time to time commits petty theft. In my opinion, the evidence accepted by the magistrate fails to establish that the appellant was . . . leading persistently a criminal life and this is sufficient to dispose of the appeal.

Hadden's victory was a narrow one. Justice Ronald Martland, who wrote for the minority of four judges, was of the opinion that Hadden was a habitual criminal. He relied on the facts that Hadden had repeatedly engaged in shoplifting and that, within three months of his last release from prison, he had committed the same offence again. This pattern of conduct was sufficient evidence, so Justice Martland said, to prove that Hadden was persisting in leading a criminal life. Justice Fauteux voted against us in both cases.

But Hadden had won by a single vote. He was a free man again, instead of facing life imprisonment.

A few months after Hadden's victory in the Supreme Court of Canada, I was visiting a client at Oakalla Prison. It was not really a surprise to run into Johnny Hadden there. He had been caught shoplifting and had received a sentence of eight months' imprisonment. I had no doubt he would continue to spend his time shoplifting and going to prison. But he could not be put away for life.

I have mentioned that my father was a policeman. He was sixteen years older than my mother, Perle. When he died, at seventy-two, my mother was only fifty-six. She came to live with Bev and me, and, because she had been a bookkeeper in Telkwa in northern British Columbia when she had met my father (he was serving in the RCMP in nearby Hazelton), she came to work in my office keeping the books. Occasionally, clients overhearing me refer to her as "Mom" thought that must be her nickname and called her "Mom" too.

Mom was skeptical of my criminal law practice. Many clients were thieves, others drug addicts, still others were prostitutes. But she rarely said anything by way of reproof. I had one client who ran a bawdy house and always came in wearing a hat large enough to be mistaken for a sombrero. They were, I suppose, pitiful creatures. I represented them often enough to know how sad their lives were. And yet they were a community. They all were to be found in the same sordid haunts—a few blocks of Vancouver's Downtown Eastside. They had friendships and alliances. They got married. There were deaths among them. They usually had no skills, no true experience of productive employment.

Often, one of them would try to give up drugs and go straight. The attempt was usually unsuccessful. The subculture to which they belonged was the only one they knew, or at least the only one in which they felt comfortable. Part of that culture was prison. For them, it held no terrors. They would prefer to be on the street. But they had friends in prison, too. They could get by there.

My mother used to drive to work with me. Then, if I did not have to work late, I'd drive her home. She was never overtly critical of my professional choices. But one day, as we headed for home, during a brief efflorescence of prostitution in my practice, she said, in her self-effacing way, "Tom, do you think it's a good idea to build a practice on cases like these?"

It probably wasn't, and I wasn't in fact much interested in making a career of such cases. But one of them, which the John Howard Society asked me to take, was as sad as any I've ever done. It suggested the irrelevance of our approach to crime and punishment. It was the first case in Canada in which a woman had been prosecuted as a habitual criminal.

My client's name was Margaret (Penny) McNeill. Though not yet forty, she had spent a lifetime as a prostitute. Her criminal record consisted almost entirely of convictions for vagrancy and possession of drugs. She had never been convicted of stealing. She had never engaged in any crime that endangered the life or property of any other person. She had sold her body hundreds of times for trifling amounts, and she had sold her soul for heroin. Her crimes were truly crimes against herself.

Prostitution itself was not a crime then, nor is it today. Prostitutes used to be charged as vagrants under clause (c) of the old vagrancy section of the Criminal Code. The charge in such cases alleged that the accused woman, "being a common prostitute, had been found in a public place and had not, when required, given a good account of herself." These cases were colloquially referred to as "vag(c)" cases. The search for customers, soliciting in a public place, has always been the target of the law. Neither is being a drug addict a crime, but being found in possession of narcotics, such as heroin (even one capsule), is enough to convict an addict of the crime of possession. Penny McNeill had been convicted of "vag(c)" and possession many times. In fact, when I went to see her at Oakalla and told her I would be defending her, she said to me, "You know, Mr. Berger, this is the first time I've ever had a lawyer and the first time that I haven't pleaded guilty."

Penny's ravaged face still retained a suggestion of sleek beauty. Born in Czechoslovakia, she was brought to Canada as a child. Her parents were unable to control her, and when she was twelve, they had her placed in the Vancouver Detention Home as an "incorrigible." She became a prostitute at fourteen and bore a child at eighteen. After that she began to use heroin.

Penny's record went back to 1946. That year she had been twice convicted of keeping a bawdy house. In 1948, she was convicted of possession of drugs. In 1951, she was convicted of possession of drugs again. Another conviction for possession of drugs followed in March 1954. In 1957, a more serious matter, a conviction for possession of drugs for the purpose of trafficking. In 1962, she was convicted of possession of drugs again. Then on March 3, 1964, came the last conviction for possession of drugs.

Of these convictions the most serious was for possession of heroin for the purpose of trafficking. It would be difficult to persuade the court to write off Penny as a drug addict and a prostitute and nothing more, unless that conviction, which made her a trafficker in drugs, could be explained. This would be essential, because she had been found in possession of twenty-four balloons, containing something like three thousand capsules of heroin.

The Crown had to establish that Penny was a habitual criminal. They obviously had enough previous convictions. They needed three, and they had about a dozen. Then they had to show that she was leading persistently a criminal life. The Crown's case, as it unfolded at the hearing, was this: Penny had been released from the women's penitentiary in Kingston, Ontario, late in 1963. On February 15, 1964, back in Vancouver, she was convicted of vagrancy. Then, on

February 20, she was convicted of vagrancy again. On March 3, she was convicted of possession of drugs. Therefore, the Crown argued, she was obviously persisting in a criminal way of life. The Crown also alleged that Penny was a drug addict and an associate of drug addicts, and that she had no gainful employment. It would be difficult to argue against any of these things. It was likely she would be found to be a habitual criminal.

But we had another string to our bow.

Even if the Crown could prove that Penny was a habitual criminal, that did not necessarily mean a sentence of preventive detention should follow. The Crown would have to establish that it was expedient for the protection of the public that such a sentence should be passed on Penny. We would argue that even if she was a habitual criminal, she was not such a threat to public safety that it was necessary to put her away for life.

The key to Penny's case was that she had tried to rehabilitate herself. It was true that she had never been successful, but the important thing was that she had tried, and we could call a number of credible witnesses to prove it.

When Penny was in Kingston Penitentiary, she sought the help of Dorothy Sheppard, a social worker in Toronto with the Elizabeth Fry Society, an organization, like the John Howard Society, dedicated to prisoners' aid. Sheppard came from Toronto to Vancouver to give evidence for Penny. She told the court that she first saw Penny in 1959. She saw her as often as she could, and they exchanged letters from time to time. When Penny was released in 1960 (after she had completed her sentence for possession for the purpose of trafficking), Sheppard and Penny discussed Penny's future. Sheppard testified:

Penny at that time indicated real concern for her future and wanted to make some concrete plans as to some sort of course or some rehabilitation—direction she could have to give her something to earn her living in the community. She had had a smattering of hairdressing at Kingston. Unfortunately the hairdressing hours that girls put in in Kingston is not given any credit when it comes to the community, so . . . there was no credit given by the Labour Department when she came out.

Dorothy Sheppard arranged for Penny to take a manicurist course at the Ontario Rehabilitation Centre when she was released. In October 1960, Penny started work in a beauty salon in Toronto. She stayed at the salon until February 1961. At Christmas, she had developed a serious kidney and liver ailment and was in constant pain. Sometimes she would be sent home from the salon because of it. But she kept on. There were, however, other problems. Sheppard explained:

She was constantly harassed, and this I have personal knowledge of, because it is the place where I go myself to have my own hair and nails done, and while I was there, there were numerous phone calls, it was not uncommon for numerous phone calls to come. The old crowd downtown would wait for Penny outside and there was pressure put on her constantly to go back downtown with the old crowd . . . Her previous associates, the drug addicts and the people downtown that she had—was trying desperately at this time to stay away from.

Penny was living at the Elizabeth Fry Residence for Young Women in Toronto. "The old crowd" sought her there, too. The housemother screened all Penny's incoming phone calls so that they wouldn't get through. This harassment went on for perhaps two weeks. On February 11, Penny left the residence of her own accord. She told Sheppard that she was in constant pain; she went back to narcotics offered to her by her old friends.

Penny was on drugs again, but she still tried to get help. According to Sheppard, she had gone to the Ontario Hospital on Queen Street West. I asked Sheppard:

Q   Did you go up to the hospital?
A   Yes, I went to visit Penny because she had filled out the initial entry form naming me as her next of kin.
Q   Now why was she in the hospital?
A   She had, as I said, gone back on drugs and Penny was asking for treatment and help at that time.
Q   Do you know how long she stayed in the hospital?
A   I believe at that time it was about a month and a half.
Q   And do you know whether there was any further treatment available to her with regard to her addiction to drugs after the period of time had elapsed that she had spent in the hospital?
A   There is no established treatment for drug addicts in Ontario Hospital. Penny did a withdrawal there. She saw the doctors on the staff and a counselling service but as far as actual treatment for drug addicts, there was none available at that time.

When Penny left the hospital, Sheppard tried to find work for her, but because Penny had no qualifications, it proved impossible. Penny became discouraged and went back on drugs once more. In June she again sought admission to Ontario Hospital. Sheppard visited her there. Penny stayed a month and when she came out, Sheppard tried again to get work for her: "Unfortunately, it was the same thing. She came out, we went to the employment office of special placement . . . As soon as there was any question of where did you work, what is your work record; and of course Penny doesn't have a work record, and there just wasn't any employment for her."

Within a few months, Penny had been again convicted of possession of drugs and once again sentenced to spend three years of her life in Kingston Penitentiary.

On cross-examination by Crown counsel, Sheppard was frank:

Q   Now I suggest to you, that part of the evidence you have given this morning, that every assistance you have given or tried to give to Margaret McNeill, every course of training has all been of no avail whatever. She has consistently gone back to her old way of life on every occasion, is that not correct?
A   Yes, there isn't any question of this at all.

Another question and answer revealed the futility of the cycle of arrest, incarceration and release.

Q   And following her release from the hospital on that occasion, you I believe yourself went to the employment office and attempted to find employment and found it wasn't available.
A   That's right. It wasn't that the employment wasn't available, if I may correct that, it was because Penny was not qualified. After her years of incarceration, she had never been trained to do anything. She wasn't qualified for any job that was available.

Neither could there be any argument about the fact that Penny's only friends were drug addicts. As Sheppard put it: "These were people that were her friends . . . She can't get friends in society because people won't be her friends."

Sheppard noted that Penny had given up the manicurist course because "she was in such terrible pain all the time, and she wouldn't go into hospital because she wanted—she tried desperately to carry on and finish that course. It was the one thing that she wanted more than anything she had ever wanted in her life, I think, and she just couldn't finish it."

Finally, the pain together with the pressure from her old acquaintances had become too much for Penny to bear. Sheppard told the court, "She herself came to me and said that she wanted to leave, because she had let me down and let herself down, and she didn't feel that it was fair to the other kids in the residence that she should stay there."

Penny's husband, Gordon Leamont, gave evidence for his wife. Leamont was forty years old. He had been a drug addict for many years but had rehabilitated himself. At the time of the trial, he was working as a truck driver for the

Salvation Army. He had met Penny in 1945 when she was still married to a man named Russ McNeill. Leamont and Penny had not often lived together. But it was not unusual for two addicts to be married and to see little of each other.

Gordon Leamont provided an explanation for Penny's conviction in 1957 of possession for the purpose of trafficking. True, it had been seven years before. But it had to be explained. Where had the three thousand capsules of heroin come from? Leamont claimed that he was responsible. He was involved in drugs at the time and was carrying the narcotics in the car. He saw the police following them: "I seen them through the mirror and saw that I was being followed and just before they pulled me over, I handed it to Penny and I said, 'Here, hide this quick,' and she stuck it in her clothes."

Leamont and Penny had gotten married in April 1957. Crown counsel asked Leamont about the marriage.

Q   This is your way of making it up to her, is that correct?
A   Not really. I was definitely in love with her and I wanted—and I still am, and I would have married her in any case.
Q   What suddenly prompted the move in 1957?
A   Because we could see that she was going to be convicted and be sent to Kingston; we cannot write back and forth unless we are married and we definitely wanted to keep in touch.

Leamont testified that when Penny's sentence was completed he picked her up at Kingston. As soon as they got back to B.C. in November, they went to the Narcotic Addiction Foundation. The foundation, a voluntary agency, provided in-residence as well as out-patient treatment for addicts. Gene Elmore, senior counsellor at the foundation, testified on Penny's behalf. He told the court that there is no such thing as a one-shot cure for an addict. The average length of time a female addict stayed in residence at the foundation was about fourteen days. This fact didn't mean that the addict was cured after fourteen days. Sometimes an addict would return again, and then again and again; sometimes an addict would never come back. Elmore said Penny had stayed in residence until Christmas, and she then was given permission to leave for two weeks. She returned in January. Altogether, she was in residence for forty-one days.

I asked Elmore if he would be willing to assist Penny again. He answered:

Yes, we would be pleased to take Margaret McNeill back as a patient, for several reasons: I am speaking here in comparative terms; comparing her to the other female patients that first of all she has shown to us a higher level of insight than many others we have treated. She has mentioned repeatedly that she realizes her problem is not entirely drugs, but why she uses drugs. She is looking more for the causes rather than the symptoms. Secondly, she has indicated in her past contacts with us that she has a better level of motivation. She has stayed with us longer and put up with a great deal in terms of her resident treatment program. Third, as I understand it from Margaret's previous history she has been using drugs for some years. At this time, she is now in her thirties, and the recent literature—I am thinking particularly of a paper presented by Dr. [Guy] Richmond of this city—indicates that the average length of use of groups of patients he has stated is around 15 years and after that period of time people seem to fall off on their use of drugs; their motivations for rehabilitation seem to be higher. Another factor in Margaret's favour is she has a job skill and this is decidedly above the average in considering her a good treatment bet.

Clayton Morehouse, who had been Penny's caseworker at the foundation, also gave evidence. He pointed out that even after Penny had left the foundation, she had kept in touch. She came to see Morehouse twice and telephoned him on three other occasions. He gave his assessment: "I feel very optimistic, as Mr. Elmore is, that Margaret has great potentiality towards receiving treatment and towards rehabilitating herself as a good citizen of the community."

Clarice Harkley, a social worker with the John Howard Society in Vancouver, also came to Penny's assistance. After she had been convicted of possession of drugs in March, Penny asked Harkley to see her during one of the social worker's visits to the women's section at Oakalla Prison. Harkley expressed the view that Margaret could rehabilitate herself: "I think the desire to rehabilitate herself is possibly stronger. I think Margaret has never been given the opportunity to rehabilitate herself. I think she has never had parole, never had the opportunity to work with a parole officer. I think her potentiality in this respect is very great."

Under cross-examination by Crown counsel, Harkley did not retreat:

Q   Do you know what her record is?

A   Yes.

Q   That is, since 1945 and in spite of that, you still would stand by your predictions?

A   I feel that given proper treatment, which this girl has never had, that her chances of—at the beginning of her record, she was very young, she did not have the desire she has now. I think given proper treatment this girl would, as I say, have a reasonable chance.

Q   Do you think perhaps your assessment of her might not be correct if other persons who had been paroled do not have the same motivation as McNeill who has not been paroled?

A I don't think she has ever had an opportunity to show us what she could do on parole.

All of the defence witnesses did not say that Penny McNeill would rehabilitate herself, if given the opportunity, but they all felt that she had a fighting chance.

I felt at the time that it would be difficult to argue that Penny was not a habitual criminal. I concentrated instead on whether Penny should be sentenced to preventive detention. My notes of argument read:

- Even if she is a habitual criminal, and it is likely that she will commit further crimes, is it necessary for the protection of the public to imprison her?
- Her crimes are all for possession of drugs and prostitution.
- These are crimes against herself.
- Does a drug addict taking a "fix" threaten the public?
- Who needs protection from a prostitute? The men who patronize her? Did Parliament, in passing the law relating to habitual criminals, truly intend that it was needed to protect men who patronize prostitutes?
- No violence.
- No theft.
- No fraud.
- No acts committed against the persons or property of the public.
- Punishment by way of preventive detention would be disproportionately severe to the gravity of the crime.

All of these points supported our argument: even if Penny were found to be a habitual criminal, and even if she would probably commit further offences, was it expedient for the protection of the public to sentence her to preventive detention?

Magistrate Douglas Hume ruled that the Crown had proved that Penny was a habitual criminal. But he could not bring himself to impose a sentence of preventive detention. He said:

The issue as I see it, is whether or not the public should be protected from the activities of the accused by sentencing her to preventive detention. And the only activity which she appeared to be engaged in, other than the isolated instance of trafficking, which might reasonably have been that of her husband, and not of herself, although she was in fact convicted of it. Aside from that isolated case there is no act that she's done from which I feel the public requires protection. I see nothing in this evidence to indicate that the accused is likely to traffic again. She certainly appears to be on drugs at this time, not of course in jail, but she appeared not to have been cured of her habit . . . I think it's only proper to infer that she will continue to try to get off the drugs. Whether or not she's successful, I don't know, but certainly this sort of evidence indicates that she's not likely to be involved in trafficking rather than that she's likely to be involved in it. And while I find that the first essential has been proved, I'm not satisfied that the second has been proved that it is expedient for the protection of the public that she be sentenced to preventive detention.

So Penny became the first woman in Canada's history to be found a habitual criminal, but she succeeded in avoiding preventive detention.

I defended two other women proceeded against as habitual criminals. Both had records similar to Penny McNeill's. Both were found to be habitual criminals, and in both cases the court refused to impose a sentence of preventive detention. The precedent set in Penny's case applied. In fact, Penny and my other two clients were the only women ever proceeded against in Canada as habitual criminals before the legislation was repealed in 1977.

Penny McNeill's case demonstrated the futility of imprisoning drug addicts. It showed how years of a woman's life were wasted, because she could not break out of the cycle of addiction and crime. When she tried to, and when people like Dorothy Sheppard tried to help her, they found that something always went wrong. "The old crowd" kept after her. There were also real barriers to gainful employment: her criminal record and her limited skills.

In cases like McNeill's the whirligig of arrest, trial and imprisonment makes little sense. For most of these people prison was a kind of home away from home; they didn't want to go, but they would survive there. They had as many friends and acquaintances inside as outside. To be sure, it was inconvenient to be in prison, and they would have much preferred liberty. But the idea of imprisonment as a deterrent had virtually no effect on their conduct. What did have an effect, even though not necessarily successful, was the help of people like Dorothy Sheppard, Clayton Morehouse, Gene Elmore and Clarice Harkley.

What happened to Penny McNeill? I don't know. I never saw her again. But the recollection of her case exemplifies, for me, the futility of pursuing, in certain categories of cases, what we choose to call crime and punishment.

2   *A Bridge Too Far*

T HE BRIDGE was a new bridge under construction, spanning the eastern end of Vancouver harbour, known as the Second Narrows. It was being built in two sections—from the north side of the harbour and from the south side. On June 17, 1958, the falsework supporting the bridge on the north side of the harbour gave way, and eighteen ironworkers on the bridge were carried to their deaths below, some drowning, others crushed by the weight of steel. A royal commission, conducted by Chief Justice Sherwood Lett, found that Dominion Bridge Company Limited, the main contractor, had failed to submit the falsework plans to the consulting engineers, as required. As for the consulting engineers, Swan, Wooster and Partners, they had not insisted that Dominion Bridge submit the falsework plans. For this failure, both Dominion Bridge and Swan, Wooster were found to have been negligent.

After the bodies of the men had been reclaimed from the water, and the wreckage had been removed, construction of the bridge went forward again. The men who were building the bridge belonged to Local 97 of the International Union of Bridge, Structural and Ornamental Ironworkers, otherwise known as the Ironworkers' Union. The following summer, in June 1959, the collective agreement between Dominion Bridge and the Ironworkers' Union expired. Management and the union could not agree on a new collective agreement. A government-supervised strike vote was held; the Ironworkers' Union voted to strike. The strike brought construction of the bridge to a halt. Dominion Bridge claimed, however, that the falsework on the south side of the bridge was in danger of collapsing, and the company went to court to get an injunction to halt the strike. Against the backdrop of the disaster at the bridge the year before, this attempt to force the ironworkers back to work, despite their legal strike, was bound to provoke a confrontation.

Clashes between labour and employers have been commonplace in B.C. The labour movement in the province has always been the most militant in Canada.

Even today, more people in B.C. belong to trade unions per capita than in any other jurisdiction in North America.

The first white settlers who came to Vancouver Island were followed by miners who worked the mines at Nanaimo, Ladysmith and Fort Rupert on Vancouver Island. These were men mainly from the United Kingdom. They brought with them the ideas that workers were entitled to a fair wage and that the way to achieve this wage was to band together in trade unions to strengthen their bargaining power. One man bargaining alone with an employer would have no leverage, but a workforce would be able to bargain on the basis of something like equal strength. All over Vancouver Island, the miners belonged to unions. The movement spread to mainland B.C. Skilled craftsmen in the building trades were organized, too. By the mid-twentieth century, the trade unions had organized the province's logging camps, sawmills and pulp mills and were moving into white-collar occupations.

Strikes occurred in the Wellington Colliery at Nanaimo as early as 1877. In 1912, miners throughout Vancouver Island went on strike. The coal companies refused to negotiate; they hired strikebreakers. Violent clashes took place. The attorney general called in the army. More than one thousand soldiers enforced martial law in the coal-mining towns, and the strike ended only with the outbreak of the First World War. With the advent of the war, one of the miners, Ginger Goodwin, who opposed conscription, refused to report for military service and fled into the woods. On July 27, 1918, he was shot dead by a special constable. In Vancouver, the Trades and Labour Council called for a general strike in sympathy.

This violent early history of B.C. labour relations set the pattern for decades of antagonism between the two sides, arguably extending to the present day.

Each year while I was at university, I had spent the summer months working in a North Vancouver sawmill on the greenchain. I belonged to the International Woodworkers of America, Local 1-217, the Vancouver local. A few years after I was called to the bar, I became Local 1-217's lawyer, and I remained their lawyer until I became a judge in 1971.

I was to spend the whole summer of 1959, not on the greenchain, but in court defending the Ironworkers' Union. Bev and I had an apartment on Broadway. Our daughter, Erin, was one year old. In the evening, we used to walk to nearby McBride Park. The weather was warm, the grass was dry. We watched our little girl taking some of her first steps. I knew that I had chosen the right profession. The ironworkers' case was in the headlines. Before the summer was out, I would become well known to the trade union movement and to much of the public.

In June 1959, the new Second Narrows Bridge was nearing completion. Steel was being laid across Burrard Inlet from both sides. The approach from the south stretched over the main line of the Canadian Pacific Railway. According to plan, in a few more days the falsework would reach Pier 16, in the water beyond the tracks. As it turned out, it would take sixty days before steel would reach Pier 16. On June 23, 1959, the ironworkers went on strike for higher wages. Work on the bridge was halted before it reached Pier 16.

Dominion Bridge moved quickly. The company asked the Supreme Court of British Columbia to issue an injunction restraining Local 97 from continuing the strike. As a matter of law, the Supreme Court had no right to interfere. The strike was a legal strike, following a government-supervised strike vote. The Trade Unions Act gave the Supreme Court the authority to issue injunctions, but no one had thought this statute applied except in the case of an illegal strike, in which case the legislation said an employer might properly seek an injunction.

The company's application to the court for an injunction to put an end to the strike should have been a forlorn hope. There was no legal footing for it. All of the conditions that had to be observed by the union and its members for a legal strike had been met. Picketing was being carried on in support of the strike, but there was no suggestion that the picketing was illegal.

The case came on for hearing before Justice A.M. Manson of the Supreme Court of B.C. This changed the whole picture. Justice Manson was in his mid-seventies, and widely regarded as being anti-labour. He was a man who had long been active in the political life of British Columbia before going on to the bench, and he had served almost a quarter of a century on the Supreme Court. A gifted lawyer, he was given to haranguing those who appeared before him: accused persons, witnesses and lawyers. He was also a fervent Presbyterian. He urged the men and women he sent to jail to turn to religion. In divorce cases, he upbraided peccant spouses. He chastised witnesses whose evidence contradicted his own views. He was sometimes known in the criminal courts as "the hanging judge."

Dominion Bridge's application for an injunction was made *ex parte;* that is, by only one side. The company relied on a provision of the Trade Unions Act that authorized the Supreme Court to issue *ex parte* injunctions to prevent irreparable damage to property or to the public interest. Because the union had not been notified, only extreme urgency could justify the court acting without hearing both sides. The lawyers for the company claimed that the condition of the bridge was precarious, that it was a matter of the utmost urgency for the approach from the south side to be completed to Pier 16.

Justice Manson was determined from the outset to see that the men returned to work on the bridge. He was no doubt impressed by the evidence put forward by the company indicating that the bridge was unsafe, and he felt it was essential to get the men back to work to ensure that a second disaster did not occur. In fact, each time the case came before him he became more entrenched in his conviction that work on the bridge must proceed. When it became plain that under the law he had no authority to force the ironworkers back to work, he decided that the law should be applied to serve the company's interest (and, as he saw it, the public interest), even if that meant bending the law out of shape. At one time or another Justice Manson threatened the union, its members, their lawyer and members of the public witnessing the trial from the public gallery. In the process he lost control of his courtroom.

If ever a judge was biased, it was Justice Manson. No one denies that there are unconscious tendencies that affect a judge's decisions on the bench, or conscious tendencies a judge usually is aware of and tries to curb. Benjamin Cardozo, a famous American judge, observed that in each person is a stream of tendency that gives coherence and direction to thought and action:

Judges cannot escape that current any more than other mortals. All their lives, forces which they do not recognize and cannot name have been tugging at them—inherited instincts, traditional beliefs, acquired convictions; and the result is an outlook on life, conception of social needs . . . which, when reasons are nicely balanced, must determine where choice shall fall. In this mental background every problem finds its setting. We may try to see things as objectively as we please. Nonetheless, we can never see them with any eyes except our own.

All judges would concede that as much could fairly be said of them. But Justice Manson's intervention in the Second Narrows Bridge case went far beyond what the great Cardozo referred to. The stream of tendency in Justice Manson's mind flooded its banks, and he was happily rowing with the current.

One of the falsework supports of the southern section of the bridge lay a few feet from the CPR line. The other falsework support was a few feet from a road where heavily laden trucks and other traffic flowed bumper to bumper during the morning and afternoon rush hours. J.S. Prescott, the erection manager for Dominion Bridge, stated in an affidavit that the structure was unsafe, sustained as it was by falsework. If the falsework were damaged, the bridge might come down again, endangering not only anyone on the bridge but any traffic on the railway track or the road. He also suggested that an earthquake tremor might result in the collapse of the falsework. He went on to say that it was not "sound engineering practice" to rely on such a temporary structure. He described the situation as "a serious hazard." Col. William Swan, senior partner of Swan, Wooster, the consulting engineers on the job, gave similar evidence.

When Justice Manson granted an *ex parte* injunction restraining the union from carrying on its strike, he did so on the ground of public safety. He agreed with the evidence filed by the company that if the southern approach was not soon extended to Pier 16, the steel extending over the railway might collapse onto the tracks or the road. The *ex parte* injunction was issued on June 23, 1959, the day the strike began. It ordered an end to the strike until the bridge could be extended to Pier 16; that is, until the southern approach could be rendered entirely safe in the opinion of the engineers.

Of course, the union's bargaining position in its contract negotiations with Dominion Bridge would be diminished once the southern approach reached Pier 16. The ironworkers did not intend to oblige the company by completing the bridge to Pier 16. That was the point of the strike.

Norman Eddison, one of the business agents of the union, had issued a statement to the press when the *ex parte* injunction was served on the union. Eddison reviewed the history of the Second Narrows Bridge disaster of the year before and the findings of the royal commission. He pointed out that the commission had found that Dominion Bridge had failed to submit falsework plans to the consulting engineers, as it was required to do, and that Swan, Wooster had not insisted that Dominion Bridge submit the falsework plans so that the company could confirm that the falsework would bear the loads as construction proceeded. As a result, the bridge collapsed, and eighteen ironworkers died. If the situation were hazardous once again, as the company had insisted when it applied for the injunction, then it was unsafe for ironworkers to resume work.

Eddison's statement asserted:

Until such time as we are personally satisfied that William George Swan, consulting engineer, has exaggerated the hazard, and is in error, and an independent engineering authority has evaluated the suggested precariousness of the structure and that further, all steps have been taken to positively prevent and make impossible damage to falsework from vehicular traffic or train wrecks, alternatively, no men to be allowed upon this structure when motor vehicle or train traffic passes under this span, an ironworker would tempt fate to resume work.

Given to self-dramatization, Norm Eddison wrapped up his statement: "I personally would rather rot in jail rather than withhold this information from our membership. Since no strike exists against this portion of the project as of 6:00 P.M. tonight in compliance with the injunction, it necessarily follows that a refusal to work by any workman on grounds of safety would not conceivably be strike action."

Eddison was making it clear that the strike might now be over, but the iron-workers might individually still decide not to go to work if they believed the bridge to be unsafe.

H.M. Wooster, one of the partners in the consulting firm, then stated in an affidavit: "That in view of the possibility that the bridge may be supported on a temporary structure for an indefinite period of time it could be considered hazardous, as all structures are during erection, but to state that it is dangerous for workers is an exaggeration completely unwarranted and unjustified by the facts."

So, Dominion Bridge was saying that the structure was hazardous but not too hazardous for the workers to complete it. Both sides were, it is fair to say, deliberately conflating considerations relating to safety with a concern about obtaining a bargaining advantage.

By this time our law firm had been retained. For the union, we had filed an application to set aside the *ex parte* injunction. Dominion Bridge had filed an application to continue the injunction, which would expire after four days.

We filed affidavits from ironworkers employed on the bridge, who stated that they had not returned to work when the injunction was issued because of Colonel Swan's and Prescott's statements. Each of the ironworkers stated that he had decided not to return to work because of a concern about the safety of the bridge.

We came before Justice Manson on June 26. Dominion Bridge wanted to renew the injunction. The union wanted it set aside. This was the first time that the union side had been heard. Ike Shulman, demonstrating once again his confidence in me, arranged that I should argue the case for the union. In court, I urged that Dominion Bridge had no right to an injunction in the first place, because it had not shown and could not show that any legal right of the company's had been infringed. Justice Manson thought otherwise. He said: "This is not novel legislation . . . The purpose is obvious. It is to take care of actions on the part of a trade union which may endanger public order or which may prevent substantial or irreparable injury to property. I do not neglect those words. They underline the purpose of the section." The judge was going to go ahead.

It may be thought that because the judge was on shaky legal ground we had nothing to fear. The trouble is that if a superior court judge, even erroneously, makes even an *ex parte* order, it must be obeyed. A failure to obey or a refusal to obey can be contempt of court, for which the court can impose a fine or a sentence of imprisonment. So long as the order stands, no matter how greatly at variance with the law, it must be treated with the same deference as if it were an order of the Supreme Court of Canada. If Justice Manson made an order, it would remain in force until the Court of Appeal set it aside, and anyone with notice of it would have to obey.

Lyle Jestley, senior counsel for Dominion Bridge, outlined why his client was entitled to an injunction putting an end to the strike until the span had been pushed onward to Pier 16. It soon became apparent that Justice Manson regarded himself, not Jestley, as senior counsel for Dominion Bridge. He took over the case from the company's lawyers. He told Jestley to read the affidavits of Swan and Prescott aloud. After Jestley had read them, Manson gave his ruling. He relied on the evidence of Swan and Prescott. He said that he had known Colonel Swan for many years: "I think he came here about the same time as I did, and that was in 1908 . . . and he unquestionably, without making comparisons, is one of our outstanding engineers in connection with bridge construction."

This was a very odd thing for a judge to say. A judge can only decide a case on the basis of the evidence brought into court. He cannot rely on his private knowledge (that is, knowledge acquired outside the courtroom), because that would mean bringing evidence forward in the courtroom would be futile. Who is to know what knowledge of the witnesses or of the dispute itself the judge has acquired outside the courtroom? This is not to say that the judge cannot take into account what everyone must be taken to know: for example, that Confederation took place in 1867, or that the Second World War lasted from 1939 to 1945, or that the terrorist attack on the World Trade Center occurred on September 11, 2001. Everyone is expected to know these things, so judges can take judicial notice of them; but not everyone knew Colonel Swan, nor was it certain that everyone would hold him in the same high regard as Justice Manson.

Justice Manson, therefore, decided that the bridge was safe enough for the men to return to work. He gave judgement, speaking from the bench in language replete with condescension.

I must find that there is nothing beyond the normal hazard in the workmen continuing their work. Officers of the union surely are as greatly interested in preventing hazards as the plaintiff is. It does not further the interest of a union for a moment to take any other attitude. Unions have their place, a place that is well established. They serve a useful purpose when their powers are properly exercised, but a union is not different from an individual. A union might be regarded as a member of society, but it has a special duty to serve. It is to serve the membership. The duty always remains, however, and it is a higher duty—to serve the public good.

Now just what is asked here? Let us see how far these men are apart. The company says: "We can finish this job, this particular piece, in ten days' work if we are given full crews and then we will all be safe, the hazard will be gone."

The company does not come forward and say: "This is an illegal strike."

Of course, if it was not an illegal strike, how could the judge order the men back to work? The judge had travelled well past that issue. He went on:

It [the company] does not seek to interfere with the strike in any way except for a period of ten days to eliminate this hazard. Now is it asking too much that the union, acting by its officers, should say to the men: "Let us go back and finish this ten days' work and get this span over on Pier 16."

That is the common sense of the thing. I venture to think there is not a man in this room, at least I hope there is not, who would not take that view of the situation.

What the judge was saying might, in the abstract, have been reasonable or prudent. But the issue before him was whether the ironworkers employed on the bridge had the right to strike; whether the courts could order back to work men who were lawfully on strike. Judges do not sit to dispense abstract justice according to what seems to be "the common sense of the thing." They can only enforce the law. The legislature can—and from time to time it does—pass legislation to put an end to a legal strike. But judges have no such power.

Now Justice Manson told the union to order its members to return to work on the bridge until the southern approach had been completed to Pier 16. Dominion Bridge had not asked for such an order. The judge was making up new remedies as he went along. Clearly, it rankled that his *ex parte* order had not resulted in the men going back to work. The judge made this new order as he left the bench. As far as our motion to set aside the *ex parte* injunction and Dominion Bridge's motion to extend the injunction were concerned, they had not been dealt with.

But the judgement that the union must order the men to return to work had been made. We filed an appeal at once; in the meantime, the judge's order had to be obeyed.

Thirty-one men were involved. These were the ironworkers who had been employed on the southern approach. I advised the union's officers to order them back to work, because they had no choice except to obey the court's order. They were, however, I said, entitled to advise the members of the union that their legal advisers felt the order made by the judge was entirely contrary to the law. They were also entitled to tell their members that we were appealing the order of the judge. As a result, the following message was read over the phone by the officers of the union to the thirty-one men employed on the south side of the bridge:

As many of the members know from the newspapers and the radio, Mr. Justice Manson has ordered the union to order the employees of Dominion Bridge Company

Limited working at the south portion of the new Second Narrows Bridge to return to work. Our solicitors have advised us that in their opinion the order granted by the judge is contrary to the law and the order is being appealed immediately.

However, we have also been advised that the order of the judge must be obeyed. We therefore have no alternative but to order the men to return to work and we now hereby do so.

The judge's order had been complied with. But nobody went to work on the bridge.

Dominion Bridge now alleged that the union had been guilty of contempt of court; that it had wilfully disobeyed the order made by Justice Manson. The company had not been able to serve the order on all of the men, only eighteen of them, but not one of those eighteen had reported for work.

The company therefore applied to the court for a writ of sequestration against the union. This ancient writ is used to enforce a judgement of the court. Dominion Bridge was asking the court to sequester the assets of the union; that is, to seize their assets and not to return them until the men were back at work.

On July 9, 1959, the application for sequestration came on for hearing before Justice Manson. For the company, Lyle Jestley told the court that not one of the eighteen men served with the injunction had returned to work. He suggested that the men had not been told by the union they must return to work but had, on the contrary, been told by the union not to go back to work. Of course, there was no evidence that the union officers had not told the men to return to work; the company's case was based on the assumption that the men would have obeyed the union officers if they had told them to return to work. Counter-affidavits were filed by Fernand Whitmore, the president of Local 97, and Norman Eddison and Thomas McGrath, the business agents for the union. These three union officers stated that they had phoned all of the men employed on the south end of the bridge and had given them the same message. They had told the men about the court order. They had told them that the union was appealing the order. But they had told each of the men that the order of the judge had to be obeyed, and they had ordered each of the men back to work.

What Justice Manson was up against was this: He had made an order requiring the union's officers to direct the men to return to work, but the ironworkers themselves were under no legal obligation to return to work. As for the union's officers, they had to order the men back to work, but once they had done so, they had no further responsibility under the court order if the men did not return to work.

I argued that there was no evidence at all to show that the union or its members had been guilty of contempt. Justice Manson intervened: "On that point the onus is clearly on you. Any sane individual sitting where I am would draw the inference in the light of what I said when this matter was before me in open court, and cannot help draw the inference that there has been deliberate defiance. The onus is on you, Mr. Berger, not Mr. Jestley."

Justice Manson by this time appeared to be aware that his order requiring the union to send its members back to work might not stand up on appeal, but he reminded all concerned that it did not matter.

Rightly or wrongly, as counsel are well aware, that order stands until the trial unless set aside by an appellate court. It is absolutely binding on all concerned for the present and until, as I have said, it is either set aside by an appellate court or until the trial, the order of the court must be obeyed. There cannot be any evasion or refusal to obey of any kind without coming into conflict with the courts.

I had been spending the evenings in the law library, looking up the old cases on sequestration. While rummaging about in these tomes, I ran into Magna Carta. At law school we had heard about Magna Carta, but I had never read the document itself. Now, reading it for the first time, I discovered a provision that seemed to apply in our case. Chapter 15 of Magna Carta said, "No free man shall be distrained to make bridges." In 1215, the barons at Runnymede had insisted that King John should not require their serfs to construct bridges for him whenever he wished to make a royal progress through the kingdom. All of this had happened seven and a half centuries before, but Magna Carta is still a revered document, even though, like me, most lawyers and judges had never read it. At the hearing on sequestration, I raised it with the judge.

MR. BERGER: If your Lordship should find that there has been disobedience to your Lordship's order, and I submit that no such finding can be made on the material, but if your Lordship should so find, your Lordship cannot issue a writ of sequestration because to do so would be contrary to our constitutional law, and I refer to Magna Carta in support of that submission.

THE COURT: Well, now, there is much later law than Magna Carta. If you look at your practice you will find that writs of sequestration—I am not going to hear you on Magna Carta. I heard about that fifty years ago in law school and need not spend any time on it.

MR. BERGER: I should like to make a submission based on Magna Carta.

THE COURT: Start at the other end and if you get back to Magna Carta, that will be all right, but start with something current. There are lots of cases on sequestration within recent times.

MR. BERGER: I am coming to those cases, but Magna Carta is current. It is as much in force in British Columbia today as it was in England in 1215. It is part of the constitution of every one of Her Majesty's realms and British Columbia is one of them.

THE COURT: This is a speech for the benefit of the gallery. You don't need to direct those remarks to me.

MR. BERGER: With respect, it is not.

THE COURT: Why bother with saying that? That is wasting my time and yours.

I persisted.

MR. BERGER: I should like to refer to Chapter 15 of Magna Carta.

THE COURT: Well, desist. I am familiar with Chapter 15 of Magna Carta. I don't want you to take my time and yours.

MR. BERGER: If your Lordship is familiar with Chapter 15 of Magna Carta then I suggest your Lordship ought, on the basis of that chapter, to rule that no writ of sequestration can go because Chapter 15 says: "No free man shall be distrained to make bridges" which means you cannot distrain on the assets of the union to compel [its] members to make bridges, which is what my learned friend seeks to have your Lordship do.

THE COURT: Well, there have been a lot of statutes passed since Magna Carta.

MR. BERGER: No statute of this province can infringe the rights or liberties granted free men by Magna Carta.

THE COURT: Yes. The Sovereign acting upon the advice of the honourable members of the Senate and the honourable members of the House of Commons can repeal Magna Carta so far as Canada is concerned, and so can the Sovereign acting upon the advice of the Legislature within the provincial field, repeal Magna Carta.

The judge was no doubt right. The provincial legislature can repeal any of the laws of England that applied in B.C. when it was first claimed and colonized. But it did no harm to show that something closely resembling the freedom the ironworkers were claiming had been insisted on at Runnymede.

In any event, Justice Manson did not make an order to sequester the union's assets. Instead, he decided that he would direct the sheriff to bring the ironworkers before him. I objected to this procedure. There was no evidence before the court to show that the union or its officers were in contempt, so there was no basis for bringing the men before the court. I said: "The court has made an order which has been complied with by the officers of the union, the only party against whom the order was made. The men apparently have not obeyed the direction of the union, but that does not . . . entitle your Lordship to say there has been defiance of the order of the court." But Justice Manson was determined to get the men back to work.

I thought I had the answer to the injunction; then I thought I had the answer to the judgement requiring the union to order the men back to work; then I thought I had the answer to the company's application for sequestration of the union's assets. But each time the judge veered off in a new direction. The judge was inventing his own procedure, because none in the books suited his purpose. This time he directed the sheriff to bring the men before him in open court the following day at ten o'clock in the morning, if they were not then back at work.

So far what I have said hasn't produced results. As referred to in the affidavits of the plaintiff, the hazard to the plaintiff continues and increases with the passage of time. All this can be resolved if tomorrow morning at the usual working hour the crew turns up and finishes the job. I would think they would show themselves good citizens and good Canadians if they would do their part in removing the hazard. If I am advised tomorrow at ten o'clock that the work is carrying on, of course that will be a happy ending.

Judges aren't appointed to hand down moral decrees, to determine what makes good citizens and good Canadians. They are supposed to act according to law. They must simply ask themselves whether one of the parties has a legal basis for asking the court to do something: to grant an injunction, to award damages or to issue some other remedy. If not, it is not a matter for the courts.

Now the judge sought to divide the men and the union:

If there is loss of life, as I pointed out, as a result of the hazard, the workmen at least, if not the union leaders, may be very sorry. Workmen are just like me, ordinarily they are men of pretty good common sense and they exercise a lot more in my experience than some of their leaders. I am sorry to say that, but I have long experience, you know, and I have seen some terrible things done.

He concluded by making an order forbidding me as counsel for the union, and the union's officers, to talk to the men on strike: "I will direct you and the union that they are not to talk to these men and if they do talk to them in the interim I shall deal with it as contempt. That is my order."

This was astonishing. The men were members of the union. The union's officers were their elected representatives. The men were on strike. Their union had retained me as its lawyer. I may have been young, I may have been inexperienced (though that ironworkers' summer was changing all that), but I was the union's legal counsel. The men were not to discuss the case with their union or the union's lawyer. Yet they were expected to be in court the following morning to face Justice Manson. What awaited them? He indicated plainly that he might find some of them guilty of contempt of court: "If they have knowledge of the direction of the court and without reason to refuse, disobey it, then they may be hailed into court to show cause why they shouldn't be dealt with."

The next morning, the sheriff advised Justice Manson that seven of the men had been served with the order directing them to be in court, but he was unable to serve the others. The judge decided to call the roll of the eighteen men who had been served with the injunction in the first place. He called out the name of each one, and there was no response. Then he said: "It would appear that none of the men whom you served, Mr. Sheriff, have responded, so I would say that constitutes contempt. You will therefore, Mr. Sheriff, with your officers bring these men into court Monday morning next at 9:30 o'clock. They must be here and it is your duty to bring them." Now the men were to be arrested. There had been no trial, no weighing of the evidence, no concern to hear both sides; in fact, there was a stubborn refusal to hear both sides.

The judge then made a speech to all of those in court. Having ordered that I, as the union's lawyer, could not speak to the men who were to be brought into court, he decided that he should urge them to obtain their own counsel.

Now, in this particular case it is my opinion the workmen should consult independent counsel. There is a conflict of interest between the union and the workmen, and there is no question about that. Apart from the fact that the men are members of the union, they are also members of society. They are citizens of our country. Their highest duty is to their country. Now, it is not for me to appoint counsel, but I would suggest this, that a senior counsel be employed, a man of ripe experience in the law. He is an officer of this court and he is sworn at the time he is called to the Bar to render faithful and true service to those who seek his advice as clients. I strongly urge that the workmen employ independent counsel.

The reference to "senior counsel . . . a man of ripe experience in the law" was intended to reflect on me, a stripling of twenty-six, as well as to secure representation for the men more amenable to the judge's views on bridge-building.

By this time Justice Manson had held all concerned—the union, its officers and the men—guilty of contempt at one time or another. I felt it was essential to make it clear that I objected, on behalf of the union and its officers, to everything the judge had done.

MR. BERGER: My Lord, may I make a number of things clear for the record . . .

THE COURT: I have adjourned the court, Mr. Berger, and I have nothing further to hear.

MR. BERGER: Your Lordship . . .

THE COURT: I called the court for a special purpose this morning and that purpose has now been resolved, and I have adjourned to Monday morning at nine o'clock.

MR. BERGER: Your Lordship . . .

THE CLERK: Order in court.

Seven of the men who were served with the injunction in the first place were arrested, but the sheriff could not find any of the others. When Justice Manson opened court on July 13 to deal with the men, he was advised of this fact. The judge then told the sheriff:

You will continue to search for them and you will report to me when you have them. It is a serious matter and this looks like a concerted evasion of service. Unless a satisfactory explanation is offered it means that they are in very definite contempt and, while I might otherwise have taken a very lenient view of their non-attendance, I certainly shall not take a lenient view if they insist on evading service. We will be building bridges for some time to come and I do not intend to have a conspiracy to evade the orders of this court.

Then he said: "As I see the situation at the present time there was no bona fide compliance on the part of the union to obey my direction to call the men back to work."

I felt I had to intervene.

MR. BERGER: May I say that the evidence before your Lordship is all to the contrary.

THE COURT: Mr. Berger, please do not tell me that. I have read the evidence and I do not want to be drawn into an argument with you about it.

But that's what you do in court. You have an argument. Then the judge decides. We had had a series of decisions, but no argument.

The judge said he had read the evidence. What evidence was there that the judge could have read? All the court knew, on the record, was that the men had been ordered to go back to work and had not done so.

Justice Manson decided to adjourn court until two-thirty.

Between now and 2:30 I shall give consideration to the conclusion to be arrived at with regard to the conduct of the union as to what penalty, if I conclude they have not obeyed my order, should be imposed. I am not closing the door to further evidence, that is why I summoned the men to attend. I direct that there be no conversations between the union and the workmen with regard to any communication with respect to the order that I made. It is not necessary for me to make any further direction. I have already told the union what they were to do and they did not do it in a *bona fide* fashion, nor in a thorough fashion. I am satisfied that, had they done so, the span would be now on Pier 16. They have counsel, he knows how to advise them—at least he should do. If I find that the crew are working at half past two this afternoon and satisfactory arrangements made I will take that into account.

I want it to be very clear that this court does not permit, does not intend to permit, the law of the land to be defied. If the court is satisfied that there is defiance the penalty will be very heavy, very heavy.

The judge was determined that, by threatening the men with the coercive power of the state, he would get them back to work. The sheriff was directed to try again to find the men that he had not been able to serve with the injunction.

At 2:30 P.M. we were back in court. Justice Manson opened court by asking whether there was any work going on at the span. He was told there was not. But all eighteen of the men who had been served were now in court.

The ironworkers couldn't talk to me. Yet they faced the possibility of imprisonment. They had to get a lawyer. So they went to Tom Hurley. Hurley was about the same age as Justice Manson. He was as courtly as Justice Manson was rude. They were old antagonists. The judge was not pleased when Tom Hurley appeared for the men.

The judge then proceeded to question the men. The first ironworker to be questioned was a young man named Eric Guttman. As the judge was about to begin his examination, Tom Hurley spoke. "With the greatest respect, may I intervene at this time as solicitor for Mr. Guttman and seventeen other people. I must confess, my Lord, I am totally at a loss as to know why this man is called here, for what purpose." Hurley was not feigning ignorance. No one knew, perhaps not even the judge, what procedure we were following.

Justice Manson answered him:

It is not necessary to disclose the detail of why he was required to be here but I propose to examine all of these men as to the notice that was given to them in compliance with my demand—if there was notice given. I want to know just how it was given, when it was given and what the whole conversation was. I propose to examine the eighteen men. If you have any objection to that I am prepared to deal with it.

I then spoke.

MR. BERGER: Would your Lordship make it clear whether your Lordship considers this
to be a criminal proceeding or a civil proceeding.

THE COURT: I will determine that later.

Eric Guttman under questioning told the judge that he had been telephoned by Norman Eddison, who ordered him to go back to work. But Guttman decided not to go back to work because he felt the bridge was unsafe. Then the judge asked Guttman whether he had talked with Eddison or McGrath since the judge had made his order that the union officers were not to talk to the men. The judge was obviously trying to find out whether the union officers had disobeyed his order. Guttman replied that he had not. Manson countered, "You realize that what you have just told me is in direct contradiction to what Mr. Eddison and Mr. McGrath said here the other day?"

I had to object to the statement that what Guttman was telling the judge had been contradicted by Eddison and McGrath. Eddison and McGrath had in fact filed affidavits saying they had talked to Guttman, but that was to order him to return to work. The judge's question was designed to make Guttman believe that Eddison and McGrath had already told the court that, in defiance of the judge's directive, they had talked to Guttman later on.

I said, "There is no evidence indicating your Lordship's statement to be correct." Manson dismissed me curtly: "Just sit down, I am doing this. You keep your seat." At this there were jeers from the public gallery. The courtroom was filled with ironworkers. They were well behaved but aware that the judge was not conducting a trial but an inquisition.

Justice Manson continued to try to lead Guttman into admitting in court that there had been a "much longer conversation" than the earlier conversation in which Eddison and McGrath had ordered him back to work. I was determined to prevent him from doing so. I interjected: "Perhaps your Lordship would put the conversation to the witness?" Manson paused, then he said, "Just a minute, Mr. Berger . . . If you keep interrupting you will be the next man facing me for contempt. I do not have to face impertinence from a comparatively young man who should know how to behave." At this exchange there were, according to the transcript, jeers and cries from the public gallery of "Three hearty British cheers, 'Rah, rah, rah, for British justice' " and "You said it, bud. Keep talking, lawyer."

I was not apprehensive. I felt that I had the legal high ground. I was determined to make sure that the judge did not, through putting trick questions, obtain any admissions from the ironworkers that might be used against the union and its officers. This is the only time in my career that I have been threatened by a judge with contempt. The fact that I was a young man seems to have been as much a cause for resentment in the judge as anything that I had said.

The judge did not press the matter any further. Instead, he wanted to know why Guttman had not returned to work when the union told him to. "Why, if you obeyed the order to go on strike, did you not obey the order to go back to work?" Guttman knew his rights; the judge was not able to intimidate him. "Because nobody can force me to go to work—I don't think so; it is a free country and nobody can force me to go to work to build a bridge if I don't want to."

In the meantime, the judge had received a wire from Premier W.A.C. Bennett stating that Phillips, Barrett and Partners, another firm of consulting engineers, had reported that the bridge was safe. The judge read it out and asked Guttman:

Q   Did you know about that?
A   That was served with the telegram.
Q   You say you were served with a copy of it?
A   Yes.
Q   And you still, in the teeth of that, are not sure whether you would go back to work if the union called you back?
A   I did say so before and I think I cannot change my mind from one minute to the next.
Q   Sometimes it is wise, you know, to have a change of mind.

Guttman's evidence was remarkable for its forthrightness. He refused to be overawed or overborne by the judge. He revealed the courage and common sense so often attributed to the ordinary working man and woman. In fact, each of the ironworkers whom the judge questioned showed the same spirited attitude.

J. A. Phillips was the second ironworker to be questioned. The judge asked him why he had not come to court when the sheriff had served him with the notice requiring him to be in court on July 10 at ten o'clock. Phillips replied: "I could not talk to the [union's] lawyer and I could not afford my own lawyer—if I could not afford my own lawyer and could not talk to the union lawyer, which is the only lawyer I can go to, I was not going to come to court, no."

Justice Manson countered: "You were prepared to defy the court in those circumstances?" At which point Tom Hurley jumped in: "I advise my client not to answer that question; it is incriminating." But the judge would not be deterred. He continued: "You will answer it or I will know the reason why. You were prepared to defy the court because you say you could not talk to a lawyer?" Phillips stood his ground: "I refuse to answer that." Manson: "On the advice of your counsel, is that correct?" Phillips replied: "I just don't think I should answer that question."

Tom Hurley then sought once more to find out what lay in store.

MR. HURLEY: My Lord, may I say I am totally at a loss as to why I and these people are here. Are they here to purge contempt . . . ?

THE COURT: I indicated why they are here and why I am examining.

MR. HURLEY: That is for what, my Lord?

The Court: I see no reason for repeating it. I stated clearly why they were here.

MR. HURLEY: Are they here to purge contempt?

THE COURT: I did not say that.

MR. HURLEY: Without a case being made out against them. I have heard no evidence against them at all.

THE COURT: These men are not on trial. Now, Mr. Hurley, you know, if I did not know you so well and if I did not know that you had been at the Bar so long . . .

MR. HURLEY: Oh, yes, my Lord.

THE COURT: . . . I would take that question seriously.

MR. HURLEY: I thought blarney was a monopoly of mine.

THE COURT: It would be hard to find a superior, Mr. Hurley, when it comes to blarney. However, let us get down to brass tacks.

MR. HURLEY: My Lord, I want to know why they should answer these questions. I speak, of course, with the greatest respect and I mean that from my heart. Why are these men here? Are they here to incriminate themselves; are they here because the Crown—I was going to say "the Crown" or "the prosecution" and I may not be so very much wrong when I say "prosecution"—cannot prove the case? But it is not Mr. Jestley that is the one trying to manufacture a case against them but your Lordship who is taking an extremely active part so far as these men are concerned. These men may finish up in gaol. And it may be, my Lord, that, rightly or wrongly, through your efforts, you may be active in getting them into gaol; not Mr. Jestley but your Lordship, and it is very, very difficult for me to speak in language of restraint.

But Tom Hurley's appeal to his old sparring partner had no effect; Justice Manson pressed on. Like Guttman, Phillips said he had not obeyed the court's order to appear because he was prevented from talking with me, the union's lawyer, and could not afford a lawyer of his own. The judge then gave another judgement, off the cuff, condemning Phillips: "Well, I might tell you that that is not a good excuse. However, I have heard it."

Phillips told the judge that Thomas McGrath, one of the business agents, had phoned and ordered him back to work. He told the judge he did not go back to work because he "did not feel the bridge was safe." The judge went after him again: "Are you saying that seriously, Phillips? . . . It could not be that you were looking for an excuse to stay away from work, could it?" Phillips replied: "That is the way I felt; the way my wife and I had talked it over." Justice Manson persisted: "How would you feel if the bridge stood there for another month or so and then collapsed and somebody was killed?" Phillips answered tartly: "I guess I would feel a lot worse if I was on it when it went down."

I then got up to ask Phillips whether he knew that the consulting engineers who had been held responsible for the failure of the bridge the year before were the same engineers who now had filed affidavits in court saying the bridge was safe. Justice Manson decided that he would rule out any questions on that issue.

Justice Manson got no further with the other ironworkers. But he kept questioning them. Typical was this exchange with Isaac Hall. The judge read to him the telegram of Phillips, Barrett and Partners and asked Hall if he knew about it.

A   I saw parts of it in the paper, yes, but can we always believe these engineers?
Q   Of course, that is a matter for you. The engineers never at any time said that the bridge was unsafe for the workmen, never at any time.
A   They told us that a year ago, that the bridge was quite safe.
Q   Quite true.
A   Eighteen of my pals got killed on that bridge a year ago.

The judge's identification with the company's cause, in his own mind, as well as in the minds of the gallery, was by this time complete. But the ironworkers were a match for him, emerging from each bout of questioning with their dignity and composure intact.

One of them, Verne Seidelman, told the court that he had been telephoned and told to report to work. On the Monday morning, he had gone out to the site and remained where the workers parked their cars till eight o'clock. There was no one on the job, so he went home. Four of his fellow workers had shown up too. Manson asked him:

Q   You were ready and willing to go to work if there had been a full crew there?
A   If there had been a crew there I would have went to work.

This evidence was important. It established that the men had been ordered to return to work, and that some of them had gone out to the bridge ready to go to work. It was evidence that the union's obedience to the injunction was sincere and not feigned. The judge's order to the union had been carried out. It may be that very few obeyed the union (they realized the union was under compulsion to order them back to work), but the union's officers had done what the judge told them to do.

Justice Manson was getting nowhere. It was evident that the ironworkers were not going to succumb to the threats he'd made. So he asked the attorney general to appoint counsel. Obviously, he wanted the attorney general to bring proceedings for contempt. As a result Meredith ("Med") McFarlane, a respected Vancouver lawyer, was appointed by the attorney general and appeared before the court on July 20. Manson reviewed the proceedings for McFarlane's benefit and concluded by saying:

> I have done my utmost to impress on all concerned that the court's order is valid until such time as it is reversed or set aside on appeal, if that should be at a later date done, and that order, of course, was, as you will see from the record, an injunction against a strike insofar as the work on the south span of the Second Narrows Bridge was concerned, and a mandatory order that the union call its men back to work, or in other words, carry out their contract with the bridge company to provide the necessary crews to enable the work to be finished. It is very difficult indeed for me to see that if the union wanted the work to proceed, it really wanted to call out the crew, that that could not be done. Indeed, I am satisfied that if the union did desire to provide the crew, it could do it. I have done my level utmost to point the way. I cannot do more than that. I will not say more at the moment.

McFarlane reviewed the evidence. He then asked the court to make an order directed to the union, its president, Fernand Whitmore, and business agents Norman Eddison and Thomas McGrath, to show cause why they should not be committed to prison for contempt of court in disobeying the court's order made on June 26.

I argued that there was no evidence to justify such an order being made. I argued that counsel for the attorney general had to make out a prima facie case before he could ask that an order be made requiring the union and its officers to show cause why they should not be committed for contempt. To no one's surprise, Manson made the order nevertheless.

On July 28, the court assembled to consider the whole question of contempt again. McFarlane was prepared to argue that there had been contempt by the union and its leaders. I was there to argue the opposite.

Justice Manson began the proceedings by reading a letter he had been sent threatening civil war if the ironworkers were sent to jail. The letter was signed "Steelworker." I pointed out that the men in the case before him were ironworkers. The steelworkers belonged to a different union, representing iron and steel foundries, not construction workers. In any event, I urged that there was no foundation for the judge suggesting that the letter had been written by one of the employees of Dominion Bridge. Even if it had, it could not be evidence in the case against the union and its officers. But the fact that the letter was read by the judge in open court, and that I was required to deal with it as if it had anything at all to do with the allegations of contempt against my clients, indicated how far the proceedings had become unhinged.

The hearing proceeded. McFarlane argued that there had been contempt; I argued that there had not been. On July 30, 1959, Justice Manson handed down his judgement. He had to determine whether the union and its officers had been guilty of disobedience to the order he had made requiring the union to direct the men back to work.

Having reviewed the evidence and the proceedings, it now becomes incumbent to put the evidence into perspective and enquire whether there was *bona fide* compliance with the mandatory portion of the order of the 26th of June, or mere literal or lip service thereto. [Were] the union and its officers guilty of disobedience to the mandatory order, and therefore guilty of contempt?

It could hardly be doubted what conclusion the judge would come to. He relied on the statement that Eddison had made, after the *ex parte* injunction had been issued, that he was prepared to rot in jail. Although that statement might have been contempt so far as the *ex parte* injunction was concerned, it could not be regarded as contempt of the order made on June 26, which required the union leaders to order the men back to work, because that order was made *after* Eddison's statement had been issued.

The judge went on to say:

And then I make reference to the behaviour of the workmen in court on the 13th and 14th of July. The fact that the behaviour was unseemly is bad enough, but what impressed me was the atmosphere of utter defiance. In a long experience I have not found workmen defiant of the orders of the court, or unreasonable. I must impute the defiance to the union and its officials.

The outbursts that had occurred in court were obviously spontaneous, and there had been no evidence whatever that the union and its officials were in any way responsible for them. The judge himself, by assuming the role of prosecutor, had provoked the outbursts. He went on: "The misbehaviour and defiance of the workmen in the courtroom—whether they were all workmen of the defendant or not is unimportant, must be laid at the door of the union and its officials. The misconduct reflected the attitude of the union officials."

Throughout his judgement, the judge was critical of my conduct of the case for the union and its officers. For instance, he gave this account in his judgement of what had occurred during Eric Guttman's evidence.

I pointed out to [Guttman] that his account of the conversation with Eddison was in direct contradiction with what Eddison and McGrath had said. There was an interruption by counsel for the union. The workmen present at this point were flagrantly defiant in their attitude—the atmosphere was crackling with defiance and there were jeers. Guttman was asked again: "You swore that that was the only conversation that you had with Mr. Eddison?" and he answered: "Yes, I do."

Mr. Berger interrupted again, obviously for the purpose of assisting the witness, and there were further jeers and violent interruptions from among the workmen. I then confronted Guttman with the statements by McGrath and Eddison that they had told the workmen that the solicitors for the union advised that in their opinion the order by the judge was contrary to law and was being appealed immediately. Asked if he was told that by Eddison, he answered "Yes," which, of course, was in flat contradiction of two previous answers made by him.

What the judge was engaged in here was unforgivable. He had tried to get Guttman to say that McGrath and Eddison had spoken to him after he had made his order prohibiting the union officers from talking to the men. He had failed. Now he was treating Guttman's denial as if it were a denial of the contents of the earlier conversation when they had ordered him back to work.

The judge also placed much store on the fact that the union would not co-operate in extending the bridge to Pier 16. Of course it would not. To do so would have destroyed its bargaining leverage.

There was a surrealistic quality about the judge's reasons for judgement. The court had not ordered the men back to work. If it had, their refusal to go back might have been contempt of the court. The court had ordered the union to direct them back to work. But they did not have to obey the union. If they decided to ignore the order made by the union because they knew it was made under compulsion, they had every right to do so. That would not be a contempt.

Justice Manson convicted the union and its officers of contempt. He fined the union $10,000 and each of its officers $3000, in default one year's imprisonment. We filed an appeal to the Court of Appeal. The appeal was on two grounds. First, there was no evidence to justify a conviction for contempt. Second, the judge had shown that he was biased against the union and its officers, and as a result they did not get a fair trial.

The appeal was heard by Chief Justice A.C. DesBrisay, Justice H.W. Davey and Justice J.A. Coady. I argued the appeal for the union and its officers. McFarlane appeared for the attorney general to uphold Justice Manson's judgement.

On November 3, 1959, the Court of Appeal handed down its decision. The court was unanimous in holding that the finding of contempt could not be justified. Chief Justice DesBrisay said: "I have carefully perused the record and with respect can find no evidence establishing the disobedience alleged nor any from which such disobedience could reasonably be inferred. The finding of contempt of court in my opinion cannot be supported." Justice Davey agreed categorically that the finding of contempt had to be set aside. He said:

The order in question did not state how the union should order the men back to work. If the officers by telephone instructed each of the men concerned to go back to work as they say they did, that, in my opinion, was, in the circumstances, a sufficient compliance with the order, unless it can be shown inferentially that the men were led, directly or indirectly, to believe that it was not intended that they should comply with the instructions.

The judge gave a number of reasons for concluding that the union did not comply in good faith with the order. With many of them, I am, with respect, obliged to disagree.

The press release by the union [Eddison's statement that he was prepared "to rot in jail"], which was published after the granting of a previous injunction restraining the strike in respect of the span, and which suggested that the bridge was unsafe for workmen was, I agree, inflammatory and contemptuous in respect of that injunction, and it was some evidence of the temper of the union and its officials concerning the injunction in question, which was made two days later. But it was not a contempt of the later order, and there was no obligation on the union under the second injunction to do anything to remove the false imputation the bridge was unsafe for workmen beyond the normal hazards of such work.

Nor can the defiant attitude and unseemly conduct of some of [the] appellants' supporters in the gallery, which occurred during the *viva voce* examination of eight of the workmen by the learned judge, be attributed to the appellants.

Justice Davey also understood the dynamics of collective bargaining. He went on:

Also, it is no evidence of contempt that before any injunction had been issued the business agent of the union refused to co-operate with the company in finishing the span. The union at that stage was entitled to any advantage from the insecurity of the span that it could get in support of the strike.

Likewise, in my respectful opinion, the appellants are not open to criticism for telling the men that they were being ordered back to work because the court had ordered the union to do so, and that their counsel had advised that the injunction had been wrongly granted and was being appealed, but in the meantime had to be obeyed.

The members were entitled to know why their union was ordering them back to work, so, among other things, that each might decide for himself whether he would comply, not with the order of the court, which in that respect was not directed to them, but with the order of the union, which they were entitled to ignore.

Justice Davey summed up: "[The union and its officers] were obliged to comply in good faith with the mandatory order, but they were not obliged to do so gracefully, and a reluctant compliance was in itself no contempt."

Justice Davey, writing for all three members of the Court of Appeal, also referred to Justice Manson's criticism of my conduct, stating: "I have read and reread the transcript, and, with respect, think the criticism was unmerited." On the occasion when I had objected to the judge's questioning of Eric Guttman and he had threatened me with contempt, Davey weighed in: "Moreover, in rising to object during the judge's examination of one of the witnesses, all that counsel sought to do was to clear up an obvious misunderstanding between judge and witness—a course which was counsel's right and duty . . . Counsel should not have been rebuked for attempting to do that."

Justice Manson was no hypocrite. He hated unions. He used his position on the bench to impede and frustrate them when he could. But he hardly took the trouble to pretend that he was dispensing even-handed justice. There were no long-winded rationales for his judgements. He was out to get you, and he did.

There are, of course, other ways of presiding, judges who know their strength is in the law, not their own predilections.

In June 1969, the trainmen working on the trains bringing coal from the Kootenays to Roberts Bank went on an illegal strike. The coal cars were unloaded onto ships at Roberts Bank by turning them upside down and yet not uncoupling them from the train. The trainmen complained that the Canadian Pacific Railway had failed to keep a promise to the union to test the braking system on each train before it returned with the empty cars to the Kootenays. The CPR, through its lawyer, Douglas McK Brown, obtained an *ex parte* injunction to halt the strike. (This was, remember, an *illegal* strike, properly the subject of an injunction.) But courts don't grant such injunctions without limitations. The court scheduled a hearing to determine if the injunction should be continued. The men, of course, had to go back to work in the meantime. Or did they?

The illegal strike could not be continued. But the CPR, to intimidate the trainmen, had not only named the union and its officers as defendants, they had named all two hundred trainmen as defendants. As their lawyer, I spoke to the men at the union hall; I told them that because they had been named as defendants and were therefore parties to the lawsuit, they were entitled to be in court at the scheduled hearing. Of course, if they had to be in court, they could not be at work.

When Douglas McK Brown saw all the men in the gallery, he asked, with some asperity, "Why aren't these men at work?" I told him his client had named them as defendants in the lawsuit, and that I had advised them that they were entitled to their day in court.

Our judge was William McIntyre, one of the ablest trial judges of his generation. Even though he was to go on to sit on the Supreme Court of Canada, he always understood that trial judges are in the front line; they are the face of justice for the public. There were two hundred trainmen in the gallery. They realized at once that they had an even-handed judge, who would decide on the evidence and the law. There was not a murmur from the gallery.

After an all-day hearing, it was apparent that the CPR had in fact misled the trainmen regarding safety. The company had promised to test the braking system on each train after the coal cars had been unloaded; but there had been no tests. The next morning, we assembled to hear Justice McIntyre's decision. He decided against the company. The court would not continue the injunction because the company itself had not come to court with "clean hands." The injunction was dissolved. Within twenty-four hours the president of the CPR was on his way from Montreal to work out a settlement of the dispute.

In the year following the decision in the Court of Appeal in the Ironworkers' case, I had come before Justice Manson again.

In a case involving Louis Battaglia, a retired hard-rock miner, I had taken the Workmen's Compensation Board to court to establish his right to a pension. The issue turned on whether Battaglia had silicosis: Were his lungs coated with silica dust after a lifetime in mining? The board said no. But a medical appeal tribunal, whose opinion under the statute was binding on the board, had sided with Battaglia. Nevertheless, the board stood by its decision: Battaglia did not have silicosis. I succeeded in persuading the Court of Appeal that the board was subject to the jurisdiction of the courts. For the first time, the court made an order of mandamus against the board; that is, an order requiring the board to accept the opinion of the medical appeal tribunal as binding. The board appealed to the Supreme Court of Canada. While the appeal was pending, Battaglia died. His case, however, was a precedent others could use; the board was forced to pay compensation to other workers suffering from silicosis.

When I came before Justice Manson again, I represented a widow named Mary Farrell, who was suing the Workmen's Compensation Board. Justice Manson hated bureaucrats as much as he hated unions. After argument in the case was over, he telephoned me. He said he hoped there were no hard feelings over the Second Narrows Bridge case. I said there were not. He then told me he was going to decide in my client's favour. He asked me to come to his office. He produced a judgement he had written, and he wanted to know if I thought it was appeal-proof. After looking it over, I told him I thought it was. The interview was wholly improper. I shouldn't even have examined his judgement. But that's the way things were when you entered Justice Manson's world. As soon as I left his office, I phoned C.C. Locke, counsel for the board, and "Med" McFarlane, who was counsel for the attorney general in the case. I told them what had happened. Neither was taken aback. Justice Manson's methods were well known. In the end, the Court of Appeal set aside Justice Manson's judgement; I appealed to the Supreme Court of Canada, but we lost.

It is tempting to look back on the Ironworkers' case as occurring in an era when we had flamboyant characters on the bench and to forgive them much because they made no particular effort to hide their biases. But that is not good enough. Justice Manson's behaviour could not be excused today, nor was it excusable in 1959.

Justice Manson was not appointed to the bench to decide when a strike was or was not in the public interest. He was there to consider the legal issues raised by Dominion Bridge and the union. Instead, he assumed the role of prosecuting counsel and decided to put the union in its place. He regarded his own biases as evidence: Workers do not want to go on strike; it is their union leaders that force them out; they don't make up their own minds; they let the union lead them by the nose.

The feisty old judge remained on the bench for two more years after the Ironworkers' case. In 1961, the Constitution of Canada was amended to force superior court judges into retirement at seventy-five. Judge Manson, then seventy-seven, was out. But not without a struggle. He threatened to sue to keep his seat on the bench. Only at the last minute was he persuaded to go quietly. In B.C., the amendment to the Constitution became known as the Manson Amendment.

Confrontation between employers and unions in British Columbia has not been confined to the bargaining table.

B.C. also has a radical tradition, going back to the turn of the twentieth century, of labour involvement in politics. From 1903 the B.C. legislature included socialist members, who sat as representatives of labour, from the mining towns on Vancouver Island. The clashes between labour and capital have reverberated in the political life of the province. The trade unions were influential in the organization of the Co-operative Commonwealth Federation (CCF) in 1933 and its successor, the New Democratic Party (NDP), in 1961.

The Liberals and the Conservatives in 1941 got together to form what they called the Coalition, to keep the CCF out of office. In 1952 Social Credit came to office, gaining one seat more than the CCF. Although Social Credit retained throughout its long term of office the trappings of populism, it had the support of the business community to serve as a political vehicle to keep the CCF and later the NDP at bay. In fact, in 1961, the government of W.A.C. Bennett sought to cut off trade union funding to the NDP, the official opposition in the province.

When the NDP was established in 1961, it made provision for membership by trade unions in the party. Each union's dues to the NDP came out of union dues paid by its members. W.A.C. Bennett's Social Credit government brought in legislation to prevent trade unions using their members' dues to aid any political party. It was done in the name of protecting trade union members' political freedom; its practical effect was to block trade union funds going to the NDP. No equivalent measures were brought in to prevent corporations, Social Credit's base of support, using corporate funds for political purposes without the consent of their shareholders.

I was retained by the B.C. Federation of Labour to argue the case. There was no Charter of Rights in those days. The issue was simply did the province have the authority under the Constitution to pass the law? The answer depended on the characterization of the law. We said the legislation related to freedom of expression, which I argued was a federal matter; moreover, the legislation related to federal elections as well as provincial elections. Counsel for the government of B.C. said the legislation related to trade unions or to labour law, subjects within provincial powers. We lost in the B.C. courts on the issue of characterization; the B.C. courts held it was labour law.

The B.C. Federation of Labour told me they wanted to retain F.R. Scott, dean of the law school at McGill University, to argue the case as senior counsel in the Supreme Court of Canada. I was delighted.

Frank Scott was a hero of mine, though I had never met him. He was one of the founders of the CCF and later of the NDP. He was an important Canadian poet and had translated French Canadian poets into English. He was famous as a defender of civil liberties, as well as a leading scholar in constitutional law. He had persuaded the Supreme Court of Canada to set aside Quebec's Padlock Act, which allowed the police to close up any premises used to disseminate Communist propaganda. He had won a renowned victory in the Supreme Court in *Roncarelli v. Duplessis,* in which the premier of Quebec, furious with the attack by the Jehovah's Witnesses on the Roman Catholic Church, had cancelled the liquor licence of Frank Roncarelli, a Jehovah's Witness restaurateur who was putting up bail for witnesses arrested by the police. The Supreme Court ordered Premier Duplessis to pay $33,000 in damages. And in a case where the cause and the choice of counsel could not have been a better fit, Frank had convinced the Supreme Court that *Lady Chatterley's Lover* was not an obscene publication.

I had drafted our written submission (known as a factum) for the Supreme Court of Canada. I sent it to Scott. A few days later he called: "Tom Berger? This is Frank Scott. I have just read your draft. It is quite good." Praise, indeed, from the great man. I travelled to Montreal for a week to work on the draft with Frank. We went out each evening to dinner. Frank was a bon vivant; in fact, he was the first diner I had ever seen taste the wine brought to the table, pronounce it unsatisfactory and send it back.

During the daytime, at Frank's office in Chancellor Day Hall at McGill University, celebrated in Frank's poem "On Leaving My Office at Chancellor Day Hall," we reviewed, revised and rewrote the factum I had drafted. Tall and angular, Frank was a member of an old Anglo Quebec family. I thought there was always about his devotion to liberal causes a sense of noblesse oblige. This did not mean that he was not as committed as others; rather it allowed him to remain at one remove, thus bringing the range of his intellect to bear. Frank was not content with merely imparting each concept that we wanted to put forward in our factum; he wanted to capture it in a phrase that would yield its meaning at a glance.

In the Supreme Court, Frank argued our case. Douglas McK Brown was senior counsel for the attorney general of B.C. The appeal was conducted in English. But when the French-speaking judges spoke to Frank, they put their questions in French, and he responded in French. All of us from B.C., I'm afraid, looked at each other, comprehending for the first time the reality of bilingualism.

Long before the Charter of Rights came into force in 1982, the personal preferences of judges—their convictions, their personal tendencies or inclinations—made a difference in their decisions. In fact, characterizing a statute like Premier Bennett's trade union legislation was almost wholly a subjective judgement. Was the legislation directed at the right of a rival political party to raise funds from the trade union movement, or was it all about trade unions only, intended to protect trade union members from having their dues conscripted for use by a political party? If it was political, the legislation was in trouble. If it was about trade unions, it fell within provincial jurisdiction.

We lost four to three. Justice Ronald Martland, writing for four judges, said the statute was properly characterized as labour law; three, for whom Chief Justice Cartwright wrote, said it was political. The legislation remained in place until 1972, when the NDP was elected in B.C. and repealed the measure. It has never been reinstated.

When I went on the bench in 1971, the contest between capital and labour was still being fiercely waged in B.C. When I returned to practice in 1985, it was still going on. Perhaps the most egregious use of state power occurred in 1987. The trade unions went on a one-day general strike, shutting down most of the province. Their action was to protest proposed legislation limiting the rights of organized labour. Attorney General Brian Smith responded by alleging that, by holding a one-day general strike, the trade unions were guilty of sedition. The writ the attorney general issued on June 2, 1987, against the labour movement was unprecedented. He charged the unions and union leaders with treason, sedition and intimidating the legislature. These were grave charges. But they were not brought under the Criminal Code; instead, the attorney general was proceeding in the civil courts and asking the Supreme Court of British Columbia to grant an injunction restraining these so-called acts of treason, sedition and intimidation by labour in B.C.

The attorney general, however, did not stop there. Sedition is defined by law as advocating the use of force to bring about a change in government. The attorney general asked the Supreme Court of British Columbia to adopt a definition of force never heard of before. He contended that force included strikes, picketing, study sessions and slowdowns. If the injunction were granted, all such activities could be prohibited by court order and punishable by contempt proceedings. In addition, he asked the court to prohibit the labour movement from advocating "governmental change." He defined "governmental change" to include such things as "showing that Her Majesty has been misled" and "pointing out errors in the government of the province." It was an attempt to stifle by court order criticism of the government of British Columbia.

I was asked to undertake the defence of the Hospital Employees' Union. I asked the court to dismiss the attorney general's lawsuit on the ground that it disclosed no reasonable claim; that it was an abuse of the process of the court.

At the hearing in the Supreme Court of B.C., the B.C. Federation of Labour and the other unions and representatives of the labour movement that had been named in the attorney general's writ supported our application to dismiss the case. I urged that the whole proceeding was "offensive to free people and free institutions."

By this time the attorney general had filed a statement of claim. In this document, however, no allegations of treason, sedition and intimidating the legislature were made. Counsel for the attorney general insisted that he had not meant to say that the trade unions had sought to overthrow the government; yet he would not withdraw the writ. He still wanted his injunction.

Justice Kenneth Meredith granted our application and dismissed the attorney general's lawsuit, including the claim for an injunction. The judge was critical of the lawsuit on a number of grounds. But in the end, the judge pointed out that the attorney general, having made allegations of treason, sedition and intimidation, had abandoned them; so the case could not proceed.

A clumsy attempt to choke off peaceful protest had been defeated. But for me, it had all started with the Ironworkers' case and the Second Narrows Bridge.

What of those ironworkers in 1959? Justice Manson did not get them back to work. They did not return to work until they had a collective agreement. Not until Dominion Bridge agreed to a fifty-seven cent an hour wage increase was the bridge completed to Pier 16. In the meantime, it had not collapsed. Safe or unsafe, it had survived. And the span across the Second Narrows was eventually completed. It is now called, in remembrance of the men who lost their lives in 1958, the Ironworkers Memorial Second Narrows Crossing.

3   *The Jones Boy*

I WAS ELECTED to Parliament in 1962, so I left daily practice at Shulman, Tupper, Southin and Gray. But my sojourn in Ottawa lasted less than a year. In 1963 I was defeated. I decided to open my own law office in the old Inns of Court Building at the corner of Georgia and Howe Streets in downtown Vancouver. You had to walk up a flight of stairs to my office on the second floor. My window looked onto Georgia Street. Essa Horswill, who had been my secretary in Ottawa, came out to Vancouver to continue as my secretary in my law office. My mother, Perle, as I have said, worked as my bookkeeper.

When you start out on your own, you wonder if anyone is going to want your services. There are hundreds of lawyers in the city. It seems unlikely that anyone will be eager to retain you. So there is an inclination to welcome a client, no matter what the problem. But you can't say yes to them all. Some types of work fell quite outside my competence: conveyancing, estates, incorporating companies, drawing commercial contracts. I soon learned that it was best to stick with what I knew. I didn't necessarily know very much, but I did know civil and criminal litigation. Even then you have to learn to say no sometimes to cases you want to do, if you already have too much on your plate. You may already be overwhelmed with work; when someone calls about a case that you believe no one else could do as well as you could, you have to say no.

One day a remarkable man came to see me. I was very busy, but I wanted to do his case.

George Ernest Pascoe Jones was not cut from the dull cloth that is supposed to typify the civil service. Everything about him was larger than life. A big man, in his mid-fifties when I first met him, he sported a big moustache, a big cigar and a big vocabulary. He served the province of B.C. as chairman of the Purchasing Commission from February 15, 1956, to March 25, 1965. By all accounts, he served ably, if flamboyantly. It was his departure from office—or, to put it more accurately, his refusal to depart his office—that made him well known to British Columbians.

He was to become an antagonist of W. A. C. Bennett, another outsize figure, who served as premier of B.C. from 1952 to 1972. During those years, Mr. Bennett dominated the political life of the province as no one had before or has since.

When W. A. C. Bennett became premier of British Columbia in 1952, he asked the legislature to pass a statute to put the office of chairman of the Purchasing Commission above politics. The Purchasing Commission was responsible for purchasing equipment and supplies for all the ministries of the government, public institutions and public buildings. The commission spent millions of dollars of public money each year; it was essential that its chairman should be able to decide when and where the government should do its purchasing without being subject to political pressure from the government or friends of the government. As a result, the legislature, at Bennett's initiative, passed a law providing that the chairman of the Purchasing Commission could only be removed from office by a resolution of the legislature itself. Bennett, the architect of this legislation, was to find it an obstacle when he would search for a way, some years later, to remove Jones from office. Frustrated by Jones's refusal to give up his office, the premier would make a speech that would leave him $15,000 poorer.

George Jones had been an officer in the Canadian Army during the Second World War, and he had served as director of Administrative Services for the federal Unemployment Insurance Commission. When he took office in 1956, the Purchasing Commission of B.C. was spending $20 million a year; when Jones left office almost a decade later, purchasing had gone up to $40 million a year. At the same time, Jones had reduced the commission staff, an unusual record.

On October 2, 1964, Robert Bonner, the attorney general of British Columbia, in his capacity as chief law enforcement officer for the province, laid a charge against Jones of accepting a benefit in violation of the Criminal Code of Canada. Jones was supposed to have bought a car from Pacific Chrysler Products at $1,577 below retail price, without having obtained the written consent of the government. The RCMP arrested Jones in his office in the legislative buildings.

On the same day, the cabinet passed an order-in-council suspending Jones as chairman of the Purchasing Commission, and his salary was stopped. Once Jones had obtained his release on bail, he returned to his office. The government appointed a new chairman, but Jones refused to give up his office. He said that under the law the chairman of the Purchasing Commission could only be removed from office by the legislature. He said that his suspension was tantamount to removal from office, and the government had therefore acted illegally. He insisted that his duty was to stay where he was. The new chairman of the Purchasing Commission did not attempt to turn Jones out; instead, he took another office. Many on Jones's staff, though obliged to report to the new chairman, continued to come to Jones for advice and even to seek his approval for purchases.

The charge against Jones was tried before Judge Montague Tyrwhitt-Drake, in the County Court Judges' Criminal Court in Victoria. Jones was represented by Hugh McGivern, one of the province's finest criminal lawyers. On January 15, 1965, three and a half months after he had been arrested, the charges against Jones were dismissed on the ground that, although the Criminal Code provided that it was an offence for an official of the government to accept a benefit from anyone doing business with the government, this provision could not be applied to Jones. Judge Tyrwhitt-Drake held that in his capacity as chairman of the Purchasing Commission, Jones was not an official of the government within the meaning of the Criminal Code. This was a question of law. But Judge Tyrwhitt-Drake went on to make a finding of fact. He held that even if the provision of the Code invoked by the prosecution did apply to Jones, he would have found him not guilty. The evidence disclosed that Jones had paid the full, regular retail price for the car. The police, when they investigated the case, had overlooked an exchange of cheques between Jones and the car dealer that accounted for the seeming discrepancy. There had never been a purchase at a discount.

Jones had been under a cloud, but now that he had been acquitted, the cloud was gone. He expected the government would repeal the order-in-council by which it had purported to remove him from office. He believed that although the government may have considered that it had been obliged to suspend him from office, it would now reinstate him. But the government did not immediately restore Jones to office. The legislature reconvened soon afterward, yet the government said nothing. Jones wrote to the premier; the premier did not reply.

On February 23, 1965—more than a month after the charges against Jones had been dismissed—the premier announced in the legislature that a bill would be introduced relating to Jones. This mystified Jones and everyone else. Why should a bill be introduced about Jones? If the government wanted him removed from office, it could ask the legislature to pass a resolution that Jones be removed from office. This was what the legislation brought in by the premier thirteen years earlier provided for. If the government were prepared to see Jones continue in office, why would there have to be a bill?

Two days later the government introduced a bill entitled An Act to Provide for the Retirement of George Ernest Pascoe Jones. This bill provided that Jones was to be deemed to have been retired and removed from office as chairman of the Purchasing Commission as of October 8, 1964. Why this date? It was on October 2, 1964, that the government had passed an order-in-council suspending Jones from office, and it was six days later, on October 8, that the new chairman had been appointed. The government was in effect conceding that it had acted illegally in purporting to suspend Jones from office and in appointing a new chairman in his place. Although it had power to appoint the chairman of the Purchasing Commission, it could not appoint a new chairman while the old chairman was still in office. Two men could not hold the same office at the same time. Therefore, to legalize what had been done on a retroactive basis, the government had brought in the bill.

Jones's salary had been stopped from the time the government passed the order-in-council suspending him. The bill provided that Jones was to be paid his salary as chairman from October 1, 1964, until February 15, 1966. At the expiration of that period, he would be treated as entitled to a civil service pension on the basis of ten years' service.

In the meantime, the attorney general had brought an appeal from Judge Tyrwhitt-Drake's decision. Before the appeal was heard, Hugh McGivern, Jones's counsel, appeared before the Court of Appeal and asked the court to dismiss the appeal. The Crown had the right to appeal the acquittal on a point of law, and the Crown had asked the Court of Appeal to hold that Judge Tyrwhitt-Drake was wrong in holding that the Criminal Code did not apply to Jones. But, McGivern argued, the Crown had no right to appeal an acquittal based on the facts. Judge Tyrwhitt-Drake had expressly said that even if the Code did apply to Jones, the evidence showed that Jones had done nothing wrong; that he had paid the full regular retail price for the car. Therefore, the appeal could serve no useful purpose, because even if the Crown won its appeal on the point of law, it was bound to lose on the facts. If the Court of Appeal found that the Code applied, it could not reverse Judge Tyrwhitt-Drake's decision, or order a new trial, because Judge Tyrwhitt-Drake's had acquitted Jones on the facts. The Court of Appeal agreed, and it dismissed the appeal by the Crown, saying that it was "frivolous and vexatious." The prosecution against Jones in the courts was now well and truly at an end.

On March 5, 1965, Premier Bennett broke his silence. He spoke to a meeting of his followers in Victoria. The attorney general was there and a crowd of perhaps two hundred people. Reporters from the two Victoria dailies, the *Times* and the *Colonist,* were there. During his speech, the premier said:

I am not going to say anything about the Jones boy. But I could tell you lots. I want to assure you that the position the government has taken is the right one.

What did Bennett mean? Obviously, he meant that he could tell the people who were there lots about why Jones should be removed from office. After all, Bennett's government was engaged in putting a bill through the legislature to remove Jones from office. What else was he talking about? He seemed to imply that Jones was unfit for office. There is an old song that began "The whole town's talking about the Jones boy." It turned out that the Jones boy was in love. Somewhere in the premier's memory bank, this song was rattling around. But when he used the phrase from the song about George Jones, he didn't mean to accuse Jones of being in love.

What was the effect of the premier's statement? It must have been to leave those who were at the meeting with the impression that Bennett had confidential information about Jones that justified Jones's removal from office. Perhaps each of those at the meeting thought they knew the reason: Was Jones guilty of the charges brought against him despite the verdict of the courts? Or was there something else? Was Jones a communist? Was he a homosexual? (Homosexual relations were a crime in those days.)

The premier knew, but he wasn't saying. His speech left Jones the victim of rumour and speculation.

This wasn't a case of one politician insulting another. Jones wasn't in politics. He was a public servant. He was working for Bennett's government. The words uttered by the premier may have seemed lighthearted, but they carried a sting. The slander against Jones may have been muffled (requiring just a bit of thought to unravel), but slander it was.

On March 26, the bill to remove Jones from office was passed. On that day, after consulting his solicitor, Jones issued a statement saying that he was going to sue the premier for damages for slander. Not long afterward, Jones came to me and asked me to represent him in court.

A suit for slander is based on oral speech. A suit for libel is based on written speech. Both are suits for defamation; that is, using language calculated to injure someone's reputation. But why sue for slander? Why didn't Jones sue for the loss of his job? The reason is that Jones had no right to claim damages for wrongful dismissal. His dismissal was perfectly legal. The government had gotten the bill through the legislature. It had been assented to by the lieutenant governor of the province. The bill was, as far as we could tell, unprecedented in Canadian history, but there were no grounds to challenge the constitutionality of the bill. The province had the power under the Constitution to pass it. The legislature had passed a law to remove Jones from office, and he had no right to sue W.A.C. Bennett, the government or anybody else for passing a valid law. That was the law in the pre-Charter era. It remains the same today.

Oddly enough, in *Wells v. Newfoundland,* the Supreme Court of Canada in 1999 held that the province of Newfoundland could not deny compensation to Andrew Wells, a member of the Public Utilities Commission of the province, by dissolving the commission and reconstituting it without Wells as a member. Because the legislature had not, in this legislative tango, provided that Wells would not be compensated, he was entitled to recover damages. Justice John Major, writing for the court, nevertheless held that the government would have been free to pass a Get Rid of Andy Wells Bill, and it would have been equally free to pass a bill to explicitly have denied him compensation. In Jones's case, we had a Get Rid of George Jones Bill, but with compensation.

George Jones's reputation had, nevertheless, been maligned. He was no longer chairman of the Purchasing Commission; there was no prospect of reinstatement. He was out of a job, and because of what the premier had said, he might not get another.

What Bennett had said was slander. Unless, of course, it was true. But what did he mean? His speech implied wrongdoing by Jones. But what? The question remained: Why had the government removed Jones from office? Once the slander suit against the premier was brought, we thought we might find out. In fact, Jones had told the media, when he launched the suit, that he wanted to get the premier into court for that very purpose; once there the premier would be required to justify the slander.

The premier, through his solicitor, had to file a statement of defence. What would it say? The premier could plead justification; that is, he could say that the implication he had made was true, that Jones was dishonest and unfit for office. If he did that, he could be required to give particulars: to say when and where Jones had been guilty of misconduct.

The premier could hardly rely on the purchase of the car from Pacific Chrysler at a discount, because the courts had found that no wrongdoing could be attributed to Jones in that case. Was there something else? Would the premier reveal it?

The premier's statement of defence didn't reveal anything. Through his solicitor, he denied having said anything about Jones, and if he had said anything about him, he denied it was defamatory. He said that even if it was defamatory, it was fair comment. These are standard defences in defamation cases. But then came the guts of the defence. The premier claimed that he was protected by qualified privilege. Statements made in the legislature are absolutely privileged. Nobody can sue for defamation for anything said in the legislature. Outside the legislature there is a privilege, but it is a qualified privilege. The law says that if someone holding a public office discusses matters of public interest, what he says is privileged, and even if he slanders someone, he cannot be sued. The reason is obvious. Public men and women must be able to make speeches, to inform the public and to report to their constituents. The public has a right to be kept informed, and politicians have a duty to keep them informed. So, under these circumstances, even if a politician says something that is untrue, he cannot be sued. But the privilege that a politician enjoys is qualified (here comes the limitation) to this extent: he cannot use a public office to say something knowing it to be untrue or reckless whether it is true or false.

All of this applied to the premier. As head of the government, he could argue that he had a duty to inform the electorate. That would bring him under the umbrella of qualified privilege. If, however, he had no honest belief in what he had said, if he did not believe that Jones was guilty of misconduct and unfit for office, then he could not claim that what he had said was privileged; he would have to pay damages for slandering Jones.

Whenever George Jones came to my office it was an event. He always smoked a cigar. He had a guardsman's mustache. George seemed to fill our small office. He would ask my mother, "How are you, Mrs. B.?" Then off we would go to lunch, Scotch with a beer chaser, several of them. I arrived once to see him in Victoria during a snowstorm. Because I was wearing light shoes, he insisted on piggybacking me from the hotel across the snow-filled parking lot to his car.

At Jones's examination for discovery, George L. Murray, the premier's counsel and one of the province's most experienced courtroom lawyers, was at pains to bring out some unusual features of Jones's past. Jones had been married four times. The first time was when he was only nineteen. The marriage lasted seventeen days. The second marriage was tumultuous, and Jones's second wife had won a divorce from him in 1948. Then, in 1951, he married her for the second time. In 1955 she left him again, for another man. Jones confronted them, and a fight ensued. Jones had brought a gun with him to the encounter but had left it in his car. (It was loaded, but only with blanks.) He was convicted of common assault and given a suspended sentence. He was also found guilty of being illegally in possession of a firearm.

Some of these items from Jones's unconventional past had been muttered about in Victoria, but it was Jones who had first made them public.

On March 15, 1965, ten days after Bennett's speech, Jones had spoken to a political science forum at the University of Victoria. He accused the government of digging up his past to find any justification for firing him. Referring to the conviction for being illegally in possession of a firearm, Jones could not resist embellishing the story: "It was a simple thing. I shot at somebody and missed.

I'm a lousy marksman. They reduced the charge and let me go free." He summed up his life story: "I've got enough skeletons in the closet to keep a Halloween party going for twenty years."

Indeed he had. But he also had a record of service to his country. Jones had joined the Royal Canadian Air Force at the outbreak of the Second World War in 1939. He left the RCAF in 1942 with the rank of flight lieutenant and shortly afterward joined the army as a gunner. When he left the army after the Second World War, he held the rank of major.

Jones's personal history was fascinating. But it had nothing to do with Jones's performance of his duties at the Purchasing Commission. Jones had been appointed to hold office during good behaviour. If there had been any evidence of misconduct, it should have—and presumably would have—been put before the legislature, and the legislature would have been asked to pass a resolution calling for Jones's removal from office. The only conclusion to be drawn was that there was no such evidence.

The government had combed Jones's past to find anything that might discredit him. Apart from a history of marital volatility, it was able to find nothing. This explained why the premier had never given any reason for Jones being removed from office: There *was* no reason to justify Jones's removal from office. Could there be any doubt that, if the government had been in possession of any evidence against Jones, the premier would not have hesitated to use it?

I conducted the premier's examination for discovery at the courthouse in Victoria. An examination for discovery is a pretrial examination under oath. It is held in private, with only a court reporter present. The premier came with his lawyer, George Murray. Bennett gave some answers that were astonishing, coming as they did from the head of the government. I asked him repeatedly why he had had Jones dismissed, my object being to show that when he slandered Jones at the meeting in Victoria he had no honest belief that Jones had been guilty of any misconduct at the Purchasing Commission. That would destroy the privilege. I asked him why Jones had been dismissed. He answered:

A   Because it was the government's decision, the government must accept the responsibility of its actions. Because we have, different from the United States, the British system of responsible government, and the government recommended to the Legislature that Mr. Jones be retired, made that decision, made that recommendation to the Legislature, then in the British system of parliament procedure it has to go through certain Bills and certain readings and certain time intervals and so forth, so everybody's rights are protected.

Q   Why did the government recommend to the Legislature that Mr. Jones be retired?

A   The government did it because it was the government's decision to make the rec-ommendation.

Q   Does the government have reasons for making recommendations to the Legislature?

A   The government brings down legislation and makes decisions and they are responsible for—the electors—for the decision. When they make a recommenda-tion then the government's recommendation goes before the Legislature, and the Legislature then either passes it or amends it or turns it down; that is our system of government.

Q   But what I want to know is why did the government recommend to the Legislature that Mr. Jones be retired?

A   That is the answer I gave you—because it was the government's decision.

Q   And that is your answer to my question?

A   Yes.

Q   Can you tell me if you concurred in the recommendation that was made to the Legislature?

A   The vote in the Legislature is a bill presented by the Provincial Secretary. There is a recorded vote taken in the Legislature and my vote was in the affirmative.

Q   Why did you vote in support of the bill for the retirement of Mr. Jones?

A   That is what I was elected for by the electors, and I took the oath of office to vote as my conscience dictated.

Q   Why did you vote as you did in the case of the bill relating to Mr. Jones?

A   Because I was in favour of the bill.

Q   Why were you in favour of the bill?

A   For the reasons I have given; it was the government decision that the bill be pre-sented and the bill was then before the Legislature at the recommendation of the government, and I and the majority of the Legislature voted with it, or for it.

Q   Did you believe in March last year that Mr. Jones was unfit for office as chairman of the Purchasing Commission?

A   What the government did when this bill was—to make a recommendation to the Legislature. I have never said anything against his character, whether he is the right man for chairman or not. All we did was to make the recommendation for this bill.

Q   Did you believe that he was unfit for office as chairman of the Purchasing Commission?

A   I am making no such statement. I never made any such statement at any time.

Q   Did you believe that Mr. Jones was guilty of the charges that had been made against him?

At this point, George Murray intervened: "Now, surely that is going a bit too far. What difference does it make whether Mr. Bennett believed or didn't believe that Mr. Jones was guilty or not guilty?" I changed my tack and asked, "Did you believe, Mr. Bennett, that Mr. Jones had accepted a benefit contrary to the provisions of the law?" Bennett replied, "I have no personal knowledge."

Round and round we went; the premier was not going to answer. It was hardly a masterpiece of evasion. No one who read his answers could regard them as anything but an exercise in obfuscation. Bennett did provide at least one straightforward answer. In exasperation I asked him, "Well, do you read the papers, Mr. Bennett?" He responded, "Not very often, because I am too busy. I make the news; I don't read the news." When his answers were read at the trial, the phrase entered the province's political currency as "I don't read the news; I make the news." But it caused the premier no political damage.

The premier's answers were ludicrous. At that point, I terminated my examination. We had enough evidence to prove that the premier had no facts to support his allegations against George Jones. I thought we had what we wanted. It was obvious that the premier had no honest belief that Jones had been guilty of any misconduct. "The Jones boy" had been unfairly maligned.

Jones was distinctly unhappy. He thought I should press on with my examination of the premier. The premier's lawyers had dug up all the dirt they could on him. Why couldn't we give the premier as rough a time? It was, however, Jones's reputation, not the premier's, that had been damaged. The premier's lawyers were entitled to show, if they could, that Jones had an unconventional, even irregular past; his reputation was not impeccable to start with; and therefore any damage to his reputation occasioned by the premier's speech would be minimal. But we had no right to ask the premier similar questions. Besides, if we had kept on questioning him, he might have come up with a reason, however implausible, for firing Jones. I didn't want to give him that chance. I thought it best to go with the answers we had.

George Murray was in no doubt. When the examination was over, he and I went to the bar at the Empress Hotel to have a drink. Nothing was said during the walk down the street from the courthouse to the hotel. We placed our orders; the drinks came; still nothing was said. Finally, Murray put his glass down and said, "Wasn't he the worst witness you ever saw?" I had the feeling that he would not be calling the premier to testify at the trial.

We had elected for trial by jury. I felt that any jury would regard the premier's answers as risible. We could read to the jury at the trial the answers the premier had given on his examination for discovery. Or we could subpoena the premier as a witness and put his answers to him.

So we went to court, seeking compensation against the premier for slander. We claimed that Jones had been disparaged in his office. This is a special category in the law of defamation. If someone has defamed you in your office, your profession or your calling, the law presumes damage in such a case. In Jones's case, there would be a presumption that Bennett's speech had caused damage to his reputation as an honest, capable administrator.

The trial opened before Justice Harold McInnes and a jury. We called Jim Hume, a reporter with the *Victoria Times*, to prove what the premier had said at the meeting in Victoria. He confirmed that, in fact, Bennett had used the very words alleged: "I am not going to say anything about the Jones boy. But I could tell you lots."

Taking the stand, George Jones testified that, since being ousted from office, he had attempted to obtain employment. He had gone to the Unemployment Insurance Commission; he had filled in an endless number of application forms. He had clipped the metropolitan newspapers religiously, answering a legion of advertisements. He had canvassed friends and relatives. He testified that he had been offered positions while he was chairman of the Purchasing Commission, but after the premier's speech the atmosphere had changed. Some employers adopted the attitude, he said, that "where there's smoke, there's fire." The premier had been responsible for the smoke, but there had been no fire.

Then I read to the jury the premier's evidence given on his examination for discovery. What you do is stand in front of the jury and read the questions and the answers from the transcript. It is not a good idea, I think, for counsel to try to do more than justice to testimony such as the premier's. Read with a straight face—as I did—it will elicit raised eyebrows, barely restrained chuckles, from judge and jury. For counsel to engage in histrionics in reading the answers would be a mistake. Let the words of the transcript speak for themselves.

Bennett had treated the lawsuit like a political campaign. His answers to questions were, perhaps, suitable to a news conference. Certainly, they were not far removed from the kind of answers the premier might have offered in the legislature in answer to opposition questions; that is, if there had been a question period in the B.C. legislature at that time. (There was none until the NDP came into office in 1972.)

In a court of law, however, in a defamation case, there must be a judgement on the meaning of words used—words become important. Political combat is one thing; the courts of law another. In a political campaign, an old stager like W.A.C. Bennett has a base of support, a record of achievement or of neglect (depending on your point of view); the public is used to his idiosyncratic use of language, the Alice in Wonderland concept of political dialogue. In the courts, however, language has to be examined on its own merits: What does it *mean*?

THE ACTUAL MEANING of words is the bedrock of the law.

In December 1989, I was asked to represent a Guatemalan refugee named Gonzalez-Davi. He had fled his own country because in Guatemala he had been assisting a Roman Catholic priest working among the Indians. Priests and other ordinary people like my client who helped the Indians and the poor were persecuted by the Guatemalan military. The military had beaten my client, then shot him and left him for dead. I was engaged by the immigration bar of British Columbia, who wished to see refugees provided with the means to retain counsel, to try to obtain a court order requiring the province's Legal Services Society to pay for legal representation for my client. The case turned on the meaning of two words in the Legal Services Society Act. Section 3(2) of the act provided that legal services are to be made available for any individual who may be imprisoned or confined through "civil proceedings." It was held that those two words include an immigration inquiry; hence, refugees are entitled to legal aid at such inquiries. The Legal Services Society was ordered to provide legal aid. As a result, in the first twelve months following the judgement, legal aid was provided to more than two thousand refugees entering Canada through B.C.; in April 1991, the Court of Appeal upheld the order of the lower court. The decision has cost the Legal Services Society $3.5 million each year since.

Or it may be a phrase in a regulation: On August 21, 1991, Brit Amos, a young man from B.C., twenty-two years old, was in Sunnyvale, California, to take a surveying course. He was driving after dark through a rough part of East Palo Alto when he had a harrowing encounter.

Brit stopped at an intersection. He had gone no farther than fifty feet when he saw three men crossing from the median into the path of his van. He slowed down and steered to the right in an attempt to get past them. As he did so, a fourth man jumped in front of his van. Brit had to slam on his brakes, but he did not bring the van to a complete stop. Two more men emerged from the shadows. He was now virtually surrounded.

Brit locked the doors on both sides of the van and kept it moving slowly ahead. His assailants were now pounding on the windows on both sides of the van. The glass on the driver's side shattered but was held in place by the door frame. One of the men walked directly in front of the van and pointed a gun at Brit. Brit ducked so as to avoid the gunman's line of fire.

The gunman then moved to the driver's side of the van and used the gun to clear away the shattered glass in the window. Brit did not hear a shot. But he felt a sudden change come over his body. He could hardly breathe. He had no control over his legs. He realized he had been hit.

With singular presence of mind, despite receiving a bullet wound that disabled him from using his legs, Brit was able to accelerate. He did this by using both hands to push his right leg down so that his right foot in turn applied pressure to the accelerator. This engaged his hands, but, slumped over the wheel, he was able to manipulate his torso to control the direction of travel of the van. He made his escape; after travelling several blocks, he used the van's emergency hand brake to bring the vehicle to a halt at a busy intersection, pulled himself out of the van and lay down on the pavement. Bystanders came to help him and he was taken to a hospital. The bullet had damaged Brit's spinal cord; he was a paraplegic, with no use of his legs.

Could he sue? He didn't know who his attackers were, so he couldn't sue them. Because Brit was from B.C., he was insured by the Insurance Corporation of British Columbia (ICBC). So he was entitled to collect no-fault medical and rehabilitative benefits payable by ICBC, according to the regulations made under the statute, if he could show that his injury was "caused by an accident that arises out of the ownership, use or operation of a vehicle." The coverage applied in the U.S. as well as in Canada.

We had to go all the way to the Supreme Court of Canada to sort out the meaning of the phrase.

Brit lost in the B.C. courts. They held that Brit's injuries were caused not by anything he did as owner of the van but by his attackers. Brit's van was simply the site of the attack.

We applied to the Supreme Court of Canada for leave to appeal. Leave was granted. In the Supreme Court, the argument was based on arcane learning about accidents and causation. I urged, however, that it was all quite simple. It may be that the attack on Brit's vehicle had been a random attack, but the *shooting* was not; it occurred because Brit Amos secured the doors and kept the vehicle moving; frustrated in his attempt to break in, one of the thugs used the butt end of his gun to shatter the window on the driver's side. The gun went off. If Brit had not been *using* his van to get from point A to point B; if he had not, as *owner,* secured the doors; if he had not continued to *operate* the van by keeping it moving, he would not have been shot.

The case could not be regarded as the same as one where a man is parked by the roadside and someone comes by and shoots him. In such a case, the motor vehicle is simply the location of the "accident." In Brit's case, the thugs may have chosen his van at random. But the shooting that followed was *not* a random shooting. It was directed at him because he would not stop his vehicle.

This was the critical error by the B.C. courts: they regarded the *attack* as random and therefore concluded the *shooting* was random. But it was not; it arose out of the locking of the doors and the continued movement of the van.

Justice John Major delivered the unanimous judgement of the court. He rejected the reasoning of the B.C. courts:

Was the attack in this case merely a random shooting, or did it arise out of the owner-ship, use or operation of the appellant's vehicle? While the appellant's van may have been singled out by his assailants on a random basis, the shooting which caused the appellant's injuries was not random. The appellant's vehicle was not merely the situs of the shooting. The shooting appears to have been the direct result of the assailants' failed attempt to gain entry to the appellant's van. It is not important whether the shooting was accidental or deliberate while entry to the vehicle was being attempted. It is important that the shooting was not random but a shooting that arose out of the appellant's ownership, use and operation of his vehicle.

Brit received his "no-fault" benefits (about $150,000). The true meaning of a word or a phrase can make all the difference.

But in a contest with Premier Bennett, words were not vessels of meaning.

As I had expected, George Murray did not call Bennett to testify on his own behalf. In fact, he introduced no evidence at all. Murray asked the judge to with-draw the case from the jury on the ground that there was no evidence. I thought the motion was bound to fail. But Justice McInnes reserved judgement. I thought he must have done so to prepare a few well-considered sentences allow-ing the case to go to the jury. A few days later, he handed down judgement with-drawing the case from the jury on the ground that the remarks of the premier could not bear a defamatory meaning. He ruled that no reasonable person would have gathered from what the premier said that Jones had been guilty of mis-conduct. Therefore, the jury should not be allowed to decide whether Bennett had slandered Jones.

This was a surprising decision. The judge had appointed himself to decide the very issue that should have gone to the jury. We appealed to the Court of Appeal. There we were successful. The Court of Appeal held that Justice McInnes had been wrong; the words might well have been regarded by many in the premier's audience as implying misconduct; and therefore it should have been left to the jury to decide whether the words were defamatory. The Court of Appeal ordered a new trial. Premier Bennett applied to the Supreme Court of Canada for leave to appeal the Court of Appeal's decision. But the Supreme Court refused to grant leave.

On January 9, 1967, the new trial opened before Justice John Ruttan. This time we did not give a jury notice. This meant that Justice Ruttan would not only have to decide the questions of law in the case, but also all questions of fact. At this second trial, Jones gave the same evidence as before. I read to the court the answers the premier had given on his examination for discovery, arguing that a man unwilling to give any reason for Jones's dismissal could not have had any honest belief in what he said when he uttered the words "I am not going to say anything about the Jones boy. But I could tell you lots." The premier, as before, did not testify on his own behalf.

Justice Ruttan found "that the words [of the premier] were slanderous and were calculated to disparage the plaintiff in his office as chairman of the Purchasing Commission." He went on:

What then was Mr. Bennett referring to when he told his listeners he could say "lots"? If he were referring merely to the legislation, why didn't he tell them "lots" about the bill, about the reasons for it, or at least that it was an Act made necessary as Mr. Murray suggested, because it would be impossible at this late date to keep Mr. Jones in the confidential position he held in the service? Perhaps the government had found someone more suitable to replace him, and was retiring him in a very generous manner. If there were reasons with no derogatory connotation attached for discharging Jones, the premier could have spoken freely either then on March 5th, in the House when he introduced the bill, on February 25th or later. Yet neither Mr. Bennett nor any of his government has ever given a reason for the legislation. If, therefore, he meant he could say lots about the reasons for the bill and also said he was going to remain silent, the most reasonable and obvious implication is that he had many good reasons, which were so derogatory to Jones, he dared not mention them.

The premier's main defence was qualified privilege. For the premier, it was argued that he was telling his political supporters what stand he had taken in the legislature. If he had a duty to convey information, and his constituents to receive it, then what he had said was privileged if he spoke believing in the truth of what he said. In this sense what he said was privileged; it was a privilege, however, that was qualified in that he must believe it to be true.

Could the premier claim qualified privilege? I conceded that if Bennett had used the occasion to inform his audience, he could claim the benefit of the defence of qualified privilege. But he did not use the occasion to inform the audience of anything. No facts were provided; in fact, the premier was at pains to say to his audience that he intended to tell it nothing.

The privilege, I argued, existed for the benefit of the public. If Bennett could claim a duty to speak, it was because his duty was to keep the public informed. Instead, he used the occasion to mock Jones ("the Jones boy") and to cast a shadow over his whole past ("I could tell you lots"). He could claim no public duty to say these things, and the public had no interest in hearing them. There is a difference, I urged, between frankness and insinuation, between saying "I have to tell you that Jones is dishonest. So he must go" and simply making derogatory insinuations.

Justice Ruttan dealt with the issue in this way:

The premier must have known that whatever he did say would be communicated to the general public. The two reporters present sat at a press table in full view of the speaker's table.

The one matter which might require the protection of special privilege, involved communication of anything the premier knew or honestly believed that would justify the government's policy towards Jones culminating in [the bill to dismiss Jones from office]. I do not suggest this was the occasion when the premier should have spoken out about Jones. If there was no need or duty to speak in the House under conditions of absolute privilege, there could hardly be any greater duty to make revelations elsewhere on the very same subject.

In any event the occasion was not used to communicate information, for the premier specifically stated he was not going to say anything. In fact he did leave them only with a slanderous imputation against Jones which cannot be justified on the grounds of interest or duty.

When he came to assess damages, Justice Ruttan suggested that Jones should not have made the speech he did at the University of Victoria ("I've got enough skeletons in the closet to keep a Halloween party going for twenty years") on the ground that it might have affected his chances of obtaining employment. He went on, however, to say that it was of no real consequence compared to the premier's slander of him.

I agree Jones showed a lack of judgement and discretion [in speaking at the university] and this would hurt his chances to secure private employment. I have taken into account also that Jones was fifty-six years old at the time of his dismissal, and that responsible jobs calling for his specific skills and training are limited in number. But these factors are of minor significance when balanced against the one overwhelming reason for his failure to secure any gainful employment. Speaking with the most authoritative voice of the government which employed Jones, Mr. Bennett in effect declared him to be unfit to continue in a position which demanded a high standard of impartiality and integrity.

Referring to the answers the premier had given on his examination for discovery, he said: "Rather than provide mitigation, Mr. Bennett's equivocation and his consistent neglect to retract or apologize served only to keep the slander alive and continue the injury to the plaintiff."

Justice Ruttan awarded damages of $15,000. This may seem by today's standards to be inadequate. It was, to that point in the province's history, however, the largest award of damages for defamation in a non-jury case.

George Jones's travail was not over. Premier Bennett appealed the decision to the Court of Appeal. In January 1968, the Court of Appeal handed down its decision. They held that the premier had been guilty of slander. Nevertheless, they said, he was entitled to claim the protection of qualified privilege. The Court of Appeal held that we had not proved that the premier had made accusations in which he had no honest belief.

Justice H. W. Davey said that the reference to "the Jones boy" added nothing to the defamatory meaning, except colour. "That description was not in keeping with the dignity of the office that Jones still occupied, but refinement of language is not required, and a certain robustness of speech is expected in political statements."

I had argued that Justice Ruttan had made a finding that the premier had no honest belief in what he said. No, said the Court of Appeal, that was a negative finding, not a positive finding. The court said that even though the premier's audience would have understood his remarks to impute misconduct to Jones, we hadn't shown the premier intended the audience should draw that conclusion. This, I thought, was splitting hairs and then splitting them again.

We applied to the Supreme Court of Canada for leave to appeal. Leave was granted. I argued the case for Jones. John J. Robinette of Toronto, regarded by many, certainly by the Ontario bar, as Canada's outstanding lawyer of his era, argued the case for Premier Bennett.

The Court of Appeal had described the premier's language as "colourful." The court excused the premier on the ground that, after all, it was simply politics. In my written submission filed in the Supreme Court, I sought to answer the Court of Appeal.

That argument might be acceptable if the premier had been discussing another politician . . . That is not to say that a public man cannot provide his audience with the facts about a public matter, and it is not to say that he cannot do so in a colourful way. But when he is discussing a matter relating to the integrity of a servant of the Crown, his words, though colourful, must also be reasonably necessary and appropriate. If his words are not really calculated to inform, but merely to denigrate, they are an abuse of the privilege.

... When a politician, especially one as powerful as the premier of the province, discusses a matter of grave importance relating to a public servant from the public platform, he not only has a duty to the electorate to inform them of the facts relating to the matter, but also has a duty to the public servant in question. What is that duty? He has a duty to be fair and to be frank. He has a duty to state the facts and not to make insinuations. He must not engage in gratuitous insults as the [premier] did when he referred to "the Jones boy." If he does, the privilege is lost.

... In such a case the courts should be diligent to see that the privilege that politicians enjoy is not exceeded, and to ensure that the privilege is not used as a vehicle for conveying insinuations in a way that goes beyond the responsible exercise of the privilege afforded. The privilege, granted for one purpose, should not be exploited for another; the duty to keep the public informed should not be regarded as a licence to slander.

On December 11, 1968, the Supreme Court of Canada handed down its judgement. The Supreme Court reversed the judgement of the Court of Appeal, reinstating the award of damages for $15,000 that Jones had won at trial. It appeared that my contention—that when a politician trains his guns on a civil servant (or any other citizen) he cannot do so with the same impunity that applies when he is exchanging insults with another politician—had prevailed.

Chief Justice John Cartwright, who gave the judgement of the court, had no difficulty finding that the premier had slandered Jones. Then he went on to the issue of qualified privilege. He was doubtful of the argument advanced on behalf of the premier. He said:

[The premier asserts] that whenever the holder of high elective political office sees fit to give an account of his stewardship and of the actions of the government of which he is a member to supporters of the political party to which he belongs he is speaking on an occasion of qualified privilege. I know of no authority for such a proposition and I am not prepared to assent to it. I will assume for the purposes of this appeal that each subject on which the defendant spoke to the meeting was one of public interest. It is not suggested that at the date of the meeting an election was pending. The claim asserted by the defence appears to me to require an unwarranted extension of the qualified privilege which has been held to attach to communications made by an elector to his fellow electors of matters regarding a candidate which he honestly believes to be true and which, if true, would be relevant to the question of such candidate's fitness for office. It is, of course, a perfectly proper proceeding for a member of the Legislature to address a meeting of his supporters at any time, but if in the course of addressing them he sees fit to make defamatory statements about another which are in fact untrue it is difficult to see why the common convenience and welfare of society requires that such statements should be protected and the person defamed left without a remedy unless he can affirmatively prove express malice on the part of the speaker.

Chief Justice Cartwright was here doubtful that any qualified privilege was claimable by the premier; such would only apply during an election. This was merely a prelude to the court's main ruling. In fact, the court went off on a narrow point. They held that because, to the knowledge of the premier, two newspaper reporters were present at the meeting, it was not in any event an occasion of qualified privilege. Chief Justice Cartwright held that it was the presence of the reporters that made all the difference. He said:

Assuming, although I am far from deciding, that had no newspaper reporters been present, the occasion would have been privileged, I am satisfied that any privilege which the defendant would have had was lost by reason of the fact that, as found by the . . . trial Judge:

The premier must have known that whatever he did say would be communicated to the general public. The two reporters present sat at a press table in full view of the speaker's table.

This meant that the premier knew he was speaking not only to his own supporters, but to the whole world. In the circumstances, what he said was not protected by privilege.

Jones had won. As a personal victory, it owed much to his pluck and persistence.

We had won because the premier's defence of qualified privilege was not claimable when he knew that the media would carry his words beyond the meeting hall to the whole province. I would have preferred to win simply on the footing that the premier had abused the privilege that would ordinarily have accompanied the occasion. Public men and women can state publicly what they honestly believe, but they cannot use the privilege they enjoy to insult their fellow citizens when they have no facts to support their insinuations. I confess that I was not altogether happy with the distinction the court made between the premier's supporters and the public beyond the meeting hall. It is difficult to see how it can be said that the premier's supporters had a greater interest than all the other citizens of the province in hearing what he had to say; that a speech to your supporters may be privileged but a speech intended to be heard by the public is not.

George Jones was not much interested in these legal niceties. He was ecstatic. He had been vindicated, his reputation restored. But he never did regain employment in his field. He became a radio hotline host for a while and then drifted from view. He came to Vancouver a few years later to take me to lunch. Though dying of cancer, he tried mightily to be his usual irrepressible self.

Premier Bennett had his revenge on me, if not on George Jones. During the course of the litigation, I had myself been elected to the legislature sitting as an NDP member in the opposition. In the legislature, Premier Bennett often referred to me as a "city slicker lawyer." Not very imaginative as invective. When the Supreme Court's decision in the Jones case came down, he went on a tirade, not altogether ill-natured, against me in the legislature. When his own members began to laugh, he said, "Oh, I admit he's good at some things." Bennett told the media that he had received thousands of telegrams of support for his stand in the Jones imbroglio. When asked by the media if they could see the telegrams, he said, "Oh no, they're confidential."

Later that same year, in 1969, I was elected leader of the New Democratic Party in B.C. Premier Bennett almost immediately called a provincial election. The NDP was soundly defeated and I lost my own seat. This led me to depart the political life and to devote myself to life in the courts, no more to toil in the political vineyards.

In fact, Premier Bennett had done me a favour. I was much better suited to law than to politics. It was not only a question of temperament. It was a question of intellectual fulfillment.

In law the cases have a beginning, a middle and an end. You undertake a case; you assemble it; shape it; decide the best way to present it. You search for the evidence. You ponder your next step. When it's over, you realize it had a trajectory that brought it from its commencement to its completion. You won it or you lost it, or perhaps it was settled somewhere along the way. But it had a shape and size of its own.

The case of *Jones v. Bennett* was like that; it had a trajectory, from a meeting hall in Victoria to the Supreme Court of Canada. It worked its way from its start to its conclusion.

But politics in B.C., certainly in the W. A. C. Bennett era, was nothing like that. It was often no more than the proclamation of slogans, a search for a phrase that would capture the difference between the parties. I preferred the cleaner lines of legal argument. It could provide a focus that went to the heart of an issue.

I have to admit, too, that I felt more comfortable in the region of legal argument than in the swirl of politics: the constant meetings, speeches, the time inevitably spent in "working the room," meeting people you'd never met before ("Nice to see you again") and would never meet again.

Once in politics, it can seem to be as important, even more important by far than any other line of work. After I had left politics, I was at a dinner with Roy Romanow, then the attorney general of Saskatchewan. He said, "Tom, don't you miss politics?" I said, no, I didn't. He wasn't satisfied with my answer: "Oh, surely you miss political life. Admit it!" I said no again. When Roy persisted, I finally said, "The trouble with you politicians is you think politics is the centre of the universe." "It is!" he said. I don't think he was being entirely facetious.

I believed there was much more for me to do, but not in politics.

In politics, however, you learn a great deal: how government works; how politicians think. You learn that fundamentally, most politicians want to do the right thing according to their lights. But the pervasive and all-consuming need to be elected and re-elected greatly affects political decisions. Perhaps that is as it should be; it is the very nature of politics. But I preferred to work in a forum where words and ideas, in and of themselves, not only carry the freight—they *are* the freight. I decided to follow Blaise Pascal's advice, "Become what you are." I was thirty-six when I left politics. I had no desire to return. I knew where I belonged. I had been cured of the political itch. I would not be tempted to re-enter political life.

4   Resurrecting a Treaty

A FTER TOM HURLEY DIED, Maisie Hurley appeared at my office, leaning on her cane. She was in her seventies but still a commanding figure. She announced, "Now, Tommy, *you* will have to defend the Indians." She was not a woman to argue with. Thus did I become a lifelong defender of Aboriginal causes.

"Defending the Indians" in those days meant defending those who were in trouble with the law. The federal government would pay for legal defence in Indian murder cases. I had done one or two of those. But Maisie announced that I was to bring an appeal for two Indian men in Nanaimo who had been convicted of hunting during the closed season. They had been found in possession of deer, in violation of the provincial Game Act. It was a summary conviction offence; they had been convicted by a magistrate, so they had the right to a new trial in the County Court. The case did not sound like an important case. But it was to be the first shot fired by the Aboriginal peoples of Canada in their campaign to reclaim Aboriginal and treaty rights.

On Sunday, July 7, 1963, Clifford White and David Bob had gone hunting. They belonged to the Nanaimo band and lived on a reserve near the city of Nanaimo on southern Vancouver Island. Clifford White had nine children; David Bob had four. They were hunting for food for their families. They did not have far to go to find deer. A few miles inland from Nanaimo, on the south slope of Mount Benson, they shot six blacktailed deer, a small deer found in large numbers on Vancouver Island. They were on their way back to the reserve with the deer when they were stopped by a game warden. It was the closed season. The warden told them they were hunting in violation of the law. Both men were charged. The law made no exception for a man with a hungry family. And no exception for Indians. On September 23, 1963, they came before the magistrate at Nanaimo. They were tried, found guilty and ordered to pay a fine of $100 each and in default to serve forty days in prison. David Bob and his family managed to put up $100 to cover his fine, but Clifford White could not. So he was sent to Oakalla Prison Farm to serve his forty-day sentence. Maisie Hurley arranged to pay Clifford White's fine, so that he could be released before the completion of his sentence. It was then that Maisie came to my office and announced I had two new clients.

It was all very well to take an appeal for two new clients. But what was our defence to the charge? The Game Act said there was to be no hunting during the closed season. There was no question that White and Bob were in possession of the deer and they had killed them during the closed season. I went to Nanaimo to see my clients. I am not sure I had ever visited an Indian reserve before. They were pleased Maisie Hurley had organized their legal defence. My conference with them took place at a meeting of the band itself. Members of the band of all ages were there, from children who ran about the hall to elders sitting gravely to hear the views of a young lawyer from Vancouver. This was not just Clifford White and David Bob's case. It was a cause that animated all those present. I soon realized why.

The elders told me that the members of the Nanaimo band had, under an old treaty, the right to hunt in the closed season. What treaty? I had never heard of such a treaty, but if it existed that would make a difference. The Indian Act, a federal statute, provided that provincial laws of general application, such as the Game Act, should apply to Indians, but they only applied subject to any treaty the Indians had signed. If a treaty existed guaranteeing the hunting rights of the Nanaimo Indians, my clients might have a defence to the charge brought under the Game Act. The Indian Act, which provided that treaty provisions would govern even in the face of provincial law, would take precedence.

But was there a treaty? The Indians of B.C. were known as "non-treaty" Indians. There were no treaties blanketing the province. To be sure, the northeastern part of B.C., lying on the eastern side of the Rockies, was covered by Treaty No. 8, signed in 1899. But that was an extension of the Prairie treaties, signed in the late nineteenth century, which covered the Prairie provinces and the northern woodlands. B.C.'s Peace River country had always been thought of as geographically part of the Prairies. The Indians of the Peace River were related to the Indians of the plains and the northern woodlands. Apart from Treaty 8, there were, as far as I knew, no treaties in B.C.

There were, however, transfers of land by some of the Indians on Vancouver Island to the Hudson's Bay Company. An old publication entitled *Papers Connected with the Indian Land Question 1850–1875* contained fourteen of these transfers to the company (known in legal parlance as conveyances) by the Indians of southern Vancouver Island. They had been signed in the 1850s. No one paid much attention to these papers; they were not seen as having any legal significance.

The transfers, however, when examined closely, seemed to be more than simple conveyances. By these transfers the Indians had given up their ancestral lands. But the transfers reserved "the right of the Indians to hunt and fish for food as formerly for themselves and their families." That seemed to open the way to a defence in our case.

But were these conveyances treaties? They had to be treaties within the meaning of the Indian Act if the hunting rights they guaranteed were to take precedence over the Game Act.

Treaties are made with the Crown. These conveyances were not agreements with the Crown, but with the Hudson's Bay Company, a private company. They could hardly, therefore, be called treaties. An Indian treaty has to be a treaty with the Crown. Vancouver Island was a Crown colony in the 1850s. If these were treaties with the Crown, why hadn't the governor of the colony signed the treaties? They had in fact been signed by James Douglas, who was governor of the colony at the time, but he had signed in his capacity as chief factor of the Hudson's Bay Company. It seemed they were nothing more than purchases of land negotiated by the Hudson's Bay Company. If the company had promised that the Indians could hunt and fish as formerly, where did that get us? Only if such a promise had been made by the Crown could it be regarded as a treaty promise. Nothing less than that was required if we were to have a defence.

To understand why the Hudson's Bay Company was obtaining conveyances from the Indians, we had to examine the history of the colonization of Vancouver Island. The first settlement on Vancouver Island was established by the Hudson's Bay Company at Fort Victoria in 1843. James Douglas was the chief factor of the company in the territory. He was a man who had spent much of his life among the Indian people.

Douglas was born in the West Indies, the son of a "free coloured woman" and a Scottish merchant. His father had him educated in Scotland. At age sixteen, he was apprenticed to the North West Company and entered the employ of the Hudson's Bay Company when the two companies merged in 1821. His wife, Amelia, was part Indian, the daughter of the company's chief factor in Rupert's Land, William Connolly. In 1828, while Douglas was at Fort St. James, Amelia and he were married according to "the custom of the country"; in 1837 their marriage was confirmed in a Church of England ceremony. Douglas was a fur trader and had always regarded the Indians as the company's partners in the enterprise. Douglas always believed in the necessity and the justice of making treaties with the Indians. To do so would be in the interest of the Crown. As early as 1851, he advised London that the Indians of Vancouver Island would "become under proper management of service to the Colony, and form a valuable auxiliary in the event of war with any foreign power."

In 1849, the Crown conveyed the whole of Vancouver Island to the Hudson's Bay Company. In the same year, the Crown Colony of Vancouver Island was established. So you had the curious situation of a Crown colony composed of land held by a single landowner. The company had a conveyance of the whole of the island from the Crown. But Douglas believed, rightly, that this conveyance was subject to the Indian title—what we now call Aboriginal title—to the island. The Indian title was a legal burden on the Crown's underlying title to the land—a burden that had to be removed. Hence Douglas obtained transfers from the Indians.

Richard Blanshard was appointed the first governor of the colony. But Douglas was the most powerful figure in the colony, because the Hudson's Bay Company was itself all-powerful. In 1851 Blanshard resigned. The Colonial Office in London appointed Douglas to replace him. So Douglas became governor of the Crown colony while remaining as chief factor of the company. He wore two hats.

Douglas himself had signed all fourteen of the conveyances, but he had plainly done so as chief factor of the company, not as governor of the colony; he had signed for the Hudson's Bay Company, not the Crown. He was, from the point of view of establishing a defence in our case, wearing the wrong hat.

Douglas believed that it was essential to obtain surrenders of land from the Indians. It had always been Britain's policy, in advancing the settlement of North America, to obtain a surrender of the Aboriginal title held by the Indians before settlement proceeded. It was a policy made explicit in the Royal Proclamation of 1763.

Although the British defeated the French on the Plains of Abraham in 1759, a peace treaty was not signed until 1763. By the Treaty of Paris, the British acquired virtually all of France's colonies in North America. The British had to issue a proclamation, under the authority of King George III, providing for the governance of the vast area that had fallen into their possession. The proclamation referred to the "several Nations or Tribes of Indians with whom we are connected," and provided that no settlement, beyond the boundaries of the colonies established by the proclamation, should take place except by a treaty with them.

There has been a continuing dispute among scholars as to whether the proclamation was intended to extend beyond the Rocky Mountains to the Pacific Coast. This has turned out to be a barren question. The significance of the proclamation lies in the fact that it exemplified the British policy of recognizing Aboriginal rights, of the necessity for treaty-making prior to settlement. That policy applied as much to the mainland of B.C. and Vancouver Island as anywhere else.

The United States, following the American War of Independence, followed the same policy. In carrying out this policy, Britain and later the United States entered into treaties with the Indians. Moreover, on Vancouver Island the Indians were far more numerous than the white settlers. Douglas realized that the Indians believed that Vancouver Island belonged to them. If the settlers were going to acquire land for farming, it would have to be from the Indians.

Douglas therefore obtained conveyances of land from the Indians in and about Victoria. As settlement extended northward, along the east coast of the island, he obtained conveyances from the Indians wherever the settlers wanted to establish their farms. In his dispatches to the Colonial Office, Douglas explained how he went about it. At a meeting with the chiefs and the people of each tribe, he would tell the Indians that he wanted their land. He told them he did not want their village sites or their cultivated fields. But he did want the remainder of their land. There were no Indian reserves in those days. The village sites and cultivated fields the Indians retained under the conveyances were the beginnings in British Columbia of the reserve system. Douglas told the Indians, however, that they would always have the right to hunt over all of the land beyond the reserves—in fact, over all of the land they were giving up—as long as the land remained unoccupied, and they would have the right to continue their fishery.

What did Douglas give the Indians for signing the treaties? Not very much. A few pounds sterling and some Hudson's Bay blankets. In exchange, he received a formal surrender of their land, permitting settlement to advance. But, as he made clear in his dispatches, this agreement was to be subject to the continuation of Indians' rights of hunting and fishing.

These conveyances may be seen today in B.C.'s Provincial Archives. The words of the instruments are usually the same. Each of the documents was written in longhand by a clerk employed by the Hudson's Bay Company. All of the Indian men in each tribe would sign. None of them could write, so each made an X, and the clerk wrote the name of each Indian beside his X mark.

Typical is the following conveyance obtained by Douglas in 1852 from the Indians of South Saanich, not far from the present-day city of Victoria:

SAANICH TRIBE—SOUTH SAANICH
Know all men that we, the chiefs and people of the Saanich Tribe, who have signed our names and made our marks to this deed on the 6th day of February, one thousand

eight hundred and fifty-two, do consent to surrender, entirely and for ever, to James Douglas, the agent of the Hudson's Bay Company in Vancouver Island, that is to say, for the Governor, Deputy Governor, and Committee of the same, the whole of the lands situate and lying between Mount Douglas and Cowichan Head, on the Canal de Haro, and extending thence to the line running through the centre of Vancouver Island, North and South.

The condition of or understanding of this sale is this, that our village sites and enclosed fields are to be kept for our own use, for the use of our children, and for those who may follow after us; and the land shall be properly surveyed hereafter. It is understood, however, that the land itself, with these small exceptions, becomes the entire property of the white people for ever; it is also understood that we are at liberty to hunt over the unoccupied lands, and to carry on our fisheries as formerly.

We have received, as payment, Forty-one pounds thirteen shillings and four pence.

In token whereof, we have signed our names and made our marks, at Fort Victoria, on the 7th day of February, one thousand eight hundred and fifty two.

[Signed] WHUT-SAY-MULLET [his X mark and nine others]

"We are at liberty to hunt over the unoccupied lands." This is precisely what Clifford White and David Bob were doing; that is, assuming there was a similar conveyance at Nanaimo. If there was such a conveyance, and if it was a treaty, White and Bob were hunting lawfully.

The question was, could we enforce the provision in favour of Indian hunting and fishing rights in these conveyances, a provision not limited to the closed season? The surrender itself was a surrender to "James Douglas, the agent of the Hudson's Bay Company," not "James Douglas, the governor of the Crown Colony of Vancouver Island." (The reference in the conveyance to "the Governor, Deputy Governor," etc., was to the governor of the Hudson's Bay Company, not the governor of the Colony of Vancouver Island.) So how could these conveyances be regarded as treaties? Indian treaties are made with the Crown, not with fur trading companies. Of course, transferring the land to "the white people for ever" looked very much like a transfer of Indian land for the benefit of the people of the colony, not just the company.

Moreover, we could argue that the conveyance at Nanaimo was, in fact, signed by the governor of the colony. Douglas was not taking off one hat and then putting on the other—metaphorically speaking. He always wore two hats. The Crown's interests were wholly mingled with the interests of the company. He could sign the conveyances as chief factor, but it made no difference—he remained the governor. Douglas exercised vast power in the colony. In fact, Douglas was isolated from London; it took two months for his dispatches to reach London and the same length of time for a reply to be received. He had his brother-in-law, James Cameron, named chief justice; Cameron was not a lawyer, but a clerk employed by the company. Douglas could not split his official identity in half.

We certainly had the makings of a case that these real estate transactions were actually treaties between the Indians and the Crown. If so, the Game Act did not apply to White and Bob. But we had a fundamental problem with regard to the question of the existence of a treaty covering Nanaimo. Though thirteen of these conveyances had been obtained between 1850 and 1852, there was no similar conveyance at Nanaimo. There was, however, in the Provincial Archives, a blank piece of paper that had been signed at Fort Nanaimo on December 23, 1854, by Douglas and by a large number of Indians. We counted the X marks: there were 159. But the Indians were not called the Nanaimo Indians; they were called the Saalequun tribe. And the body of the paper was blank. There were only the marks of the men who had signed it and, beside each man's mark, the number of blankets he was to receive. The Indians at Nanaimo received 638 blankets in all. They did not receive any money, only blankets.

If this document was a treaty, it was unique: a blank piece of paper and 159 X marks. But perhaps it was enforceable despite its poverty of information.

Douglas and the Saalequun Indians at Fort Nanaimo had signed something in 1854, but what had Douglas and these Indians agreed to? Even if we were able to find out, what good would it do Clifford White and David Bob? How could we show that they were the descendants of the Saalequun Indians who had signed the conveyances?

We enlisted the provincial archivist, Willard Ireland, a historian, in the search for the true meaning of the document. He pointed us towards a letter that Archibald Barclay, the secretary of the Hudson's Bay Company in London, had sent to Douglas in December 1849. In it, Barclay authorized Douglas to take conveyances from the Indians. He gave him copious instructions on compensating the Indians for their land, the chief object of these instructions being to ensure that the scale of compensation should be limited. Then Barclay went on to say: "The Natives will be confirmed in the possession of their lands as long as they occupy and cultivate them themselves, but will not be allowed to sell or dispose of them to any private person, the right to the entire soil having been granted to the Company by the Crown." This stipulation was in keeping with what had been British policy since 1763. That is, the Crown did not recognize any sales of land by the Indians to private persons. Only the Crown could acquire Indian land. Given Barclay's letter, the company was behaving suspiciously like the Crown itself.

Barclay continued: "The right of fishing and hunting will be continued to them, and when their lands are registered, and they conform to the same conditions with which other settlers are required to comply, they will enjoy the same rights and privileges." These instructions were given in 1849, before any of the conveyances had been obtained. Douglas had obviously followed them in obtaining the thirteen surrenders.

Then we looked at a dispatch Douglas had sent on May 16, 1850, acknowledging Barclay's instructions. Douglas told him that he had already made three purchases with Indian bands in and about Fort Victoria. He had arranged these purchases, at a total cost to the Hudson's Bay Company's exchequer of 150 pounds, three shillings and fourpence. Then he said: "I informed the Natives that they would not be disturbed in the possession of their Village sites and enclosed fields, which are of small extent, and that they were at liberty to hunt over the unoccupied lands, and to carry on their fisheries with the same freedom as when they were the sole occupants of the country." Thirteen of the conveyances in the archives do in fact faithfully reflect Douglas's promises regarding the right of the Indians to continue to hunt and to fish. He concluded his dispatch: "I attached the signatures of the Native Chief's [sic] and others who subscribed the deed of purchase to a blank piece on which will be copied the contract or Deed of conveyance, as soon as we receive a proper form, which I beg may be sent off by return of Post. The other matters referred to in your letter will be duly attended to."

Thus it appeared that Douglas had gotten the first three conveyances around Fort Victoria signed on blank sheets of paper, and, when the proper form of wording to be used had been sent from London, he had arranged for the words of the conveyances to be filled in. If he had done that in 1850, why not in 1854 at Nanaimo? In 1854, he might well have followed the same procedure, except that he never got around to filling in the terms of the "contract or Deed of conveyance" with the Indians at Nanaimo. It would explain why the instrument made in 1854 consisted simply of a blank piece of paper with the Indians' X marks and nothing more. If we were right, there had been fourteen conveyances, not thirteen; fourteen treaties, not thirteen.

If the Nanaimo conveyance was secured from the Indians on the strength of a promise that the Indians would have the right to hunt over the unoccupied lands, the Indians had the right to hunt over the whole of their ancient tribal territory wherever the white settlers had not yet occupied the land. All of the thirteen conveyances made between 1850 and 1852 had guaranteed in the same language the hunting rights of the Indians. Archibald Barclay of the Hudson's Bay Company had given Douglas instructions that the Indians should continue to have the right to hunt, and Douglas had carried out those instructions. We knew what had been agreed to, even if it had not been confirmed in writing.

Douglas's transactions with the Indians may look one-sided, and they were: a few pounds sterling and some blankets in exchange for all the Indians' land, except the reserves. But Douglas, at least, understood the Indians to have rights that had to be recognized, and that there had to be compensation; the white people could not simply enter their land and take it. That, however, was not the view of the settlers.

After the Hudson's Bay Company had obtained these fourteen conveyances from the Indians, the policy of obtaining surrenders and providing compensation and guarantees of Native hunting and fishing rights was abandoned (against Douglas's advice), even though vast tracts of lands on Vancouver Island were still occupied by the Indians and even though the whole of what is now the mainland of British Columbia was occupied by them. The Colony of Vancouver Island, and subsequently the mainland Colony of British Columbia established in 1858, and the united Colony of British Columbia established in 1866 took the position that no surrenders of land had to be obtained from the Indians, and none ever were. When B.C. entered Confederation in 1871, the provincial government adhered to the same policy—there would be no treaties with the Indians. In fact, the rights of the Indians under these fourteen conveyances were never recognized by the province after B.C. entered Confederation.

The settlers, who were growing in numbers, were not prepared to appropriate the money to pay for any more conveyances of land. They wanted London to pay. In a dispatch that Douglas sent to Lord Newcastle, the secretary of state for the colonies, on March 25, 1861, accompanying a petition from the House of Assembly of Vancouver Island requesting the aid of the imperial government in extinguishing the Indian title, he said:

My Lord Duke

I have the honour of transmitting a Petition from the House of Assembly of Vancouver Island to Your Grace praying for the aid of Her Majesty's Government in extinguishing the Indian Title to the public lands in this Colony: and setting forth, with much force and truth, the evils that may arise from the neglect of that very necessary precaution . . .

2. As the Native Indian population of Vancouver Island have *distinct ideas of property in land, and mutually recognize their several exclusive possessory rights in certain districts*, they would not fail to regard the occupation of such portions of the Colony by white settlers, unless with the full consent of the proprietary Tribes, as national wrongs; and the sense of injury might produce a feeling of irritation against the

Settlers, and perhaps dissatisfaction to the government, that would endanger the peace of the Country. [emphasis added]

Douglas then explained why he had obtained the conveyances on southern Vancouver Island.

3. Knowing their feelings on that subject, *I made it a practice, up to the year 1859, to purchase the Native rights in the land,* in every case, prior to the settlement of any District: but since that time in consequence of the termination of the Hudson's Bay Company's Charter, and the want of funds, it has not been in my power to continue it. Your Grace must indeed be well aware that I have, since then, had the utmost difficulty in raising money enough to defray the most indispensable wants of Government. [emphasis added]

So this brought us to 1859. The blank piece of paper signed at Nanaimo in 1854 must have been "to purchase the Native rights in the land" before settlement. It all seemed to fit.

Douglas continued:

4. *All the settled Districts of the Colony,* with the exception of Cowitchen [sic], Chemainis [sic], and Barclay Sound, *have been already bought from the Indians,* at a cost in no case exceeding £2.10 sterling for each family. As the land has since then increased in value, the expense would be relatively somewhat greater now, but I think that their claims might be satisfied with a payment of £3 to each family: so that taking the Native population of those districts at 1000 families, the sum of £3000 would meet the whole charge.
5. It would be improper to conceal from Your Grace the importance of carrying that vital measure into effect without delay.
I have the honour to be
My Lord Duke
Your Grace's most obedient
and humble Servant
James Douglas
[emphasis added]

Here was evidence that Governor Douglas believed the Indians had their own legal system, each tribe had title to its own territory, and its rights with regard to its territory were recognized by all other tribes. In fact, this evidence raised a much larger legal issue—that of Aboriginal title. According to Douglas, the Indians had their own "distinct ideas of property in land," and they "mutu-ally recognize[d] their several exclusive possessory rights in certain districts." This was a not unsophisticated land title system. Douglas did not see how the settlers could superimpose their own land title system without first extinguish-ing Indian title.

Back in London, the secretary of state for the colonies, though unwilling to comply with the request for aid in extinguishing the Indian title, acknowledged the existence of that title and the necessity for funds being raised for the purpose of obtaining its surrender. Lord Newcastle wrote:

Sirs,
I am fully sensible of the great importance of purchasing without loss of time *the native title to the soil of Vancouver Island,* but the acquisition of the title is a purely colo-nial interest, and the Legislature must not entertain any expectation that the British taxpayer will be burdened to supply the funds or British credit pledged for the purpose. I would earnestly recommend therefore to the House of Assembly, that they should enable you to procure the requisite means, but if they should not think proper to do so, Her Majesty's Government cannot undertake to supply the money requisite for an object which whilst it is essential to the interests of the people of Vancouver Island, is at the same time purely Colonial in its character, and trifling in the charge that it would entail.
I have etc.
[signed] NEWCASTLE
[emphasis added]

The Colony of Vancouver Island wanted London to pay; London said it was up to the legislature. In the end, no one paid. But the colonial secretary in London, like Douglas, believed there was an Aboriginal title to the island and that it had to be extinguished.

When I took on *White and Bob* I had just opened my own office. I did not at first have a lot of clients. I had time to spend in the law library in the old court-house (now the Vancouver Art Gallery) across the street from my office. While I was looking into the question of whether the Nanaimo conveyance was a treaty, another question kept coming up. If it was a treaty, why did we make treaties? In the law library, I found the judgements of John Marshall, chief justice of the United States from 1801 to 1836. He had surveyed the history of British North America as it stood before the American War of Independence, and he had held, in a series of judgements in the 1820s and 1830s, that the Indian tribes were sov-ereign nations. Their sovereignty had been diminished by the coming of the

Europeans, but their Aboriginal title to the land constituted an interest recognized by English and American law. We made treaties with the Indians, he said, because we regarded them as nations possessed of title to the land they occupied, and the treaties were a lawful means of extinguishing that title. This was the law that Marshall claimed had been inherited by the Americans from Great Britain. It accounted for the fact that the American government made treaties with the Indians throughout the lower forty-eight states. It must also, I thought, be the law passed on to Canadians. If the conveyance signed by the Nanaimo Indians was not a treaty because it had not been made with the Crown, then the Nanaimo Indians had never surrendered their Aboriginal title and rights, including the right to hunt. It was an alternative argument that opened up immense possibilities.

But all of this lay in the future. My job at the time was to win an appeal for Clifford White and David Bob. To show that they had a treaty right to hunt was the most straightforward way of doing it.

We could read the blank piece of paper signed at Nanaimo in 1854 as if it had contained the same promise about hunting as the other thirteen instruments. But we still had to establish a link between Clifford White and David Bob and the Saalequun Indians, who had signed the conveyance in 1854. Even if the Saalequun had retained the right to hunt, how could White and Bob claim any such right? The conveyance had been made at Fort Nanaimo, but who were the Saalequun, where had they lived, and where had their hunting grounds been?

It was at this point that Willard Ireland and I went to see Wilson Duff at the Provincial Museum in Victoria. Duff, at that time curator of anthropology at the museum, was an anthropologist specializing in the culture of the Indians of the Northwest Coast. In 1963, he was highly regarded, his reputation approaching its pinnacle. On the arts and culture of the Indians of the Northwest Coast, Duff was one of the world's acknowledged experts. He was one of a handful of ethnologists who had urged us to rediscover the civilization that had flourished on the Northwest Coast little more than a hundred years earlier.

Duff was well acquainted with the history of the Indian land question in B.C. In his book *The Indian History of B.C.: The Impact of the White Man,* he said—at a time when it would have seemed of merely academic interest to many—that the Indian land question in B.C. was not closed, that it already "to an increasing extent formed a rallying point for a growing Indian 'nationalism.'"

Duff told us that the Saalequun had lived at Nanaimo, but they were only one of the five tribes living there in the 1850s. There were four other tribes. We did not know whether Clifford White and David Bob were descendants of the Saalequun tribe or of one of the other tribes; unless we could show that they were descendants of the Saalequun, we could not claim that they had any right to hunt under the treaty.

Duff looked at the names on the treaty. He told us the next step would be to examine the census that Governor Douglas had carried out in the early 1850s. We examined Douglas's census, and it showed more than one tribe at Nanaimo. In fact, Douglas's census listed four tribes: the Sumlumalcha, the Whewhulla, the Akmainis and the Saalequun. The census showed that there were 159 "men with beards," 160 women, 300 boys and 324 girls. The figure 159 in Douglas's census stood out because there were 159 Indian Xs on the blank paper that Douglas had had the Indians sign at Nanaimo in 1854. Quite obviously the treaty of 1854 had been signed by the men of all the tribes at Nanaimo (whether there were only four, as Douglas thought, or five as Duff maintained), not just the Saalequun. So all the Indians at Nanaimo who could claim descent from any of the tribes that lived there in 1854 could claim the right to hunt. And my clients were undoubtedly descended from Indian people who had lived there in 1854.

White and Bob had already been tried and convicted by the magistrate. But they had the right to appeal by way of what is called a trial *de novo*—a new trial— in the County Court of Nanaimo. Willard Ireland and Wilson Duff could be called as witnesses.

Wilson Duff demonstrated in *White and Bob* the relevance to Native claims of anthropological knowledge. It is now not at all unusual for anthropologists to give evidence in cases involving the rights of Aboriginal people. Anthropological evidence has often been of great assistance to Aboriginal peoples in establishing their rights in the courts and in fleshing out the land claims they are now pursuing with Canadian governments. But Wilson Duff was, I think, the first anthropologist to demonstrate the importance of such evidence. And for many years it was essential. It was not until 1997, in *Delgamuukw*, that the Supreme Court of Canada held that the oral history of Indian people, passed on from generation to generation, could be treated as evidence in its own right.

The trial in the County Court began in March 1963, before Judge H.A. Swencisky. During his evidence, Duff laid the groundwork for the argument to be advanced on behalf of White and Bob. He told the court:

DUFF: In brief, there were five local bands or groups in this immediate area. They were together known as the Nanaimo tribe. The name of one of these local groups was Saliquin, or Saliquil, or variations of that name. These tribes, or groups, were quite migratory in their habits. Each of them had a village on the Nanaimo River, where they would fish for dog salmon in the fall. They had a winter village right here on Nanaimo Harbour. The other four groups had their winter villages on Departure

Bay, quite close by. In the springtime all of these groups would move out to Gabriola Island for various kinds of fish and clams and other food, and in mid-summer they would all go over to the Fraser River for other kinds of salmon. Now the name Saliquin correctly applies just to one of these five groups. However, I am convinced that Governor Douglas used the name to apply to the Nanaimo tribe.

BERGER: What use would the Indians have made of their tribal territories?

DUFF: . . . They used different kinds of territories in—with different intensity. They would use the rivers, of course, for fish with great intensity, and the beaches with great intensity, and the mountains and forest with somewhat less intensity, yet they would go at least that far back, not only to hunt the land mammal, deer, and also other land mammals, but to get bark and roots for basketry and matting and such things. These territories would be definitely used by them and would be recognized by other tribes as belonging to them.

Just before we went into court, I had said to Duff, "I have one more concern. Was Mount Benson [where White and Bob had shot the deer] within the ancient tribal territories of the four or five groups?" He looked out the window, pointed and said, "That's Mount Benson, right there." In court I asked:

BERGER: And Mount Benson would be within the area the Nanaimo Indians used in 1854 for these purposes?

DUFF: Mount Benson is so close that there is no doubt but that it would be within the Nanaimo tribe area.

On our theory, Mount Benson would be covered by the guarantee of hunting rights contained in the conveyance signed by Douglas and the Indians in 1854.

We knew now that the conveyance was one entered into by all of the Nanaimo tribes. White and Bob could claim that they were covered by the guarantee of Indian hunting rights made in 1854. That would do them no good, however, unless we could establish that the instrument that had been signed in 1854 was a treaty. The Game Act, which prohibited hunting during the closed season for any purpose, applied to hunters, white or Indian, throughout the province. Only if White and Bob's hunting rights were guaranteed by a treaty within the meaning of the Indian Act would they have a defence to a charge brought under the Game Act.

This was the key issue. The Crown argued that it was no treaty in the legal sense, merely a transfer of land from the Indians to the Hudson's Bay Company. And treaties were made by the Crown, not by the Hudson's Bay Company.

I argued that the conveyance made in 1854 was indeed a treaty. Douglas was the governor of the colony at the time. The intention was, according to the wording of the other thirteen conveyances, that the Indian lands should become "the entire property of the white people for ever." The surrender was obtained not only for the benefit of the Hudson's Bay Company but for the benefit of the Crown itself. In this instance, the Hudson's Bay Company was an agent of the imperial government. These were treaties, not mere conveyances.

I also advanced our alternative argument. If this document wasn't a treaty, then the Indian title had not been extinguished, nor had the Indians' right to hunt over the land. Douglas believed in Aboriginal title. The Colonial Office in London knew it had to be extinguished. That was why the federal government had signed treaties with the Indians everywhere on the Prairies. If there was no treaty, if the Indians had no rights under the conveyance at Nanaimo, then neither did the province. The point was clear enough: It had always been the policy of the Crown that the Indians could not sell their lands to anyone except the Crown; since 1763 and before the Indians had been prohibited from conveying their land to anyone except the Crown. If the Hudson's Bay Company was not obtaining a surrender of Indian title on behalf of the Crown at Nanaimo back in 1854, then no surrender recognized by the law was ever obtained from the Indians. If the Crown did not recognize the instrument as a treaty, then the Indians could stand on their Aboriginal rights.

Aboriginal title was the title of the Indians to their tribal territories. Members of each tribe had an Aboriginal right to hunt over their tribal territory. These were rights they had enjoyed for centuries before the coming of the white man. If we could establish that Aboriginal title and Aboriginal rights had never been extinguished, then we could argue that the right to hunt had never been extinguished. After B.C. entered Confederation in 1871, only Parliament could extinguish Aboriginal rights, and it never had. Certainly, the province could not, by passing the Game Act, extinguish Aboriginal rights. The Indian people regarded themselves as the rightful owners of the land when the white people came. If the treaty was no good, then they had never surrendered the land, and they could claim ownership of the land today—and with it the right to hunt. This theory brought us into the midst of the Indian land question.

If the theory was sound, it was daunting: the Indians could assert their title not only at Nanaimo but throughout B.C., except for the northeastern part of the province covered by Treaty No. 8. None of the surrenders on southern Vancouver Island would be binding—and there were no other surrenders obtained in B.C.

The appeal was heard in the old courthouse in Nanaimo, which has a beautiful dark-panelled courtroom with a gallery for spectators, not at the back, but at the side of the room, closely overlooking the lawyers and the judge. The case aroused a great deal of interest among the Native people on southern Vancouver Island. It gave rise to the formation of the Southern Vancouver Island Tribal Federation. The appeal was brought with the support of the federation and of the Native Brotherhood of B.C. as well.

Argument was completed on December 10, 1963, International Human Rights Day. The case had begun to attract attention. Newspaper reporters were there to hear the final addresses. But, more tellingly, the large gallery was filled with Indians. They had never heard their treaties discussed in court. I did my best to lay before the judge the tangled history of the Indian land question in B.C. I pieced together the evidence that Wilson Duff and Willard Ireland had assembled. I realized that all those faces in the gallery belonged to people who had a stake in the outcome. It wasn't any longer a question of whether or not the charges laid against Clifford White and David Bob were to be dismissed, or even whether or not the treaties were to be upheld. The Native people in the gallery sensed that, for the first time in the twentieth century, Aboriginal rights were being treated as something more than a quaint and faintly amusing notion but one of no consequence in the practical world. Guy Williams, president of the Native Brotherhood of B.C., shook hands with me as the trial concluded and told me he had never thought he would live to see the Indian land question aired in a court of law.

Judge Swencisky accepted the evidence of Ireland and Duff and ruled for the Indians. He found that the guarantee of hunting rights by the Hudson's Bay Company was binding on the Crown and that the conveyance was indeed a treaty under the Indian Act. Clifford White and David Bob had been acquitted; they and the Nanaimo Indian band were jubilant. But no less jubilant were the other Indians of southern Vancouver Island who had made treaties with Governor Douglas. The hunting and fishing rights contained in all fourteen conveyances would now have to be recognized as treaty rights taking precedence over provincial legislation.

B.C.'s attorney general appealed. The Court of Appeal agreed with Judge Swencisky that a treaty had been made at Fort Nanaimo in 1854, ruling three to two (two judges held there was no treaty) in our favour. Justice H.W. Davey for the majority held that the Hudson's Bay Company was "an instrument of Imperial policy." He said:

In the Charter granting Vancouver Island to the Hudson's Bay Company, it was charged with the settlement and colonization of that island. That was clearly part of the Imperial policy to head off American settlement of and claims to the territory. In that sense the Hudson's Bay Company was an instrument of Imperial policy . . .

Considering the relationship between the Crown and the Hudson's Bay Company in the colonization of this country . . . I cannot regard [the conveyance at Nanaimo] as a mere agreement for the sale of land made between a private vendor and a private purchaser . . . I entertain no doubt that Parliament intended the word "treaty" in sec. 87 [of the Indian Act] to include all such agreements . . .

Justice Thomas Norris agreed that we had a treaty. In a wide-ranging concurring judgement, he held that every promise that constituted "the word of the white man" was a treaty.

Lawyers are sometimes critical of the practice by judges of writing concurring judgements. If you agree with the majority, just say so; there is no need to expatiate on your particular approach to the case. All it does is add to the confusion. But Justice Norris's concurring judgement has shown the value of the practice. His definition of a treaty has since been adopted by the Supreme Court of Canada. Referring to section 87 of the Indian Act, which gave precedence to Indian treaties, Justice Norris said:

In determining what the intention of Parliament was at the time of enactment of sec. 87 of the *Indian Act*, Parliament is to be taken to have had in mind the common understanding of the parties to the document at the time it was executed. In the section "treaty" is not a word of art and, in my respectful opinion, it embraces all such engagements made by persons in authority as may be brought within the term "the word of the white man," the sanctity of which was, at the time of British exploration and settlement, the most important means of obtaining the goodwill and cooperation of the native tribes and ensuring that the colonists would be protected from death and destruction. On such assurance the Indians relied.

Moreover, Justice Norris explored our alternative argument. He held that Aboriginal hunting rights in B.C. had never been extinguished. His judgement laid the groundwork for the law to come. He held that "Aboriginal rights existed in favour of Indians from time immemorial." He went on:

Prior to British Columbia entering into *Confederation* in 1871, no provincial legislation had been passed extinguishing the aboriginal rights of the Indians to hunt. By Ordinances of the Colony of Vancouver Island in 1859 and 1862, statutes dealing with the preservation of game were passed and in 1870 the United Colony of British Columbia passed a further Act for the protection of game. In none of these statutes was there any prohibition applying specifically to Indians. It would have required specific legislation to extinguish the aboriginal rights, and it is doubtful whether Colonial legislation, even of a specific kind, could extinguish these rights in view of the fact that such rights had been confirmed by the *Royal Proclamation* of 1763.

Thus, he concluded, "the said rights have never been surrendered or extinguished."

Now the B.C. courts had vindicated the right of White and Bob to hunt on unoccupied Crown land. The fourteen "Douglas treaties," as they came to be called, had been upheld by the B.C. courts, and the hunting and fishing rights recognized in them have been enforced by the courts of the province ever since.

What is achieved in the courts affects public opinion too. When the courts uphold Aboriginal and treaty rights, the public comprehends that these aren't ephemeral notions, something invented by lawyers on a dull day; they are tangible, they are contemporary, and they have to be taken seriously.

The Crown appealed to the Supreme Court of Canada. Douglas Sanders, newly called to the bar, had joined me in working on the factum to be submitted to the Supreme Court. Doug came with me to Ottawa for the presentation of oral argument. Doug left me soon afterward to become a law teacher and, in due course, an international authority on the rights of Aboriginal peoples. But he caught the scent for the first time in *White and Bob.*

In the Supreme Court we faced a bench of seven judges. T. G. Bowen-Colthurst, arguing the case for the Crown, said that the document signed at Nanaimo in 1854 was a mere deed of conveyance. This argument brought a reaction from Chief Justice Cartwright. He referred to the language of the conveyances that ran, "Know all men that we, the chiefs and people . . . do consent to surrender . . . the whole of the lands . . . It is understood . . . that the land . . . becomes the entire property of the white people for ever." Addressing Bowen-Colthurst, he said, "You say this is a mere deed, but it seems to me very like a surrender by a people of their land. Isn't that what a treaty is?"

The Supreme Court did not leave the bench to give judgement. Chief Justice Cartwright announced, after the Crown had completed its argument, that it did not need to call on me to answer Bowen-Colthurst. Speaking for the court, he said there could be no doubt the document to which the Indians had put their Xs in 1854 was a treaty. The attorney general's appeal was dismissed.

But suppose the Supreme Court had rejected the argument that there was a treaty? Suppose the courts had held that the conveyance was not a treaty within the meaning of the Indian Act? Suppose the Supreme Court had been obliged to consider the alternative argument, based on Aboriginal rights?

It was not a pipe dream. Justice Norris, in the Court of Appeal, had held that Aboriginal rights had not been extinguished. And if Aboriginal rights to hunt and fish had not been extinguished, then it seemed to follow that Aboriginal title had not been extinguished.

Justice Norris was a formidable figure in British Columbia jurisprudence. A member of the Conservative Party, Norris was thought of as an old Tory. This impression wasn't helped by his manner, which could be belligerent. In the 1950s, there was a public inquiry into the conduct of Vancouver's police chief. The chief's name was Walter Mulligan, and Norris was the lawyer who represented him at the inquiry. One of the witnesses against Mulligan was Ray Munro, the publisher of *Flash,* a tabloid weekly. Munro, while under cross-examination by Norris, over a weekend adjournment, had published an article referring to the fact that Norris's daughter was a recovering mental patient. Norris taxed him with this point and, when Munro refused to answer, said, "Sir, you are a contemptible cur." I was spending the summer working on the green-chain at a sawmill in North Vancouver at the time; we all followed the inquiry avidly. I still remember reading about the encounter, and Norris's denunciation of Munro. In fact, when Norris not long afterward withdrew as counsel for Mulligan, one of my co-workers, known as "Big Frank," laughed and said to me, "Now you'll have to take over."

I did my first civil jury trial before Justice Norris, when he had been a trial judge. It was a negligence action on behalf of a boy riding a bicycle who had turned left without signalling and been hit by an oncoming truck. There was a suggestion that his companion, another boy riding ahead of him, had also turned without signalling. So the truck driver should have expected the second boy to turn, even if there was no signal. That was all we had to go on. I cross-examined the truck driver to show that he had a poor driving record. Justice Norris thought this tactic was unfair. Putting a man's offences to him in cross-examination is permitted to challenge his credibility. But Justice Norris believed that only offences such as forgery, fraud or false pretences—offences going to show that a man is perfectly willing to lie—should be put to him. Otherwise, you are using a man's record to prove that he is the kind of man who is likely to have been driving negligently. He told the jury members that they could not conclude, on the basis of a poor driving record, that the defendant had been negligent. Of course, Norris was right about the unfairness of putting a man's record to him in that way. The Supreme Court has since 1988 curbed this practice in criminal cases, but it remains unrestricted in civil cases.

After the jury brought in a verdict against my client, Norris sent me a message to see him in his chambers. "I've had these hopeless cases, too," he said. "Come on, let me buy you a drink." He did his best to cheer me up. I was to appear before him often when he went to the Court of Appeal. I cannot recall any judge on the Court of Appeal as unafraid as he was to hold in favour of the trade unions, the Indians or accused persons (three of the staples of my practice) if the evidence and the law pointed in that direction.

Clifford White and David Bob had not only resurrected the southern Vancouver Island treaties, they had obtained a judgement by Justice Norris that gave new life to claims of Aboriginal rights.

In the Supreme Court of Canada, that court had simply upheld the treaty as binding on the Crown but had not expressed any view regarding Aboriginal rights. That would have to wait for another case. The other case came along, in a suit filed two years later by the Nisga'a Indians, seeking a declaration that their Aboriginal title to the Nass Valley had never been extinguished.

Looking back, I can see how far we have travelled in a comparatively short time. In 1965 the Supreme Court of Canada upheld the treaty made at Nanaimo in 1854. The treaty was a single page with no writing on it except 159 X marks, signed in an afternoon at Fort Nanaimo in the middle of the nineteenth century. The next case I was to argue for the Indians would be on behalf of the Nisga'a people of northwestern B.C. Their case, too, went to the Supreme Court of Canada. The judgement there would lead to the adoption by the federal government of a land claims policy with a view to settling claims of Aboriginal title. The Nisga'a would sign a treaty, 714 pages in all, including appendices, with the federal government and the province of B.C., which would come into force on May 11, 2000. Yet both the Nisga'a agreement and the agreement made at Nanaimo nearly 150 years earlier are treaties; both are enforced today by the courts. Commitments made by the Crown, by officers of Her Majesty, whether in 1854 or in 2000, are not to be regarded as empty promises.

But this reassessment had all started when Clifford White and David Bob went hunting on the slopes of Mount Benson to put food on the table.

5 The Nisga'a Odyssey

IN 1966, I WAS ELECTED to B.C.'s Legislative Assembly. One of my colleagues in the New Democratic Party caucus was Frank Calder, a Nisga'a man first elected to the legislature in 1949. At the time, Frank was the first Indian in Canada to hold elective office in any provincial legislature. (Indians could not vote in B.C.; hence, they were not eligible to run for office until 1949; the same held true in federal elections until 1960.) Frank was always genial, describing himself as the "Little Chief" and greeting everyone with a "Hi, pardner." His constituency included the Nass Valley, homeland of the Nisga'a people, and he was president of the Nisga'a Tribal Council. My political career was brief, but Frank remained to become a cabinet minister in 1972, when the NDP formed its first government in British Columbia.

Nowadays, the Nisga'a are well known to Canadians, but in the 1960s they were marginal, at best, to the consciousness of the average Canadian. The Nisga'a Treaty, which came into force on May 11, 2000, represented the culmination of a struggle that had taken the Nisga'a more than a hundred years. That struggle emerged out of B.C.'s history.

We have seen how Governor James Douglas's policy of extinguishing Indian title was abandoned on Vancouver Island. In 1858, when the mainland Colony of British Columbia was established, Douglas was named governor of that colony, too. Lord Carnarvon, the colonial secretary, in a dispatch to Governor Douglas in 1859, had given him these instructions with regard to the Indians:

In the case of the Indians of Vancouver Island, and of British Columbia, Her Majesty's government earnestly wish that when the advancing requirements of colonization press upon the lands occupied by members of that race, measures of liberality and justice may be adopted for compensating them for the territory which they have been taught to regard as their own.

If they had been "taught to regard [the territory] as their own," it was by their own teaching: they had their own laws and institutions. As for the British, it had always been their policy to make treaties—to obtain the surrender of the Indian title to the territory.

The mainland colony, however, was no more willing to recognize Indian title than the island colony had been, because if you recognized Indian title you would have to extinguish it, and that would involve paying for it. In 1866 the two colonies were united, with Douglas as governor. But the policy remained the same. The settlers were adamant in their opposition to any settlement of land claims. In 1867, Joseph Trutch, chief commissioner of lands and works of the newly united colony, wrote: "The Indians have really no right to the lands they claim, nor are they of any actual value or utility to them, and I cannot see why they should either retain those lands to the prejudice of the general interests of the Colony, or be allowed to make a market of them either to the Government or to the Individuals." Trutch's attitude was one adopted by generations of B.C. politicians.

By the time B.C. entered Confederation in 1871, the province had set its face against recognition of Aboriginal title. The views of James Douglas had been rejected by men who recognized no legal obligation to compensate the First Nations for their land. The fourteen "Douglas treaties" on Vancouver Island covered less than one per cent of the new province. After the last of them was signed in 1854, no further treaties were made. The government of the province did agree that the Indians had to live somewhere, and reserves were set aside for them. The question of Aboriginal title, however, remained outstanding.

Under the Constitution of Canada, jurisdiction over Indians and lands reserved for the Indians is assigned to the federal government. Accordingly, as settlement moved westward across the prairies and into the northern woodlands, which now constitute Manitoba, Saskatchewan and Alberta, Canada made a series of treaties with the Indians. In 1880, Alexander Morris, who as one of Canada's treaty commissioners negotiated many of the treaties on the Prairies, wrote: "One of the gravest of the questions presented for solution by the Dominion of Canada, when the enormous region of country formerly known as the North-West Territories and Rupert's Land, was entrusted [in 1870] to her rule, was securing the alliance of the Indian tribes, and maintaining friendly relations with them."

Alliances were made, friendly relations maintained, and land opened up for settlement by entering into treaties with the Indians.

In B.C., however, opposition to treaty-making had become entrenched. Ottawa was no more successful than James Douglas had been in persuading the government of British Columbia to modify its position. It was a policy that was to persist for 120 years.

The dispute over Indian title became a continuing source of acrimony between Canada and the province. In 1872, Trutch, by then lieutenant governor of B.C., wrote to Prime Minister John A. Macdonald: "If you now commence to buy out Indian title to the lands of B.C. you would go back on all that has been done here for 30 years past and would be equitably bound to compensate the tribes who inhabited the districts now settled [and] farmed by white people equally with those in the more remote and uncultivated portions." In 1873, Macdonald was driven from office as a result of the Pacific Scandal. He was succeeded by a Liberal, Alexander Mackenzie. To the Liberals, the claims of the Indians were not a purely academic question. Télesphore Fornier, Mackenzie's minister of justice, raised the question of Aboriginal rights in British Columbia in an opinion he wrote recommending federal disallowance of the province's 1874 Land Act. Referring to the policy exemplified by the Royal Proclamation of 1763, Fournier said: "There is not a shadow of doubt, that from the earliest times, England has always felt it imperative to meet the Indians in council, and to obtain surrenders of tracts of Canada, as from time to time such were required for the purposes of settlement."

In B.C., however, no progress whatever could be made. As it is for First Nations throughout Canada, for the Nisga'a the "land question" was paramount. Aboriginal people feel an attachment to their land, a sense of belonging to a part of the earth. Their land is not a commodity but the heritage of the community, the dwelling place of generations. For them, to lose their land may be a misfortune beyond measure.

In 1885, the completion of the Canadian Pacific Railway had brought a rush of new European immigrants. By the end of the century, B.C.'s white population had greatly increased, and the resource industries and the road and rail networks extended throughout much of the province.

In 1887, the provincial government appointed a royal commission "To Enquire into the Conditions of the Indians of the Northwest Coast." Reserves had been allotted, but no treaties made. When the royal commission visited the Nass Valley, the Nisga'a chiefs raised the question of Aboriginal rights. They had never signed a treaty with the Crown. They believed the land was theirs. David Mackay, one of the chiefs, summed up the Nisga'a point of view:

What we don't like about the Government is their saying this: "We will give you this much land." How can they give it when it is our own? We cannot understand it. They have never bought it from us or our forefathers. They have never fought and conquered our people and taken the land in that way, and yet they say now that they will give us so much land—our own land. [Our] chiefs do not talk foolishly, they know the land is their own; our forefathers for generations and generations past had their land here all around us; chiefs have had their own hunting grounds, their salmon streams, and places where they got their berries; it has always been so . . . it has been ours for thousands of years.

But the settlers and their government were adamant in their refusal to recognize that the land that had belonged to the Indians "for thousands of years" could form the basis of a legal right to be compensated for its loss.

The Indians of the Northwest Coast were defenceless against the diseases brought by the Europeans. Smallpox and tuberculosis took an enormous toll. By 1890, the Indian population of the Northwest Coast, which at mid-century had stood at more than fifty thousand, was reduced to perhaps no more than ten thousand, many of whom were enfeebled by disease. The startling decline in the Indian population led to the conclusion, widely held among whites, that the Indians were a people condemned by history, who would soon become extinct. This belief was to prevail until the mid-twentieth century.

Wilson Duff, in 1960, described one of the coastal villages decimated by disease:

Little remains of the thriving community . . . A few fragments of memory, a few bright glimpses in the writings of the past, some old and weathered totem poles in a storage shed, and the mouldering remnants of once-magnificent carved posts and houses on the site of the old village . . . What was destroyed here was not just a few thousand individual human lives. Human beings must die anyway. It was something even more complex and even more human—a vigorous and functioning society, the product of just as long an evolution as our own, well suited to its environment and vital enough to participate in human cultural achievements not duplicated anywhere else. What was destroyed was one more bright tile in the complicated and wonderful mosaic of man's achievement on earth. Mankind is the loser. We are the losers.

The Native peoples of the Northwest Coast, however, refused to die. In 1890, the Nisga'a had established the Nisga'a Land Committee in an attempt to reopen the Indian land question. The province would not change its position. In 1909, the premier of British Columbia, Richard McBride, said, "Of course it would be madness to think of conceding to the Indians' demands. It is too late to discuss the equity of dispossessing the Red man in America." Prime Minister Wilfrid

Laurier was prepared to consider referring the dispute regarding Aboriginal title to the Privy Council. But in the election of 1911, he was defeated.

In 1913, the Nisga'a Land Committee sent a petition to the imperial government in London, urging that the Privy Council should determine the matter. The Nisga'a said they would be prepared to enter into a reasonable settlement.

We are not opposed to the coming of the white people into our territory, provided this be carried out justly and in accordance with the British principles embodied in the Royal Proclamation [of 1763]. *If therefore as we expect the aboriginal rights which we claim should be established by the decision of His Majesty's Privy Council, we would be prepared to take a moderate and reasonable position.* In that event, while claiming the right to decide for ourselves, the terms upon which we would deal with our territory, we would be willing that all matters outstanding between the province and ourselves should be finally adjusted by some equitable method to be agreed upon which should include representation of the Indian Tribes upon any commission which might then be appointed [emphasis added].

On January 22, 1913, this statement was unanimously adopted at a meeting of the Nisga'a people at the village of Kincolith. Here is the manifestation of a political tradition—an approach that the Nisga'a would follow decade after decade. Here we can locate the spirit of the Nisga'a Treaty of 2000. The Nisga'a would take "a moderate and reasonable position." But the Nisga'a would have the right to decide for themselves "the terms upon which [they] would deal with [their] territory."

In 1912, the federal government and the province agreed to establish a royal commission to make a final and complete "adjustment" of Indian lands in British Columbia. But the mandate of the commission was not to settle the land question, merely to adjust reserve boundaries. From 1912 to 1916, the McKenna-McBride Commission travelled throughout the province to take evidence. In 1915, its members visited the Nass Valley, where Gideon Minesque spoke for the Nisga'a:

We haven't got any ill feelings in our hearts, but we are just waiting for this thing to be settled and we have been waiting for the last five years—it is not only a short time that we have lived here; we have been living here from time immemorial—it has been handed down in legends from the old people and that is what hurts us very much because the White people have come along and taken this land away from us . . . We have heard that some White men . . . said that the [Nisga'a] must be dreaming when they say they own the land upon which they live. It is not a dream—we are certain that this land belongs to us. Right up to this day the government never made any treaty, not even to our grandfathers or our great-grandfathers.

Over the next half century, the issue had long been forgotten by most Canadians—but not by the Nisga'a. In 1966, Frank Calder and the four chiefs of the Nisga'a villages crowded into my walk-up law office on Georgia Street to tell me that they wanted to proceed with a lawsuit to prove that their Aboriginal title had never been extinguished.

The Nisga'a have had the good fortune to be led by generations of statesmen. There had been David Mackay in 1887, then Gideon Minesque in 1915. When they came to see me, Frank Calder was president of the Nisga'a Tribal Council. James Gosnell was chief of the New Aiyansh band; he was to succeed Frank as president of the Nisga'a Tribal Council. As well, on that day in 1966, there was Maurice Nyce of the Canyon City band, W. D. McKay of the Greenville band and Anthony Robinson of the Kincolith band. After James Gosnell died in 1988, he was succeeded as president of the Nisga'a Tribal Council by Alvin McKay, and then by his younger brother Joseph Gosnell, who in 2000 would become, under the provisions of the Nisga'a Treaty, the first president of the Nisga'a Lisims Government.

But the Nisga'a would have to go it alone in any lawsuit. Indian bands throughout B.C. were opposed to the Nisga'a bringing a suit to establish Aboriginal title. They said to the Nisga'a, "You'll lose, and then our claim to Aboriginal title will be lost forever." The Nisga'a, however, decided to go ahead. The lawsuit was brought in Frank Calder's name and in the names of the four village chiefs. Because Frank's name led the list of plaintiffs, the case became known as *Calder*.

Why did the Nisga'a come to me? Of course, Frank knew me. I think, however, the main reason was that I had been successful in *White and Bob*. In that case, the door to recognition of Aboriginal title had been opened a crack by Justice Norris. The Nisga'a wanted to see if we could open it wide.

The *White and Bob* decision was handed down in 1965. It meant that the rights of the Indian bands who had signed the fourteen treaties on Vancouver Island could now be enforced. But these treaties covered only a few hundred square miles in a vast province. What about the rest of the province, where there were no treaties? What rights could be enforced there?

All along in *White and Bob* we had advanced an alternative argument. We said that the treaty at Nanaimo had been signed to extinguish the Indians' Aboriginal rights. If, as the Crown argued, the treaty was unenforceable, if it was not binding on the Crown, then the Indians were not bound either. They had never signed over their Aboriginal rights, so their Aboriginal rights had not been extinguished. Justice Norris agreed. The same reasoning would apply to their Aboriginal title, for they had never signed it over. If Aboriginal title still existed in B.C., its footprint would cover most of the province (except for the area covered by the Douglas treaties and the northeastern corner of B.C., lying beyond the Rockies, which was covered by Treaty No. 8).

In *Calder,* we sued the province for a declaration that the Aboriginal title of the Nisga'a people had never been extinguished. The existence of Aboriginal title would be the sole issue before the court. If we succeeded, there would have to be negotiations—and a treaty.

It may seem improbable that a legal question as basic as Aboriginal title should have survived unresolved for so long. One reason, of course, was the marginalization of Indian people. Moreover, Parliament, to put the issue to rest, had passed an amendment to the Indian Act in 1927 that made it an offence for Indians to raise money for the purpose of suing in the courts to establish Aboriginal title to their land. This provision of the Indian Act remained in force until 1951.

Lawyers knew little or nothing about the subject. Aboriginal rights were not taught at UBC's law school when I went there in the mid-1950s. How did we acquire the country from the Indians? Did they have their own legal system? Do we have any obligations to them today? The subject never came up. It was the lawsuit brought by the Nisga'a in 1967, and decided by the Supreme Court of Canada in 1973, that finally placed Aboriginal rights on the law school curriculum and, more importantly, on the Canadian agenda.

Aboriginal title has a lengthy pedigree in North America. Its greatest exponent was John Marshall, chief justice of the United States from 1803 to 1836. The most famous of the cases he decided arose out of Georgia's annexation of the lands of the Cherokee Nation within the state. Georgia had annulled all tribal laws and imprisoned tribal officials. In 1832, Chief Justice Marshall, in *Worcester v. Georgia,* writing for the U.S. Supreme Court, held that Georgia's laws were "repugnant to the Constitution, laws and treaties of the United States" and could not be applied to the Cherokee Nation. Marshall said, relying on the Royal Proclamation of 1763 and the policy the British had adopted towards the Indians in the years before the American Revolution:

The Indian nations had always been considered as distinct, independent political communities, retaining their original natural rights, as the undisputed possessors of the soil, from time immemorial, with the single exception of that imposed by irresistible power, which excluded them from intercourse with any other European potentate than the first discoverer of the coast of the particular region claimed.

Marshall's judgements are still followed in the U.S. In that country, treaties now blanket the lower forty-eight states. In Canada, when the Nisga'a filed their lawsuit, much of our country, not only B.C., had no treaties. Treaties had not been made in Quebec. There were treaties in the Northwest Territories, but under them no reserves had ever been set aside for the Indians. The same was true of the Yukon. There were no treaties in the Eastern Arctic. Claims could be made to Aboriginal title by the Indians and Inuit, not to mention the Metis, in these vast territories. If we succeeded in *Calder,* all of these claims would have to be dealt with.

At the time the Nisga'a filed their suit, Canadians believed that claims to Aboriginal title were nothing more than make-believe. Prime Minister Pierre Trudeau, speaking in Vancouver on August 8, 1969, said: "Our answer is no. We can't recognize Aboriginal rights because no society can be built on historical 'might have beens.' "

But the belief of the Native peoples that their future lay in the assertion of their common identity and the defence of their common interests proved stronger than anyone had realized. Policies worked out by the practical men and women in Ottawa, without any knowledge of the true state of mind of Native people, were annulled as events impinged on the bureaucratic construct. The policy of the government was overthrown by the Native peoples' determination to reject it. A principal instrument in that overthrow was the suit brought by the Nisga'a people to establish their Aboriginal title.

The difficulty, at first, in arguing a case like *Calder* was to have the courts take it seriously. Because Aboriginal rights had not been taught in the law schools, the judges had no background in the field, no frame of reference for the subject. They were schooled in torts, contracts, trusts and property. They were at first unwilling even to consider Aboriginal title as understood by Native people. But we had, in the judgement of Justice Norris in *White and Bob,* convinced at least one jurist that the idea should be taken seriously.

On March 31, 1969, *Calder* opened in the Supreme Court of British Columbia in the old courthouse in Vancouver. Professor Kenneth Lysyk, who taught constitutional law at UBC, had brought his class to join members of the Nisga'a Tribal Council and other spectators in the gallery.

The media were there in force, believing something important was going on, though they were not sure exactly what. Douglas McK Brown represented the province. He was at the time widely regarded as B.C.'s leading litigator in civil cases. He was a man who made up his mind regarding the main issues in a case. He therefore conceded that the Nisga'a people had inhabited the Nass Valley since time immemorial. He also admitted on behalf of the attorney general that the Nisga'a people had obtained a living since time immemorial from the lands and waters of the Nass Valley. These were vital concessions. To concede them was no more than common sense, but today no such concessions would be made. Instead, the courts would have to sit for weeks, months or years while elders of the tribe, together with anthropologists and other experts in disciplines unknown in 1969, struggle to advance extensive and tedious proof of the obvious.

Brown's argument went: There never was such a thing as Aboriginal *title* that was required to be extinguished, and alternatively, if any such title had ever existed, it had been extinguished between 1858 (when the mainland Colony of British Columbia was established) and B.C.'s entry into Confederation in 1871. The argument of the attorney general was that, by passing a series of laws relating to the disposition of Crown lands, and legislating for the settlement by pre-emption of all vacant lands, the government of the old colony had acted in a way that was consistent only with an intention to extinguish Aboriginal title. The attorney general admitted, however, that once B.C. entered Confederation only the federal government could extinguish the Aboriginal title of the Nisga'a, and that the federal government had not since Confederation adopted any measures to extinguish that title.

Frank Calder, as president of the Nisga'a Tribal Council, testified:

From time immemorial the Nishgas [sic] [that was the form in which the word "Nisga'a" was rendered in English in 1969] have used the Naas River and all its tributaries within the boundaries so submitted, the lands in Observatory Inlet, the lands in Portland Canal and part of Portland Inlet. We still hunt within those lands and fish in the waters, streams and rivers, we still do, as in time past, have our campsites in these areas and we go there periodically, seasonally, according to the game and the fishing season, and we still maintain these sites and as far back as we can remember.

We still roam these territories, we still pitch our homes there whenever it is required according to our livelihood and we use the land as in times past, we bury our dead within the territory so defined and we still exercise the privilege of free men within the territory so defined . . .

The Nishgas have never ceded or extinguished their Aboriginal title within this territory.

Calder and the chief councillors of the four villages gave evidence. Calder's evidence is typical.

Q Are you on the band list?
A I am.

Q   Would you tell his lordship where you were born?

A   I was born in Nass Bay, near the mouth of the Nass River.

Q   Where were you raised?

A   I was raised at Nass Bay and mostly at Greenville.

Q   Were your parents members of the Greenville Indian Band?

A   Yes they are.

Q   Going back beyond your own parents, are you able to say whether your forefathers lived on the Nass River?

A   Yes, they did.

Q   Now, Mr. Calder, are you a member of the Nishga Tribe?

A   Yes, I am.

Q   What Indians compose the Nishga Tribe?

A   The Nishga Indians that live in the four villages of the Nass River.

Q   What are the names of the four villages?

A   Kincolith . . .

Q   Kincolith?

A   That's correct, Greenville, Canyon City and [New] Aiyansh.

Q   Can you tell his lordship, Mr. Calder, whether all of the Indians who live in the four communities on the Nass River are members of the Nishga Tribe?

A   Yes, they are members of the Nishga Tribe.

Q   Do you include not only the men and women but the children as well?

A   Yes.

Q   What language do the members of the Nishga Tribe speak?

A   They speak Nishga, known as Nishga today.

Q   Is that language related to any other languages that are spoken on the North Pacific Coast?

A   It is not the exact—our neighbouring two tribes, we more or less understand each other, but Nishga itself is in the Nass River, and there is no other neighbouring tribe that has that language.

Q   What are the names of the two neighbouring tribes who have a limited understanding of your language?

A   Gitksan and Tsimshian.

Q   Do you regard yourself as a member of the Nishga Tribe?

A   Yes, I do.

Q   Do you know if the Indian people who are members of the four Indian bands on the Nass River regard themselves as members of the Nishga Tribe?

A   Yes, they do.

Q   Apart from their language, do they share anything else in common?

A   Besides the language they share our whole way of life . . .

Q   Now, Mr. Calder, I am showing you . . . a map. Does the territory outlined in the map constitute the ancient territory of the Nishga people?

A   Yes, it does.

Q   Have the Nishga people ever signed any document or treaty surrendering their aboriginal title to the territory outlined in the map?

A   The Nishgas have not signed any treaty or any document that would indicate extinguishment of the title.

We also called Wilson Duff to show what use the Nisga'a made of their ancient tribal territories. I questioned Duff:

Q   Now, prior to the establishment of these reserves what use would the Indian people have made of the areas which flow into the mouths of the streams and rivers?

A   The general pattern in these cases would be that the ownership of the mouth of the stream and the seasonal villages or habitations that were built there, signify the ownership and use of the entire valley. It would be used as a fishing site itself and a fishing site on the river, but in addition to that the people who made use of this area would have the right to go up the valley for berry picking up on the slopes, for hunting and trapping in the valley and up to forest slopes, usually for the hunting of mountain goats. In other words they made use, more or less intensive use of the entire valley rather than just the point at the mouth of the stream.

Duff quoted what he had written in his book *The Indian History of British Columbia:*

It is not correct to say that the Indians did not "own" the land but only roamed over the face of it and "used it." The patterns of ownership and utilization which they imposed upon the land and waters were different from those recognized by our system of law, but were nonetheless clearly defined and mutually respected. Even if they didn't subdivide and cultivate the land, they did recognize ownership of plots used for village sites, fishing places, berry and root patches, and similar purposes. Even if they didn't subject the forests to wholesale logging, they did establish ownership of tracts used for hunting, trapping, and food gathering. Even if they didn't sink mine shafts into the mountains, they did own peaks and valleys for mountain goat hunting and as sources of raw materials. Except for barren and inaccessible areas which are not utilized even today, every part of the Province was formerly within the owned and recognized territory of one or other of the Indian tribes.

Duff then went on to explain the pre-contact Nisga'a economy.

The territories in general were recognized by the people themselves and by other tribes as the territory of the Nishga Tribe. Certain of these territories were used in common for certain purposes, for example, obtaining of logs and timber for houses, and canoes, totem poles and the other parts of the culture that were made of wood, like the dishes and the boxes and masks, and a great variety of other things, and the obtainment of bark, which was made into forms of cloth and mats and ceremonial gear. These would tend to be used in common.

Other areas weren't tribal territories, would be allotted or owned by family groups of the tribe and these would be used, different parts, with different degrees of intensity. For example, the beaches where the shell fish were gathered would be intensively used. The salmon streams would be most intensively used, sometimes at different times of the year, because different kinds of salmon can run at different times of the year.

The lower parts of the valley where hunting and trapping were done would be intensively used, not just for food and the hides and skins and bone and horn material that was used by the Indian culture, but for furs of different kinds of large and small animals which were either used by the Indians or traded by them.

These people were great traders and they exploited their territories to a great degree for materials to trade to other Indians and later to the white man.

The farther slopes up the valleys, many of them would be good mountain goat hunting areas. This was an important animal for hunting. Other slopes would be good places for trapping of marmots, the marmot being equally important, and there are a great number of lesser resources, things like minerals of certain kinds for tools and lichen and mosses of certain kinds that were made into dyes. It becomes a very long list.

Now, in addition to this, the waterways were used for the hunting of sea animals as well as fishing of different kinds. They were used also as highways, routes of travel for trade amongst themselves and for their annual migration from winter to summer villages, and a great variety of minor resources from water, like shell fish of different kinds, fish eggs, herring eggs—there is a great list of such minor resources in addition.

Duff concluded by providing an insight into the way in which Nisga'a title to the Nass Valley was recognized by other First Nations. I asked him: "To what extent would the use and exploitation of the resources of the Nishga territory have extended in terms of that territory? Would it have extended only through a limited part of the territory or through the whole territory?" He answered:

To a greater or lesser degree of intensity it would extend through a whole territory except for the most barren and inaccessible parts, which were not used or wanted by anyone. But the ownership of an entire drainage basin marked out by the mountain peaks would be recognized as resting within one or other groups of Nishga Indians and these boundaries, this ownership would be respected by others.

Douglas McK Brown did not call any evidence for the defence except that of an official who described the extent of Crown grants, licences, leases and other tenures throughout the province. He had no doubt what the key to the defence was: the pre-Confederation statutes passed by the Colony of British Columbia, which enabled the Crown to make grants of land to the settlers. He argued that these statutes had put an end to Aboriginal title before B.C. entered Confederation. If Aboriginal title had existed, it had not survived the legislative axe wielded by the pre-Confederation governments established by the settlers.

These old statutes made no mention of Aboriginal title; nevertheless, the province contended that this exercise of legislative power had extinguished whatever interest the Indians may have had in the lands constituting British Columbia. After all, how could it be said that Indian title still existed when the pre-Confederation governments had assumed the power to dispose of the very lands the Indians claimed? By disregarding Aboriginal title, Douglas McK Brown argued, the Crown had extinguished it. This was extinguishment by implication.

I have said that the first difficulty in these cases is to have the courts take the claim seriously. The second difficulty arises from the first: The consequences of a decision in favour of Native rights are hard to foresee. Will a verdict upholding Native rights disrupt existing land titles? Will it impinge on existing tenures? Where is all of this legal activity headed? Douglas McK Brown sought to exploit this concern. He told the trial judge that the claim advanced by the Nisga'a threatened all land titles in the province. He argued that the grant of a declaration that Aboriginal title had not been extinguished could yield mischievous, even dire consequences. Land titles in the province would be cast into a state of uncertainty. "Why," he said, "the Indians may be in a position to claim the very land beneath this courthouse." It is idle to say that judges are not affected by such arguments.

Justice Jay Gould was the trial judge. He dismissed the Nisga'a case. He did not purport to decide whether Indian title existed in B.C. at the time white settlement began. He simply held that if it had existed, it had been extinguished by the pre-Confederation statutes passed by the old Colony of British Columbia. But he well understood that the issue was one of the greatest importance. He expected the case to be appealed, and he made it clear that he accepted entirely the evidence we had placed on the record before him.

I find that all witnesses gave their respective testimony as to facts, opinions, and historical and other documents, with total integrity. Thus there is no issue of credibility as to the witnesses in this case, and an appellate Court, with transcript and exhibits in hand, would be under no comparable disadvantage in evaluating the evidence from not having heard the witnesses in person.

So an appeal could go forward on the record we had established.

In the meantime, I had been elected leader of the British Columbia NDP. A few months later, when W. A. C. Bennett called a provincial election, I had lost not only the election but also my own seat in Vancouver-Burrard, and I had resigned as leader of the party. A busy life. But the fact that my political career, such as it was, had crashed and burned freed me to devote myself to the appeal for the Nisga'a.

In the Court of Appeal, however, we suffered another setback. The trial judge had left to the higher courts the determination of whether Aboriginal title was a concept recognized by Canadian law. The Court of Appeal was ready to address the question. The judges of that court held that the law had never acknowledged any such concept as Aboriginal title; that although governments might choose as a matter of policy to deal with Indians as if they did have a legal interest in land, there was, in reality, no such legal interest—no Aboriginal title—and there never had been. Thus the Nisga'a had never had Aboriginal title to the Nass Valley. The Court of Appeal went on to say that, even if there had been such a title, it had been extinguished by the statutes passed by the old Colony of British Columbia during the pre-Confederation era. Justice Davey had in *White and Bob* upheld the treaty rights of the Nanaimo Indians. But he could not grasp the idea of Aboriginal title. His judgement exemplified the attitude of the court, an attitude of ancient lineage. Observing the Nisga'a across an ethnographic gulf, he declined to believe that the Nisga'a had their own ideas of land ownership, saying, "They were undoubtedly at the time of settlement a very primitive people with few institutions of civilized society, and none at all of our notions of private property."

It was difficult to convince lawyers and judges that the Aboriginal peoples of Canada possess rights based on the indisputable fact that they used and occupied vast areas of if not the whole of this continent before the Europeans colonized it. They had their own institutions, their own laws. But of this fact many lawyers and judges remained unaware. They could not accept that people without a written language could have an elaborate legal system. And, as for their Aboriginal title, how could the court acknowledge it? It was ill defined; it was not recorded in a system of title deeds and land registration; most importantly, it was not a form of private property but property held communally by the tribe.

So there was no relief to be had in the B.C. courts and, given Prime Minister Trudeau's view that Aboriginal title was nothing more than an historical "might have been," no acknowledgement of Indian claims by the federal government. But the Native peoples' belief that their past had a place in their future—that their Aboriginal title was not a chimera—led the Nisga'a to appeal to the Supreme Court of Canada.

Was there any chance of winning in that court? We felt there was a chance, though the odds were against us. I approached Jean Chrétien, then minister of Indian affairs, urging the federal government to intervene in support of the Nisga'a. He indicated that, given the rejection by the prime minister of the concept of Aboriginal title, they could not intervene to support the Nisga'a. I suppose we should have been grateful that the federal government was, at least, not coming in against us.

I travelled to Ottawa to argue the appeal with two colleagues, Don Rosenbloom and John Baigent. We were on the same flight as the B.C. government's lawyers, Douglas McK Brown and William Hobbs. They travelled in the first-class section; we travelled economy. During the flight they visited us at the back of the plane. We chatted. Brown said they were showing a movie in the first-class cabin. John Wayne, he said, was busily engaged in extinguishing Indian title. Brown seemed confident that the Supreme Court of Canada would do the same.

But Brown and Hobbs had something more serious to tell us. They said they had learned that not all nine judges of the court would sit on our appeal. Justice Emmett Hall, they said, was about to retire and would not sit on the case; to avoid sitting with only eight judges, an even number, which could result in a tie, and therefore no decision, the most junior judge, Justice Bora Laskin, would be dropped. This was dreadful news. Hall was known by this time as the most liberally minded member of the court, and Bora Laskin, a leading scholar and teacher, newly appointed to the court, was regarded as a defender of civil liberties and minority rights.

Stopping in Toronto, we spent an evening at the home of Kenneth Lysyk, who was by this time teaching at the law school at the University of Toronto, and two other law professors, experts in the field of Native law, as the nascent subject was called in the law schools, where it was beginning to find its way on to the curriculum. I rehearsed the argument I intended to present to the Supreme Court. Afterwards, we mentioned what we had heard about the composition of the court for our appeal. One of the professors immediately got up and went to the phone to call a former student, who was clerking for Emmett Hall. He came back, excited, and said that Emmett Hall, far from retiring, had postponed his retirement to sit on the Nisga'a appeal. The following day, when we arrived in Ottawa, we were told that the court was sitting with only seven judges. But it was Chief Justice Gerald Fauteux and Justice Douglas Abbott who were not going to sit. This news was more than welcome, because even the most optimistic prediction of how the court would deal with our appeal would have located both of these judges on the side of the provincial government. Our prospects had improved.

Frank Calder and the chiefs of the four villages in the Nass Valley, together with village elders, travelled to Ottawa for the hearing in the Supreme Court. They were grave, respectful, a poignant presence. These chiefs and elders represented in a sense the Aboriginal peoples of Canada, whose interests the judges, for the first time in the twentieth century, would have to confront—to consider what Wilson Duff called "Canada's unfinished business."

In the Supreme Court, when the great doors open behind the bench, the entrance of the judges is announced, in English and in French: "The Court. La Cour." It is a moment that I always find thrilling. If there is a fighting chance of obtaining justice, it is here, where the judges know they are the last stop on the judicial railway, where they will make or unmake history. They know they are writing for all of Canada and for a posterity that will read what they have written.

I don't know how many times I have told clients to dress properly for court, to call the judge "sir" or "ma'am." But it hadn't occurred to me at any stage to give this little speech to the Nisga'a. In their own way, they invested the courtroom scene with as much dignity as the entrance of the judges. Wearing their ceremonial sashes, they had not the slightest self-consciousness about appearing to be anachronisms. They believed in their case, and they believed that any fair-minded tribunal would see the force of it. They placed their interests in the hands of the highest tribunal in the land, just as they had been prepared to do in 1913, when the Privy Council was still the last stop on the judicial railway.

I made the argument on behalf of the Nisga'a. Douglas McK Brown argued for the province. The hearing took four days. The judges were considering Aboriginal title for the first time in a hundred years. It was obviously going to be a case of historic importance. Each evening we were allowed to use the courtroom, where our papers covered the counsel table, to prepare for the following day. Each day brought questions from the bench; the judges were obviously ready to deal with a subject that Canadian law throughout the twentieth century had ignored.

In the B.C. courts, our argument had been met by skepticism, even by incomprehension. In the Supreme Court, however, the judges were intellectually engaged. Justice Emmett Hall and Justice Bora Laskin put questions to Douglas McK Brown indicating that Aboriginal title must have a place in Canadian law. The courts would no longer treat the legal history of our country as if we had started with a clean slate with the coming of the Europeans; as if before our land title system was established there had been no recognized title to land. Our legal system was not created out of the void.

When the hearing had concluded, we left the courtroom elated. We could not be at all sure of the outcome. But we had the feeling that Aboriginal title, one way or the other, would be on Canada's legal and political agenda.

While I was in Toronto, on my way to Ottawa to argue the Nisga'a case, I received a call from the office of John Turner, then minister of justice. If asked, would I accept an appointment to the Supreme Court of British Columbia? I prevaricated, requesting that I be allowed to give my answer after the Nisga'a case was over. As I prepared my argument, I was wondering whether to accept John Turner's offer. But it was a thought I managed to put to one side. A few years later, Emmett Hall, speaking as chancellor of the University of Saskatchewan when I was receiving an honorary degree, said that my argument in *Calder* was in the opinion of the Supreme Court judges the finest they had heard. Perhaps it was. Very likely it was not. However it is ranked, I do not think it suffered because I was at the same time bound to consider whether to accept an appointment to the bench.

The judges had reserved their decision, and we all went home to wait. We would wait thirteen months.

In January 1973, when the Supreme Court of Canada finally handed down judgement, the Nisga'a had lost, four to three. At last, they had reached the end of the road. Or had they? Sometimes a loss is almost as good as a win. Six of the seven judges held that Aboriginal title existed in Canadian law, and that the Nisga'a held Aboriginal title when the Europeans came. Three judges held that the Nisga'a still had Aboriginal title; three held that they did not. The seventh judge, Louis-Phillipe Pigeon, rejected the claim by the Nisga'a for procedural reasons and did not vote on the Aboriginal title question. He held that the lawsuit had not been properly brought because the Nisga'a had not first obtained a "fiat" (the permission that you had to obtain from the cabinet in order to sue the province, a relic removed by the NDP when they came to office). He therefore voted to dismiss the appeal without addressing the issue of Aboriginal title. So the count was three with us, three against. It was effectively a hung jury in the highest court in the land.

Justice Wilfred Judson, writing for himself, Justice Ronald Martland and Justice Roland Ritchie, held against the Nisga'a claim. But his judgement was not a rejection of the concept of Indian title. In the nineteenth century, the Privy Council had persuaded itself that Indian title in Canada was based on the Royal Proclamation of 1763. Justice Judson rejected this proposition and, relying on

Wilson Duff's evidence, stated: "Although I think that it is clear that Indian title in British Columbia cannot owe its origin to the Proclamation of 1763, the fact is that when the settlers came, the Indians were there, organized in societies and occupying the land as their forefathers had done for centuries. This is what Indian title means." This was a refreshing demystification.

Justice Judson went on to rule that the introduction of general land legislation in the colony before B.C. entered Confederation in 1871 constituted a termination of whatever rights the Nisga'a had to land outside their reserves. "In my opinion, in the present case, the sovereign authority elected to exercise complete dominion over the lands in question, adverse to any right of occupancy which the Nishga Tribe might have had, when, by legislation, it opened up such lands for settlement, subject to the reserves of land set aside for Indian occupation." Thus was extinguishment by implication upheld.

But there were three judges who supported the Nisga'a. Justice Emmett Hall wrote on behalf of himself and Justice Willard Spence and Justice Bora Laskin. He discussed the importance of rising above the cultural biases evident in many judicial pronouncements about Indian people.

The assessment and interpretation of the historical documents and enactments tendered in evidence must be approached in the light of present-day research and knowledge disregarding ancient concepts formulated when understanding of the customs and culture of our original people was rudimentary and incomplete and when they were thought to be wholly without cohesion, laws or culture, in effect a subhuman species. We now know that the assessment was ill-founded.

Did they make war? He answered: "The Indians did in fact at times engage in some tribal wars but war was not their vocation, and it can be said that their preoccupation with war pales into insignificance when compared to the religious and dynastic wars of 'civilized' Europe of the 16th and 17th centuries." He was critical of Chief Justice Davey:

Chief Justice Davey in the judgement under appeal, with all the historical research and material available . . . and notwithstanding the evidence in the record which [the trial judge] found was given "with total integrity" said of the Indians of the mainland of British Columbia:
"They were undoubtedly at the time of settlement a very primitive people with few of the institutions of civilized society and none at all of our notions of private property."

In so saying this in 1970, he was assessing the Indian culture of 1858 by the same standards that the Europeans applied to the Indians of North America two or more centuries before.

Justice Hall, like Justice Judson, thought it was important to demystify the issue of Aboriginal title. He pointed out that possession is of itself proof of ownership: "*Prima facie,* therefore, the Nishgas are the owners of the lands that have been in their possession from time immemorial and, therefore, the burden of establishing that their right has been extinguished rests squarely on [B.C.]." He concluded that the Nisga'a had their own concept of Aboriginal title before the coming of the white man and were entitled to assert it today. Relying on Wilson Duff's testimony, he said:

What emerges from the . . . evidence is that the Nishgas in fact are and were from time immemorial a distinctive cultural entity with concepts of ownership indigenous to their culture and capable of articulation under the common law, having "developed their cultures to higher peaks in many respects than in any other part of the continent north of Mexico."

The rights of such a people could not be extinguished by implication. Extinguishment had to be "clear and plain." The pre-Confederation statutes did not "clearly and plainly" extinguish Indian title; they didn't refer to it at all. As a result, Justice Hall would have granted the claim by the Nisga'a to a declaration

that the appellant's right to possession of the lands delineated . . . and their right to enjoy the fruits of the soil of the forest, and of the rivers and streams within the boundaries of said lands have not been extinguished by the Province of British Columbia or by its predecessor, the Colony of British Columbia, or by the Governors of that Colony.

Emmett Hall's contributions to Canadian life were numerous. Perhaps none was more important than his judgement in the Nisga'a case. For he held that the Aboriginal title of the Nisga'a could be asserted in our own time. No matter that the province would be faced with innumerable legal tangles. What was right was right. The law was the law.

Thus Aboriginal title arises from Aboriginal ownership, possession, use and occupation of the land. It does not depend on the Royal Proclamation of 1763 or any legislative enactment. It could, of course, be extinguished by competent legislative authority. It was on the latter point that Justice Judson and Justice Hall were in disagreement: Justice Judson held that the title of the Nisga'a had been extinguished before Confederation, whereas Justice Hall held that their title was still good today.

Moreover, all six judges who had addressed the question had supported the view that the Nisga'a title had been recognized by English law in force in B.C. at the time of the coming of the white settlers. For the first time, Canada's highest court had unequivocally affirmed the concept of Aboriginal title.

The split decision of the Supreme Court of Canada bolstered in a dramatic way the legal credibility of Indian land claims. Prime Minister Trudeau met with Frank Calder and the Nisga'a Tribal Council. The prime minister conceded that the Supreme Court's judgement meant that "perhaps" the Indians had more "legal rights" than he had thought. He still refused to use the terms "Aboriginal title" or "Aboriginal rights." He advised the Indians to speak of "legal rights." Well, the whole point of the lawsuit was to show that when Aboriginal people speak of Aboriginal title and Aboriginal rights, they are talking about legal rights enforceable in the courts. We were making progress.

The Supreme Court's judgement came at a propitious moment. The election of 1972 had returned the Liberals to power, but as a minority government. To remain in office, the Liberals depended on the goodwill of the opposition parties. The Nisga'a decision now catapulted the question of Aboriginal title into the political arena. In Parliament, both the Progressive Conservatives and the New Democrats insisted that the federal government must recognize its obligation to settle Native claims. The all-party Standing Committee on Indian and Northern Affairs passed a motion approving the principle that a settlement of Native claims should be made in regions where treaties had not already extinguished Aboriginal title. On August 8, 1973, Jean Chrétien as minister of Indian affairs announced that the federal government intended to settle Native land claims in all parts of Canada where no treaties had yet been made. Chrétien announced that the government had accepted the principle that there ought to be compensation for the loss of an Indian "traditional interest in land." This statement applied especially to claims in British Columbia, Quebec, the Yukon and the Northwest Territories.

I believe that the Supreme Court's decision in *Calder* was instrumental in changing the course of Canadian history.

After the decision in *Calder*, land claims agreements were reached in James Bay and Northern Quebec in 1975, in the Western Arctic in 1984, in the Yukon in 1990, in Nunavut in 1994 and with the majority of the Dene along the Mackenzie River in the 1980s and 1990s—agreements covering more than half the Canadian land mass. Our institutions do work, and lawyers can make them work.

Today the law schools teach Aboriginal rights. There is a thriving Aboriginal rights bar—many of whose members belong to First Nations—and major law firms advertise the fact that they employ specialists in Aboriginal rights.

Calder was the Supreme Court's first crack at Aboriginal title in the twentieth century. The vote on whether Aboriginal title in B.C. had been extinguished was a tie. Three judges said Aboriginal title could be extinguished by implication. Three said no, lawmakers have to say plainly and obviously that they intend to extinguish Indian title, or it remains unextinguished. That is where it stood. In a series of decisions in the 1980s and 1990s, the Supreme Court explained the origin, scope and meaning of Aboriginal title and Aboriginal rights. In 1997, in *Delgamuukw,* the Supreme Court broke the tie in unmistakable fashion, coming down unanimously on the side of Emmett Hall. Aboriginal title cannot be extinguished by implication; it therefore remains unextinguished in B.C.

Since 1982, decisions of the Supreme Court on Canada's Charter of Rights, particularly in relation to equality rights, have fundamentally altered the legal landscape. But perhaps an undertaking of comparable importance in the decade before 1982 and since has been the Supreme Court's exploration and elaboration of the nature of Aboriginal rights and treaty rights. This activity has conferred a legitimacy on the cause of First Nations—a legitimacy that politicians and the public would not, I think, otherwise have acknowledged.

The Constitution Act, 1982 recognized three Aboriginal peoples in Canada: the Indians, the Inuit and the Metis. The land claims movement, growing out of *Calder,* led to settlements not only with Indians but also with the Inuit in the Eastern Arctic, because the Inuit are understood to enjoy the same rights under the Constitution as the Indians. But not the Metis. Except in the Northwest Territories, the federal government has not so far been prepared to negotiate land claims settlements with them.

The Metis, however, are taking their claims to court. One of the keys to Metis claims lies in the uprising led by Louis Riel in 1869, the establishment of the provisional government at Red River and the entry of Manitoba into Confederation in 1870. In 1990, I appeared before the Supreme Court of Canada seeking to overturn a decision of the Manitoba Court of Appeal denying the Metis the right to raise the question whether their land rights under the Manitoba Act of 1870 had been violated by Canada and Manitoba. It was necessary to argue that the claim of the Metis, though more than a century old, had a contemporary relevance. The Supreme Court agreed, and it decided from the bench, without reserving judgement, that the Metis could proceed with their lawsuit.

As a result of *Calder,* the federal government was now ready to negotiate with the Nisga'a. The Nisga'a, true to the policy they had announced in 1913 in their petition to the imperial government, were prepared to take "a moderate and reasonable position." They knew that they would not be able to have the whole of the Nass Valley restored to them; that resources had already been extracted; that white people had made their homes in the valley in the intervening years.

So the Nisga'a embarked on years of negotiations with Canada. In the meantime, almost as soon as I had completed the argument in the Supreme Court in *Calder,* I had accepted John Turner's offer and been appointed to the Supreme Court of British Columbia. When I left the bench in 1983, twelve years later, negotiations between the federal government and the Nisga'a were going on. In that same year, I went to Alaska to head the Alaska Native Review Commission, returning to B.C. in 1985 to resume the practice of law. The negotiations were still proceeding between Canada and the Nisga'a, but B.C. had still not agreed to participate.

For there to be a treaty resolving land claims, British Columbia had to participate. Crown land is held by the province. If land was to be part of a settlement with the Nisga'a, B.C. had to be involved. In 1990, B.C. finally agreed to join the negotiations. At last, all three parties—Canada, the Nisga'a and B.C.—were at the table together.

I was not the legal adviser to the Nisga'a for these negotiations. Don Rosenbloom was their legal adviser from 1972 until the early 1980s. His colleague, Jim Aldridge, became the legal adviser to the Nisga'a Tribal Council soon after his call to the bar in 1980. He was to remain their legal mainstay throughout the years of negotiations that ensued. After B.C. joined the treaty table in 1990, Jim devoted virtually his entire professional life to the negotiations. Jim's work in this regard is unique. No other lawyer I know has ever devoted the best part of twenty years of his career to such a vital national undertaking, with such success.

But Jim took direction, as I had done, from the generations of statesmen who have led the Nisga'a Nation throughout its long saga. The negotiators on the side of Canada, and those on the side of the province, had to protect the interests of their two governments. For the Nisga'a negotiators, however, the very idea of the Nisga'a Nation had to be preserved—the history of a people and of a culture that had never died.

Beneath their grave exteriors, their willingness to wait upon the interminable processes of federal and provincial negotiations, the Nisga'a leaders had a deep concern for the future of their people. They were conscious of, but not preoccupied with, the grievances of the past. They had no interest in representing themselves as, or being characterized as, victims. And they always maintained their sense of humour—they could not have made it through if they had not.

They weren't negotiating merely a land claim—though their claim was characterized as such—but the future of their people. They were engaged in redefining the relationship between the Nisga'a and the dominant Canadian society. That was what was always at stake and what remained at stake through the negotiations. I never had clients who were steadier, more composed, or possessed of a greater determination to see their struggle through to the end.

The federal government and the provincial government realized the Nisga'a would not give up, that theirs was not an erratic or inconstant goal. They meant to persevere until they achieved a treaty. But once the two governments had accepted that there must be a settlement, they saw that there was another side to this coin. They came to realize the Nisga'a meant business. That meant the two governments could in turn do business with the Nisga'a. A deal would be a deal. In 1996 an agreement in principle was reached. Even when the *Delgamuukw* decision came down in 1997, raising expectations about what might be achieved by persevering in the courts, the Nisga'a decided that, having already reached an agreement in principle, they could not renege. In 1998 the treaty—the Nisga'a Final Agreement—had been achieved.

The treaty represents a hard-fought compromise. Under the treaty, the Nisga'a own 1992 square kilometres of land, known as Nisga'a Lands. The Nisga'a are to receive $190 million in cash, paid over fifteen years. The treaty also provides for Nisga'a entitlements to forestry, fishery and wildlife resources extending beyond the Nisga'a Lands into the remainder of their ancient territory. Over time, the Nisga'a will give up their exemptions from taxation.

As the negotiations moved towards consummation, the issue of self-government emerged as one of critical importance. It was an issue overarching the treaty process. For the Nisga'a did not wish to continue to be subject to the Indian Act. As Joe Gosnell was to say many times, "We want to be free to make our own mistakes." The Nisga'a wished to govern themselves. This was not a claim to independence, to constitute themselves a kind of nation-state within Canada. It was founded on a belief that they were a political community, one that existed before the Europeans came and survived to the present day. Every attempt to shatter it had failed. They believed that the Nisga'a Nation should determine, for itself, issues related to Nisga'a land, resources, language and culture.

This is an issue entwined with every comprehensive land claim. If First Nations are to move from being isolated populations on pocket-sized reserves to peoples disposing of substantial land and resources, the Indian Act scheme of federal supervision and veto is for many of them no longer relevant.

In the case of the Nisga'a, the issue came to this: Was the Nisga'a government to be a kind of municipal government, with powers of self-government, even in areas vital to Nisga'a interests, subject to withdrawal by the federal and provincial governments, or was the Nisga'a government to be acknowledged as an institution exercising, on behalf of the Nisga'a Nation, an inherent right of self-government, originating in the history of the Nisga'a people, and not a right conferred by the federal government or by the province?

Who is to govern on Nisga'a lands? Who will regulate the Nisga'a fishery? Who will regulate hunting on Nisga'a lands? The answer inevitably had to be the Nisga'a Nation. What would be the point of a treaty that established Nisga'a title to an extended land base, Nisga'a forests, a Nisga'a fishery, Nisga'a wildlife, but left these matters to others to govern?

Moreover, the treaty covered such subjects as Nisga'a citizenship, language, culture, adoption, heritage and artifacts. How were these matters to be dealt with? By the Nisga'a, claimed the Nisga'a.

In 1982, Canada had adopted the Charter of Rights. At the same time, there had been entrenched, in section 35 of the Constitution Act, 1982, "existing aboriginal and treaty rights." The Nisga'a claimed that the inherent right of self-government was an "existing" Aboriginal right; moreover, once the Nisga'a Treaty was signed, it became a treaty right. And Aboriginal rights and treaty rights now had constitutional protection.

The federal government since 1995 has taken the position that First Nations have an inherent right to self-government. If you think about it, this must be so. The Aboriginal people were here, governing themselves, before the Europeans came. They had their own societies, their own political institutions. The NDP government in B.C. was, like Canada, prepared to recognize that the Nisga'a are entitled to govern themselves on their own land and, where it is necessary to protect their identity, in respect of their culture, their language and their future. The Nisga'a Treaty so provided.

The treaty was immensely controversial.

In 1998, the Nisga'a ratified the treaty. In 1999, the treaty was ratified by the B.C. legislature, after the longest debate in the history of that body. The B.C. Liberals, the official opposition, were adamant in their opposition to the treaty. In 2000, Parliament ratified the treaty. The Reform Party, the official opposition in Ottawa, opposed the treaty with a ferocity equal to that of the B.C. Liberals, moving more than four hundred amendments to the bill. It was the provision for Nisga'a self-government that especially attracted the antipathy of the B.C. Liberals and the Reform Party.

Both parties carried on a public campaign against the treaty based on their singular view of Canadian history and the Canadian Constitution. Perhaps the most misguided of their characterizations of the Nisga'a Treaty is that it is race-based. This was a theme that they could not be persuaded to give up. They did not understand that you can't subjugate a people who happen to be of one race, take their land, destroy their institutions and then turn around a hundred years later and say, "To restore the institutions you once had would be contrary to our principles. We don't hold with race-based institutions. It's bad luck that you were all of one race when we came here. But any restoration of your institutions would necessarily be limited to descendants of the First Nations inhabiting the province a century ago. So we are going to deny you the right to govern yourselves on your own land, except to the extent that we decide from time to time to delegate power to you—power that we can withdraw at any time." This argument, of course, ignores the fact that treaties with First Nations are treaties not with a race of people but, as Chief Justice John Marshall said, with distinct political communities that have survived in our midst.

Throughout the controversy, the Nisga'a leadership and the Nisga'a Nation remained steadfast. Still another generation of Nisga'a statesmen was determined to see the thing through. In 1998, the Nisga'a Tribal Council asked me to represent the Nisga'a again. Gordon Campbell, then provincial leader of the opposition, and two Liberal MLAs had brought a lawsuit challenging the constitutionality of the self-government provisions of the Nisga'a treaty. Jim Aldridge joined the Nisga'a in asking me to act as lead counsel in defending the treaty.

The world had changed since the Nisga'a had first come to see me in 1966. Then it was Aboriginal title. Now it was Aboriginal self-government. This time, however, we had the federal government and the province on our side. The treaty was a tripartite treaty, signed by Canada and B.C. as well as the Nisga'a. So Gordon Campbell's lawsuit had necessarily to be brought against Canada, British Columbia and the Nisga'a.

The trial of Campbell's lawsuit took place before Justice Paul Williamson in May 2000, commencing on May 15, four days after the treaty had come into force. Frank Calder, now eighty-two years of age, the oldest of the Nisga'a statesmen, was in court, thirty-one years after *Calder* had been tried in the old courthouse in Vancouver before Justice Gould. I shared the presentation of the argument with Jim Aldridge. Counsel for Canada and B.C. supported us.

Campbell's claim was that the self-government provisions of the treaty were unconstitutional. His main argument was that the dividing up of legislative powers between Parliament and the provinces, at Confederation in 1867, was an exhaustive division of all powers of self-government—of all law-making authority. All the law-making power there was had been parcelled out; there could be no law-making power left for Indian nations to exercise.

Campbell's argument was founded on the rejection of the proposition that an inherent right of Aboriginal self-government can be asserted today. Bradley Armstrong, Campbell's lawyer, argued that any such right had been extinguished in 1871 when B.C. entered Confederation, and the division of powers provided for in the Constitution Act, 1867, applied to B.C. So no such right could be an "existing" Aboriginal right that had been recognized and affirmed in 1982 under section 35(1) of the Constitution Act, 1982. Nor, he argued, could an inherent right of self-government be a treaty right under section 35(1).

On behalf of the Nisga'a, we argued that an inherent right of self-government survived Confederation. There had been no legislation by Canada extinguishing the right. It was therefore an "existing" Aboriginal right in 1982, and it was recognized and affirmed by section 35(1) of the Constitution Act, 1982. It was properly the subject of a treaty.

We also made the argument that, even if the inherent right of self-government was not an "existing" Aboriginal right in 1982, all of the rights of the Nisga'a set out in the Nisga'a Treaty are nonetheless treaty rights under section 35(1).

That section recognizes and affirms existing Aboriginal rights and treaty rights. It is obvious that if an Aboriginal right is sought to be enforced under section 35(1), it must have "existed" at April 17, 1982 when the Constitution Act, 1982 came into force. The nature of an Aboriginal right means it cannot be created after contact. Not so with treaty rights. The rights contained in a treaty signed before 1982 would, of course, be "existing" treaty rights and entitled to the constitutional protection of section 35(1). But treaties signed thereafter, like the Nisga'a Treaty, can create section 35 rights. And rights that may be acquired in contemporary land claims agreements are to receive the same constitutional protection as existing Aboriginal or treaty rights. This protection was provided for in section 35(3) of the Constitution Act, 1982, which came into force by constitutional amendment in 1983. Once a treaty specifying rights in its Indian signatories comes into force, those rights are called into existence; they become "existing" treaty rights. This is exactly what the Nisga'a Treaty provided.

Since *Calder*, the courts had been working out the implications of the doctrine of Aboriginal title and Aboriginal rights. When Aboriginal title was asserted by the Nisga'a, in *Calder*, it was said that there was only one title to land, that of the Crown, and that the existence of the Crown's title necessarily excluded recognition of Aboriginal title. But now, as the result of *Calder*, we pointed out, it is accepted that Aboriginal title is a burden on the Crown's underlying title. Moreover, it is acknowledged that Aboriginal title is derived not by grant from the Crown but from Aboriginal peoples' immemorial use and occupation of the land. In the same way, we argued, there is a right of self-government exercisable by First Nations that is not derived by delegation from the Crown but from the fact that First Nations were here governing themselves at the time the British claimed sovereignty over what is now British Columbia.

To express this argument conceptually: In *Calder* we argued that title to land can be derived otherwise than from the Crown—by Aboriginal use and occupation by the Aboriginal societies that were here first; in *Campbell* we argued that the right of self-government or authority to make laws can be derived otherwise than from a grant of power by the Crown, but rather from those selfsame Aboriginal societies that are still in our midst.

Once again, Chief Justice John Marshall had put it best. Before the coming of the Europeans, he said, "America, separated from Europe by a wide ocean, was inhabited by a distinct people, divided into separate nations, independent of each other and of the rest of the world, *having institutions of their own and governing themselves by their own laws*" [emphasis added].

So it could not be argued that the First Nations had not governed themselves before the coming of the white man. If they did so, it was because they had, as sovereign political communities, an inherent right to do so. Of course, the Nisga'a had to accept, as Chief Justice Marshall had said, that with the coming of the Europeans: "They were admitted to be the rightful occupants of the soil, with a legal as well as a just claim to retain possession of it, and to use it according to their own discretion; *but their rights to complete sovereignty, as independent nations, were necessarily diminished*" [emphasis added]. But this was in no way inconsistent with the survival of a measure of political autonomy, a right of self-government. The word that Chief Justice Marshall had used was "diminished," not "extinguished." And the Supreme Court of Canada had, in a series of recent decisions, adopted the language of Chief Justice Marshall.

In 1990, in *R. v. Sioui*, Chief Justice Antonio Lamer, giving judgement for all members of the Supreme Court of Canada, wrote:

As the Chief Justice of the United States Supreme Court said in 1832 in *Worcester v. State of Georgia* . . . about British policy towards the Indians in the mid-eighteenth century:

"Such was the policy of Great Britain towards the Indian nations inhabiting the territory from which she excluded all other Europeans; such her claim, and such her practical exposition of the charters she had granted: *she considered them as nations capable of maintaining the relations of peace and war; of governing themselves under her protection; and she made treaties with them, the obligation of which she acknowledged*" [emphasis is the court's].

Moreover, Chief Justice Lamer indicated that "political rights" could be included in a treaty. He said:

There is no reason why an agreement concerning something other than a territory, such as an agreement about political or social rights, cannot be a treaty within the meaning of s. 88 of the Indian Act.

Treaty-making began long before Confederation. It was not brought to an end by Confederation. The process continued in the 1870s with the signing of the numbered treaties on the plains, and it was extended into B.C. when Treaty No. 8 was signed in 1899. Why would Canada make treaties with people who had no authority as self-governing peoples to enter into treaties?

Every treaty, whether made before or after Confederation, acknowledges a measure of Aboriginal sovereignty by the very fact that a treaty is entered into; that is, every treaty acknowledges the existence of Aboriginal political communities. Why else make a treaty? This acknowledgement marks off Aboriginal peoples from other minorities. Are there any treaties with the Ukrainians, the Poles, the Greeks in Canada?

Moreover, for First Nations, the right to make laws has survived into our own time. Aboriginal customary laws have often been enforced since Confederation, particularly in relation to marriage and adoption—laws made by Aboriginal communities that the courts have held are enforceable not only within the Aboriginal community but against the world. Continuing recognition of customary law, enforceable in the courts, is a recognition of political structures that do not derive their authority from the allocation of legislative power in 1867. Such a right, which still exists today and is constitutionally protected by section 35(1), is the very essence of self-government—the authority to make laws. Even the Indian Act all along recognized the continuing vitality of Indian self-government, including for many Indian bands the authority to determine for themselves, by customary law, as a matter of inherent right, how their chiefs and councils would be chosen.

An important piece of evidence that we had, in sorting out these historical conundrums, was the statement by Prime Minister Trudeau, on March 15–16, 1983, in opening the Conference of First Ministers—a conference mandated by the Constitution Act, 1982—which led to the adoption of section 35(3). Trudeau's statement is entitled "The Constitution and the Rights of Aboriginal Peoples." In it, he said that since becoming prime minister he had given more thought to this issue than any other. He went on:

Clearly our aboriginal people each occupied a special place in history. To my way of thinking, this entitles them to special recognition in the Constitution . . .

But the heart of the matter, the crux of our efforts to improve the condition of our aboriginal peoples and strengthen their relationships with other Canadians, is found within the set of issues concerning aboriginal government . . .

We shall have to put aside notions or perceptions that have surfaced in the past: that we can have systems of aboriginal government functioning somehow in parallel with, or separate from, other governments within our federation. Our system of government is based on interdependence and cooperation among the several orders of government, each with its responsibilities, powers and functions flowing from provisions of the Constitution, whether in the form of exclusive or concurrent powers.

Aboriginal government, in whatever form or model, will have to fit into that system. It should fit smoothly, comfortably and effectively. The complexity of jurisdictional issues is at once obvious and formidable. It can only be addressed through careful negotiations, based on full and frank expression of aims and needs and a determination to get a set of intergovernmental relationships that will work well for the benefit of all concerned [emphasis added].

Pierre Trudeau had come a long way since 1969, when he had treated Aboriginal rights as "historical 'might have beens.'" In 1983, he concluded his presentation: "All options revolve around the semi-autonomous Aboriginal community, the hub and heart of the system."

The framework to be established by section 35, according to Trudeau, would sustain Aboriginal peoples in their "political . . . uniqueness."

Gordon Campbell claimed that he was only attacking the self-government provisions of the Nisga'a Treaty. But under the treaty the powers of Nisga'a self-government are essential to the scheme for administering funds, land, fish and wildlife, and the other treaty rights and assets, and for fulfilling Nisga'a obligations to Canada, B.C. and third parties. If Campbell's argument were to succeed, the Nisga'a Nation would be left with land the Nisga'a could not manage or administer, money they could not spend or invest, forests they could not harvest or protect, fish and wildlife they could not distribute or conserve. The treaty would be reduced to an empty shell.

The court was confronted with a demand that it render a dead letter what had been achieved after a hundred years of struggle and more than twenty years of negotiation. Campbell's attack on the treaty, if successful, could have only one outcome: effectively setting aside the whole treaty. We pointed out that the courts have repeatedly said that Aboriginal claims must be settled by negotiation. The

Nisga'a Treaty is a sensitively crafted response to that call; it is designed to acknowledge and reconcile the Nisga'a Nation, its political tradition and culture, with the sovereignty of the Crown. The powers of the Nisga'a to legislate under the treaty are not absolute. The Supreme Court has laid it down that the federal and provincial governments can interfere with the exercise of those powers if they can show that it is necessary to do so in the national interest and if they can justify such interference as being consistent with the honour of the Crown.

Campbell's argument, however, came to this: Parliament or the provincial legislature must be free at any time to infringe or even to nullify the exercise of any Aboriginal powers of self-government, without justification. We argued that this contention, viewed in the light of our history and the development of our constitutional law, could not be supported.

In 1969, the Nisga'a had asked the courts to answer the question "Has Aboriginal title been extinguished?" Now, in 2000, Gordon Campbell asked the courts to answer the question "Has the Aboriginal right of self-government been extinguished?"

On July 24, 2000, Justice Paul Williamson dismissed Campbell's claim. He upheld the inherent right of the Nisga'a Nation to a measure of self-government under the Constitution. He held:

The continued existence of indigenous legal systems in North America after the arrival of Europeans was articulated as early as the 1820s by the Supreme Court of the United States. But the most salient fact, for the purposes of the question of whether a power to make and rely upon aboriginal law survived Canadian Confederation, is that since 1867 courts in Canada have enforced laws made by aboriginal societies. This demonstrates not only that at least a limited right to self-government, or a limited degree of legislative power, remained with aboriginal peoples after the assertion of sovereignty and after Confederation, but also that such rules, whether they result from custom, tradition, agreement, or some other decision-making process, are "laws" in the . . . constitutional sense . . .

In summary, these authorities [the decisions of Chief Justice John Marshall and of the Supreme Court of Canada] mandate that any consideration of the continued existence, after the assertion of sovereignty by the Crown, of some right to aboriginal self-government must take into account that: (1) the indigenous nations of North America were recognized as political communities; (2) the assertion of sovereignty diminished but did not extinguish aboriginal powers and rights; (3) among the powers retained by aboriginal nations was the authority to make treaties binding upon their people; and (4) any interference with the diminished rights which remained with aboriginal peoples was to be "minimal."

He went on:

I have concluded that after the assertion of sovereignty by the British Crown, and continuing to and after the time of Confederation, although the right of aboriginal people to govern themselves was diminished, it was not extinguished. Any aboriginal right to self-government could be extinguished after Confederation and before 1982 by federal legislation which plainly expressed that intention, or it could be replaced or modified by the negotiation of a treaty. Post-1982, such rights cannot be extinguished, but they may be defined (given content) in a treaty. The Nisga'a [Treaty] does the latter expressly.

Campbell appealed, but before his appeal came on for hearing, he had won the 2001 provincial election and become premier of B.C. His two co-plaintiffs, Geoff Plant and Michael De Jong, were now attorney general and minister of forests. The plaintiffs could hardly continue with their appeal. How could they give instructions on one side as plaintiffs, and at the same time give instructions to the province's lawyers on the other side? In the treaty itself, the parties agreed that none of them would contest its validity. Patently, they could not.

This might be thought to be a technical point. But it encompassed a much more important consideration: under the treaty B.C. was honour bound not to challenge its validity. Engagements made by one government must be kept by its successors. For the province to turn around and, in violation of the treaty itself, contest its validity, would be inconsistent with the honour of the Crown. In December 2001, Campbell formally abandoned his appeal. The provincial government would not, the attorney general announced, contest the validity of the treaty. This meant a good deal more than the abandonment of a lawsuit. The treaty's most committed opponents could not, once in office, mount any further legal attack on the treaty signed by the province.

There was a coda to this litigation. The Nisga'a wanted Premier Campbell and his two co-plaintiffs to pay their taxable costs. These are costs that a losing party has to pay the winner. They are based on a tariff; the tariff in only a few cases will fully compensate a winning client; that is, their legal fees will ordinarily be a lot more than the taxable costs that are claimable. But an award of taxable costs is not insubstantial.

We came before Justice Williamson again. Bradley Armstrong said that Campbell's lawsuit had been brought as a disinterested public service. We said that, although it had no doubt been brought as a matter of sincere conviction, it was nevertheless a political undertaking. The leader of the opposition had the right to conduct his campaign against the Nisga'a Treaty in the courts as well as the legislature, but if he lost in the courts he had to pay. The courts have held that public interest groups that challenge legislation may sometimes be excused from paying costs when they lose; by no stretch of the imagination could the leader of the opposition bring himself and the B.C. Liberals within that limited category. The ordinary rules should apply: he had lost the case and he must pay taxable costs.

The courthouse in Vancouver is built around a great hall that spans the length of the building. The courtrooms are situated on galleries above the great hall. On the day of the argument on costs in *Campbell*, in the great hall a throng of new lawyers were being called to the bar. Family and friends were present. My peroration must have coincided with the presentation of the new lawyers in the great hall because, as I concluded with a plea that the ordinary rule must apply, that Premier Campbell must pay, there was a wave of applause from the ceremony below that swept into our courtroom. An omen?

Justice Williamson held that Campbell and his colleagues must pay costs. Their challenge to the legislation was, he held, a political undertaking.

In 1997, in Gitwinksihlkw (which used to be known as Canyon City), one of the four Nisga'a villages in the Nass Valley, at an assembly of the Nisga'a Nation, I was given a Nisga'a name, Halaydim Xhlaawit. This is a mark of distinction I treasure.

The ceremony took place at the school gym. I stood below the stage. First, Rod Robinson, a Nisga'a elder, had me don a long-sleeved shirt embroidered with Nisga'a designs. Then he wrapped an apron around my waist; the apron was fringed with dried deer hooves that produced a crackle of sound. Lastly, a button blanket was placed around my shoulders.

After I had been thus prepared, a procession of chiefs accompanied me around the hall. As the drums throbbed, the dancers on the stage were moving back and forth in a sea of red and black. The hall was crowded. Bev sat on the stage behind me; she felt swept up in the intensity of the occasion.

In front of the stage Rod Robinson spoke. He said that my name, Halaydim Xhlaawit, meant "Man of the Mountain." In Nisga'a legend, a great flood had forced the Nisga'a to flee to a nearby mountain, where they had found refuge. At Gitwinksihlkw, the mountain was visible across the valley. Rod Robinson, in making the presentation, spoke of the flood and the escape to the mountain. In the same way, he said, I had saved the Nisga'a by taking their case to the Supreme Court of Canada and obtaining the means for the Nisga'a to vindicate their Aboriginal title.

Now the treaty has been achieved. The Nisga'a will have to confront a new set of realities, to undertake the rebuilding of their institutions and their economy. Practical voices will say it is out of the question, that their only future lies in assimilation. But unless that occurs by enforced social engineering on a Stalinist scale, there will be no assimilation, for the Nisga'a or for any other First Nation.

At bottom, this new reality is a question of human rights. In 1987, Pope John Paul II said, speaking to Canada's Native peoples at Fort Simpson, "You are entitled to take your rightful place among the peoples of the earth." In Canada, through the negotiation of treaties, Native peoples have begun to assume that rightful place. Land claims and self-government are not ancient, forgotten and specious, but current and contemporary.

Canada has tried to be a good citizen of the world. Indeed, many countries look for guidance to Canada's policies regarding the recognition of the rights of Aboriginal peoples. The Nisga'a Treaty, as Joseph Gosnell, speaking for the Nisga'a, told the B.C. legislature in 1998, can be "a beacon of hope for Aboriginal people around the world"—proof, he said that "reasonable people can sit down and settle historical wrongs."

6 *To the Bench and Back*

MY WORK AS A LAWYER came to an end—so I thought at the time—in November 1971. Once I had finished arguing *Calder* in the Supreme Court of Canada, I accepted Minister of Justice John Turner's offer of an appointment to the Supreme Court of B.C. So *Calder* should have been the last time I appeared in court as an advocate. Superior court judges used to serve for life. Since the so-called Manson Amendment of 1961, they must retire at seventy-five. I could, nevertheless, at thirty-eight, look forward to spending the next thirty-seven years sitting as a judge. As it turned out, I was to spend only twelve years on the bench.

When John Turner called me, he made it clear that he wanted to establish two things by my appointment. First, it would demonstrate that federal judicial appointments would not necessarily go to the usual alternating cycles of Liberals and Conservatives, depending on which party was in office, but that he was prepared to reach out to lawyers connected to the NDP. Moreover, he wanted to set a precedent for bringing younger lawyers to the bench. At the time I was appointed, I was the youngest judge named to the Supreme Court of British Columbia in the twentieth century.

Although my father seldom spoke of his early life in Sweden, he did tell me that his father had been a judge. We realized, without him ever saying so, that he must have become estranged from his father, because he never corresponded with his family in Göteborg. On the day of my call to the bar in 1957, my father asked me to write to his family in Sweden. I did, announcing who I was and telling them that Theodore, now retired from the RCMP, was now living in Vancouver, married for many years, with children and grandchildren. They were amazed. He had left home forty-six years before and, after a few desultory letters to his stepmother, had never been heard of again. My father died a few years after my letter to his family, but Bev and I have been to Sweden. We learned that Theodore's father, Ivar, who had sent him away, had, when there was no news from his son, spent the rest of his life trying to locate him. I did not have to be very insightful to realize that my father regarded my becoming a lawyer as a kind of vindication of his own life. Had he lived until I went on the bench, he would have seen the wheel come full circle.

I had reservations about going on the bench. I still had much to do as a lawyer. A multitude of causes still remained, and, I believed, I was the lawyer who might transform them into lawsuits, to make the law work on their behalf. Well, such is the vanity, the ambition of a man not yet forty.

I wondered whether on the bench I would enjoy the work. No longer an advocate, would I be prepared to listen and adjudicate? Or would I yearn for the role of the courtroom lawyer? Would I wish that I could still be at my law office waiting for new legal adventures? What about researching the cases, looking for the niche in the law that would provide a foothold for a new legal construct? To assemble a case that would move the law forward, to calculate how to present the case, and to astonish the courts with my capacity for invention—would I miss all that?

I am afraid I made a mess of it. I was to be sworn in on January 10, 1972, along with two excellent lawyers: Richard Anderson, a prominent member of the bar, and Harry McKay, a much-admired county court judge who was being moved up to the Supreme Court. Friends called to congratulate me, but I had misgivings.

My doubts grew. Arthur Maloney, a leading criminal lawyer in Toronto and a friend, phoned to congratulate me. I think Arthur realized I was apprehensive. He told me that John Robinette had once accepted an appointment to the Ontario Court of Appeal, the appointment had been announced, and he then begged off before being sworn in. Arthur didn't suggest that was a course to be followed, but he said that if I didn't enjoy the work I could always leave the bench after six months.

On the morning I was to be sworn in, I spoke on the telephone with Allan McEachern (then a well-known Vancouver lawyer, who had urged Turner to appoint me) and told him that I had changed my mind. Allan was alarmed. He, like Maloney, told me that I should go ahead and take my seat on the court. If it turned out that I wasn't suited to the bench, I could resign in six months.

Six months. It would have been feckless to resign within six months of my appointment. I felt I should either commit myself to the bench wholeheartedly or turn down the appointment. I decided to make the commitment. Bev and I and my daughter, Erin, my son, David and, of course, my mother, Perle, went to the courthouse for the swearing-in ceremony.

Now I was a judge.

I soon realized that I was enjoying the work. It was a more measured life, a much more regular routine than I had enjoyed at the bar. And with a salary cheque coming in every month, there was no need to worry about office overhead, sending bills and collecting delinquent accounts. Nor was it necessary each day to dash back from the courthouse to the office to interview witnesses for the following day. Or to spend every Sunday night reviewing a transcript of evidence in preparation for a trial, civil or criminal, to begin on the Monday morning.

And judges have to write. This I discovered I delighted in. Of course, I had written countless briefs and delivered innumerable arguments. But as a judge there was time to reflect. It wasn't necessary to persuade anyone of the soundness of my point of view. I could put down on paper exactly where I thought the evidence and the law should come out.

One of my colleagues was Justice David Verchere, whose office was next to mine. He had been on the bench many years. Convivial, literate, never taking himself altogether seriously, David often had lunch with me. I looked in at his door one day, suggesting we step out for a bite to eat. He was busily writing. As he had been hearing a high-profile civil dispute, much discussed in the media, and had reserved judgement, I asked him, "David, what are you going to do in that case?" He looked up from his desk, pen still in hand, and said, "You know, Tommy, I can't wait to see how it turns out."

Work on the bench is solitary. The phone doesn't ring. You realize that the clients who thought you were indispensable find other legal help soon enough. There are a lot of good lawyers to whom they can turn. You don't want to trouble your old comrades at the bar to go to lunch: for lawyers, lunches are an occasion to recruit allies; to talk settlement; to assess an opposing lawyer's position. In such a milieu, judges are supercargo. On the other hand, my work on the bench was always interesting, sometimes fascinating.

I intend to say nothing here, however, about the cases that I decided, for two reasons. The first is that, having pronounced judgement in a case, there is nothing more for a judge to say; in fact, it would be altogether inappropriate for a judge to say anything more. This does not mean that a judge cannot, in speeches or articles or books, discuss the progress or the lack of progress of the law in a given field. But he or she must not offer any explanation of a judgement already handed down. When the litigants and their lawyers hear what the judge has to say, or when they read the judge's reasons for judgement, that is the basis on which they can decide whether to appeal. But they would have a justifiable grievance if, after the period allowed for an appeal had elapsed, the judge were to provide what would appear to the litigants to be additional reasons, reasons that should have been provided to them earlier—because that is the judge's first task, to determine fairly the dispute between the litigants before the court.

There is a second reason. Despite its name, the Supreme Court of British Columbia is a trial court. Judges of the court sit to hear witnesses and arguments by lawyers, either alone or with a jury. If there is an appeal, the case goes to the province's Court of Appeal, where the judges, sitting in panels of three, consider the record. They don't hear from any witnesses, only from the lawyers, whose job it is to persuade them that the judgement at trial is erroneous or sound, as the case may be. From there, a case may go to the Supreme Court of Canada.

I was a trial judge, and not very much of the work of a trial judge survives. A trial judge's job is to decide a particular dispute. The judge's take on the law may, in a given case, be of interest beyond the confines of a particular dispute. Usually, it will be of no significance to anyone except the parties who brought the dispute to the court in the first place. Judge-made law is made in the appellate courts, especially the Supreme Court of Canada.

Being a judge also meant that I was called on to conduct royal commissions. During my twelve years on the bench, I headed three royal commissions of inquiry. This is work that judges often do. Why judges? There are two good reasons. First, they have the time. If judges are allowed to absent themselves from judicial duty, they can devote their full time to the task assigned to the commission. Lawyers with busy practices or persons employed in business or the trade unions or the universities simply cannot absent themselves from their ordinary round of obligations for months or years.

In 1972, the NDP, under the leadership of Dave Barrett, elected its first provincial government in B.C. and asked me to head a Royal Commission on Family and Children's Law. With four colleagues and an excellent staff, we held hearings all over the province and issued thirteen reports, dealing with everything from division of family property to illegitimacy to custody and guardianship. Many of the recommendations of the commission were enacted into law by the Barrett government and its successors.

From 1974 to 1977, under the Liberal government of Prime Minister Pierre Trudeau, I conducted the Mackenzie Valley Pipeline Inquiry. My mandate was to determine the social, environmental and economic impact of the proposed Arctic Gas pipeline to be built from Prudhoe Bay in Alaska across the north slope of the Yukon and along the Mackenzie Valley to Alberta for the purpose of transporting natural gas from the Arctic to the metropolitan centres of North America. I held hearings in every city, every town and every village in the Mackenzie Valley and the Western Arctic, and in hunting and fishing camps as well. In 1977, on my recommendation, the government rejected the Arctic Gas pipeline proposal. I recommended that a national wilderness park be established in the northern Yukon to protect the calving grounds of the Porcupine Caribou herd; a wilderness park called Ivvavit was established in the northern Yukon in 1984, and another wilderness park called Vuntut established in 1995. In fact, they were established as part of the Inuvaluit and Vuntut Gwichin land claims settlements. As a result, both parks are constitutionally entrenched: their character and their boundaries cannot be altered except by constitutional amendment.

I found that, given appropriate environmental safeguards, a pipeline could be built along the Mackenzie Valley. I recommended a ten-year moratorium to enable the land claims of the Dene and the Inuvaluit along the route to be settled before any major pipeline project was undertaken. No formal moratorium was imposed, but, because the Arctic Gas project had been rejected, there has been a de facto moratorium of twenty-five years. As a result, Dene and Inuvaluit land claims have been settled throughout most of the region.

At the time there were many critics of my recommendations. Some said I had exceeded my terms of reference. I would concede, if pressed, that I gave them a liberal interpretation. But, as Emmett Hall told me at the time: "Tom, if they don't accuse you of exceeding your terms of reference, you haven't done your job."

In 1979, I headed a third royal commission, under the Conservative government of Prime Minister Joe Clark, this time dealing with Indian and Inuit health-care programs. My recommendation—for greater consultation with Indians and Inuit regarding the delivery of such programs—was made to Clark's minister of health, David Crombie, and, with the Liberal restoration in 1980, adopted by Crombie's successor, Monique Bégin.

A commission of inquiry has—or ought to have—an advantage that ministers and senior officials in the public service do not have: an opportunity to hear all the evidence, to reflect on it, to weigh it and to make a judgement on it. Ministers and their deputies, given the demands that the management of their departments impose on them, usually have no such opportunity.

Commissions of inquiry, both through their hearings and in their reports, have brought new thinking into the public consciousness; expanded the vocabulary of politics, education and social science. They have added to the furniture that we now expect to find in Canada's storefront of ideas. And, contrary to popular mythology, they have always had real importance in providing considered advice to governments.

There is a widely held view that royal commissions are nothing but a means to enable governments to avoid confronting issues, to put a judge to work holding interminable hearings and then to file any recommendations in a waste basket. But this is not a true picture. The report of the Rowell-Sirois Commission in the 1940s led to a rearrangement of taxing powers between the federal and the provincial governments. The Massey Commission in the 1950s led to the establishment of the Canada Council and federal funding for universities. The recommendations of Emmett Hall's Commission on Health Care in the 1960s led to medicare spreading from Saskatchewan to become a national program. The MacDonald Commission in the 1980s provided the blueprint for free trade with the United States. And my own commissions have had, I think, a demonstrable influence on public policy.

I wrote there were two reasons for appointing judges to royal commissions. The second reason is that judges are independent. They're not looking for political reward. They're not dependent on government for legal business. So they can call it as they see it. When I conducted the Mackenzie Valley Pipeline Inquiry, I said, more than once, at the hearings, "My only client is the truth." That statement may have seemed sententious and self-important, but I thought it was necessary to emphasize that I was independent of the federal government and all the interested parties. That meant, of course, I would search for the truth as I might see it, because the views of judges, like those of everybody else, reflect their life experience. But that is a limitation built into any royal commission, indeed, any human endeavour. The recommendations of royal commissions may be good or bad, but they should be the result of a truly independent examination of the issues.

Prime Minister Trudeau told me, when the two of us had lunch at his home on Sussex Drive, that he felt the same way about the Mackenzie Valley Pipeline Inquiry. I was under some criticism on the ground that the inquiry was going too slowly. He told me to take the time to do a proper job. "I wanted you," he said, "because I knew you would not be a patsy."

After I left the bench, I was invited to conduct inquiries very much along the lines of royal commissions, but for non-governmental organizations. I had learned enough about the need for independence to insist on it in these new undertakings.

In August 1983, I was asked to head the Alaska Native Review Commission, sponsored by the Inuit Circumpolar Conference, an international organization of Inuit from Alaska, Canada and Greenland, to look into the impact of the Alaskan land claims settlement enacted by Congress in 1971. This commission took me to Alaska for two years. I insisted on my independence, requiring that my fee be paid in advance. I travelled for two years, throughout Alaska, to sixty Aleut, Indian and Eskimo Villages (in Alaska, the Yupik and Inupiat preferred, when referred to generically, to be called Eskimo). My recommendations were intended to be submitted to Congress. They were not adopted by Congress, but my report, published under the title *Village Journey*, is still used by the Aboriginal people of Alaska as a manual in their continuing campaign for tribal self-government and restoration of their land to tribal ownership.

In 1991, I was appointed deputy chairman of the first Independent Review commissioned by the World Bank. Our job was to examine the implementation of resettlement and environmental measures in the Sardar Sarovar dam and irrigation projects in western India. The chairman, Bradford Morse, an American, was a former undersecretary general of the United Nations, an international public servant living in retirement in Florida. I was practising law in Vancouver. We were, to the bank's consternation, truly independent. Neither of us belonged to the bank's universe of consultants, located in virtually every country of the world, many of whom looked to the bank as the motherlode. In 1992, the report of the Independent Review was made public. We found that the projects were flawed in that they failed to take adequate measures to resettle the villagers in the Narmada Valley who were being flooded out; we also found that India had not taken adequate measures to protect the environment. As a result, the World Bank discontinued funding.

But it was the Mackenzie Valley Pipeline Inquiry that had the greatest effect on my career. It attracted a great deal of attention. *Northern Frontier, Northern Homeland,* the report of the inquiry, became the best-selling volume ever published by the government of Canada. It was a controversial report, but its recommendations against the proposed Arctic Gas pipeline, for protection of the environment and for settlement of Aboriginal claims, were adopted by the federal government. The inquiry sharpened my profile as a champion of Aboriginal rights.

When, therefore, Pierre Trudeau brought in a new Constitution and Charter of Rights in 1981, I spoke in support of it at the annual meeting in Vancouver of the Canadian Bar Association on September 2, 1981. The draft Constitution included a guarantee of Aboriginal and treaty rights: "The aboriginal and treaty rights of the aboriginal peoples of Canada are hereby recognized and affirmed."

I have found the presentation I made at the time; it is an endorsement of Trudeau's constitutional proposals. I said:

So democratic institutions, the rule of law, and due process do count. When all is said and done, it is not a question of economic arrangements alone. The achievement and the strength of the Western nations, indeed, their right to call for the judgement of history, lies in our willingness to examine and re-examine the assumptions by which we live, and in our openness to the winds that bring new ideas. The spirit of free speech and free inquiry in politics, religion, science and the arts informs our ideal of democracy; it depends on the affirmation and reaffirmation of our conviction in the virtues of diversity and the right of dissent. The Constitution and the Charter affirm these principles.

I added:

The Charter of Rights offers persons who are under attack by the majority a place to stand, ground to defend, and the means for others to help them. Many have said that the entrenchment of these rights, placing them beyond the reach of Parliament and the provinces, will enhance the power of the courts. And, of course, it does precisely that. In a federal state the courts interpret the provisions of the Constitution that divide legislative power. Why should they not also have the task of interpreting the nature and scope of the rights that belong to the people and lie beyond the reach of legislative authority?

If the rights of minorities and dissenters are to be entrenched, if there are to be limits on the powers of both Parliament and the provinces, the judges will always have the last word on where these limits are. Judges may not always be wiser than the politicians, but they should be able to stand more firmly against the angry winds blowing in the streets; at any rate they should have no reason to take the bellows to them.

No one took offence at my remarks. Perhaps no one noticed them. But there I was, a sitting judge, speaking out, if you will.

At the last minute, Trudeau and the premiers dropped Aboriginal and treaty rights from the document. I felt that I had to make a public declaration opposing the action of the First Ministers. I had become known as someone who had articulated the idea of Aboriginal rights in *Calder* and treaty rights in *White and Bob*. As commissioner of the Mackenzie Valley Pipeline Inquiry, I had urged the importance of settling land claims in the Northwest Territories. I realized that if I spoke out against what had been done, two things might result. First, it would raise a lot of flak. I would no longer be offering an innocuous endorsement of the original document, but a specific criticism of the amended document. At the same time, however, my intervention, I thought, might be helpful in getting Aboriginal and treaty rights restored to the Constitution.

I realized that what I had in mind to say would be controversial. But it seemed to me I had no choice.

I had been invited to speak at the University of Guelph, on November 11, 1981. Here is what I said:

The agreement reached in February this year by all parties in the House of Commons, to entrench aboriginal rights and treaty rights in the new Constitution, has been repudiated by the Prime Minister and the premiers.

In fact, they were unanimous on this question. The Prime Minister and all the premiers were in agreement—not only the nine premiers of the English-speaking provinces, but Premier Lévesque [of Quebec], too, for the reasons he gave for his refusal to sign the constitutional agreement did not include any reference to native rights. There was, at the end, not one of our Canadian statesmen willing to take a stand for the rights of the Indians, the Inuit and the Metis.

I went on:

Why were native rights affirmed in February [in the original document] and rejected in November? I think it is because the native peoples lie beyond the narrow political world of the Prime Minister and the premiers, a world bounded by advisers, memoranda, *non obstante* clauses and photostat machines. It is, in fact, in our relations with the peoples from whom we took this land that we can discover the truth about ourselves and the society we have built. Do our brave words about the Third World carry conviction when we will not take a stand for the peoples of our own domestic Third World? How can anyone believe us when we say that we wish to see poverty eradicated in native communities, an end to enforced dependence and a fair settlement of native claims?

The constitutional agreement is a defeat for the native peoples, but it is also a defeat for all Canadians. The agreement reveals the true limits of the Canadian conscience and the Canadian imagination. For the statesmen who signed the agreement of November 5, 1981, represent us. They know us well, and they believed they could, with impunity, delete native rights from the Constitution.

I concluded:

In the end, no matter what ideology they profess, our leaders share one firm conviction: that native rights should not be inviolable; the power of the state must encompass them. Their treatment of native peoples reveals how essential it is to entrench minority rights, without qualification.

No words can disguise what has happened. The first Canadians—a million people and more—have had their answer from Canada's statesmen: they cannot look to any of our governments to defend the idea that they are entitled to a distinct and contemporary place in Canadian life. Under the new Constitution the first Canadians shall be last.

This is not the end of the story. The native peoples have not come this far to turn back now. But it is an abject and mean-spirited chapter. No one can rejoice that it was written in Canada.

I spoke at a time when the proposals agreed to by the First Ministers were about to come before Parliament. It was my hope that it might be possible for me to influence the course that Parliament was to take. Though I was driven to speak, I was distressed that I felt compelled to do so.

There were justifiable reasons for remaining silent. Judges do not make public utterances on matters of political controversy. The conventions guiding the conduct of judges are inimical to offering such utterances. I was aware of the rules, and aware that many would regard my foray into the constitutional debate as imprudent, unwise and uncaring of the importance of upholding the impartiality of the judiciary.

But I felt there was a distinction between the ordinary round of partisan politics on the one hand and overarching issues of human rights and fundamental freedoms on the other. Such issues do transcend partisan politics. The constitutional debate was an occasion of constitutional renewal, unique in our national life. Having supported Aboriginal and treaty rights in fair weather, I had no choice but to offer my support when the weather turned foul.

I also prepared an op-ed piece for the *Globe and Mail*, to the same effect as my Guelph speech. In it, I not only urged restoration of Aboriginal and treaty rights but also recognition of Quebec's veto over constitutional amendments. This latter was a bit of impudence, and no one paid it the slightest attention. I was in Toronto at the time. I had to get the piece typed. I was staying at a hotel near the University of Toronto. I asked Frank Iacobucci, the dean of law of the University of Toronto, to have his secretary type it. He read it over and said, "Tom, there'll be hell to pay over this."

I told him I realized there would be. As he handed my handwritten notes to his secretary, he said, "You know, Tom, I hoped to see you go to the Court of Appeal and then to the Supreme Court of Canada." Unspoken was the implication that none of this would happen now. It was Frank Iacobucci who was to sit on the Supreme Court of Canada.

Many others spoke out as I did—Aboriginal leaders themselves, and other voices around the country. As a result, Trudeau and the premiers met once more and agreed to restore Aboriginal and treaty rights to what is now section 35 of the Constitution Act, 1982. My intervention, I think, helped to produce this outcome. But it did raise a serious question for the judiciary. Should a judge remain silent when, by speaking out, he may help to prevent a grave injustice to a minority? If he does speak out, is this act to be condemned as a venture into partisan politics and an abuse of his office?

Some thought so. On November 19, 1981, a judge of the Federal Court named George Addy filed a complaint with the Canadian Judicial Council. He said: "It appears to me that Mr. Justice Berger has not the faintest idea of the position and role of a judge in the British parliamentary system to-day. On the other hand, if he has, then he is guilty of misconduct which, in my view at least, would tend to cause far greater harm to the administration of justice than sleeping with a prostitute or driving whilst impaired." (One B.C. judge had recently been guilty of the one, a second judge of the other.) A few days later, Prime Minister Trudeau held a news conference in Vancouver. When the local media asked him about my intervention, he said that I had no business becoming involved in a political dispute, and he "hoped the judges would do something about it."

So what was the Judicial Council going to do? At the outset, Allan McEachern, who in 1979 had become chief justice of the Supreme Court of B.C., spoke to me. He said Bora Laskin, now chief justice of the Supreme Court of Canada, had phoned him and urged me to apologize. It was clear that if I did so, Judge Addy's complaint would not be proceeded with. I said I would not, that I believed I had no other course, that I would do it again. "I did it and I'm glad."

That may have been a frivolous way of putting it. I had struggled with the question whether I should speak out. The fact is I thought that I was uniquely placed to draw to the country's attention the injustice that had been done. My credentials were such that I had good reason to expect that by speaking out I could make a difference. In fact, the prime minister and the premiers had given way. Aboriginal and treaty rights had now been restored to the Constitution. Why should I apologize for saying something I believed in and that had achieved the outcome I had in mind?

Chief Justice McEachern spoke to me again a day or two later, saying that Laskin still urged an apology be made. I declined.

On January 25, 1982, the Judicial Council appointed a Committee of Investigation consisting of three chief justices, chaired by Associate Chief Justice B.J. Robertson of Ontario, to look into the complaint. The committee in turn appointed John J. Robinette as counsel to the committee. When Robinette phoned me, I told him that I did not intend to appear before the committee members or make representations of any kind to them. They knew what I had said at Guelph; they had read my piece in the *Globe and Mail*. I had nothing to add.

I know that Chief Justice McEachern was deeply troubled by what was occurring. One weekend, he telephoned me at home and said: "Tom, I've thought a great deal about this. I think you're right and they're wrong. If you won't defend yourself, will you let me defend you?" I said, by all means. He made a lengthy submission to the committee, urging that I had not acted in a way that warranted any action on its part. Reading the committee's report again for the first time in many years, I realize how thorough Chief Justice McEachern's defence had been. He had put up a valiant fight. I think the most telling point was made when he wrote:

I also ask the Committee to consider whether this entire procedure is not fraught with danger for the independence of the Judiciary. Is it the role of Council to impose its will upon the conscience of a judge who went unnoticed when he spoke up for the constitutional package, but who, when he speaks critically of later developments in the process, feels the full weight of the judicial establishment coming down on him—possibly destroying his career—merely because one judge has made a formal complaint?

He concluded:

Lastly I wish to remind the Committee that several members of Council have suggested that Berger, J. has shown no evidence of regret or contrition, and that all this might have been avoided if he had apologized, or had adopted a more conciliatory attitude to the complaint and to Council. I hope the Committee will put any such thoughts out of its mind . . . [Berger] denies that the conduct complained of has anything to do with the condition of good behaviour in his commission and, that being so, he disputes the jurisdiction of Council to discipline him.

Should an independent judge take any other position in the face of insulting allegations by the complainant that his conduct is worse than sleeping with a prostitute?

Nevertheless, the committee concluded that the complaint of Judge Addy was well founded, and that my conduct had been such as to support a recommendation for my removal from office. Judges are appointed during good behaviour. They cannot be removed except by a joint resolution of the House of Commons and the Senate. The committee said, however, that "this is the first time this issue has arisen for determination in Canada." They did not think it would be "fair" to set standards *ex post facto* to support a recommendation for removal in my case. The committee, nevertheless, convicted me of abusing my office, of using it as a political platform, and questioned whether the public could have confidence in my impartiality. This conviction was tantamount to a vote of censure and, were I to accept it, would in my view have required my resignation.

I was not supplied with a copy of the committee's report. The Judicial Council did not send one to me. Was this because I had not appeared before the committee? The committee's report would necessarily go to the Judicial Council. Why shouldn't I have a chance to read it and make a submission to the council?

Chief Justice McEachern made sure I received a copy, or else I would have had no opportunity of responding to the committee's findings.

The committee had held that I was guilty of a breach of the condition of good behaviour on which I had been appointed; there were grounds for impeachment. Yet the committee said that nothing further should be done; Parliament should not be asked to remove me from office. This was on the footing that nothing quite like this had happened before, and the rules governing judicial conduct had not been altogether clear. The committee might have thought this recommendation would be a satisfactory outcome, but a moment's reflection showed that it was untenable.

I wrote to the Judicial Council. I said that you cannot have a judiciary where a breach of good behaviour is excused. You cannot have judges continuing in office, on probation, so to speak. Parliament is the final arbiter of good behaviour. The committee had, in effect, urged the council to arrogate to itself the right to determine what is or is not a breach of the condition of good behaviour and, by not recommending removal, to withhold the judgement of the council from parliamentary review, thereby denying me the opportunity for exoneration.

The odd thing is that it *had* happened before. There were Canadian precedents. But the committee had refused to consider them. The Judicial Council is composed of the chief justice of Canada and the chief justices of the provinces. In 1970, Chief Justice Samuel Freedman of Manitoba, a member of the council, had gone on television to express his public support for Prime Minister Trudeau's invocation of the War Measures Act. In 1979, Chief Justice Jules Deschênes of Quebec, in *The Sword and the Scales,* published a collection of his speeches—to which Chief Justice Bora Laskin had written the foreword—including "The Rights of the Child," an eloquent plea for the recognition of the rights of the unborn child, which was unsparingly critical of judges who had refused to recognize the rights of the fetus. This speech was a lance hurled into a subject of perennial controversy. It seemed to me that the committee had proclaimed a rule of conduct, and condemned me thereby, that had not always been observed by members of the Judicial Council themselves.

I did not raise these previous instances to show how smart I was. These instances showed that judges might on rare occasions comment on matters of public controversy.

I asked the council: What if I had waited until Parliament had acted, and then criticized what they had done? Perhaps that would have been all right. In fact, it would have explained why Chief Justice Deschênes could second the motion to have me investigated and then travel to Vancouver in the same month to give a speech denouncing the failure of Parliament to entrench the independence of the judiciary in the new Constitution. To intervene when one may be effective is apparently an offence, but to paw the air in exasperation after the event is not. The one will impair public confidence in the judiciary; the other will not. I suggested that the public would not see the usefulness of the distinction.

I turned to the real question: Had my speech undermined public confidence in the judiciary? I felt the committee had failed to give the public credit for understanding that judges hold strong opinions, but that they do their best to ensure that these opinions do not determine the content of their judgements. Occasionally, judges may feel that, on a question with respect to which they may claim to be qualified to speak, they must give expression to those views. Couldn't we trust the public to understand that, notwithstanding our own convictions, we determine each case on the evidence and the law? After all, this is what we tell jury members they must do.

The committee said that the independence of the judiciary would be undermined if judges were constantly engaged in such activity. It said, "It would be possible to have judges speaking out in conflict one with the other." But that had not happened in the past when judges had spoken out; the committee had not given any reason to be fearful of it in future. In fact, such interventions by judges had been infrequent. I added that, if interventions by members of the Judicial Council were not included in the count, the number would be very, very few.

I told the council that public confidence in the judiciary had survived generations of political appointments, unconscionable delays by judges in handing down their judgements, and various kinds of scandalous activity by judges. The proposition that public confidence in the judiciary would be impaired because a judge had urged our political leaders to reconsider their rejection of the rights of Aboriginal peoples was not easy to justify.

I did not accept the council's authority to censure me—for this is what the committee had urged the council to do. I submitted that the council had no statutory power to do so. Chief Justice McEachern had tried to persuade the committee of this point. Parliament had not conferred any authority upon the Judicial Council to declare that judges should be gagged (the word that the committee chose), as if they were civil servants subject to the council's supervision. I said that if the council desired to assert such authority, it should seek it from Parliament.

I told the council that a judge has the right to speak out, on an appropriate occasion, on questions of human rights and fundamental freedoms. Parliament and the legislatures represent majorities; they are not always mindful of the interests of minorities. This fact is central to the dilemma of the democratic system: How can the majority rule without unduly impairing or extinguishing the rights of minorities? The rule enunciated by the committee would forever bar any judge from speaking in that cause.

I then asked, suppose that in 1942 one of the judges of the Supreme Court of British Columbia had spoken out against the internment of the Japanese Canadians following the Japanese attack on Pearl Harbor? No doubt there would have been a complaint, an investigation by somebody or other, and condemnation would have followed. I do not think that any act of mine required the moral courage that would have been needed to speak out in 1942. But the issue raised was the same. If a judge does speak out, is it grounds for removing him or her from the bench?

There are times when, convention notwithstanding, certain things must be said. Occasionally, it will fall to a judge to say them. I acknowledged, however, that reasonable people might take a different view. I urged the council members that, if that was their view, they must have the courage of their convictions and recommend my removal from office so that the issue could be brought before Parliament.

Curiously, Trudeau at this point had more or less withdrawn his criticism of my conduct. He was offended at my remarks, it turned out, because he thought I had never supported his new Constitution in the first place. But when he realized I had, he recanted.

Ian Waddell, a Vancouver lawyer who had been special counsel to the Mackenzie Valley Pipeline Inquiry and was now an MP for the New Democratic Party, wrote to Trudeau on December 15, 1981. He said:

I am writing to you to ask you to recall our short conversation on the evening of the historic vote on Canada's new Constitution. You may recall that, at that time, I asked you about your recent criticism of Justice Berger.

I got the impression that you were unaware that at the Annual Meeting of the Canadian Bar Association on September 2, 1981, Mr. Justice Berger defended your original constitutional package during the course of a panel discussion. His remarks were widely circulated in the lawyers' journals and appeared in the press in Western Canada. He was virtually the only voice in Western Canada to so strongly support unilateral action.

You may be right that, as a judge, Justice Berger should not have made comments on native matters during the constitutional debate, but you must remember the absolutely special place Justice Berger has in the hearts of our native people. Your government had the foresight—as it turns out—to appoint him to the Mackenzie Valley Pipeline Inquiry which now has given Canada a worldwide reputation as a country that honestly tried to struggle with the implications of development on the frontier.

Who knows what the future holds for the eventual settlement on matters concerning our native people, but I remain convinced that your initiative in putting the native guarantees in the Constitution (no matter how much criticized now) will be seen as a statesmanlike act. Judge Berger takes that view and said so. He also defended your Charter of Rights. Considering his position of trust among native people, Canada may need him in the future to work with our native people.

Your remarks could potentially undercut his position and I would hope that, at some time, somewhere, in your future public remarks you might take the opportunity to temper your criticism with some positive comments. Otherwise, I feel an injustice may be done.

Trudeau responded to Waddell:

You are right: I was unaware of Justice Berger's statement to the Canadian Bar, on September 2, 1981. It was a superb statement, and I am thankful that you brought it to my attention.

But it was made late in the game, and in a forum scarcely designed to get wide coverage. Whereas Berger's attack on the accord was made in the *Globe and Mail*, and at a time when even your Party was not certain of supporting the accord so painfully reached.

The paradox remains. Berger supports us in an esoteric forum, perhaps as might befit a member of the Judiciary. But Berger attacks us in a hostile "national" political newspaper, as hardly befits a judge.

But have no fear. I have no lasting grudges, nor have I the disposition to pursue them. And Berger will suffer no injustice on my account!

Ian Waddell made public his correspondence with Trudeau. Now the council members, having given the impression that they were proceeding against me at Trudeau's behest, could hardly wind up the case without it appearing that they were acting a second time at Trudeau's command.

The Judicial Council met and, rejecting the committee's conclusion, decided that I had been guilty of a mere indiscretion. Pierre Chamberland, the secretary to the Judiciary Council, sent me a copy of the council's resolution. It read:

(1) The Judicial Council is of the opinion that it was an indiscretion on the part of Mr. Justice Berger to express his views as to matters of a political nature, when such matters were in controversy.

(2) While the Judicial Council is of the opinion that Mr. Justice Berger's actions were indiscreet, they constitute no basis for a recommendation that he be removed from office.

The resolution passed by the Judicial Council seemed straightforward. It was a retreat from the committee's view that, all other things being equal, I should have been impeached. But still, I had, the council said, been guilty of an indiscretion.

My son, David, and I were watching television that night. *Hamlet* was on, starring Derek Jacobi. Hamlet had just made his way back to Denmark and was about to confront Claudius the King. Horatio urges caution, and Hamlet speaks; at that point a reporter phoned to ask me how I felt about the council's decision. I said: "The Council should remember what Hamlet said: 'Our indiscretion sometimes serves us well, when our deep plots do pall.'" I suppose this was over-the-top. But they had put me through the wringer.

On May 4, 1982, Jean Chrétien, then minister of justice, in making public the Canadian Judicial Council's resolution, said the council had "accepted" the report of the Committee of Investigation. This statement was puzzling. If so, the council would not have decided that I had been merely "indiscreet." Chrétien had, in language unmistakably his own, added: "In my judgement any guys who will become judges will be well advised to read that report because they will know that if they do not follow it their fellow judges will ask them why they didn't read it, because most of the judges feel very strongly that the separation of powers is extremely important to our system."

I telephoned Chamberland to find out what the council had done. I was advised that the committee's report had been received, not adopted by the council. I asked Chamberland if this is what the council's minutes said. As the judge accused in the case, I felt I had the right to know exactly what the council had decided. Chief Justice Gregory Evans of Ontario, a member of the Judicial Council, had by that time given an extensive interview to the CBC, and another to the *Globe and Mail,* about the council's deliberations. He went so far as to say to the CBC that a minority of council was opposed to the resolution that had been passed, indicating the grounds on which they were opposed, yet he temporized on the question whether the report of the committee had been adopted.

Jean Chrétien had left the impression that the committee's report had in fact been adopted by the Judicial Council, and Chief Justice Evans had done nothing to dispel that impression. Many news media carried the story as if the report had been adopted. For instance, the *Toronto Star* ran an editorial citing the words of the committee but attributing them to the Judicial Council, and the newspaper then called for my resignation. The council did not straighten out this misshapen record of events; nor did the council take steps to see that Jean Chrétien was properly informed as to what had occurred.

I wrote to Chief Justice Bora Laskin:

The Minister stated in the House, as spokesman for the Government, that the Council had accepted the Committee's report. He also said in the Commons, as spokesman for the Government of Canada, that "we welcome this report," a statement that clearly referred to the report of the Committee. It may be that the Government welcomed the report but, if so, it was wrong to leave the impression that this quite dreadful piece of legal craftsmanship had been accepted by the Judicial Council. The Council was bound to make this plain to the Minister and to the public. It failed to do so. This failure was an abdication of its claim to act as custodian of the independence of the judiciary.

Chief Justice Laskin, however, took the position that if the minister of justice had made an error in a public statement regarding the council's decision in my case, it was not up to the council publicly to correct the error. I thought this reasoning was not only unsound but unforgivable. At least one member of the council agreed with me. Chief Justice William McGillivray of Alberta wrote to Laskin, taking issue with his refusal to clarify the council's decision.

Two things concern me. The first is that, as I understand it, Chief Justice Evans made a statement publicly, to the effect that the decision of Council was the same in the result as the report of the Investigating Committee . . . Now to leave the impression, as I think Chief Justice Evans' statement has done, that the Judicial Council was of the view that Mr. Justice Berger's conduct would justify his removal from office, is unfair to Mr. Justice Berger. It seems to me it is not so much a matter of correcting a statement made by the Minister of Justice, as a statement made by a spokesman for the Judicial Council. This, it seems to me, is our responsibility.

The second matter that concerns me is that I feel that as a matter of just plain fairness, we are bound to correct an injustice done to a member of the judiciary by making it clear exactly what our body has done. I think it desirable that a brief statement be made to the effect that as there seems to be uncertainty as to the view the Judicial Council took of Mr. Justice Berger's conduct, it should be stated that the Judicial Council's opinion was that Mr. Justice Berger had done nothing to justify removal from office and that his public statements in respect to political matters in controversy were regarded as an indiscretion, and no more.

Laskin took no steps to clarify the situation. But he was agitated that I had called Pierre Chamberland, the executive secretary of the Judicial Council, to find out what had happened. Laskin wrote to me:

Unfortunately owing to a recent illness I was unable to participate fully in the proceedings relating to the complaint against you. The purpose of this letter is not to deal with the complaint because the Canadian Judicial Council has made its decision and that is where the matter rests.

What I wish to raise with you is to indicate my complete revulsion of your conduct for your inquiry of Mr. Pierre Chamberland, our Executive Secretary, of certain decisions and positions that were taken during the meetings of the Canadian Judicial Council. You should know better than anyone that Mr. Chamberland is engaged in a confidential operation and that he has no authority to divulge to anyone the course of proceedings before meetings of the Canadian Judicial Council. This is a shameful intrusion by you on confidential matters to which Mr. Chamberland is privy. I wish to say to you as plainly as I can that you are to refrain from any attempt to obtain disclosure from Mr. Chamberland of matters pertaining to the Canadian Judicial Council which Mr. Chamberland is, in any event, precluded from divulging. I hope I will not hear of another such intrusion by you again.

This response seemed an overreaction to my call to Chamberland. I replied to Laskin:

I do not think it would serve any purpose to reply to the personal animadversions in your letter of June 17, except to say that it became necessary for me to telephone Mr. Chamberland to find out whether or not the Judicial Council had adopted the report of the Committee of Investigation. You will recall that the Committee had said that there were grounds for recommending my removal from office. The Minister of Justice said on a number of occasions that the Council had accepted the report of the Committee, leaving the impression that the Committee's strictures had found favour with the Council.

The resolution passed by the Council, giving its opinion that I had been indiscreet, did not deal with the issue addressed by the Minister and discussed in the House of Commons. As the judge who was the subject of the controversy, I felt that I had the right to know what disposition the Council had made of the Committee's report. So I called Mr. Chamberland; it turned out that the Council had only received the Committee's report, and not adopted it.

I added: "I am sorry to read that you have fallen ill again. I express the hope—I do so quite sincerely—that this misfortune will soon pass and that you will be able to continue to serve."

Laskin replied:

I quite agree with what you say in your letter of July 7 that no purpose will be served to pursue any of the matters arising from the complaint against you. The Canadian

Judicial Council has made its determination and it matters little that you take exception to the way in which it handled the matter.

Then cryptically, and apparently forgetting how he'd begun his earlier letter, he added:

I appreciate your reference to my illness which was really an alleged illness wrongly reported by the press.

Reaction of editors and columnists was, on the whole, favourable to me and critical of Laskin and the Judicial Council. Charles Lynch, senior political correspondent of Southam News Services, wrote:

Even such an old Berger baiter as I cannot read the transcript of the proceedings against him without coming down on his side, and against his judicial persecutors.

My own feud with Berger stems from his work as a Trudeau-appointed royal commissioner, assigned to study the implications of the proposed pipeline in the valley of the Mackenzie River. Berger's anti-development bias was well known at the time of his appointment, and he wrote a completely predictable report whose effect was to stifle economic development in the Mackenzie valley for a decade, and perhaps forever.

In my view, Berger did the native peoples of the north a grave disservice, though by espousing their claimed rights and prerogatives he became their hero.

Now, the judges have made him my hero, as well.

They have displayed the workings of justice at its worst, following the lead of Pierre Trudeau at his most petulant.

Berger, once Trudeau's darling, fell out of favour by making a speech to the Canadian Bar Association supporting Trudeau's constitutional package, and then turning critical when Trudeau deleted the clause protecting native peoples' rights.

What Trudeau said was that he hoped the judges would "do something about" Berger's meddling.

The effect was the same as the infamous words of King Henry II about his old supporter, Thomas à Becket: "Who will free me from this turbulent priest?" To oblige the king, four knights of the court slew Becket forthwith . . .

The published evidence not only clears him, but establishes Berger as one of the most distinguished thinkers of our time. His speech to the annual meeting of the Canadian Bar Association in Vancouver last September is one of the most vivid utterances from anybody on the merits of Trudeau's proposed constitution and charter of rights.

The judges kiss off the bar association speech by saying: "It is true that it appears that judges, in speaking to legal bodies, are accorded somewhat greater leeway in expressing their views than they are in speaking to the general public."

Baloney, your lordships.

You would have done much better to have read Berger's eloquent address to the bar association, and to urge your fellow judges and all citizens to do the same.

And you should have turned your wrath on Trudeau, instead of responding to his bidding, like the bonehead knights of Henry II.

Berger lives on, awaiting what Chief Justice McEachern calls future opportunities for greatness.

I supposed that the Judicial Council's censure might have been the end of the matter. But Laskin, perhaps stung by the criticism, insisted on bringing the matter up again and again, each time publicly, and each time criticizing me by name.

In September 1982, Laskin had been invited to speak at the closing banquet at the annual meeting of the Canadian Bar Association in Toronto. The day before Laskin was to speak, Paul Fraser, a Vancouver lawyer who was serving as the president of the organization, phoned me to say that he suspected Laskin was going to make me the subject of his speech. He said that Laskin would not tell him the subject of his address or provide him with a copy of the speech.

At the banquet, Laskin said he wanted to set the record straight. Despite the fact that the Judicial Council had found that in my case there was "no basis for a recommendation that he be removed from office," Laskin said that a judge who "feels so strongly on political issues that he must speak out is best advised to resign from the bench." He went on, "He cannot be allowed to speak from the shelter of a judgeship."

This statement was difficult to interpret as anything but a call for my resignation.

Laskin was nettled by the fact that the coincidence of George Addy's complaint and Prime Minister Trudeau's expressed hope that the judges would do something about Berger had left the public with the impression that Laskin was acting on Trudeau's orders. Relying on the fact that Judge Addy's complaints about me were made on November 18 and 19, while it was not until November 24 that Trudeau had spoken, he denounced the media. "It is therefore mischief-making to suggest that the Judicial Council was moved to action by the Prime Minister."

Laskin said of the widespread support for my stand: "Would the same support be offered to a judge who intervenes in a political matter in an opposite way? Surely there must be one standard, and that is absolute abstention, except possibly where the role of the Court itself is brought into question." He went on to lacerate the media's support for me: "Was there ever such ignorance of history and of principle?" If you read the transcript of his speech, it appears he was referring to the ignorance of the media. But the *Vancouver Sun,* and most everyone, thought he was talking about me.

Looking back, Laskin obviously had a case. I always thought that reasonable men and women might come down on one side or the other of the issue. Friends of mine on the bench agreed with me; other friends on the bench agreed with Laskin. It was the same among members of the bar. At a meeting of the B.C. bar's provincial council, there was a spirited debate. Bryan Williams moved and Cec Branson seconded a motion expressing confidence in me. Others argued against it. But it passed. The Law Society of B.C. also expressed confidence in my capacity to continue to sit on the bench.

If Laskin was right, and the rule ought to be "absolute abstention," he should have made the case. A good case could have been made. But he seemed not to appreciate that such a rule had not always been observed by his colleagues on the Judicial Council. And he never did come to grips with the argument I had advanced: What if you could, by intervening, make a difference, not on an ordinary political question (should the old age pension be increased? should Canada adopt the GST? should Canada join NAFTA?), but one involving human rights and fundamental freedoms?

What Laskin seemed unwilling to consider was that this was an occasion when a judge could make a difference: not because I was a judge, but because of work I had done in other capacities. He might well believe in his hard and fast rule, applicable in all circumstances and in every case. And if a judge were to use his office to act as busybody, feeling that his views had to be considered by the nation, and if it were simply a question of an out-of-control ego, the judge would deserve censure. But I felt that I had a moral obligation to speak out on this single issue. It may be that Michael Valpy, a columnist with the *Globe and Mail,* put it best. He said: "It was possibly, if you like, a rare case for civil disobedience."

The evening of Laskin's speech to the bar in Toronto, Bev and I were visiting friends in Victoria. The day following, as we walked back to our hotel, we saw the evening edition of the *Vancouver Sun,* with a front-page headline: "Laskin lashes Berger's ignorance." My offence may have been a hanging offence, but it need not have been accompanied by a campaign of vilification. Bev and I both realized I must now leave the bench. I told Chief Justice McEachern I would be resigning.

McEachern maintained his good humour throughout. We were at lunch one day with Justices William Esson and Harry McKay. The chief justice said, "You know, only a bunch of judges could have made such a mess of this affair." Harry McKay responded, "No sir, only a bunch of chief justices could have made such a mess of it."

It was time to go. I suppose I could have remained, ignoring Laskin's tin lightning bolts. But as long as Laskin remained Canada's chief justice, the dispute would remain a live issue. It would be unseemly to carry on a feud with the chief justice of Canada. It would do the bench no good. It would do Laskin no good. And it would do me no good.

Why did I leave? I looked up my letter of resignation, dated April 25, 1983, to Mark MacGuigan, the minister of justice. It was written after I had had time to think about all that had occurred. I said:

It used to be thought that an appointment to the bench was for a lifetime. But the judiciary, like all of our institutions, is changing. When I went on the bench I was 38. I am 50 now, a good time of life to consider a change.

My differences with Chief Justice Laskin and the Canadian Judicial Council are well known. They have adopted a view of judicial service that I cannot share. This extends beyond the dispute over the propriety of my intervention in the constitutional debate in November, 1981. Then, I said—and I still firmly believe—that on rare occasions a judge may have an obligation to speak out on human rights and fundamental freedoms. That is, I think, in keeping with Canadian experience. The Judicial Council disagreed. The issue is not a simple one, as may be illustrated by the fact that the Judicial Council relied on the writings of Lord Denning [England's most revered judge]; yet when Lord Denning was asked about my intervention in the constitutional debate . . . he said:

"At all events, there are times, I think, when the judges have a responsibility to express their views on matters of great moment even though it is not in the law courts."

Some people asked, given the fact I had championed the cause of First Nations, how could I sit as a judge in cases involving Indians? I never felt that, had I continued on the bench, I would have been disqualified from hearing cases involving Aboriginal or treaty rights. Why don't they ask similar questions of judges who have spent their careers representing insurance companies? Or as prosecutors? Or who have spent their careers employed in government departments?

Mind you, a conflict did arise on one occasion.

During the years I was on the bench, my wife, Bev, was a counsellor at the Native Indian Teacher Education Program at UBC. One evening, some of the students came to the door. I was upstairs. I heard some discussion and laughter at the front door. Then they were gone. I asked what it was all about. Bev said, "It was Angie Todd-Dennis and some of the students. They're going to occupy the offices of Indian Affairs downtown. They expect to stay overnight and wanted to borrow cooking utensils, so I loaned them a frying pan."

The next day I had a call from Chief Justice McEachern. He said, "I think the federal government is going to be applying for an injunction to remove some women who have occupied the offices of Indian Affairs. Would you hear the application?" I said, "Chief, I'm afraid I can't. I have a conflict here. As we speak, our frying pan is being held hostage at Indian Affairs' offices."

I remain puzzled: Why was George Addy's diatribe ever taken seriously? For me, Bora Laskin, together with Frank Scott, represented a flowering of a distinctly Canadian approach to the development of the law. Laskin did not defer to English precedents, as many of his generation did. He knew that we were capable of a distinctly Canadian jurisprudence. He had as a professor at the University of Toronto Law School taught hundreds of Canadian lawyers, and many of them became his ardent admirers.

Once, at a banquet for judges held in Vancouver, when Laskin was new to the Supreme Court of Canada, we had suffered through a tiresome speech by Geoffrey Howe, an English Chancery barrister, later a cabinet minister in Margaret Thatcher's government. The judges present dutifully applauded the dry, English non-humour. I left for the washroom and encountered Laskin in the corridor. "Why," I asked, "do we have to listen to these tedious speeches by English mediocrities?" "Not me!" he said, with feeling.

Laskin made a formidable contribution to Canadian law. He was a scholar, an arbitrator of renown and a great teacher. He was a civil libertarian. On the bench, however, he displayed a devotion to rank, status and hierarchy. Inside the skin of the civil libertarian was an authoritarian struggling to get out.

Looking back, however, I think I was mainly tired of the whole episode—and wanted to put as much distance as I could between the controversy and my career. I had, I think, resigned on a question of principle or, at least, spoken out on a question of principle knowing that it might well lead to my departure from the bench. The episode had been wearying. At the time I believed that I was doing the right thing; with the passage of time, I am even more convinced of this belief.

Aboriginal and treaty rights had been restored to the Constitution. As a result, what is now section 35 of the Constitution, affirming existing Aboriginal rights and treaty rights, is argued in courtrooms in every province every day and enforced every day. Indeed, I would find myself before the courts in the year

2000 urging that it afforded constitutional protection to the Nisga'a under the Nisga'a Treaty. In any event, even if the section had not been restored, it would have been right to protest its deletion.

These events concerning my departure from the bench happened two decades ago. I realize that they may have some of the qualities of a soap opera. But there were profound issues at stake. At least I thought so. And so did the Aboriginal peoples of Canada. In countless ways, they have indicated that they, too, remember these events. Once, a few years ago, while I was waiting for a flight in the Calgary airport, a group of First Nations people passed by, obviously heading for a destination of their own. They stopped when they were passing by and said, "Aren't you Judge Berger?" I said, "Well, I'm not a judge now, but I used to be Judge Berger." One of them produced two beautiful, framed pieces of art (one a design embroidery made of moose-hair tufts and one of porcupine quills) and said, "We'd like you to have these. We just want to thank you for all you've done for our people."

Having left the bench, I had to make a living. Resigning after twelve years' service meant that I would not be eligible for a pension. I was starting over. Under the Law Society's rules, I could not appear in court again for three years. I had to consider whether it would be awkward to appear in court before judges who had been colleagues on the bench. I was also concerned that, when I did return to the bar, I might be retained to argue a case that required a consideration of one of the judgements I had written during my twelve years on the bench.

I needn't have worried. Law is protean, multifarious. The possibilities of new disputes are endless. The permutations and combinations go on and on. As a lawyer, when you get a new case, you think it must be subject to a precedent, that the point at the heart of the dispute has already been decided. Surprisingly often, it is not so. In fact, in none of the cases in my second career was I embarrassed by having to rely on or, worse still, disparage any decision I had made on the bench. The controlling authorities had been written by the judges of the appellate courts. My contribution as a judge to the development of the law, my few pages in the volumes of law reports filling the stacks and shelves of every legal library, might as well have drifted down a legal black hole.

When I left the bench in 1983, I headed to Alaska for two years to conduct the Alaska Native Review Commission. But, in 1985, I would return to Vancouver to the practice of law, to commence a second career at the bar.

7 Questions of Conscience

UPON RETURNING to legal practice, I was almost immediately retained by a civil servant in a case involving a question of conscience, one not too far removed from my own case.

Richard Price was director of policy and program consultation for the Department of Indian and Northern Affairs (DINA). He was also an ordained United Church minister. He had, however, followed a career in academe and the public service, having been employed as research director for the Indian Association of Alberta, then as executive director for the same organization. From there, he went to DINA, serving as director of long-range planning and liaison for Alberta, then to Ottawa as director of policy and program consultation. This position gave him access to confidential information.

In April 1985, he deliberately leaked a confidential cabinet report. It was a report of the Ministerial Task Force on Native Programs, recommending draconian cuts to DINA's budget. Price believed implementation of the cuts would mean breaking faith with Indian bands all over the country. The authors of the report themselves referred to their work as "The Buffalo Jump of the 1980s." Dismayed by the damage he believed the implementation of this report would create in Indian communities, Price decided to break his oath of confidentiality and turned the report over to Dr. Terence Anderson, a friend, mentor and at the time professor of Christian social ethics at UBC's Vancouver School of Theology. He asked Dr. Anderson to pass it on to Nisga'a leaders, who gave it to James Fulton, MP for Skeena. Fulton brought it up in the House of Commons, where not only the contents of the document but also the circumstances of its disclosure became the subject of debate.

Price had committed an act for which he knew he would be fired. And he was. Fred R. Drummie, assistant deputy minister, wrote to him:

I have satisfied myself that in the month of April 1985 you released a classified document to an unauthorized person. Such action represents a serious breach of trust and
of your Oaths of Office and Secrecy.

As a senior public service manager, such an act must be viewed as a most serious
offence. Consequently, by the authority vested in me by Section 106 of the Public
Service Terms and Conditions of Employment Regulations, I hereby discharge you
from the Public Service effective July 23, 1985.

But losing his job was not all that awaited Price. On July 19, 1985, a criminal
charge had already been laid against him. It alleged that he

at or near the City of Vancouver, in the County of Vancouver, in the Province of British
Columbia on April the 17th, 1985, being an Official, to wit, the director of policy and program consultation for the Department of Indian and Northern Affairs Canada of the
Government of Canada, in connection with the duties of his office, did unlawfully commit a breach of trust by giving, without due authority in that behalf, to an unauthorized
person, to wit, Terry Anderson, a copy of a document entitled Memorandum to Cabinet,
Report of the Ministerial Task Force on Native Programs, knowing the said document to
be classified as "secret" contrary to Section 111 of the Criminal Code of Canada.

Firing a man is one thing. To then charge him with criminal breach of trust
is quite another.

For Richard Price, it was a matter of conscience. He felt that he had a higher
duty to the public interest than the duty he owed to the government of the day.
But is it as simple as that? Doesn't a civil servant owe a paramount duty of loyalty to the government he serves? It would be hard to argue otherwise. The
orderly administration of government affairs depends on the loyalty of the public service, and loyalty means keeping the government's secrets.

It may be said that a civil servant has an obligation to the public interest, to
advise the public of malfeasance in the government, but does this obligation
extend to advising the public that the government has under consideration proposals that a civil servant may think are wrong-headed, even if the consequences
of their adoption might in his opinion be extremely harmful? Isn't it for the government to determine matters of policy and to decide for itself at what stage to
make its intentions public?

Richard Price was dismissed from his post and charged with criminal breach
of trust. But he was not the only civil servant to disclose secret documents.

Perhaps the most compelling case of leaking confidential government documents occurred in the United Kingdom in the 1930s. In the House of Commons,

Winston Churchill, then a Conservative MP but not a member of the government, repeatedly warned the nation of the menace that Nazi Germany represented. In 1934, when Stanley Baldwin, the prime minister of the day, claimed that the strength of Germany's air force did not amount even to fifty per cent of Britain's, a civil servant named Desmond Morton, who knew of the rapidity with which Hitler was rebuilding the Luftwaffe, supplied Churchill with figures revealing Baldwin's claim to be false. When Churchill disclosed the information he had received, Baldwin's government promptly announced it would expand the air force by forty-one and a half squadrons.

Churchill received fresh information that even this action would be inadequate. Ralph Wigram, a senior Foreign Office official, travelled to Churchill's country home at Chartwell. There he revealed secret Air Ministry projections showing that by October 1936 Germany would have almost twice the first-line air strength of Britain. By the autumn of 1937, Churchill was, according to his biographer Martin Gilbert, receiving information from serving army and naval officers, including Commander Lord Louis Mountbatten.

Churchill was sufficiently concerned about the air force's weaknesses that he passed on details, without naming his sources, to the cabinet secretary, Sir Maurice Hankey. Hankey's reply is a document fit for the bureaucratic hall of fame.

It shocks me not a little that high Officers in disciplined Forces should be in direct communication with a leading Statesman who, though notoriously patriotic beyond criticism, is nevertheless in popular estimation regarded as a critic of the Departments under whom these Officers serve . . . They jeopardise their official careers by their action, for a slip might prove disastrous to them, and even though they escape this possibility, it may all come out years after and damage their reputations before posterity.

Richard Price was not disclosing documents to Winston Churchill. And the safety of the country was not at stake. But it is safe to say that there are times when it is right for a public servant, as a matter of conscience, to breach his oath of confidentiality.

Daniel Ellsberg, an employee of the U.S. Department of Defense, became famous for leaking what became known as the Pentagon Papers in 1971 because he believed Americans were being misled by their government about the conduct of the Vietnam War. He was charged with espionage and acquitted.

I was retained by Richard Price, but I could not yet appear in court. Under the rules of the Law Society, I would have to wait for three years following my resignation from the bench. That would be in September 1986. But I thought the prosecution was uncalled for, exceeding altogether what might have been necessary to make the point regarding the civil service oath of confidentiality. I thought I should do what I could to bring the prosecution to an end before it proceeded any further.

To begin with, Richard Price's case was only the most recent in a series of leaks of federal government information. The Conservatives had come into office in 1984. Before that, as the long Liberal ascendancy in Canadian politics drew to a close, members of the official opposition had seized on a series of leaks. Two civil servants had leaked copiously to the Conservatives while they were in opposition, and once the Conservatives gained office, they were singled out for advancement.

James Wood, a member of the RCMP security service who had fed information on the state of the RCMP to Elmer MacKay, a leading Conservative spokesman in the Commons, had, once the Conservatives gained office, been given a seat on the Canadian Pension Commission, an appointment made by cabinet. Aditya Varma, a post office employee, had been fired by the Liberal government for leaking information about the internal problems of Canada Post. Once the Conservatives were in office, Varma was reinstated and then employed by a firm of consultants retained by the government to investigate the post office.

There was much to be said in Richard Price's defence: It was clear that he had acted out of conscience—he felt that he had no choice in the matter. He had not been engaged in a partisan effort to embarrass the government. Moreover, it was not a case where national security had been affected in any way. No citizen's privacy had been compromised.

The principle of confidentiality had been upheld: Richard Price had been fired for violating it. Surely that was sufficient. But the Conservatives, new to office, believed that by prosecuting him, they would put the fear of God into any others tempted to engage in leaking. In their government, there would be no plain brown envelopes arriving over the transom or under the door.

But none of these considerations was a defence to the charge of breach of trust. There was, of course, a question whether what Price had done was, in the circumstances, a "breach of trust." Here we could raise a series of questions relating to the duty of a civil servant in the circumstances in which Price found himself. Does his duty extend only to the government of the day? Can he claim a duty to the public interest? To his department's constituents? To Parliament? And so on. I had no real confidence that any of these defences would be successful.

But there was one possibility. It seemed hypocritical for the Conservatives while in opposition to welcome leaks and then once in government to anathematize them. John Crosbie, the minister of justice, had led the way in welcoming the leaks by civil servants under the previous Liberal government. Now, as minister of justice, he was insisting that Richard Price should be prosecuted. If we were to go to trial, I wanted a trial by jury, and I wanted to lay before the jury the hypocrisy of Crosbie and the Conservatives. Ordinary men and women, I believed, would find it repellent that their political masters could pick and choose whom to prosecute and whom to celebrate among members of the public service who were willing to take the risk—for reasons they believed sufficient—of violating their oath of loyalty.

My last case as a lawyer before going on the bench had been *Calder* in 1971. Canada's Charter of Rights had come into force on April 17, 1982. The coming into force of Section 15 of the Charter, known as the equality section, guaranteeing equality before the law, had been postponed for three years and had taken place only a few months earlier, on April 17, 1985, the very day Richard Price had committed the act for which he was charged. The equality section prohibited discrimination on enumerated grounds: race, national or ethnic origin, colour, religion, sex, age or mental or physical disability. But it did not say that these were the only grounds. Section 15 expressly provides that "every individual is equal before and under the law and has the right to the equal protection and equal benefit of the law without discrimination." That would cover Richard Price. To be sure, section 15 went on to list prohibited grounds of discrimination, but these were said to be "in particular." That meant that other grounds, which had not necessarily been listed, could be relied on. I thought Richard was entitled to equality before the law: the authorities had to prosecute all the leakers or none of them; to prosecute him when the others had not been was selective prosecution, a form of discrimination I would argue was prohibited by section 15. But the forms of discrimination listed were illustrative, not exclusive; that would be the argument. Equality before the law must mean that law enforcement would be even-handed, and where it could be demonstrated that it was not, there must be a remedy.

On August 7, 1985, I wrote to John Crosbie, the minister of justice:

[Richard Price's] case raises the issue of selective prosecution. Under Section 15 of the *Canadian Charter of Rights and Freedoms* every Canadian is equal before and under the law and has the right to the equal protection and equal benefit of the law without discrimination. This means that governments cannot arbitrarily pick and choose those whom they wish to prosecute and punish. The law must be enforced with an even hand . . .

You and I are both lawyers. We both know that the office of Minister of Justice and Attorney-General of Canada is not political in the same sense as other Cabinet offices. The Minister of Justice is obliged, according to well-established traditions: J. Ll J. Edwards, *The Law Officers of the Crown*, 1964, (chapter 10), to see that the law is not abused, that it is not made to serve partisan purposes. I do not know whether Wood and Varma disclosed documents that were classified as 'secret', but clearly if what my client is alleged to have done is a crime, so also were the actions of Wood and Varma. The provisions of the section of the Code under which my client is charged are sufficiently wide to encompass all three cases.

Section 15 of the Charter had been in force only since April 17, 1985. There were virtually no decided cases under it. Why not claim that Richard Price's prosecution was discriminatory? I had chosen the phrase "selective prosecution." A good phrase, I thought. Crosbie would realize that, if a judge allowed me to lay the evidence before a jury, the government would be as much on trial as Price. I continued:

I take the view that this is a case of selective prosecution and therefore a violation of the Charter guarantee of equal protection. I request that the prosecution against my client be stayed; to pursue it is likely to diminish public confidence in the fairness with which justice is administered. Not only was my client dismissed, he was charged with a very serious crime—but [the document] he is alleged to have "leaked" is a document that the government was at pains to repudiate as soon as it was made public. There is no slightest suggestion that what my client is alleged to have done affected the national security in any way, or that he sought any sordid personal gain—all agreed that he was actuated by Christian conscience.

It may be that those who advised the RCMP to proceed against my client were not aware of the implications of Section 15 of the Charter in cases such as this. Section 15 not only affects the conduct of proceedings in court, it also informs the exercise of prosecutorial discretion. Whatever the extent, before April 17, 1985, of prosecutorial discretion to decide whom to charge and whom not to charge, clearly that discretion must now be exercised without discrimination. I urge therefore that the Crown direct, when the matter comes on for hearing, that the charge against Richard Price be stayed.

I went on:

This will not prevent the government from disciplining civil servants in cases where it is appropriate to do so. It has the power to dismiss them. It can prosecute under the Code. But only if its policy is clear and only if it is enforced even-handedly.

If the case against my client is to proceed, however, the defence of selective prosecution will be advanced. In that event, I request that you provide me with full details of the Wood and Varma cases. I also request that you let me know whether there are other similar cases that have come to the attention of you or your officials. It is the Crown's obligation to make full disclosure to the Defence in such a case as this: *Boucher vs. The Queen* (1954) 110 C.C.C. 263, Rand J. at p. 270 (S.C.C.); *Re Bledsoe and Law Society of B.C.* (1984) 13 C.C.C. (3d) 560 (B.C.C.A.).

Though the prosecution is in the hands of the Crown Provincial, it clearly has been brought by federal instigation. It is therefore appropriate that I turn to you, as Minister of Justice and Attorney-General of Canada, to secure this information, rather than to the Attorney-General of British Columbia, whose participation in the matter, as well as his access to the information I am seeking, is nominal.

I look forward to hearing from you.

Now I wanted an opportunity to make my letter public.

Crosbie gave me an opening. He told the media that there was no comparison between Richard Price's case and Aditya Varma's case. I sent him the following telegram: "RE: RICHARD PRICE. As you have publicly stated (Vancouver *Sun*, August 15), that there is no comparison between my client's case and the Varma case, I think it is in my client's interest that I make public the submission I sent to you on August 7, 1985."

I gave my letter to Crosbie to the media; it received wide publicity.

Crosbie's position had become untenable. Having lionized those responsible for leaks to his own party when in opposition, he could hardly justify his prosecution of Richard Price. By the end of the month, Crosbie had advised B.C.'s attorney general that he did not wish the case to proceed. A formal stay was entered.

As Charter jurisprudence unfolded, it turned out that I was wrong about section 15 of the Charter. The Supreme Court has made it plain that section 15 cannot be invoked except on the grounds enumerated in section 15 or on grounds that are analogous, and only by members of "discrete and insular minorities" and where the discrimination complained of demeans the complainant's human dignity. Richard Price would not have qualified as a member of a discrete and insular minority. Section 15 cannot now be used as a foundation for challenging selective prosecution, unless it is a case of selective prosecution on grounds of race, religion, age, disability and so on or an analogous ground. In the meantime, Richard Price was free.

How important is conscience in a citizen's life? Richard Price was an employee of the government. He believed that its proposed policy for cuts in funding to Indian bands was not only wrong but immoral. His conscience impelled him to act, at the risk of losing his job. What about an ordinary citizen who conscientiously believes that the government is spending her taxes in a cause she rejects?

Dr. Jerilynn Prior is one of Canada's leading physicians, a professor in the

Faculty of Medicine at the University of British Columbia, an expert in the study of ovulation and menstrual cycles in women, and scientific director of the Centre for Menstrual Cycle and Ovulation Research at UBC. She is also a member of the Quakers, a religious sect whose members believe in non-violence. They are pacifists. The Vietnam War made Jerilynn Prior a Quaker. She demonstrated against the war while she was a medical student in Boston in the 1960s. It was then she joined the Religious Society of Friends—the Quakers—which opposed American involvement in the conflict. She brought her anti-war beliefs with her when she came to Canada in 1976.

As a Quaker, Dr. Prior opposes the use of force. She is a citizen of Canada now. She pays her taxes and pays them willingly. But she opposes the use of any of her tax money for military purposes. In 1981, Dr. Prior and 532 other Canadians who shared her faith decided to act on their beliefs. They established a Peace Tax Fund Trust Account and paid into that account the portion of their taxes that would otherwise be used by the federal government for national defence. They didn't expect to retain the money going to the trust account, but they were anxious that it should not be used for military purposes. As Dr. Prior stated: "It's against my conscience and deeply held religious beliefs to participate in any way in war, military preparations or military means of defence."

Section 2(a) of the Charter offers a guarantee of "freedom of conscience and religion." Dr. Prior and her fellow Quakers claimed that the Income Tax Act, to the extent that the act required them to pay taxes to be used for military expenditures, violated their freedom of conscience.

Dr. Prior and her friends had filed an objection to their tax assessments and had brought their case before the Tax Court. From there, it had come before the Federal Court Trial Division. They had lost in both courts. In the Federal Court Trial Division, Justice George Addy had dismissed their claim, without a trial.

Why no trial? Because the rules of the Federal Court, and most other courts, provide that if a case has no chance of success the court can dismiss it "on the pleadings"; that is, the court will look at the claim that the plaintiff hopes to prove when the case goes to trial, and it may say, "Well, even if you proved everything you say here, the court would not hold in your favour, because the law is plainly and obviously against you—the law recognizes no such claim." This is what had happened to Dr. Prior.

She had appealed, and she asked me to represent her in the Federal Court of Appeal.

Not a promising case on the face of it. After all, wasn't Justice Addy right? How could there possibly be a legal right to have your tax money diverted from expenditures that you, as a citizen, abhorred? Any more than Richard Price had a right to decide for himself which policies of the government he served justified the breach of his oath of loyalty?

The argument we faced was: If Dr. Prior is right, couldn't we all then decide where we wanted our tax money to go and not to go? In Dr. Prior's case, it wasn't a matter of the taxpayer's whims or wishes, or even of philosophical differences. It was a matter of freedom of conscience or religion. That is what is guaranteed by the Charter. Where the taxpayer as a matter of conscience or religion opposes the expenditure of tax money for certain purposes, that, arguably, is a violation of Charter rights. But such an objection must be properly founded on conscience or religion. As a Quaker, Dr. Prior regarded herself as morally responsible for the expenditures made by her government. Her Quaker conscience forbade her to make war or to support in any way the cause of war.

The Quaker belief had a lengthy pedigree. Jerilynn Prior and her friends relied on the tradition of Christian and Quaker pacifism. In 1661, only a year after the restoration of the monarchy in England, a religious movement known as the Fifth Monarchy, anticipating the Second Coming, sought by force of arms to take control of the city of London and did so for three days. The movement was swiftly put down; there were then wholesale arrests, and four thousand members of the Society of Friends were imprisoned.

Members of the Society of Friends had not been involved in the uprising. They rejected the use of armed force. In a declaration presented to King Charles II, in which they described themselves as "the Harmless and Innocent People of God, called Quakers," they declared:

We utterly deny all outward wars and strife and fightings with outward weapons, for any end or under any pretence whatsoever. And this is our testimony to the whole world. The spirit of Christ, by which we are guided, is not changeable, so as once to command us from a thing as evil, and again to move unto it; and we do certainly know, and so testify to the world, that the spirit of Christ, which leads us into all Truth, will never move us to fight and war against any man with outward weapons, neither for the kingdom of Christ, nor for the kingdoms of this world.

But not only Quakers believe that the followers of Christ must be pacifists. Leo Tolstoy, in *What I Believe*, reminded us that the Bible teaches "Resist not him who is evil." Tolstoy argued that Christ had supported the principle of non-violence. According to Matthew 5.39, Jesus taught: "Resist not evil: but whosoever shall smite thee on thy right cheek, turn to him the other also." Mahatma Gandhi, though he did not derive his beliefs exclusively from Christian doctrine, spread the idea of non-violent resistance to armed force. Martin Luther King Jr., the leader of the American civil rights movement in the 1950s and 1960s, was an exemplar of that same principle.

The tradition of Christian pacifism, central to Quaker belief, is certainly not unknown in Canada. The Mennonites came from Russia to Manitoba in the 1870s on the strength, among other things, of a guaranteed exemption from military service. The Doukhobors, a sect of Russian dissenters, believers in pacifism, who were persecuted in their native land, emigrated to Canada in 1898–99, settling in Saskatchewan and later B.C. They were aided in their passage to Canada by Leo Tolstoy and by the Quakers in the United Kingdom and the United States. When they came to Canada, they were exempted from military service. The Hutterites, also believers in non-violence, migrated from Central Europe and Russia to the U.S. From there, some moved to Canada in 1918, because in the U.S. they had been persecuted for refusing military service. They settled in the Prairie provinces.

James Shaver Woodsworth, once an ordained Methodist minister and the first leader of the CCF, spoke out against Canada's involvement in armed conflict. His famous speech to the House of Commons in September 1939 at the outbreak of the Second World War, as the sole MP opposing Canada's declaration of war against Germany, included these words:

I left the ministry of the church during the last war because of my ideas on war. Today I do not belong to any church organization. I am afraid that my creed is pretty vague. But even in this assembly I venture to say that I still believe in some of the principles underlying the teachings of Jesus, and the other great world teachers throughout the centuries . . . War is an absolute negation of anything Christian. The Prime Minister, as a great many do, trotted out the "mad dog" idea; said that in the last analysis there must be a resort to force. It requires a great deal of courage to trust to moral force. But there was a time when people thought that there were other and higher types of force than brute force. Yes, if I may use the very quotation the Prime Minister used today, in spite of tyrants, tyrants as bad as even Hitler is today, in spite of war-makers—and every nation has them—as Lowell reminds us:

Truth forever on the scaffold, Wrong forever on the throne,
Yet that scaffold sways the future, and, behind the dim unknown,
Standeth God within the shadow, keeping watch above his own.

Quakers object, on grounds of conscience, to fighting. They are not cowards; indeed, they display a form of civil courage that requires the most admirable firmness in the face of the call of patriotism and the ties of nationalism. We have always found a place for conscientious objectors in war. Canada established tribunals in the First and Second World Wars to consider the claims of conscientious objectors and gave these tribunals the power to excuse them from service in the armed forces. Some of them served as stretcher bearers or ambulance drivers, engaged in activity on the battlefield requiring as much fortitude as was expected of those fighting in the front line.

No one was about to draft Dr. Prior to serve in the armed forces. Canada has not had any form of conscription since the Second World War. But Dr. Prior wished to apply the idea of conscientious objection to her taxes. This idea also is intrinsic to Quaker faith: John Woolman, one of the founders of the Society of Friends in North America in the mid-eighteenth century, had long-standing scruples against paying taxes "for carrying on wars." He could see no effective difference between fighting in a war and supporting it with his taxes. In his *Journal,* he wrote: "To refuse the active payment of a tax which our society generally paid was exceeding disagreeable, but to do a thing contrary to my conscience appeared yet more dreadful . . . Thus, by small degrees, we might approach so near to fighting that a distinction would be little else but the name of a peaceable people." These were not trivial ideas. They had been espoused by some of the most admired figures in history.

But could we bring the Quaker belief that their taxes should not go to the military under the rubric of freedom of conscience and religion?

In 1985, in *R. v. Big M Drug Mart,* Chief Justice Brian Dickson, writing for the Supreme Court of Canada, had offered a broad definition of freedom of religion under the Charter.

A truly free society is one which can accommodate a wide variety of beliefs, diversity of tastes and pursuits, customs and codes of conduct . . . The essence of the concept of freedom of religion is the right to entertain such religious beliefs as a person chooses, the right to declare religious beliefs openly and without fear of hindrance or reprisal, and the right to manifest belief by worship and practice or by teaching and dissemination.

No one was preventing Dr. Prior from espousing her beliefs. She could hold whatever beliefs she wanted, pray for the achievement of those beliefs and seek converts where she would.

Chief Justice Dickson, however, went on to say: "All coercive burdens on the exercise of religious beliefs are potentially within the ambit of s. 2(a)." He wrote: "Freedom [of conscience and religion] means that, subject to such limitations as are necessary to protect public safety, order, health, or morals or the fundamental rights and freedoms of others, no one is to be forced to act in a way contrary to his beliefs or his conscience." We could argue that Dr. Prior could not be forced to act in a way contrary to her beliefs or her conscience. If it was against her conscience to have her tax money used for military purposes, couldn't we argue that applying her tax money to those purposes forced her to act in a way contrary to her conscience?

This strategy offered us a measure of comfort. How had this argument fared before Justice Addy? The issue had never been reached. Instead, Justice Addy had simply held that there was no connection between Dr. Prior's taxes and expenditures made for national defence.

The existence of a connection was critical to our appeal. If there was a connection, then the argument could be made that requiring Dr. Prior to contribute to military expenditures was forcing her to act in a way contrary to her beliefs or her conscience.

Under the Charter of Rights, if a violation of a freedom guaranteed by the Charter is established, the government is entitled to show—if it can—that the infringement on freedom is reasonable and one justifiable in a free and democratic society. Justice Addy, however, had declared Dr. Prior's case to be without legal merit. He had heard no evidence; he simply held that, as a matter of law, Dr. Prior's claim could not on the face of it succeed; there was no "nexus" (a fancy word—but useful—meaning "connection") between Dr. Prior's payment of taxes and Parliament's appropriation of money for military purposes. Her taxes, like all revenue collected by the federal government, were paid into the consolidated revenue fund. Parliament then appropriated money and used it for various proposed items of expenditure—not as her money, but as part of a pool of money to which all taxpayers contribute.

Referring to the money that Dr. Prior had withheld, Justice Addy said: "Any money withheld by the plaintiff is not withheld from military expenditures but from the sum of all of the moneys in the Consolidated Revenue Fund, from which all government expenditures are financed by reason of the operation of the *Financial Administration Act* and of our very system of government." He went on:

The plaintiff is merely being taxed for general federal purposes and the expenditures for military purposes are made entirely by the federal authority without any personal participation by the plaintiff in any way.

Her freedom to practice the tenets of her religion cannot reasonably be held to be affected since she neither directly nor indirectly participates in the expending for military purposes of the moneys collected by the Receiver General.

In other words, the government of the day collects money from all taxpayers; then it decides how to spend the money, and its choices in that respect are its responsibility and not the taxpayers'. At that point, the nexus is broken.

Justice Addy made two other points: he characterized Dr. Prior's action as a challenge to the federal government's legislative power over taxation and military and defence matters. He reasoned that if Dr. Prior's action were successful, the constitutional authority of Parliament to levy taxes for military purposes would be frustrated, at least as far as conscientious objectors were concerned.

Justice Addy also held that none of the remedies requested by Dr. Prior could be legally granted. By asking for an order that she be allowed to redirect some of her taxes to the Peace Tax Fund, Dr. Prior, he said, "in effect, is requesting that the court usurp the powers of Parliament and actually appropriate moneys destined by law to the Consolidated Revenue Fund for appropriation by Parliament. This would fly directly against one of the most basic tenets of our Constitution, namely, the separation of powers."

Apart from this point, there were "very practical obstacles to the remedies requested by the plaintiff being granted," Justice Addy observed. "One can easily envisage government actions and policies, both present and proposed, to which certain taxpayers and possibly a great number of taxpayers might conscientiously and out of deep and sincere moral and religious convictions, consider to be totally wrong, reprehensible, unjustified and even evil." Inevitably, the judge referred to the issue of abortion. "One such issue on which public attention is being focussed today is the extremely divisive question of whether public moneys should be expended for abortions. If each of those taxpayers who might be conscientiously objecting to this policy were entitled by law to withhold a percentage of income tax, complete chaos would result and orderly government would break down."

But Judge Addy was getting ahead of himself. The framers of the Charter realized that not *every* violation of Charter rights ought to result in legislation being set aside. So they passed section 1, which provides that the rights guaranteed by the Charter are "subject to such reasonable limitations as may be demonstrably justified in a free and democratic society." Indeed, Justice Addy said, in conclusion: "If the freedom of conscience of the plaintiff were in fact being infringed, section 1 of the *Charter* could probably be successfully invoked since it would appear to be a reasonable limit on the plaintiff's freedom, which could be demonstrably justified in a free and democratic society."

Dr. Prior, however, had not been given a chance to show an infringement; nor had the federal government, for that matter, been given a chance to show that under section 1, it could justify the infringement.

Dr. Prior believed that her case truly engaged freedom of conscience; she wished to have her day in court to submit evidence regarding the tenets of the Quaker faith and the violation of her conscience entailed by forcing her to contribute to military expenditures. If she succeeded, the federal government might well invoke section 1. It might prevail under section 1. But Dr. Prior was entitled to take a crack at establishing that there had been a violation of her conscience. After that, Ottawa could seek to establish—the onus would lie on the government—that the enforcement of the Income Tax Act was a reasonable limit on her freedom of conscience and religion.

It seemed to me, however, that the case had to be considered in a historical context. In Dr. Prior's case, this would include the history of Christian pacifism and the history of warfare.

We should have been given an opportunity to provide evidence of the history of the development of Quaker beliefs, including Quaker pacifism. We could show that many civilized countries had, in wartime, acknowledged the connection between pacifist beliefs and the bearing of arms; it was obvious that to require a pacifist to bear arms with a view to killing others was a means by which he would be "forced to act in a way contrary to his beliefs or his conscience." Was there no similar connection in the case of being required to provide money for taxes used to send soldiers into battle? We believed we could show that there was.

Canadian statutes and orders-in-council have for more than a century acknowledged the rights of conscientious objectors. In the First and Second World Wars, as noted, conscientious objectors were allowed to do alternative service. Dr. Prior simply wished to have her tax money do alternative service.

We amended Dr. Prior's statement of claim to allege: "A Quaker paying taxes to government regards himself or herself as morally responsible for the military expenditures of that government." This statement was an allegation of fact, of the state of Dr. Prior's own beliefs. It was, to use an old legal phrase, as much a matter of fact as the state of her digestion.

We would ask the Federal Court of Appeal to allow the case to go to trial. If allowed, Dr. Prior would testify as to the tenets of her faith. She could be cross-examined. Experts might be called as to the Quaker faith and cross-examined. Experts might also be called by the Crown to dispute the allegations of fact in the statement of claim. At the end of the day, the court would have to adjudicate on this question of fact. Was it contrary to Dr. Prior's conscience? Did she in her conscience regard herself as morally responsible for the military expenditures of the government? If that responsibility gave rise to a violation of the Charter, the federal government could always invoke section 1, on the footing that the violation was a reasonable one and demonstrably justifiable in a free and democratic society. The government could say, "Well, we have to be able to do this; we couldn't run the country otherwise. What if everybody wanted to ride their conscientious or religious hobby-horse?" That might present a formidable argument. We had to be ready to meet it. But it wouldn't be reached until the court determined the question of whether there had been a violation of Dr. Prior's freedom of conscience.

Justice Addy had said it was unnecessary to determine the issue of conscience. He said there was no connection between Dr. Prior's conscience and her taxes. That, of course, depended on Dr. Prior's belief. Her belief would establish the connection between her faith and the violation of her conscience. If she truly believed—and if it were an article of her faith—that she was morally responsible for the military expenditures of the government and that it is as wrong to contribute taxes for military purposes as it is to go to war yourself, then we would have some evidence of a nexus. But the court had heard no evidence as to her belief. Given our amendment—asserting that the belief established the nexus and a motion to strike had to be based on the allegations in Dr. Prior's statement of claim—the Federal Court of Appeal would be obliged to accept as a fact what we had now pleaded; that is, Dr. Prior regarded herself as morally responsible for the military expenditures of the government of Canada. That would allow the case to go to trial. That would be the basis of our appeal.

To the Quaker, conscience is the essential link between faith and practice. Quakers try to live a sacramental life according to an internal yardstick, that inner light to which individual choices are subjected. To quote eighteenth-century American Quaker leader William Penn:

In that day we judged not after the sight of the eye, or after the hearing of the ear, but according to the light and sense this blessed principle gave us, we judged and acted in reference to things and persons, ourselves and others, yea, towards God our Maker. For being quickened by it in our inward man, we could easily discern the difference of things; and feel what was right and what was wrong, what was fit and what not, both in reference to religious and civil concerns.

Conscience would dictate the Quakers' choices between right and wrong; these choices would be outward manifestations of that inner light.

But we had to persuade the Federal Court of Appeal that Justice Addy had been wrong to say, at the outset and without hearing evidence, that there was no connection—no nexus—between Dr. Prior's taxes and the military expenditures of the federal government. The judge said this issue was a question of law. How could it be, when the connection depended on a question of fact—Dr. Prior's beliefs?

There was a lively hearing in the Federal Court of Appeal. Dr. Prior and her friends attended, as well as representatives of the Society of Friends from the United States. John Power of the Department of Justice in Ottawa appeared for Canada. I argued that because the government collected taxes from Dr. Prior and devoted them, in part, to military purposes, this activity established a nexus. It was clear from the wording of the Financial Administration Act that the consolidated revenue fund was an aggregate of all public monies, including the taxes paid by Dr. Prior. John Power said that this fact of a consolidated fund was the whole point; Dr. Prior's taxes could not be treated as if they were directed to any specific item of expenditure.

I replied that it merely required a calculation to determine what portion of Dr. Prior's taxes would go to each of the expenditures, including military expenditures, made by the federal government. Dr. Prior had made the calculation and sent to the Peace Trust the portion of her federal taxes that would otherwise go to military expenditures.

Ordinary taxpayers, I urged, would have no doubt about it; they know that their money in some small proportion goes to pay the salaries of MPs, or the salaries of federal judges, or the cost of national defence, and so on. If you told them there was no connection, they would think you were being obtuse. Those same ordinary taxpayers might also say that they would be opposed to allowing Dr. Prior's claim, because they might think it would require that a throng of religious whims and whimsies would have to be considered in determining who should pay what, and that determination would require the hiring of a thousand accountants. Justice Addy had specifically relied on this argument ("complete chaos would result and orderly government would break down"). But that issue would come later; it would arise when the court had to consider whether requiring Dr. Prior to live with the violation of her belief was a reasonable and justifiable limitation on her freedom of conscience.

On first impression, the argument that might be made against us under section 1 seemed formidable. But we had the right to get to that issue!

Dr. Prior's case was heard at an early stage of Charter jurisprudence, when the Canadian courts relied extensively on decisions of the U.S. Supreme Court on the U.S. Bill of Rights, which had been in force since 1791, as a guide to the interpretation of our own Charter of Rights. The U.S. Supreme Court, in *U.S. v. Lee,* had said in 1981: "The tax system could not function if denominations were allowed to challenge the tax system because tax payments were spent in a manner that violates their religious belief."

But the U.S. Bill of Rights contains no section 1. In the U.S., the two stages of analysis are rolled into one. The judges carry out a balancing function. The court at the outset weighs the conflicting interests: on the one hand the interests of the state, and on the other those of the religious minority whose belief has run up against the mandate of the state. In the U.S., the question of a citizen's right and a state interest that justifies its infringement are considered together. In Canada, we consider these issues in two stages. The onus of establishing a Charter violation would be on Dr. Prior. The onus of justifying the violation under section 1 as a reasonable limit on her freedom of conscience would be on the Crown.

A determination under section 1 would ordinarily be made only after the citizen's evidence of a Charter violation had been considered and a violation found. If there were no violation established, section 1 would not enter into it. But Justice Addy had found, without considering the evidence, that Dr. Prior could not establish a violation (there being no nexus), and that the Crown would, at the second stage, probably have succeeded under section 1. He relied on American cases. But to use American authorities where these questions are dealt with not separately but concurrently was to deny Dr. Prior a hearing on the question arising at the outset of an infringement of her Charter rights.

In *Andrews,* an early Charter decision decided in 1987, Justice William McIntyre, writing for the Supreme Court of Canada, held that this point was a critical distinction between the Canadian Charter and the U.S. Bill of Rights. I argued in the Federal Court of Appeal that the only issue the court had to consider was whether Dr. Prior's claim of a nexus was sufficiently plausible that we should have a chance to go to trial to prove it.

Dr. Prior *was* entitled to go to trial and to call evidence on the subject of Quaker belief, shared by many Christian pacifists, in non-violence, and its ramifications for ethical choices in their daily life. If the Charter were to be interpreted properly by the courts, such evidence was essential. Justice Addy had no evidence before him, no historical materials. The court was left to speculate, which was what the court had done. In support of this contention, I urged that, for Quakers, the inner light represented conscience, the link between faith and practice. It was a link that could not be severed by the Financial Administration Act.

We did not suggest that the Income Tax Act is legislation in relation to freedom of conscience and religion; that is, that Parliament had sat down and said, "Let's pass a law to collect taxes, for the express purpose of infringing freedom of conscience." Yet if the effect of legislation was to violate Dr. Prior's freedom of conscience, then it had been a violation of the Charter. That is the way the Charter works: it is the *effect* that counts. Dr. Prior needed only to show the special impact of the legislation on her own situation; she did not need to show that infringement of her freedom of conscience was the purpose of the legislation. Only she, and other pacifists like her, were affected. Others who did not share the same beliefs would not find their freedom of conscience affected. To grant Dr. Prior a remedy would not leave the Income Tax Act shot full of holes.

Dr. Prior believed she was morally responsible for what the government did with her tax money. Sophistical distinctions did not alter the fact. She was entitled to go to trial on the issue, unless it was plain and obvious that she could not succeed. I urged it on the court that, once the issue was properly cast as one of fact and not of law, the case had to be allowed to proceed.

Proving as a fact that there was a connection depended not only on Dr. Prior's beliefs. It also depended on the progress of the technology of war. Until the mid-twentieth century, wars were fought by standing armies augmented by conscripts. That was certainly Canada's experience in both world wars. But today armed forces are not maintained by a stream of raw recruits; they are maintained by a stream of new devices and instruments designed specifically to destroy. The direct service of ordinary citizens has become far less relevant than it used to be to the maintenance of the armies of modern technological societies. It is the citizen's resources that the government now wants to enable it to pay for these new devices and instruments. As William Stringfellow wrote in 1973 about the Vietnam War:

The use of apparently anonymous automated weapons exposes the common and equal culpability for slaughter of those who pull the trigger and those who press the button with those who manufacture the means and those who pay the taxes. The fact that a person does not see, and cannot foresee, the consequences of an action does not make the action either innocuous or innocent. Automated warfare, so sophisticated in Vietnam, dramatizes the corporate guilt of all Americans, civilian as much as serviceman, in the genocide of the war.

This seems still to be true today: like Vietnam, the Gulf War and the wars in Kosovo and Afghanistan have been wars in which technology has been predominant.

Justice Addy treated Dr. Prior's case as a challenge to Parliament's power to tax under section 91(3) of the Constitution Act, 1867. This finding was patently unsound. Dr. Prior was not challenging the power of the government to collect taxes for military purposes; she claimed instead the right to be protected in her freedom of conscience.

The court would not have to strike down the Income Tax Act. All that was required by way of remedy, should it come to that, was a means to enable Dr. Prior's tax money to do alternative service. As early as 1841 this provision had been made for Quaker and Mennonite conscientious objectors in Upper Canada. The old Province of Canada had passed a law to provide that Quakers and Mennonites who objected to military service on grounds of conscience would make a special payment of tax recorded on a separate tax roll and paid into a fund for building roads, highways and bridges. The statute provided:

III. And be it enacted, that it shall be the duty of the Assessor or Assessors in each Township within the said portion of this Province, and they are hereby required to *annex a column to each and every Assessment roll* of each and every Town, Township or Place in his or their respective District, and *therein to insert the names of every such Quaker, Mennonist or Tunker, and also affix the sum of money so to be paid opposite thereunto* . . .

IV. And be it enacted, that it shall be lawful to and for the said *Town Clerk* for such Town, Township or Place, and *he is hereby required to pay out the said monies from time to time, to the order of the Road or Path Master of the division wherein such fine shall have been levied, and to be expended on the public Roads, Highways and Bridges within such division* [emphasis added].

This situation was not exactly the same as our own. In 1841, payment was made in lieu of military service by a person otherwise required to spend a certain time each year in the militia. In Dr. Prior's case, she was not herself required to enlist, but her taxes had been enlisted, and she wanted them to be used for the equivalent of road-building and bridge-building.

The legislators of Upper Canada had managed to arrange, in a frontier province, a simple means of diverting Quaker and Mennonite taxes from military expenditure to the Path Master, for roads and bridges. In our age of computers, it should be possible to ensure that the portion of Dr. Prior's tax money that would otherwise go to military expenditure could be accounted for separately, and that it then could be assigned to the support of a benign governmental purpose (foreign aid, for instance, or some other peaceful purpose, or even, as in 1841, on roads, highways and bridges).

The Federal Court of Appeal rejected the appeal. The court, like Justice Addy, in its eagerness to dispose of this prickly issue, mixed up the issue of whether Dr. Prior's freedom of conscience had been violated (the first stage) with the question of whether the limitation on her freedom was a reasonable limit under section 1 (the second stage). Justice Louis Marceau wrote the judgement of the court. He adopted Justice Addy's reasoning, adding embellishments of his own.

The Federal Court of Appeal concluded that Justice Addy was correct in determining that the issue of whether there was a sufficient nexus between taxes and actual military expenditures such as to constitute a violation of Dr. Prior's freedom of conscience was strictly a question of law. Justice Marceau said:

Neither the payment of income tax nor the defence expenditures of the Government of Canada in any way affect, curtail, diminish or infringe the Appellant's conscience or religion within the meaning of paragraph 2(a) of the *Charter*. The income tax paid by her under the secular scheme of the *Income Tax Act* charging her business or employment income to tax, in no way identifies her with any of the functions of the Government of Canada be they political, social, economic, defence or for the Peace Order and Good Government of Canada.

Justice Marceau then held that Dr. Prior's lawsuit was a challenge to the taxing power itself, rather than simply a challenge to the way the taxing power was exercised under the Income Tax Act. He elaborated:

The declaration sought would mean that the power given to Parliament by s. 91 of the *Constitution Act, 1867* to levy taxes is lawful, in relation to certain taxpayers, only if the monies collected are not used for certain types of defence expenditures. The challenge is formally directed against the *Income Tax Act* but, in reality, it extends to any legislation levying taxes. It is the power itself which is put in question.

Justice Marceau went on:

To give effect to the Appellant's argument, the Court must either amend the rate provisions of the *Income Tax Act*, or create a credit scheme exempting the Appellant from payment of a portion of her income tax otherwise payable, to the Receiver General of Canada, under the provisions of that Act. A change in the statutory scheme of the *Income Tax Act* would therefore have to be devised. That is not the role of the Court.

Of course that would not be the role of the court. It would be the role of Parliament. Under section 52(1) of the Constitution Act, 1982, legislation that violates the Charter is of no force and effect to the extent that it is inconsistent with the Charter. Dr. Prior did not seek to set aside the Income Tax Act as unconstitutional, but merely to obtain a declaration that to the extent that it violated her freedom of conscience it was of no force or effect.

What the courts do—where they hold that legislation is in violation of the Charter, but they do not wish to strike it down—is to leave it to the legislature to devise a remedy and to rule that for now the legislation is to remain in force.

The order sought by Dr. Prior would not mean that she and others would not have to pay their taxes. Parliament could fashion a legislative remedy, just as Upper Canada had done 175 years before, and the court's order regarding the constitutional exemption would be suspended for a time to enable Parliament to do so.

The judgement of the Federal Court of Appeal took a narrow view of the guarantee of freedom of conscience. It defined freedom of conscience as a matter to be determined by law and not according to an individual's beliefs; it treated a challenge to the application of tax legislation as a challenge to Parliament's power to tax. It rejected the idea that legislation could be held of no force and effect unless the court itself could fashion a legislative remedy.

The *Lawyers Weekly*, on November 10, 1989, carried a report of the case, including an extensive interview with me.

Mr. Berger criticized the court's suggestion that his client is challenging the state's power to tax as "patently unsound." "I think that's nonsense. It would mean that any time you challenged legislation under the Charter the Crown can simply say 'Oh no, you're really challenging the constitutional power to enact the legislation.' "

He noted: "We now have four judges of the Federal Court adopting this position, so there must be something in it, but for myself I don't follow it."

The appeal court, he added, "just missed the point. They're three nice judges. They came out to Vancouver to listen, but clearly I made no impression on them.

"They never did come to grips intellectually with the issues in the case.

"It's unfortunate because there are 500 Quakers and Christian pacifists who have been withholding their taxes, and they deserved, I think, a judgement that came to grips with the real issues here. This was simply a reiteration of the trial judge's decision."

I think the language I used was gratuitous and intemperate. But even now, thirteen years later, I still think my analysis holds up. Perhaps it illustrates a saying often attributed to advocates: "I've never lost a case that wasn't wrongly decided."

The article continued:

According to Mr. Berger, the nub of the case is whether freedom of conscience under the Charter is a matter of law to be determined by judges, or whether it is concerned with what the individual really believes, as a matter of fact.

"If the courts can finesse the whole issue by characterizing it as a question of law then there is nothing left to talk about," Mr. Berger contended.

Rather than allowing the issue to go to trial to test what Dr. Prior actually believes, "they treated this [case] as if it were a tracing action, as if Dr. Prior was obliged to show that she could trace the very dollars that she contributes as a taxpayer to military expenditures," he said.

Such a narrow view of freedom of conscience "will gladden the heart of every bureaucrat. But it eviscerates the guarantee of freedom of conscience entrenched in s. 2(a) of the Charter," Mr. Berger concluded.

Jerilynn Prior was deeply disappointed in the outcome. "I believe that there is a pure and simple accounting connection," she said. "But the important connection between my taxes and Canada's military expenditures is in my conscience."

We applied to the Supreme Court of Canada for leave to appeal. The court turned us down. So we applied for reconsideration and were turned down again. I thought there were sufficient grounds for granting leave: the Federal Court of Appeal was wrong in holding that a question of conscience is a question of law and not a question of fact; the Federal Court of appeal was wrong in treating Jerilynn Prior's case as a challenge to Parliament's power to levy taxes; the Federal Court of Appeal was wrong in determining that only the court could devise a remedy; and the Federal Court of Appeal was wrong in bringing section 1 of the Charter into consideration on a motion to strike out the plaintiff's statement of claim that there had been a violation of her freedom of conscience. The Supreme Court was not interested.

I have emphasized Dr. Prior's side here. My point is that her side should have been heard in court; her evidence should have been considered. My complaint is that Justice Addy and the Federal Court of Appeal had decided, at this early stage and without evidence, issues that should have been considered at trial.

I have no doubt that the issue of abortion continued to stalk Dr. Prior's case in the higher courts. Justice Addy had warned specifically about abortion; it was the egregious example. On our part, we relied on the decision of the Supreme Court in 1988 in *R. v. Morgentaler*. In that case, Justice Bertha Wilson had said:

I believe that the decision whether or not to terminate a pregnancy is essentially a moral decision, a matter of conscience. I do not think there is or can be any dispute about that. The question is: whose conscience? Is the conscience of the woman to be paramount or the conscience of the state? I believe, for the reasons I gave in discussing the right to liberty, that in a free and democratic society *it must be the conscience of the individual*. Indeed, s.2(a) makes it clear that this freedom belongs to "everyone," i.e., to each of us individually [emphasis added].

The unstated question was: If Dr. Prior and her friends could claim that, as a matter of conscience, they could refuse to have their taxes go to national defence, why could not taxpayers opposed to abortion (as a matter of conscience) call for the diversion of their taxes from paying for abortions? It might come to that. But that was an issue that would arise in its own time and in a future case. In the meantime, we wanted to try the issue of alternative service for taxes.

The courts are obviously concerned about the consequences of the decisions they make. Would other exceptions have to be made on religious grounds? Perhaps. There might be other causes placed squarely within the articles of one faith or another. These things are impossible to foretell. But these questions could be worked out case by case. Judges should scan the horizon, but they shouldn't try to peer around corners. In its own way, this judicial caution can amount to judicial activism.

It might be asked, what difference would it all make? If five or ten per cent of Dr. Prior's tax money were specifically dedicated to roads and bridges, wouldn't the balance of her taxes still be spread over the whole panoply of federal expenditure, including military expenditure? And, if Dr. Prior's five or ten per cent did not go to military expenditure, the deficiency in the military budget would be made up by the taxes of others.

Dr. Prior's tax money, diverted to a benign purpose, would be replaced by money collected from other taxpayers. But the same could be said of alternative service for conscientious objectors. By toting stretchers on the field of battle, they free others to engage in killing. Yet we have excused them from actively engaging in killing. Dr. Prior's tax money could in the same fashion be permitted to do alternative service.

How would Jerilynn Prior and her friends have fared at trial? We don't know, because we were thrown off the bus at the first turn.

The Quakers remind us of our personal responsibility for the military operations of our governments. In the eighteenth century, John Woolman worried that civilians would "by small degrees . . . approach so near to fighting that the distinction would be little else but the name of a peaceable people."

Dr. Prior's lawsuit represented one woman's struggle to remain true to her faith in a violent world, a world constantly shadowed by war. It may be said that her lawsuit was a futile gesture. But gestures are important. And this lawsuit was more than a gesture. Dr. Prior had to proclaim her faith to the world, or at least to the bureaucracy of Revenue Canada and before the judges of the Federal Court.

All this trouble then to accommodate Dr. Prior and 532 other taxpayers. Why not? Canada did it in 1841 in peacetime. And we have done it in wartime for conscientious objectors. Would this case have opened the floodgates?

If we had won, would those opposed to abortion have been allowed through? Yes, if they could show that it was a matter of conscience or an article of their faith that none of their tax money should go to government funding for abortion procedures. But the Crown could invoke section 1. The burden would be on the Crown to show, as it ought to have been required to do in Dr. Prior's case, that a limitation on a taxpayer's freedom of conscience would be a reasonable one and "demonstrably justifiable in a free and democratic society."

If the Crown were unable to justify the limitation, and Parliament believed that we were on the verge of "the breakdown of orderly government," it could invoke section 33 of the Charter, which allows Parliament to legislate in violation of Charter rights.

Lying at the heart of the Quaker belief is a faith in human nature, a belief that, in settling conflicts between nations, there is a better way than war. The Quakers do not claim to be paragons of virtue. They themselves have not always been consistent in their commitment to non-violence. They have been divided from time to time over the issue of whether defensive wars, as opposed to offensive wars, can be justified. During the United States Civil War, Quakers in that country who had been active in the campaign against slavery decided—some of them—that it was more important to end slavery than to remain steadfast in their commitment to non-violence, so they enlisted in Lincoln's armies; others paid substitutes to take their place (a common practice at the time); still others served in a non-military capacity.

Nevertheless, the Quakers have demonstrated a faith in the capacity of human beings to turn away from the use of force. In 1994, John Keegan, the West's leading military historian, wrote in *A History of Warfare:* "Despite confusion and uncertainty, it seems just possible to glimpse the emerging outline of a world without war." This goal entails a profound cultural transformation. The Quakers were among the first to campaign against slavery. Slavery, as Keegan points out, was, until two hundred years ago, an institution integral to human societies. Yet it has now almost disappeared from the world.

In the age of nuclear weapons, says John Keegan, war "may well be ceasing to commend itself to human beings as a desirable or productive, let alone rational, means of reconciling their discontents. This is not mere idealism. Mankind does have the capacity, over time, to correlate the costs and benefits of large and universal undertakings." Keegan foresees the weighing of the costs and the benefits producing a "cultural transformation." He says:

Throughout much of the time for which we have a record of human behaviour, mankind can clearly be seen to have judged that war's benefits outweighed its costs ... Now the computation works in the opposite direction ... War truly has become a scourge, as was disease throughout most of human history . . . As most cultures of which we have knowledge were transfused by the warrior spirit, such a cultural transformation demands a break with the past for which there are no precedents. There is no precedent, however, for the menace with which future war now confronts the world.

All of this would require a profound shift in moral perception. But if war is the continuation of politics by other means, then, as Keegan puts it: "Politics must continue; war cannot."

In 1998, in *War and Our World,* John Keegan returned to this theme. To be sure, Keegan argues that the United Nations and governments that support that organization must continue to maintain armed forces to secure the peace and be willing to use deadly force if necessary. But he argues that "war, until very recent times, was not among life's great enemies." The great enemies were famine and disease. They are still with us, but it is possible, as it once was unimaginable, to contemplate their eradication. Why not war?

Those who, like Jerilynn Prior, make a signal gesture in rejecting the cause of war remind us of the possibility that what John Keegan foresees may be achievable.

8 A Fair Trial

WHAT IS A FAIR TRIAL? In criminal law, we continue to define and redefine the rules for achieving a fair trial.

There cannot be anyone who isn't able to repeat the warning given on television a hundred times a week: "You have the right to remain silent, but anything you do say may be taken down and given in evidence." When you've heard it often enough, you begin to think of it as pro forma, merely a ritual. But there is a reason for it. The warning is given because anyone arrested *does* have a right to keep silent. If you keep silent, the fact that you offered no explanation, did not protest your innocence when arrested, cannot be used against you later on. This right is essential to a fair trial.

The police are not entitled to coerce a confession. You are not required to be a witness against yourself. What is most valuable to the prosecution is an incriminating statement from the mouth of the accused. But an accused does not have to say anything to the police. He or she has the right to remain silent.

One of the first cases I argued, upon returning to practice, was that of Martin Chambers. He was a prominent commercial lawyer in Vancouver, who had been charged, together with six other persons, with conspiracy to import cocaine into Canada. I was still on the bench when his saga began. He had already been tried twice when he retained me.

The case against him consisted almost entirely of telephone intercepts. At his first trial, these intercepts were ruled inadmissible; without them, there was no case, so he was acquitted. But the Court of Appeal for British Columbia reversed the decision of the trial judge, ruling that the telephone intercepts should not have been excluded, and ordered a new trial. The Supreme Court of Canada upheld the order for a new trial.

Chambers was brought to trial a second time; it was a jury trial. His case was discussed every day in the media. It certainly had features that caught the public's attention.

Chambers had an affair, which started in 1980, with a woman named Zena Pocius. She was from Miami, and he kept her in an apartment in Vancouver. Chambers's involvement in the conspiracy came about in the following year, 1981, in this way. He leased office space to a man called Dumyn. Through Dumyn, Chambers was retained to go to Panama to see if he could arrange for Barudin, an associate of Dumyn, to be released from jail.

He went to Panama and succeeded in his mission: Barudin and his cellmate, a man named Jay Gonzalez, were released. Chambers had to bribe Panamanian authorities to get them released. The evidence was that this procedure was at the time normal in the Panamanian justice system.

Chambers, Barudin and Gonzalez returned to Miami to celebrate. The evidence indicated that a conspiracy among Barudin, Dumyn, Gonzalez and Pocius to import cocaine into Canada germinated in Panama, and that they discussed it again in Miami, the idea being to bring cocaine from Miami to Vancouver. Barudin and Dumyn were Vancouverites.

Chambers testified that while he was in Panama, he was unaware of the hatching of the conspiracy. When, after they reached Miami, he became aware of the conspiracy, he pretended to go along with it to maintain his connection with Pocius, who was implicated in the conspiracy and whom he wished to extricate.

A conspiracy is an agreement by two or more persons to commit a criminal offence. There must be an intention by two or more persons to agree to commit what is called an overt act, and an intention to put the agreement into effect. It is not necessary, however, that there be proof that any overt act was committed in furtherance of the conspiracy. Even if the conspirators do not carry out the overt act, they are nevertheless guilty of the crime of conspiracy. If, therefore, you agree with others to bring cocaine into Canada, you are guilty of conspiracy even if none of those who have conspired transport any cocaine across the border.

Was Chambers part of the conspiracy? Chambers relied on the so-called double intent rule: he pretended to agree with the others in the conspiracy but claimed that he himself had no intention of carrying out the agreement to commit the unlawful act. His purpose was not to import cocaine into Canada but to recapture the affections of Pocius, who by this time was transferring her fondness to Gonzalez. The trial proceeded on the footing that if Chambers raised a reasonable doubt on the point, he should be acquitted. In 1954, the Supreme Court held in *R. v. O'Brien* that a double intent is a defence to a charge of conspiracy. It is a defence that is almost Jesuitical; the accused may outwardly have been a member of the conspiracy, but inwardly he withheld any intention of conscientiously participating.

There were voluminous transcripts of telephone intercepts that, on the face of it, indicated that Chambers was a member of the conspiracy. But there was also evidence in the transcripts to support Chambers's defence.

Jay Gonzalez, whom Chambers had freed from custody in Panama, had supplanted Chambers in Zena Pocius's affections. After the celebration in Miami, Chambers returned to Vancouver, but Pocius remained in Miami. So Chambers went back to Miami. He confronted Pocius and Gonzalez. They were having a picnic. Gonzalez pulled a gun. Chambers was thus prevented from reclaiming his mistress, but he was still determined to get her back.

After Chambers returned to Vancouver, he made phone calls to Pocius in Miami. The police were investigating by this time. Chambers's calls to Pocius were tapped. The calls confirmed his agitated state of mind about his relationship with her. Calls placed between Zena Pocius and Jay Gonzalez were also tapped. Pocius told Gonzalez that Chambers was "obsessed" about getting her back.

The conspiracy was still afoot. The conspirators agreed that Gonzalez would bring the cocaine to Vancouver. Chambers, however, remained inwardly opposed. Moreover, there was evidence that Chambers took steps to prevent the object of the conspiracy from being realized.

Chambers claimed that he hired Santiez Tabbance, a Cuban also known as Kuko, to intercept Gonzalez in Florida. Kuko did not succeed. But during an intercepted telephone call made by Jay Gonzalez to Zena Pocius from Atlanta, Gonzalez told Pocius that somebody had tried to hold him up but failed. So Chambers's story was apparently not a fabrication. Somebody had tried to stop Gonzalez. It must have been Kuko.

Uncertain about what to do next, Gonzalez went to ground in Atlanta. While there, he called Pocius a number of times. These calls, too, were intercepted. They revealed that Gonzalez was apprehensive that someone was attempting to rob him. Chambers had Kuko try again to intercept Gonzalez. This second time, at the Atlanta airport, Kuko succeeded. The evidence of the police confirmed that Gonzalez did not arrive as expected in Seattle, the next leg on his route to Vancouver, with the cocaine.

The earlier intercepted calls indicated that someone had attempted to rob Gonzalez in Florida. Now there were calls indicating that he had been robbed in Atlanta, that his jaw was injured in the robbery, and that on his return to Miami he was unable to speak owing to the injury.

At Chambers's trial, the defence called Jay Gonzalez. The Crown had agreed that if he came to Vancouver to testify for the defence, he would be given immunity from prosecution. No doubt Crown counsel believed that Gonzalez, under cross-examination, would implicate Chambers as a true conspirator, that his shelter in the double intent rule would collapse. Gonzalez instead confirmed

Chambers's defence: he testified that he was attacked and robbed of the cocaine in the Atlanta airport. He showed the jury a scar on the inside of his mouth that he had received in the attack. In cross-examination, Crown counsel put it to Gonzalez that there had never been an attempted robbery in Florida and no actual robbery in Atlanta; that there was one reason and one reason only that Gonzalez had come to Canada to testify—money that Chambers had paid him to give false testimony on his behalf.

Chambers's defence may have seemed a tall tale. But the telephone intercepts showed there might be something to it. And Chambers went into the witness box to back it up.

His conduct, though perhaps irrational, is not unprecedented. He was not the first respectable man to risk everything for a woman of the demimonde.

Robert DeBou, who was prosecuting, accused Chambers of being a full member of the conspiracy. DeBou had accused Gonzalez, when he testified, of coming forward only because he'd been paid to do so. Now, Crown counsel accused Chambers of bribing Gonzalez. He brought out the fact that, after Gonzalez testified, Chambers had driven him to the U.S. border, and there Gonzalez had $10,000 in his possession. Where had he gotten it, if not from Chambers?

Crown counsel's cross-examination of Chambers lasted two weeks. This was the critical stage of the trial. Would Chambers's testimony, even if he did not convince the jury members of his truthfulness, raise in their minds at least a reasonable doubt? Was there reason to think the testimony might be true? That was all Chambers needed for an acquittal.

After a fifty-day trial, the jury convicted Chambers. The trial judge sentenced him to nine years' imprisonment. I was retained to represent Chambers in the Court of Appeal. My colleague on the appeal was David Martin, a criminal lawyer specializing in Charter cases.

David and I combed the record. The most serious flaw in the trial was this: Crown counsel had asked a series of questions implying that Chambers's defence should not be believed because he had not disclosed it to the police when he was arrested.

Chambers had been warned by the police when he was arrested. He didn't *have* to say anything. And he didn't. But Crown counsel tried to use this fact against him. Why hadn't he told the police of his double intent? Why, if it were true, save it for the trial? Why not speak up right away?

This argument was dangerous territory for the prosecution. If you are arrested, you are under no obligation to offer an explanation to the police of your behaviour. You are entitled to keep your silence. And when you go into the witness box to tell your story, it cannot be held against you that you didn't explain yourself to the police at the time of arrest. In other words, you can't be asked, "How can you expect us to believe you now when you had a chance to disclose all this at the very beginning? You've come here and made it all up. You've concocted the whole story."

That would be a telling question. But Crown counsel is not allowed to put it to an accused, or it would render meaningless the right to silence. It would hardly be fair—indeed, it would be misleading—to tell an accused that he has the right to remain silent, and then turn around and use his silence against him. In Chambers's case, the prosecutor did just that.

DeBou made a straightforward accusation in his cross-examination of Chambers. Six years had passed since Chambers had been arrested. Chambers, he alleged, had concocted the whole story.

> Q Let me be plain, Mr. Chambers. I'm suggesting to you that your defence is a contrived one, it's a lie. This didn't happen the way you've described it, and you've been fine-tuning a defence for the last six years and you came up with this Kuko idea, this Kuko idea at the last moment?
>
> A That's not so, Mr. DeBou.

Well, there's nothing wrong in the prosecution making an accusation of concoction. But you have to be careful. The accusation that Chambers had been "fine-tuning a defence for the last six years" did not cross the line.

Crown counsel went further, however, cross-examining Chambers as to why he had not made a statement at the time of his arrest.

> Q Mr. Chambers, if that's the case, why did you not tell the authorities as soon as you were arrested that it may look bad, but you have an explanation for why it looks so bad. Why didn't you?
>
> A Mr. DeBou, as a lawyer I would never talk to the authorities under any condition where they've laid conspiracy charges and arrested a whole bunch of people.

Crown counsel continued: "Isn't this the first time, sir, in court, in these proceedings that you've actually told someone in authority your story about what happened?" Chambers's lawyer, Howard Rubin, objected: "I think that's totally inaccurate." Crown counsel responded: "My friend is quite wrong. This is an improper objection, I think, my lord."

Rubin objected because Chambers had, through his lawyer, disclosed at an earlier stage of the case, when it was determined that he would be tried separately from the other alleged conspirators, that he would be relying on a defence of double intent. Rubin, in saying "that's totally inaccurate," was absolutely right. DeBou, who responded by saying "My friend is quite wrong," was himself "quite wrong."

Crown counsel continued to develop the theme. Why hadn't Chambers lobbied the police and the prosecution with his explanations?

Q Mr. Chambers, when was it that you first raised this whole subject of Kuko with anyone? Maybe you don't understand that question? I am referring to the subject of you arranging for Kuko to take down the drugs at the Atlanta airport. When was it that you first raised that topic . . . ?

Rubin told the judge he wanted to re-examine Chambers to bring out the fact that he had on an earlier occasion disclosed his defence of a double intent.

The jury was excluded for almost two hours while legal argument ensued, ultimately without any ruling by the trial judge, because DeBou realized, belatedly, he had crossed the line. He requested the judge to direct the jury to completely ignore the questions he had put and the answers Chambers had given as to his earlier silence. On this basis, Rubin stated that he would not re-examine Chambers to bring out the fact that he had in the severance proceedings before his first trial disclosed his defence of double intent. Justice William Trainor, the trial judge, undertook that in his charge to the jury, he would direct the jury to ignore the whole exchange between DeBou and Chambers. This was the very least he could do.

In a lengthy trial, the ball is sometimes dropped. The judge never gave the promised direction to the jury to disregard the questions by DeBou that violated Chambers's right to remain silent. In the meantime, Rubin, relying on the judge's promised direction, did not bring out in his re-examination of Chambers that he had earlier told the authorities he would be claiming that he had only pretended to go along with the conspiracy. The jury brought in a verdict of guilty.

On appeal, therefore, we had a good argument that there was a flaw in the trial. Crown counsel had sought to establish by improper questioning that Chambers acted as a guilty person by not protesting his innocence. The Crown sought to imply that an innocent man would have cried out upon arrest, lobbied prosecution authorities with explanations of his innocence, seized the first opportunity to make disclosure. The Crown, by putting these questions, had asked the jury to accept that Chambers had, by his silence at the time of his arrest, communicated his guilt. This suggestion undermined Chambers's right to remain silent.

The Court of Appeal agreed with us. Chambers had been denied a fair trial. Ordinarily, there would then be a new trial.

But what about a case where the evidence is overwhelming; a case in which a mistake by counsel or by the judge has made no difference; where the verdict would undoubtedly have been a verdict of guilty anyway? In such a case, should the accused go free?

The Criminal Code provides for this contingency. It gives an appellate court authority to allow an appeal where the judgement of the trial court should be set aside on the ground of a wrong decision on a question of law. But there is also a provision that allows an appellate court, even in a case where a mistake has been made—evidence improperly admitted or a mistaken direction by the judge—to uphold the verdict if there has been no "substantial wrong or miscarriage of justice." Many appeals are about this question. If the appellate court believes the evidence was so overwhelming that the accused would have inevitably been convicted, fair trial or no, there is no need to try the case again. If it is merely a situation where an "i" has not been dotted or a "t" crossed, a guilty verdict will not be set aside. The rule book may not have been observed in every particular, but no harm done.

There seemed to be no doubt that the judge had erred. But had there been a miscarriage of justice? Should there be a new trial? Or would Chambers have been convicted anyway? The Court of Appeal, by a majority of four to one, thought a conviction was inevitable. They were impressed by the weight of the evidence against Chambers. They thought that the few questions to which Rubin had objected would not, in a cross-examination lasting fourteen days, have seemed significant to the jury. Justice William Esson, in a concurring judgement, best expressed the view of the majority. He conceded that the questions should never have been asked, but he went on:

When the jury came to deliberate more than a month later, it may have seen some significance in Chamber's [sic] own evidence in direct [examination] that he had not told anyone this strange story until shortly before the second trial. That was a proper matter for their consideration. But it was in my view beyond the bounds of reasonable possibility that the jury attached significance to the questions relating to silence after arrest. Given the great length of time, and the mounds of evidence and argument which had been piled up between the time of the offending question and the judge's charge, it may well have been an act of charity to the accused to say nothing.

We did, however, obtain a dissent from Justice Douglas Lambert, a meticulous, scholarly member of the court. He pointed out that if DeBou's questions were permissible, "the police warning about the right to remain silent would be a trap."

As to the issue of whether there had been a miscarriage of justice, Justice Lambert said:

Was the inadmissible evidence which was wrongly admitted capable of influencing the reasoning of a member of the jury? . . . The jury must have been aware of the importance attached by both counsel to the questions and answers relating to the time when Chambers first offered his explanation of events to the police or to anyone else . . . And the members of the jury may have independently concluded that the evidence was important. It was evidence that Chambers did not disclose his defence or tell his story to the police from 1982 until 1986. A member of the jury might reasonably have concluded that the prolonged failure to say that he was only trying to bring Zena Pocius back to Vancouver and that he had no criminal intention with respect to carrying out the criminal design of the conspirators and, indeed, that he intended, from the outset, to frustrate it, turned a story that might have been worth the benefit of the doubt into one that was wholly incredible.

Justice Lambert dealt with the majority view that the evidence against Chambers was massive.

I do not see why the effect of the wrongful admission of this inadmissible evidence in breach of Chambers's right to silence should be regarded as any less damaging because it represents only a small portion of the totality of the evidence. The jury would not be weighing the evidence by bulk.

He concluded:

In my opinion it is impossible to say that the violation of Chambers's right to silence which occurred in the course of the trial in this case could not have possibly had any effect on the jury. It was capable of influencing the reasoning of a member of the jury. I consider that a properly instructed jury, acting judicially on admissible evidence, might possibly have concluded that Chambers's guilt had not been proved beyond a reasonable doubt.

We appealed to the Supreme Court of Canada. We didn't have to seek leave to appeal on this point, because there had been a dissenting judgement in the Court of Appeal. We argued the right to keep silent is a right enshrined in section 7 of the Charter, which provides that "Everyone has the right to life, liberty and security of the person and the right not to be deprived thereof except in accordance with the principles of fundamental justice." One of these fundamental principles must surely be the right of silence. In the Supreme Court, by a majority of eight to one, we won a new trial. The Supreme Court felt it could not safely say that the verdict would have been the same had Chambers's right to silence not been violated.

Justice Peter Cory wrote for the majority. He dealt with the right to silence:

It has as well been recognized that since there is a right to silence, it would be a snare and a delusion to caution the accused that he need not say anything in response to a police officer's question but nonetheless put in evidence that the accused clearly exercised his right and remained silent in the face of a question which suggested his guilt.

He went on:

The questions were improper and the evidence inadmissible. The failure of the trial judge to so instruct the jury, pursuant to his undertaking, compounded the error and caused, I fear, irreparable damage to the defence . . . The jury were deprived of the evidence that would establish that the so-called double intent defence to which the "Kuko" evidence related was not of recent concoction. As a result of the Crown's cross-examination, the jury could well have been left with the erroneous impression that Chambers was under a duty to disclose the Kuko story to a person in authority . . . The failure to correct such an impression by direction from the trial judge rendered the right to silence *a snare of silence* for the appellant. Without any direction to ignore these questions and answers, it is impossible to say that the verdict would necessarily have been the same [emphasis added].

Justice Cory located the right to silence squarely within "the fundamental principles of justice" guaranteed by section 7 of the Charter. The accused has the right under section 7 to remain silent. It is not open to the Crown to put in evidence that the accused remained silent in the face of a question that suggested his guilt. Neither questions by investigating officers nor evidence as to the ensuing silence of an accused person should be admitted at trial.

Justice Cory was aware that Chambers had already been tried twice. The second trial had spanned three months. It was unlikely that, if the Supreme Court ordered yet a third trial, the Crown would proceed. The case would necessarily be left in an inconclusive state. Justice Cory said:

It is not without considerable regret that I reach this conclusion. The trial was lengthy. The conduct of the trial judge throughout the long case was exemplary. Much of the charge was beyond reproach. Nonetheless, the failure [of the judge] to charge on this issue in the circumstances of the case constituted a serious miscarriage of justice that requires the direction of a new trial.

The Crown had had enough. They did not proceed with a third trial.

Is this an unsatisfactory outcome? Shouldn't there have been a third trial? Well, there may not have been a third trial and a final verdict, but due process had been affirmed. We don't allow a guilty verdict to stand unless the accused has had a fair trial; unless there has been no substantial wrong or miscarriage of justice. And we screen such cases carefully. The test is a stringent one. Can we say that the verdict was inevitable? As Justice Lambert asked, was it "reasonably possible" to say that if the questions violating Chambers's right to silence had not been asked, Chambers would have been acquitted? The jury had been out for a day and a half considering its verdict. Justice Lambert could not say the jury would inevitably have convicted Chambers. Eight of nine judges in the Supreme Court of Canada had agreed. So the verdict of guilty had to go.

The right to silence is protected by the Charter. You don't have to explain yourself to the police when you are placed under arrest. And at your trial, your failure to do so cannot be used against you. In 1997, in *R. v. Noble*, Justice John Sopinka, for the majority in the Supreme Court, wrote that as far as the question of whether the silence of the accused on arrest or while detained could later be used at trial as evidence of guilt is concerned, Chambers's case had "settled the matter."

So the police have to build their case in other ways. But what if you told the whole story; what if you spilled the beans to confederates? In such a case, of course, they could be subpoenaed to testify about an incriminating statement you may have made. But the police do not often acquire such evidence. Confederates usually keep their mouths shut.

Suppose, however, that you told the whole story—made an incriminating statement to a confederate or to a friend or to someone else over the telephone— and the police had tapped the phone? The police would have the evidence from your own lips.

Wiretaps occur every day in Canada; thousands of them in a year. Listening in on someone's phone is an extraordinary invasion of privacy. The law is that the police must get a court order. Only judges can issue orders authorizing wiretaps. The police and the prosecution go before a judge, with an affidavit or affidavits sworn by a police officer, to justify tapping someone's phone. After the judge authorizes the wiretap, the packet containing the affidavits that have been brought before the judge is sealed.

Of course, a request to a judge for a wiretap has to be made *ex parte*. There would be no point in notifying a suspect that he was invited to the courthouse to explain to a judge why his phone should not be tapped. He would, unless incorrigibly stupid, be discreet thereafter about what he might say on the telephone if he failed to persuade the judge that his phone should not be tapped. But because the procedure is necessarily *ex parte,* it is open to the kind of abuse that can occur when the court hears only one side.

If a wiretap is to be used as evidence at a trial, there is a preliminary question of whether it is admissible. What if the judge who granted the wiretap was not told the whole story? What if the prosecution told the judge what they knew implicating the wiretap target, but they did not disclose other information they had that showed the opposite? Suppose they withheld crucial evidence that, if shown to the judge, might have undermined the argument for a wiretap?

A wiretap obtained without any proper basis is a violation of section 8 of the Charter, which says that "Everyone has the right to be secure against unreasonable search or seizure." A search and seizure is what occurs when the police enter a home, search the premises and seize letters, accounts or records. The interception of telephone conversations falls into the same category—it is an appropriation of private information. The courts have held that it amounts to search and seizure.

Before the trial, the prosecution has to disclose the contents of the intercepted conversations. There is a tape of the conversation or conversations, and a typed transcript is made up. But is it fair to allow the tape and the transcript to be introduced in evidence? That depends *not* on what was said on the phone by the accused, incriminating or otherwise, but on whether the wiretap was lawfully obtained.

If the accused can show that the police misled the judge when they obtained the order for a wiretap, the wiretap evidence may be excluded on the ground that it has been obtained in violation of the Charter. A search warrant obtained by a failure to make full disclosure is a violation of section 8 of the Charter, making the search and seizure unreasonable. The same applies to wiretaps. It may be the difference between a verdict of guilty and not guilty, because the evidence of the tapped conversation may be vital to the prosecution's case—in some cases, like that of Martin Chambers, it may be the only evidence.

Section 178.16(1) of the Code at the time made wiretap evidence absolutely inadmissible unless lawfully obtained. Ordinarily, where evidence is unlawfully obtained, it will be admissible under section 24 of the Charter unless admitting the evidence would bring the "administration of justice into disrepute." The wiretap provisions were at the time unique. If the wiretap evidence were to be unlawfully obtained, it had to be excluded whether or not to admit it would bring the administration of justice into disrepute. If the authorization was not lawfully obtained, that was the end of the matter: there was no discretion to be exercised; the evidence would be absolutely inadmissible.

At trial, an accused person may object to the admissibility of evidence: the evidence may be irrelevant; it may be hearsay; it may be in the form of a confession not voluntarily made. Or it may have been unlawfully obtained.

An accused person whose phone has been tapped may therefore object to the introduction of wiretap evidence, of the tape and the transcript, on the ground that the police did not make full disclosure; that they misled the judge who issued the wiretap authorization. But how would the accused find out whether the police had made full disclosure to the court to obtain the wiretap order? The accused would need to see the affidavits used to obtain the wiretap. If the accused and his lawyer can examine those affidavits, they may be in a position to object to the introduction of the wiretap evidence. But what if they are not allowed to see them? What can they do? This issue arose squarely in the case of Wilfred Wayne Dersch.

Dersch had been charged with trafficking in drugs. The case for the Crown depended on wiretap evidence obtained under twenty-two wiretap authorizations. A transcript was provided to Dersch and his lawyer, and the tapes themselves made available. But not the affidavits used by the police to obtain the wiretap order in the first place. They remained in the sealed packet.

Could Dersch see the affidavits? Could he go through them, and if he found that they contained false statements, could he show that the court had been gulled? And then argue that the evidence of his intercepted telephone conversations should be excluded? Without the evidence of the tapped conversations, there would be no case against him.

Dersch argued that he should have the *right* to inspect the packet. How else would he know if the wiretap order had been lawfully obtained? But the packet had been sealed. Would the courts open the packet?

In B.C., the answer was no; not unless the accused made out a prima facie case of fraud or misrepresentation by the police. Then—and only then—would he be allowed to see the affidavits. But how could the accused do that unless the packet were opened so that he could find out what the police had in their affidavits told the judge to get the wiretap order?

The circumstances left the accused in a Catch-22: Yes, the wiretap evidence will be excluded if you can show that it was obtained by fraud or misrepresentation. No, you can't see the affidavits the police presented to the court to obtain the wiretap in order to determine if there was fraud or misrepresentation. Kafka could not have said it better.

Dersch's lawyers asked me to argue his case in the Supreme Court of Canada.

We had to get leave to appeal, because the B.C. Court of Appeal had been unanimous in upholding Dersch's conviction. On December 3, 1987, the Supreme Court of Canada granted leave to appeal.

The Supreme Court had already upheld, at the request of the media, a right of access in search warrant cases (that is, after the search has been carried out). In a 1982 case called *A.G.N.S. v. MacIntyre*, Justice Dickson, writing for the Supreme Court of Canada, concluded: "The presumption, however, is in favour of public access and the burden of contrary proof lies upon the person who would deny the exercise of the right."

Thus far had the law proceeded in search warrant cases. It established a prima facie right to disclosure in such cases (that is, after the warrant had been executed). We argued on behalf of Dersch that the reasoning in those cases applied to wiretap cases. To impose a requirement that there had to be a prima facie case of fraud or non-disclosure effectively nullified a defendant's right of access to the packet and the right to challenge the admissibility of the wiretap. Why should there be a presumption of disclosure in a search warrant case and not in a wiretap case?

Justice William Esson, writing for the Court of Appeal, had invoked the need for the maintenance of a complete armoury of detection in the war against crime, especially drug trafficking, and the urgency of protecting informers at all costs. He stated what he conceived to be "the facts of life": "One is that most accused persons, including some of those who are acquitted, committed the crimes charged against them."

That being so, the procedural safeguards for those accused of crimes could safely be dismissed. There is a kind of sturdy common sense about this approach. But it does not hold up on examination.

To start with, innocent persons do get charged with crimes they did not commit. Usually, they are found not guilty. We have learned since, in at least four famous Canadian murder cases—*Donald Marshall, David Milgaard, Guy Paul Morin* and *Thomas Sophonow*—that some of those convicted did not commit the crimes charged against them. In all four of these cases, men were found guilty of murder and had served lengthy sentences before it was discovered that they were innocent. It may well be, of course, that most persons arrested may be guilty of something. But what? Is it murder? Or is there an absence of the requisite intent? So is it instead manslaughter? Was there provocation? Was the killing in self-defence?

Consider trafficking in drugs. Did the accused purchase the drugs for his or her own use? Or did the accused purchase such a quantity that the purpose must have been for trafficking?

You have trials to figure these things out. And every trial starts with the presumption of innocence, even for drug traffickers. The words "drug trafficker" sound menacing. But most traffickers are addicts themselves, selling drugs to buy drugs.

In Canada, a fair trial is based on the idea of proof. The necessity for the police and the prosecution to prove their case is where our freedom lies: proof beyond a reasonable doubt. Proof is what our system is about. Those who are acquitted have not been proved guilty. These are not just stock phrases trotted out to impress visitors to the courthouse. Unless proof is required, where are you? And the police and the prosecution have to gather their proof lawfully. They can't obtain confessions by force or intimidation. They have to go to a judge to obtain a search warrant. And when they want to listen in on private conversations on the telephone, they have to persuade a judge that they are justified in engaging in electronic eavesdropping. When a person makes a telephone call, he ought to be able to assume that the state is not intercepting the call.

The necessity for obtaining *lawful* proof is a check on the power of the state—for the police are the agents of the state, agents authorized and equipped to enforce the law, and possessing a monopoly on the use of force in society.

In the Supreme Court of Canada, the issue would have to be squarely faced.

We argued that section 7 of the Charter of Rights applied. Section 7, as we have seen, provides that no one is to be deprived of liberty "except in accordance with the principles of fundamental justice." The right to a fair trial is guaranteed by section 7 of the Charter, and by section 8 of the Charter everyone is to be secure against unreasonable search and seizure. Thus, I argued, the wiretap provisions of the Code must be interpreted to permit a right of access to the packet. If a person charged with a crime has no means of determining whether material evidence has been obtained by a violation of the Charter, the trial is not a fair trial under section 7. And, in a wiretap case, unless the person has access to the packet containing the affidavits used to obtain the wiretap, he cannot know whether there has been a violation of Charter rights under section 8.

The case involved the perennial issue of means and ends. Once property is seized under a search warrant, you've got it; if it's incriminating nothing can change that. The same goes for conversations recorded by wiretap. If an accused has incriminated himself in a conversation on the telephone, well, there is the transcript; that's what he said; let's use it.

In Dersch's case, to justify its refusal to acknowledge a right of the accused to disclosure of the contents of the packet, the Court of Appeal invoked the war on crime, the ruthlessness of drug dealers, and so on. But how could the considerations relied on by Justice Esson be invoked to justify a ban on access to *all* authorizations? These arguments could equally be used to justify discarding other safeguards, including the presumption of innocence itself.

We argued that to formulate legal principles on such a footing could draw the law into an evil tendency. Such a proposition could be used to undermine every procedural safeguard in the Code and the Charter.

The judgement of Justice Esson meant that, though a person has the right to be secure against unreasonable searches and seizures, no such right can be enforced in the case of wiretaps. By this interpretation, what is secured is precisely the opposite of what the Charter intended. It is not the right of a person to be spared unreasonable search and seizure that is secured, but the right of law enforcement authorities to engage in the most prolific modern form of search and seizure (in other words, electronic surveillance) that is secured.

The reasons for disclosing to an accused the contents of the packet of affidavits used to obtain a wiretap and the reasons for disclosing to an accused affidavits used to obtain a search warrant are the same. But the invasion of privacy by means of electronic surveillance is a more pervasive intrusion on the accused's reasonable expectation of privacy. This explains why Parliament imposed an absolute rule of exclusion where the wiretap has been unlawfully obtained. In a search warrant case, even if the evidence has been obtained by a Charter violation, it may still be introduced in evidence unless to do so would, to use the words of section 24(2) of the Charter, "bring the administration of justice into disrepute."

Justice Esson ruled that denial of access to the packet was merely "technical." He said:

It follows, in my view, that refusal of the opportunity to demonstrate a defect in the proceedings leading to the authorization does not affect the right to make full answer and defence or the right to fair trial. It merely deprives the accused of an opportunity to have relevant evidence excluded on a technical ground. That opportunity is not a constitutionally protected right.

Of course, no one had argued that access to the affidavits would be unlimited. The identity of informers would have to be safeguarded. This protection could be done by editing. The practice of editing had been adopted generally in Canada, except in British Columbia. Justice Esson discussed judicial editing and suggested that it could not work. Yet it was in fact working in other provinces.

The Court of Appeal's approach entailed unwarranted judicial deference to the executive branch and to the law enforcement authorities. Not only did it compromise the right to a fair trial, the approach meant that there would be no judicial means to ensure that the police obey the law; no disincentive to law-breaking by the police.

Justice Esson argued the case for secrecy and immunity from scrutiny, and he argued it well. But to proceed on the footing that "most accused persons, including some of those who are acquitted, committed the crimes charged against them"; that the protection intended by Parliament against the abuse of power by law enforcement authorities should be nullified; that the accused should have no right to invoke the rule laid down regarding the absolute exclusion of wiretap evidence—these are the hallmarks of a police state.

When I was preparing my presentation to the court, I thought we had the better argument. In addition, we had the Ontario Court of Appeal on our side. In *R. v. Playford*, Justice Allan Goodman, writing for the Ontario Court of Appeal, held that denial of access to the packet is a denial of a fair trial under section 7 of the Charter. Justice Goodman said:

The essence of a fair trial includes as a fundamental principle that only evidence properly admissible in law will be admitted in evidence at trial. If relevant and material evidence is admitted by a trial judge where it should be excluded it cannot be said that an accused has had a fair trial. An accused is entitled to be tried according to law. That is a principle of fundamental justice. If Parliament does not wish to automatically exclude unlawfully intercepted communications as evidence it will be necessary for it to amend the provisions of section 178.16(1).

Parliament did amend the Code in 1993, making extensive changes to the rules relating to the interception of private communications. The admissibility of intercepts is now governed by section 24(2) of the Charter. Even if an order for an intercept is not lawfully made, the evidence may still be admissible if to do so would not bring the administration of justice into disrepute. But in Dersch's case, we were able to rely on the rule in section 178.16(1) in force at the time that evidence on a wiretap unlawfully obtained is absolutely inadmissible.

I thought we would be able to persuade the Supreme Court that Justice Esson had got it wrong. So would it be a slam dunk? I didn't think so. Judges are properly concerned that law enforcement should not be frustrated by defence lawyers spinning a web of restrictions that would unduly fetter the freedom of police action. The appeal to law and order may weigh too heavily on the side of order. We argued for the law.

There is such a thing as the right time to deliver an argument.

Usually, at trial, in a jury case, or a non-jury case, when the right moment presents itself, you proceed swiftly. The evidence has been heard. You know where you think it leads. You know the law you want the judge to apply. So you head over the top of the trenches.

There is always a point at which you sense that you are ready, that you must trust yourself in the flow of the argument to hit upon the phrase or emphasize the point that will carry the day. The task was to capture this moment in Dersch's case.

In 1991 and 1992 I went to India for the World Bank as deputy chairman of the Independent Review of the Sardar Sarovar Projects. Sardar Sarovar was then the world's largest water project. The review was to consider the adequacy of measures taken there for resettlement of the villagers in the Narmada Valley who were being flooded out and the adequacy of measures adopted for the protection of the environment. The task was a vast one, involving travelling to the construction sites, holding meetings in many rural villages and, together with Bradford Morse, the chairman, and Don Gamble and Hugh Brody, two veterans of my commissions in the Mackenzie Valley and Alaska, preparing a report for the president and directors of the World Bank. After our work in western India was complete, I was headed home to Vancouver. After flying from our headquarters in Baroda, I stayed overnight at a hotel in Bombay. I knew on the following day there would be the flight to Hong Kong and then across the Pacific to Vancouver. I was scheduled to argue a case in the Court of Appeal in Vancouver the day after my return. The case was an important case because millions of dollars were at stake. Of course, every case is important—important to the client, and that means for the lawyer it must always be an important case.

My client, Bob Lundy, a lumberman, phoned me in Bombay. He said, "Look, Tom, if you're exhausted after your work in India, go ahead and try to get an adjournment of the appeal. I want you at your best. If it means the appeal won't be heard until a year from now, don't worry. I'll understand."

I thought about it and said, "No, Bob, I'll be ready to go. This is the right time to do it."

Bob was general partner in a corporation together with a group of limited partners. He had been sued by the limited partners. The trial judge had held against him. It had cost him millions. The judgement ran to four hundred pages.

The case entailed a consideration of a vast panorama of evidence and law. But I had been reflecting on our approach to the appeal. Even while I was intensely involved in my work for the World Bank in India, my mind would revert to Bob's case. I knew exactly how I thought we could win the appeal. My partner Gary Nelson had been working with me, and he would be at my side in the Court of Appeal.

I reviewed the file on the flight home across the Pacific. A flight halfway around the world, and a not-very-good night's rest, together with jet lag, is not the best preparation. But in the Court of Appeal, I took a day and a half to present the case. All went well. I confess I was weary, to the point where once or twice while I was on my feet I thought it was possible I might faint. I simply held on tightly to the lectern and the moment passed.

Why not adjourn and wait a year? Because it would be like rewriting an examination paper. It would mean getting up the case again in a year, reviewing once more the vast record and the plethora of decided cases. It would be like eating regurgitated porridge.

We were successful. The Court of Appeal found in Bob Lundy's favour.

My point is that there can be such a thing as too much preparation.

This very thing had happened in the Dersch case. I argued the case on April 27, 1988.

I spent the first twenty minutes of my hour-long argument reading straight from the wiretap provisions of the Criminal Code. There had been a number of decided cases—the Court of Appeal for British Columbia had gone one way; the Ontario Court of Appeal the other—but if you subjected the provisions of the Code to a close reading, Parliament's intention, in light of the Charter, became clear enough: fairness required that the accused should have access to the packet. Sometimes, it is best simply to look at the statute itself, carefully, and not turn at once to the grand edifices of legal reasoning built on it.

A year passed. No judgement had come down. Chief Justice Antonio Lamer scheduled a new hearing for October 2, 1989.

The reason, as Chief Justice Lamer told us, was that some of the judges who had heard the argument the year before had retired, and new judges had been appointed in their place. He thought that the issue raised in the case was of the first importance, and the new judges should participate in the determination of the issue.

We reviewed the evidence and the arguments all over again. I believe I did a competent job in presenting the appeal. We won the case. But the appeal did not have the excitement of a year and a half before. I did, however, have what I believed was an approach that would shed new light on the case, or at least give it a graphic dimension it would not otherwise have.

On October 2, 1989, tumultuous events outside the courtroom formed a backdrop to the hearing in the Supreme Court. The argument took place while freedom was arriving in Eastern Europe. The Berlin Wall didn't come down until November, the following month, but an appeal could be made based on events there: all over Eastern Europe the grim hand of the secret police was being lifted.

Law might now accompany order in the region. Many of these countries were looking to Canada's Charter of Rights and to Canadian lawyers and judges for help in refashioning their legal systems.

I urged that events in Eastern Europe showed that there the idea of the rule of law had not been allowed to die. I pointed out that law reformers in Poland, Hungary and the Soviet Union were seeking to make the law enforcement authorities accountable, to replace the rule of secrecy with the rule of law.

I believe these were not idle musings. Ensuring that law enforcement authorities must play by the same rules as the citizenry is basic to our system. We ought not to sanction a regime where there is no accountability, a regime that substitutes the rule of secrecy for the rule of law.

On November 22, 1990, the court handed down its judgement. They had unanimously decided to allow Dersch's appeal.

Dersch's case was of signal importance in the unfolding of the law. The court removed the previous restrictions on the accused's ability to gain access to the packet of affidavits. There is now a right to have the packet opened for the twin purposes of making full answer and defence under section 7 of the Charter and to contest the reasonableness of the search and seizure under section 8 of the Charter.

Justice John Sopinka, writing for the court, agreed with Justice Goodman in the Ontario Court of Appeal in *Playford*. He went on:

The accused is placed in this dilemma in virtually every case. If placing him or her in this dilemma is a denial of the right to make full answer and defence, then in every case in which access is denied, the accused is denied the right to make full answer and defence. Consequently, there would be in every such case a breach of s. 7 of the *Charter*, which includes among its principles of fundamental justice the right to make full answer and defence. If the restricted access cases are right in their interpretation of the section, then Parliament has authorized a procedure which uniformly results in a breach of the *Charter*. It follows that either the section is unconstitutional or the interpretation of the restrictive access cases cannot stand . . . It is fundamental to this view that denial of access constitutes a denial to make full answer and defence.

Then he dealt with Justice Esson's contention that the issue was merely technical.

The presumption of innocence requires the prosecution to prove that the accused is guilty beyond a reasonable doubt. This must be done by admissible evidence . . . Under s. 8 of the Charter, the accused has acquired a constitutional right to be secure against unreasonable search or seizure. Because an unlawful search will be an unreasonable one, s. 8 also confers on the accused the right to challenge the lawfulness of a search or seizure of which the accused is the target. That right would be hollow if it did not permit access to the sealed packet.

What happened to Dersch? In the end, the prosecution—for reasons they never disclosed—was not prepared to divulge the contents of the packet. The charges against Dersch were stayed.

The public often thinks of criminal cases as a struggle to find a loophole in the law—to discover some technicality that will allow guilty persons to wriggle out of convictions. But these are not loopholes. They are the outcome of the application of fundamental principles. These principles may be asserted on behalf of accused persons who do not necessarily attract our sympathy. But they are principles that exist to protect us all.

9 *Linda Macdonald*

In OCTOBER 1988, Linda Macdonald came to see me. She was a Shirley MacLaine look-alike, intelligent, vivacious, altogether charming. But Linda had a harrowing story to tell: As a young woman she had been a victim of brainwashing experiments at the Allan Memorial Institute (AMI), a psychiatric hospital at McGill University in Montreal. The experiments were spearheaded by Dr. Ewan Cameron, the institute's director. Admitted to AMI at twenty-five for postpartum depression, Linda had been the subject of experiments intended to establish that "brainwashing" was an achievable goal. The experiment succeeded: in Linda's case she emerged from AMI without any recollection of the first quarter century of her life. She had lost the memory of her past. All the signposts—the stored knowledge that enables us to know who we are—were taken from her.

Linda Macdonald wasn't the only victim of these experiments at AMI. Initiated by the American Central Intelligence Agency (CIA) but conducted in Canada, the experiments had ruined the lives of scores of patients. The story goes back to the early 1950s, when the United States and its allies, including Canada, had sent troops to defend South Korea after it had been invaded by the Communist regime in North Korea. The CIA's interest in the experiments at AMI lay in duplicating the brainwashing they believed the Chinese Communists, who had come into the war on the side of North Korea, were conducting on captive American servicemen. The CIA obtained the co-operation of the Canadian government and funded the research at AMI throughout the 1950s. In the CIA, the project was designated MK-Ultra.

As for AMI personnel, they were happy to organize and conduct the experiments. Dr. Ewan Cameron was a formidable figure in Canadian psychiatry; as head of AMI, he, logically, should be in charge of the experiments. After the CIA funding ended, the government of Canada continued to provide Cameron and AMI with financial support for the work.

News of what had gone on at AMI began to emerge after some years. The government of Canada provided financial aid for nine Canadian victims of the AMI experiments to sue the CIA in the American courts. This financial aid was on the footing that the CIA ought properly to have supervised Cameron's experiments. But Linda Macdonald had entered AMI in 1963, when the CIA was no longer funding the experiments. Canada's Department of National Health and Welfare was, however, still funding them. Any suit by Linda would have to be brought against the government of Canada. But Canada was not prepared to admit any liability for its own part in funding the experiments.

Why had Canada decided it had no legal responsibility? The federal government had commissioned a report by George Cooper, a Nova Scotia lawyer and former MP. He empanelled three psychiatrists as consultants and investigated what had happened at AMI. Cooper's report, made public in 1986, found that the federal government had no legal liability. Cooper wrote:

In my formal opinion on this matter, I concluded that the federal government has neither legal nor moral responsibility towards former patients at the Allan Memorial Institute. This opinion rested on the ground that *Cameron's research procedures were, in general, within acceptable bounds when judged by the standards of the day.* The opinion remains valid, even if it could be shown in the case of a particular patient or patients that Cameron transgressed the bounds of the acceptable, because there was *no knowledge on the part of Canadian government officials of any improper conduct,* and because their procedures in processing grant applications were fully adequate [emphasis added].

When Linda Macdonald came to see me in 1988, the AMI horror story was already well known. Books had been written about it. There had been TV documentaries. There was the ongoing lawsuit in the U.S. There was the Cooper Report. In a sense, everyone knew all about it. But one question had never been answered or even tested in court: *Did* the federal government have any legal responsibility? Cooper said no; the federal government said no. Linda Macdonald thought otherwise.

Linda told her story to me and to Ron Shulman ("Ike" Shulman's son), who had joined our practice. She had been born in Vancouver in 1937. When she was four, her family moved to Ottawa, where her father worked for the National Film Board and the CBC. Linda went to school in Ottawa. She was an accomplished classical singer and, from the ages of twelve through eighteen, together with her sister, she won the local Kiwanis Festival musical competition each year.

She met her husband when both were students at Glebe Collegiate in

Ottawa; they were married in 1955, when Linda was eighteen. They started a family two years later. While her husband studied engineering at Queen's, Princeton and Stanford Research Institute, Linda cared for their young family in married students' quarters. She was happy, energetic and devoted to her children. She had five children, including twins. After the birth of the twins, Linda collapsed. Her family doctor sent her to AMI to be treated for postpartum depression. Her medical records indicated that at the time schizophrenia was suspected, but this illness was mere conjecture.

When she entered AMI, Linda had signed a general consent to treatment. But now, ostensibly for the purpose of treatment for schizophrenia, she was to be subjected to a series of experiments intended to serve the interests of the West in its struggle against Communism and, by the perverted lights of Dr. Ewan Cameron, the advance of psychiatric science. At AMI, the injunction "Do no harm," to which all physicians are expected to subscribe, was no longer observed. But the public didn't know. Linda didn't know. Her family doctor didn't know.

The experiments at AMI had their genesis at a meeting at the Ritz-Carlton Hotel in Montreal held on June 1, 1951. This meeting was to lead to a co-operative effort by the U.S., Canada and the United Kingdom in defence-related research into problems of the mind. The defence ministries of the three countries wished to focus on brainwashing techniques in the context of the Cold War and the Korean War. They were concerned about the "totalitarian advantage" in brainwashing. Present at the meeting were Dr. Omond Solandt, first chairman of the Defence Research Board of Canada; Donald Hebb, chairman of the Department of Psychology at McGill University; Dr. Travis Dancey, head of psychiatry at Montreal's Queen Mary Veterans' Hospital; Sir Henry Tizard, British physicist and wartime adviser to the government of the United Kingdom; Dr. James Tyhurst, a Vancouver psychiatrist; and Dr. Carl Haskins and Commander R. J. Williams, representing the CIA.

According to the minutes, those present wished "to investigate the general phenomenon of change of idea and attitude with particular respect to individuals and insofar as this may become an important item in psychological warfare"—a fairly innocuous description of the project. But how was this investigation to be done? One way, according to the minutes, involved a "chemical approach through the use of depressing drugs of one kind or another" and experimental isolation of various forms "for the purpose of placing individuals in such a position psychologically that they would [be] susceptible to the implantation of new or different ideas." Not so innocuous.

These notions of brainwashing were widespread at the time, not only in psychiatry but in popular culture. In 1962, a film called *The Manchurian Candidate* was released, starring Frank Sinatra. It was about a captured American soldier who had been brainwashed by the Communists while a prisoner of war in Korea and programmed to act as a Communist agent in the U.S. upon his release. The public hadn't the slightest notion whether brainwashing was a real threat. It is hard to know whether the CIA did. Frank Sinatra was, after all, portraying a fictitious character.

In any event, the procedure discussed at meetings at the Ritz-Carlton—drugs, isolation, fatigue, confession—prefigured the experiments to which Linda and others would be subjected at AMI. Dr. Ewan Cameron was recruited to run the program. A man of impressive bearing and reputation, Dr. Cameron was at the time the pre-eminent figure in Canadian psychiatry. He had served as president of the Canadian Psychiatric Association and the American Psychiatric Association, and in 1963 he became the founding president of the World Psychiatric Association. Cameron was chair of the Department of Psychiatry in the Faculty of Medicine at McGill. The AMI was the psychiatric wing of the Royal Victoria Hospital, the teaching hospital of McGill's Faculty of Medicine.

Then, as now, there were competing schools of psychiatric thought. One, the "physical" school, regarded mental illness as physical in origin and believed that it could be treated by physical therapy. Another, the "psychoanalytical" school, placed reliance on psychological therapy. Dr. Cameron was a proponent of the physical school.

According to the Cooper Report, Cameron's theory was that mental illness came about through learning "incorrect" ways of responding to the world. The pathways of the brain therefore developed a set of "learned responses" that were not socially acceptable and resulted in the patient being classified as mentally ill. Cameron relied on evidence that persons subject to convulsions of the brain did not become mentally ill. He believed that these naturally occurring convulsions cleared the brain pathways and eliminated the "incorrect" thought processes. So he thought that if he subjected mentally ill patients to artificially induced convulsions through electroconvulsive therapy (ECT), the brain pathways would be broken up and the patient's illness relieved.

Cameron was not alone in believing this. But Cameron's experiments extended well beyond existing psychiatric frontiers. He decided to apply massive electroshock therapy, twenty to thirty or even forty times as intense as normal ECT, until the patient's brain had been "depatterned." Then, through a process he called "psychic driving," the brain would be "repatterned." Cameron believed that he could rewire the brain.

But, of course, he had to have subjects for his experiments. These he found among the patients admitted to AMI. Patients suffering from schizophrenia qualified as mentally ill. Cameron's patients would be placed in a state of prolonged sleep. To do this required the use of barbiturates in heavy doses. This drug treatment was accompanied by massive electroshock treatments. When the patients had been reduced to a childlike state, they would be placed on drugs to ensure they remained immobilized. Sensory deprivation was also used to achieve depatterning. Once in this state, they would be subjected to psychic driving.

Psychic driving consisted of messages played on tape recorders and repeated thousands of times to patients by means of pillow microphones and stenographic headphones. At this stage, too, drugs were used to keep the patient receptive.

Cameron was determined to find a cure for mental illness, to win the Nobel Prize for Medicine. His ambition converged with the desire of the CIA to achieve what they believed the Chinese Communists had done. In his pursuit of a cure for mental illness, Cameron lost sight completely of the injury he was causing to patients. Memory deficit, sometimes slight, sometimes substantial, had often been the result of ECT. But Cameron's experiments entailed a grave risk of complete memory loss.

Cameron's patients were entitled to know that they were the subject of experiments. So also were their families. They were entitled to know that Cameron was working not only on their behalf but also for the CIA—that he wasn't necessarily looking to their own best interests where those conflicted with those of his paymasters. They were entitled to know that the treatment was not necessarily therapeutic, that the relentless logic of the Cold War was the motivation for the treatment. Yet they were never informed.

In Linda's case, there was a further problem. She was treated as if she were schizophrenic, but AMI had no evidence of schizophrenia in Linda's case. She also had the additional misfortune to arrive at AMI after Cameron had begun to appreciate that his methods had failed in repatterning the brain. In Linda's case, therefore, he intensified the program.

Linda had been admitted to AMI on March 25, 1963. Her "treatment" began on May 1, 1963. It was to consist of four months of brainwashing experiments. Under Dr. Cameron's direction, she was subjected to over one hundred massive electroconvulsive shocks, untested combinations of barbiturates and antipsychotic drugs, and put into a drug-induced sleep for at least eighty-six days.

This course of treatment was embarked upon *without a diagnosis*. No one at AMI thought to wait until they found out what, if anything, was wrong with Linda. The important thing was that she would do as a subject for Dr. Cameron's experiments.

The absence of any affirmative diagnosis of schizophrenia in Linda's case can be seen from the notes of the physicians made at the time Linda's treatment began and at the time, four months later, of her discharge. Dr. Robert Cleghorn, on May 6, 1963, one week after Linda had begun her "cure," stated that no firm diagnosis had been reached.

Considerable time was spent in discussing this case, and no firm conclusion was arrived at as far as the diagnosis. Certainly she shows schizophrenic elements, but has been under very considerable stress with her five young children. A decision was made last week for her to have depatterning treatment, and on May 1st she had her first Page Russell [electroshock treatments]. She has had six since then, making a total of seven to date.

The reference to Page-Russell is significant. Standard electroconvulsive therapy (ECT) entailed administering up to 110 volts through the patient's brain to produce a generalized seizure. The Page-Russell consisted of an initial jolt of 150 volts for one second. This jolt was followed by five shocks of a hundred volts administered during the primary convulsion triggered by the initial jolt: the aim was to produce multiple convulsions.

On September 5, 1963, one week before Linda's discharge, Dr. Cameron noted:

In working over her case on April 5, 1963, the psychologists felt that the general impression was that of a notable hysterical overlay to an early schizophrenic pathology. *Our examinations of her clinically, however, have failed thus far to show any evidence of schizophrenia. Due to the dangers of neglecting a possible schizophrenia, we put her through extensive therapy* [emphasis added].

Cameron, still without a diagnosis of schizophrenia, was justifying "extensive therapy," that is, prolonged drug-induced sleep, intensive electroshock, sensory deprivation, depatterning and psychic driving—all for a non-existent condition.

Linda's consent was not obtained for any of these "treatments."

As Anne Collins wrote in *In the Sleep Room,* a book that tells the story of Cameron's experiments:

Cameron did not have either the patience or the ability to accept the fact that symptom relief for certain kinds of patients may take a significant time. Consequently, at the Allan, patients who were not severely disturbed did not receive a cautious and careful therapy; instead they were subjected to extreme physical procedures designed to force an entry into their minds by breaking down their defences.

On September 12, 1963, Linda was discharged. She had regressed to a child-like state. She had to be toilet trained. She could no longer read or write. She did not know her husband and her children. She could not look after herself or her family. Now twenty-six, she had lost those years—that life—forever. There was no counselling, no further contact and no follow-up plan. She had been "depat-terned" and then abandoned.

Linda's medical record at AMI contains repeated references to increased epileptiform activity during electroencephalogram (EEG) monitoring of Linda through the depatterning process. Three months after leaving AMI, Linda began having intense seizures and was admitted to the Ottawa Civic Hospital. When, in January 1964, she was again hospitalized following the onset of seizures, nobody suspected that her illness might be traced to the "treatment" she had received at AMI. It was only when, in June 1964, she attempted suicide, that she was diag-nosed as an epileptic and received medication that brought her seizures to an end.

Her life continued its downward spiral. She had suffered a complete change of personality; now she was moody, opinionated, insecure and, not surprisingly, terrified of becoming ill again. She had another child in 1966, but eventually her marriage broke up and she lost contact with her children. She supported herself by singing in nightclubs, moving between cities in the United States and Canada before settling in 1978 in Vancouver.

Over the years, her parents and friends helped Linda to piece together frag-ments of her lost past. She had to learn again how to read, to write, to cook. Fear was her constant companion, fear that she would succumb to the unnamed "ill-ness" that had already cost her so much.

The brainwashing had worked. A woman had, through depatterning, lost all memory of her own life. It was for Cameron success of a kind.

On the face of it, you would think that AMI, Cameron, and Health and Welfare Canada should be responsible under the law for Linda's misfortune. But who knew the full story? Linda didn't know that her plight was the outcome of the machinations of the CIA and the government of Canada, and that Canada's leading psychiatrist had been conducting experiments on her to advance the interests of the West in the Cold War. Then, on January 16, 1983, two decades later, Linda read in the Vancouver *Province* of Dr. Cameron's brainwashing experiments at the Allan Memorial Institute. Only then did the first glimpse of what had happened to her begin to take shape in her mind.

In a letter written in 1987, Linda described what occurred:

I have no memory of my first life; the only life I remember began sometime in 1964. I was told then and many times since that I had been an "acute schizophrenic" when I was admitted to the Allan Memorial Institute as one of Ewan Cameron's patients in March, 1963.

I mention the above to try to communicate some measure of the confusion, the disbelief, and the horror I experienced when I finally fully realized that I had never been "sick" . . . that I had been duped, criminally abused, experimented upon and left to fumble my way through this second life still believing that I had been and probably still was a "sick" woman. The first real sense that perhaps I had been a guinea pig in experiments paid for by the c.i.a. began for me in January, 1983. I sought legal counsel because I did not know my rights. I secured my medical file but I could not find anyone to translate it for me. Reading it myself did nothing to dissuade my original belief that I had been as sick as I had been told I was. The c.i.a. was something I used to watch unfold in t.v. drama. Part of me sensed, in 1984 and 1985, that what I was reading in the newspapers and hearing on t.v. concerning the c.i.a. and Cameron's victims . . . concerned me and that I should be doing something about it. Most of me, for those years, could not "take hold" of the moment. I needed all my energy to maintain emotional stability, my life and to keep my job.

What had happened at AMI was appalling. But it was routinely defended as accepted psychiatric practice at the time. You can't, it was said, judge what occurred at AMI in the 1950s and 1960s by the standards of the present day. Moreover, even if there had been negligence, malpractice or worse, how could you hold Canada at fault? Canada's minister of justice, Ramon Hnatyshyn, refused to make any payment by way of compensation to any of the persons such as Linda Macdonald who had been victimized while Canada was funding AMI. He relied on the Cooper Report, which absolved Canada of any culpability.

When the federal government had provided $20,000 to each of the nine former AMI patients suing the U.S. government in the U.S. Federal District Court, Joe Clark, Canada's foreign minister, said it was "to help cover their legal expenses and as a mark of our continuing support." Linda Macdonald had by this time hired a lawyer, who asked for similar assistance to enable Linda to bring a suit in Canada. But Mary Dawson, assistant deputy minister of justice, wrote on May 16, 1988:

Unlike the c.i.a., the Canadian government did not act secretly in funding [AMI]. Also, the funding [by the government of Canada] was provided in the normal course of supporting medical activities. In addition the Canadian government has made great efforts to investigate and make public all information regarding its involvement and no basis has been shown for a payment by the Canadian government.

So Canada was prepared to help Canadians sue the CIA in the American courts, but Canada did not want to encourage anyone to sue in Canada. Canada was innocent. And it had the Cooper Report to back up its verdict.

Thus Linda's story to the day in October 1988 when she came to our office. What were we to do?

Our contention would have to be that this story was a case of medical malpractice. But there were complications occasioned by questions of jurisdiction and limitations. Cameron had died in 1964. The CIA was out of the picture because it had ceased funding the experiments before Linda was admitted to AMI. So we couldn't sue the CIA. We could sue AMI but only in the Quebec courts. We could sue the federal government but only in the Federal Court of Canada.

One of Dr. Cameron's patients, Mary Morrow, had already sued AMI in Quebec. In *Morrow v. Royal Victoria Hospital and the Estate of Ewan Cameron*, the Superior Court of Quebec dismissed her claim. At the time Cooper wrote his report, he relied on the judgement of the trial judge in *Morrow* dismissing her claim. But Mary Morrow was herself, at the time she agreed to treatment at AMI, a psychiatrist in training. She interned with Dr. Cameron at AMI, and she apparently understood the risks she was taking. The case of Linda Macdonald was not at all similar. Mary Morrow's case was, however, an unfortunate precedent.

We had obtained an opinion from a Montreal law firm that under Quebec's statute of limitations time had run out for bringing a suit. We could, however, sue Canada in the Federal Court, if we could show that Canada at the time had a duty to supervise and monitor the experiments at AMI. Our case would have to be that Canada had failed in its duty. But there, too, we would face a limitations problem: Canada could argue that Quebec's statute of limitations applied to any federal claim arising in Quebec. Canada would argue that time had run out. Nevertheless, we decided that a lawsuit in the Federal Court was Linda's best hope.

Canada, of course, relied on the Cooper Report. We would have to study that document. Cooper had been a Conservative MP in the government of Brian Mulroney—perhaps not the best choice to conduct an investigation into the liability of the government he had supported in the House of Commons. But the events at AMI had occurred long before the Mulroney government came to office. There was no reason to doubt the impartiality of Cooper's report.

The Cooper Report had dealt with two main issues. The first was whether Dr. Ewan Cameron was guilty of malpractice. Cooper had found there was no malpractice, that in the 1950s and 1960s Cameron's methods had been acceptable in Canadian psychiatry. The second issue was if there had been malpractice, did the government of Canada, as the granting agency, have any legal responsibility to Cameron's victims? Cooper's report answered this question, like the first, in the negative.

Nevertheless, as Ron Shulman and I studied the case, it seemed very, very odd. How had psychiatry reached the point that experiments conducted on unwitting patients, with catastrophic results, could be justified as conforming to reasonable psychiatric practice?

We decided to start at the beginning.

The Hippocratic Oath goes back to 460 B.C. It binds physicians to the following promise:

I will follow that system of regimen which, according to my ability and judgement, I consider for the benefit of my patients, and abstain from whatever is deleterious and mischievous.

The French medical philosopher Claude Bernard wrote in 1865: "The principle of medical and surgical morality, therefore, consists in never performing on man an experiment which might be harmful to him to any extent, even though the result might be highly advantageous to science."

Out of the Nuremburg trials, arising from Nazi doctors' experiments on Jewish prisoners in the Second World War, emerged the Nuremburg Code. The code established the patient's right to be informed and the requirement of voluntary consent for experimental or unorthodox treatment. From Nuremberg onward, that requirement was, or should have been, in every psychiatric practitioner's mind. In fact, it was widely recognized in uncodified form long before the Nuremberg trials. The Nuremberg Code merely formalized it.

In 1949, the World Medical Association adopted an international code of medical ethics recognizing the primacy of the patient, the necessity for the patient's right to treatment to take precedence over experiments even when such experiments may be believed to be in the national interest or for the benefit of humankind, and the duty to abstain from procedures that bring harm to the patient.

Then there is the United Nations Covenant on Civil and Political Rights, adopted by the U.N. General Assembly in 1958. The covenant provides:

No one shall be subjected to torture or to cruel, inhuman or degrading treatment or punishment. In particular, no one shall be subjected without his free consent to medical or scientific experimentation.

All these exhortations to the medical profession were well known and well understood *before* Linda was admitted to AMI. Dr. Cameron deviated radically from these principles. He was engaged in experimentation. The risk of harm to the patient was obvious, the outcome for many of his victims disastrous. And he had not informed any of them or obtained their consent.

Dr. Cameron might be dead, but we had his own evidence of his methods.

In Cameron's grant application filed with the Department of National Health and Welfare, dated January 21, 1957, entitled innocently enough "An Application for a Grant to Study Effects upon Human Behaviour of the Repetition of Verbal Signals," he described his attempts to establish lasting changes in a patient's behaviour using verbal signals, which, he wrote, *"in the most successful case* has produced behavioural changes lasting up to two months" [emphasis added]. He described his method in some detail:

The procedure requires:
i.   The breaking down of on-going patterns of the patient's behaviour by means of particularly intensive electroshocks (depatterning).
ii. The intensive repetition (16 hours a day for 6 or 7 days) of the prearranged verbal signal.
iii. During this period of intensive repetition the patient is kept in partial sensory isolation.
iv. Repression of the driving period is carried out by putting the patient, after the conclusion of the period, in continuous sleep for 7 to 10 days.

Dr. Cameron's grant application, expressed in clinical language, does not foretell, except in merest outline, the dreadful experimentation to which Linda would be subjected. But he did use the tell-tale word "depatterning." Depatterning was a coinage used in the literature on brainwashing. It had not, however, found its way into accepted psychiatric literature.

Then we had the records of AMI, recording the observations of Dr. Cameron and his associates. These observations, too, are couched in clinical language. But the detachment of the observers at AMI cannot disguise the horror of Linda's ordeal.

The depatterning took place in three stages: In the first stage, there was some memory loss, but the patient was still oriented with respect to time, place and self. In the second stage, space and time were lost, provoking great anxiety in the patient, who was severely incapacitated. Then there was the third stage, when the patient was reduced to a childlike state.

By June 13, six weeks after her treatment began, Linda had been brought to the third stage. The doctor's notes describe Linda in the third stage of de-patterning: "June 25, 1963: She has been on sleep for 28 days. She has had 67 Page Russells as of today." Page and Russell, developers of the treatment, admin-istered it once a day, occasionally twice, but only in the most severe cases. In Linda's case, even though no mental illness had been diagnosed, Page-Russells were administered twice, sometimes three times a day.

On June 26, after Linda had been thirteen days in the third stage, it was noted: "According to the nurse's notes, the p.t. [patient] shows the best third stage features. She is completely disoriented and needs complete nursing assis-tance. However, she swallows well and can drink fluids well. She is incontinent of both urine and feces."

On July 4, Dr. Cameron himself made these notes:

She has had her 47th day of sleep. She has had 76 ECTS, 68 of which have been Page Russell. She is having an Offner [the machine that delivers electroconvulsive treatment].

She passed into her turbulent stage about 2 days ago, and we are now beginning to increase her sleep medication in order to prevent excessive turbulence and a ten-dency to relapse . . . on June 12th, after she had 15 days of sleep and 47 Page Russells, there was clear epileptiform activity . . . on June 25th, at which time the p.t. [patient] had had 67 Page Russells and had 28 days of sleep, there was some increase in the amount of epileptiform activity.

Some further notes of Dr. Cameron's on the same day, July 4, reveal how per-nicious the treatment was: "Reviewing the EEG's, we find on March 29th, 1963 (her admission EEG) that there was no evidence of focal or cerebral damage or epileptiform activity." So Linda, when she entered AMI, had no brain damage. She did not have schizophrenia. She did not have epilepsy. But, by administer-ing the Page-Russells, AMI had managed to induce epilepsy. This, of course, was Cameron's fundamental theory: artificially induced convulsions would clear the brain pathways, thus relieving a patient's mental illness. Cameron had not the slightest evidence that his theory could be made to work with persons who were mentally ill. In Linda's case, of course, there was no evidence of mental ill-ness to begin with.

Having observed Linda's disintegration, Dr. Cameron kept on. On July 16, 1963, he noted:

She has now had 49 days of sleep.

She has had 88 ECT, 68 being Page Russell. The last ECT was today, and she is running on a daily Offner . . . She is quite turbulent. Her speech is very slurred.

She shows no definite evidence of delusional ideas . . . In view of the fact that her EEG shows an increase in epileptiform activity, we are going to reduce the ECT rate to every second day.

The epileptiform activity revealed in Linda's EEG was reported to be still increasing by the last week of July 1963. In August, the rate of this activity began to decline, presumably due to the reduction in the use of Page-Russell ECTs. According to Dr. Cameron's notes, there were no further Page-Russells after July 14, but ordinary ECT continued: Linda received her one hundred and second ECT on September 10.

Linda's medical records indicated that throughout her stay at AMI, she was on chlorpromazine, also known as largactil, an anti-psychotic drug prescribed for schizophrenia and other psychotic disorders. In addition to chlorpromazine, a variety of barbiturates and sleep-inducing drugs were administered. These included, while Linda was under Dr. Cameron's care, chloralol, Nembutal, Seconal, veronal, phenergan, artane, beminal and sodium amytal. This was an amazing combination of drugs for that time or any time.

Linda had been "depatterned." Now she was to be subjected to "psychic driving" to implant new thoughts and ideas, to rewire her brain.

All of these procedures were carried on while Linda was asleep. We are not certain how long Linda was in what was called, with macabre understatement, the "sleep room." By August 9, the doctors reported that she had had seventy-three sleep days. Two weeks later, on August 22, Dr. Cameron noted, "She is now entirely all asleep." Eighty-six days of sleep up to that point, but for how many days after? The medical records were silent.

In *In the Sleep Room*, Peggy Edwards, head nurse on the ward, is quoted:

And in the psychic driving—these people were put to sleep, of course, and they had this combination of chlorpromazine and barbiturates, this cocktail, this whole big cocktail. And with that they were given ECT's, and the Page-Russell ECT's, and the button was often pressed several times, and they were given Page-Russell's at least a couple of times a day until the point that they were confused in all three spheres [time, place and self]. Which is totally horrifying to think back on.

There was an enormous difference between the standard dose for therapeutic electroshock and the dose used by Dr. Cameron. According to Dr. Leon Salzman, who testified in the U.S. District Court in the case brought by nine of Dr. Cameron's victims: "The standard dose for therapeutic electroshock is 110 volts, once a day . . . *Dr. Cameron used a 20–40 times higher dosage, three times a day"* [emphasis added]. Sir Aubrey Lewis, for many years a leader in psychiatric research in England, told Dr. Robert Cleghorn as early as 1957 that Cameron's depatterning treatments were "barbaric." Dr. Cleghorn, who succeeded Cameron as director of AMI, in his private papers described Cameron's practice as "therapy gone wild with scant criteria."

But Cleghorn's was, in truth, too generous an assessment. It was not "therapy gone wild." There was no true therapeutic purpose; that is, no purpose centred on the well-being of the patient. It was, in fact, experimentation "gone wild."

After Cameron left AMI in August 1964, Dr. Cleghorn, as the new director, immediately reduced the frequency of the ECTs to be administered to patients. In due course, Cleghorn brought depatterning to a complete halt. But it was too late for Linda Macdonald.

The conclusion of the Cooper Report was that Cameron acted "incautiously, but not irresponsibly." Yet Cooper followed with this sentence:

Most psychiatrists did not make the mistake he did in developing and applying the depatterning and psychic driving techniques, but this was out of a sense of caution in the face of the highly intrusive and extremely intensive nature of the treatments.

Nevertheless, Cooper took the view that Dr. Cameron's practices were "within acceptable bounds when judged by the standards of the day." How could this be, unless the 1950s and 1960s had been the dark ages of Canadian psychiatry? Even if Dr. Cameron's experiments were in conformity with Canadian standards of psychiatry, those same standards must have been altogether inconsistent with the standards proclaimed by the international psychiatric community.

Cooper had relied on three consultants, whose advice he published with his report. Dr. F. Grunberg was a professor of psychiatry at the University of Montreal. Grunberg summarized Cameron's work:

The theoretical framework of Dr. Cameron is quite weak and somewhat naive based on an oversimplified extrapolation of neurophysiological concepts to a complex behavioural level.

Also from a methodological standpoint the testing of the therapeutic value of this treatment was totally uncontrolled based essentially on biased subjective evaluation and on irrelevant pseudo-objective parameters such as movies taken in four different and standardized situations, a battery of conditioned reflex tests and the use of the plethsymograph to measure skin resistance.

By today's standards this was bad science with heavy reliance on gadgetry rather than on reflective scientific thinking.

Grunberg's assessment was devastating. Did he therefore proceed to the logical conclusion that it was "bad science" at the time? No. He referred to "the standards of the fifties." Cameron's treatment of his patients was excusable given those standards. Nevertheless, Grunberg said: "I personally disagree and disagreed then with the *intrusiveness and lack of scientific rigor* of [Cameron's] work" [emphasis added].

Grunberg concluded: "In my opinion in spite of all the media noise there is no evidence that psychic driving did any irreparable harm to patients who voluntarily submitted to it. The Canadian Government should not bear any moral responsibility for supporting a project that was essentially therapeutic in its aims." Although Grunberg acquitted Cameron, and found that no one had suffered "irreparable harm," there is no indication that he ever examined any of Cameron's patients. His statement that, notwithstanding all that had gone before, the project was "essentially therapeutic in its aims" was nonsense. Linda Macdonald did not voluntarily submit to Cameron's quackery; it seemed unlikely that anyone else had done so. Moreover, Grunberg's dismissal of the suffering of Cameron's victims was telling.

After the publication of the Cooper Report, evidence emerged in the U.S. District Court that Dr. Grunberg was a man with a history of countenancing the abuse of patients. When he was deputy commissioner of mental retardation in New York, he had acquiesced in the Willowbrook State School experiments. At Willowbrook, a state-run institution in New Jersey, beginning in the 1950s, mentally retarded children were injected with a live hepatitis virus and then with an experimental vaccine. Dr. Grunberg acknowledged that, although he did not come on the scene until 1967, he knew that these experiments were going on and should have brought them to a halt on ethical grounds.

Q What did you do?
A I did nothing. I didn't stop it. I let it continue. We only stopped it after the second Willowbrook scandal came public.
Q Now, you say you should have stopped because it was not a direct benefit to the children.
A Yes.
Q Is the other part of it, not only was it not a direct benefit, but it had a serious potential for harm?
A Yes, it had a potential for harm. He was injecting an illness.

Because Dr. Grunberg had a previous history of ignoring the use of captive patients, without their consent, for experimental purposes, how could his clean bill of health for Dr. Cameron possibly be accepted?

Cooper's other two psychiatric advisers came to their task without the flawed credentials of Grunberg. But their analyses were not convincing.

Dr. Ian McDonald was dean of medicine at the University of Saskatchewan. Dr. McDonald, in his report, reviewed the medical principles applicable to human experimentation. His touchstone was the findings of a working group established in 1977 by the Medical Research Council of Canada, which proposed guidelines for research carried on in Canadian institutions by Canadian researchers. McDonald said:

I would point out only that this report established that the *sine qua non* for all research involving human subjects is that it be scientifically valid. "Without scientific merit, placing human beings at risk to perform an experiment cannot ethically be justified" . . . In my opinion, had these guidelines been in place at the time of Cameron's work in the Allan Memorial, I have serious doubts as to whether he would have been able to proceed with his work. Certainly not in the fashion described in his papers.

So what Cameron had done in the 1960s would not have been acceptable in 1977.

McDonald went on:

I believe it is now quite clearly recognized that the responsibility for ensuring the quality (both from scientific and ethical standpoints) of research involving human beings lies jointly with the investigator, the institution in which he works, and the granting agency that supports his research activity. In my opinion, all three could and would be currently held accountable for research projects that do not meet the current standards of research practice in Canada.

This statement was helpful, as far as it went. In our case, the "granting agency" was the Department of National Health and Welfare. But McDonald, writing in 1986, relied on standards established in 1977, standards he did not think applied to AMI in 1963.

Cooper's third expert, Dr. F.H. Lowy, wrote as dean of medicine at the University of Toronto. He also acquitted Cameron, though he acknowledged his own skepticism at the time (he had worked for Cameron as an intern). Dr. Lowy said:

There can be no doubt that, in retrospect, Cameron's more extreme experimental treatments were misguided and ineffective, certainly in the long run. Controversial even at the time, they may have produced short term benefits for some patients but it is also quite possible that they resulted in emotional and, perhaps, organic damage to many others. I do not believe that any of these treatments has survived anywhere in the world.

The key paragraph of Dr. Lowy's report to Cooper read:

It is not useful, in my view, to evaluate the use of procedures in the late 1940s, the 1950s and the early 1960s by the application of today's standards. Certainly, none of these treatments could be used today in a major teaching hospital and they would not be supported by a responsible granting agency.

Lowy went on to say, however:

Fundamental ethical principles governing the practice of medicine have not changed during the past thirty years, having been established over the centuries since the teachings of Hippocrates, Maimonides and many others. The physician in Cameron's time, as now, was ethically bound to place the welfare of his patients above all considerations including personal advantage, research objectives and the purposes of agencies supporting the research. Further, the doctrine of *primum non noers* (above all do no harm to the patient) was taught to medical students then as it is now. *It may indeed be argued that Dr. Cameron's treatments transgressed both of these well accepted ethical precepts* [emphasis added].

Here Lowy was on the verge of condemning Cameron. But he would not draw the logical conclusion to which his own analysis pointed.

Lowy's defence of Dr. Cameron was remarkable, given a passage in which he wrote:

[Dr. Cameron's] criteria for the selection of patients for these controversial treatments seemed to broaden. By the time I became personally involved with his patients (1961) it was my own view that many of the schizophrenic patients who were "depatterned" had not had adequate trials of appropriate phenothiazine medications that were then available and many of the psycho-neurotic patients who received hallucinogenic drugs and psychic driving could have been helped by conventional psychotherapy. Of course, at the time, I was very junior in status and quite inexperienced in psychiatry; nevertheless, even in hindsight after more than twenty years of practicing and teaching psychiatry I still hold this view.

No one at AMI, including Dr. Lowy, was prepared to challenge the lunacy of the great man.

Cooper, relying on Doctors Grunberg, McDonald and Lowy, said that Dr. Cameron's experiments were not a marked departure from the accepted standard of psychiatric practice in Canada at the time. The three consultants conceded that in the 1950s and 1960s, psychiatrists were obliged to do no harm to patients, and that they were obliged to obtain informed consent for experiments on patients. They conceded that Dr. Cameron had failed on both counts. Nevertheless, they were of the opinion that Canada had no responsibility to Cameron's victims. None of Cooper's expert advisers were prepared to acknowledge that two plus two equals four.

Cooper held that Canada was not legally or morally responsible for what had occurred at AMI. Yet tucked away in an appendix to his report was a suggestion that Canada should make an *ex gratia* payment of $100,000 to each of Cameron's victims. The suggestion was ignored.

We were determined to proceed, and so was Linda. On April 29, 1990, Linda gave an interview to Lyn Cockburn of the Vancouver *Province*. The concluding paragraphs of the interview read:

"There is no doubt we're going to win. I wrote a letter to Mulroney several years ago before I knew half of what I know now and I told him that I was not old and that I was not dying and that I was not going to stop doing what I am doing until the truth is out in the open. And I told him then that if I needed to go to the International Court of the Hague I was on my way. I meant it then and I mean it now."

Does she ever wish she could get her hands on the now-dead Cameron, surely a Mengele-like figure. "There were moments," she says.

Macdonald believes that Cameron decided at some point in his life that he was going to do something important for mankind and after that anything was justifiable.

"And we have to take our share of the responsibility for putting such people on pedestals," she says. "Doctors, lawyers, judges, politicians. We have to be much more aware about who we worship and who we support in positions of power."

By now we had the evidence obtained in the American proceedings, which had not been available to Cooper. The suit by the nine Canadians, brought with the support of the government of Canada against the CIA, was called *Orlikow v. U.S.A.* It was brought in the U.S. District Court for the District of Columbia. Joseph Rauh Jr., a renowned lawyer who for decades had been a champion of civil liberties in the U.S., represented the plaintiffs.

I knew something of Rauh's reputation. When I left the bench in 1983, I was asked by the United Steelworkers of America to sit on their Campaign Conduct Administration Committee. The committee consists of two Americans and a

Canadian, and it supervises the steelworkers' elections held every four years for international and district offices in Canada and the U.S. The committee enforces two rules: office-holders cannot use union offices, media, automobiles, staff or assets to obtain an electoral advantage; and union insurgents cannot obtain funds or assistance outside the union with which to campaign against office-holders. Joseph Rauh Jr., on behalf of a group of insurgents who objected to any restriction on raising funds on the ground that it interfered with their freedom of speech, took their case to the U.S. Supreme Court. There, the court upheld the establishment of the Campaign Conduct Administration Committee by a single vote. It was at this time that I joined the committee, a few months after it had narrowly avoided an early eclipse at Rauh's hands.

I went to Washington, D.C., to see James Turner, a lawyer in Rauh's office. (Rauh was ill at the time.) Turner made available the evidence they had assembled—evidence that had not been considered in the Cooper Report. The American proceedings included the testimony of a number of eminent psychiatrists, which refuted the views of Cooper's panel. Their testimony showed that, even if the 1950s and the 1960s were benighted years in the field of psychiatry, the experiments that Dr. Cameron carried out at AMI were not in accordance with accepted practice even then; indeed, they were barbarous by the standards of those earlier decades.

Dr. Paul Termansen, a Vancouver psychiatrist, had worked at AMI for Ewan Cameron. He gave a deposition in the American proceedings. It was suggested to Dr. Termansen that Cameron's methods constituted "extreme attempts to help patients who were not benefitting from more conventional treatments." Termansen replied: "Well, I disagree with that because, from my study of the charts, it appeared to me that they were indeed extreme attempts, but it was not clear that they were exclusively for patients who were not benefitting from more conventional treatments." In Linda Macdonald's case, of course, she had not received any conventional treatment at all.

Dr. Termansen, like Dr. Lowy, had worked at AMI under Cameron. He was unreserved in his condemnation. Termansen gave it as his view that Cameron transgressed the ethical standards of the profession as they stood *at that time*. He testified:

I believed that the state of regression that the patients were reduced to and the benefits that were derived from that were just not proportionate. The risks of the treatment and the sort of dehumanized state that the patient got into was just not warranted either by the patient's condition or by any possible outcome of that treatment.

As early as 1967, Dr. Termansen and Dr. A. E. Schwartzman had established the non-therapeutic nature of Cameron's work and the "memory difficulty" engendered in patients. This is what had happened to Linda, except that her memory difficulty consisted of the loss of memory of her whole life before AMI. Their report, entitled Intensive Electroconvulsive Therapy: Follow-up Study, investigated seventy-nine former patients of Dr. Cameron who were known to have reached the third stage of depatterning.

Dr. Termansen, in an affidavit filed in the U.S. District Court, referred to the 1967 follow-up study: "We concluded that the incidence of memory loss attributable to the intensive electroshock was higher than that encountered with standard therapeutic electroshock, and that the 'depatterning' procedure, therefore, was not an acceptable form of therapy." Regarding the granting agency's responsibilities, Termansen discussed Cameron's 1957 "Application for a Grant to Study Effects upon Human Behaviour of the Repetition of Verbal Signals." He mentioned specifically "paragraph D, Section 1: the breakdown of ongoing patterns of the patient's behaviour by means of particular electroshock, i.e., depatterning." He referred to that giveaway word: "depatterning, I think somebody's eyebrows should have probably [raised]." Termansen also pointed to another part of Cameron's grant application:

Can we find chemical agents which will serve to break down the ongoing patterns of behaviour more rapidly, more transitorily, with less damage to the perceptive and cognitive qualities of the . . . individual than the present physiological agents?

Termansen testified: "That would raise, should raise the question as to how much damage was being done to the cognitive capacities of the individual with these experimentations, when you think the cognitive capacities of the individual are the essence of his being."

A number of American psychiatrists provided depositions. Two of them are representative. Dr. David Joseph, a practising psychiatrist and an associate clinical professor of psychiatry and behavioural science at the George Washington University School of Medicine in Washington, D.C., categorically rejected the legitimacy of Dr. Cameron's methods.

To my knowledge, intensive electroshock, psychic driving procedures, long drug-induced sleep and sensory deprivation would not have been prescribed for treatment for any psychiatric diagnosis. [They] were not standard treatments, *then or now*, but were clearly experimental . . . The closest approximation to the combined experimental procedures . . . of which I am aware, is described in the literature on various methods of brainwashing in Korea and elsewhere [emphasis added].

It is hardly surprising that Dr. Joseph would compare Cameron's methods to brainwashing in Korea, because Cameron's experiments had their genesis in the military's desire to develop brainwashing techniques, which it was believed had already conferred a "totalitarian advantage" on the Chinese Communists.

Dr. David J. Rothman, a professor of social medicine and director of the Center for the Study of Society and Medicine, College of Physicians and Surgeons, Columbia University, also testified. His specialty was the study of medical ethics and the patient's rights. He cited the well-known principle that the health and welfare of the patient is paramount. He explained:

The ethical requirement that physicians solely serve their patients' interests was explicitly recognized in the Hippocratic Oath, and has been stressed in virtually every statement on medical ethics issued during the 20th century.

Dr. Rothman then reviewed the development of risk disclosure and voluntary consent in the twentieth century.

By the end of the Second World War, the voluntary consent requirement was a well-established medico-legal obligation of physicians. During the first half of this century, legal scholars and professional medical associations recognized this ethical consent requirement and by the 1940's were setting it out in specific detail.

In the face of such evidence, could anyone accept the view of Cooper's psychiatric panel? We could show that Grunberg, McDonald and Lowy, in providing their opinions, did not do justice to the standards of their own profession. In exonerating Cameron, they would have had us believe that in Canada in the early 1960s psychiatry was being practised in a way that contravened every known principle of medical research on human beings.

The use of intensive ECT, drug-induced sleep, sensory deprivation to achieve depatterning and the mad notion of "psychic driving"—how could it credibly be argued that this treatment was acceptable psychiatric practice? If Cooper and his advisers were right, the generally approved standard of practice in Canadian psychiatry in the early 1960s was lamentable.

Even if they were right, we had another argument we could advance. The law of malpractice has always been that if accepted practice falls below *any* reasonable standard of medical practice, it is no excuse that a particular defendant measured up to such a wretched standard of accepted practice. Admittedly, in the face of a wall of expert opinion, this argument would be hard to advance, but we clearly had a fighting chance of showing that, even if Cooper and his consultants were right, there was no defence. The testimony of Dr. Grunberg regarding the hepatitis experiments with mentally retarded children at Willowbrook demonstrated why it is necessary to guard against the justification of standards that, objectively considered, made no sense at all. The medical profession cannot be allowed to write its own ticket, cannot be the ultimate judge of its own standards.

The strength of our case on the merits had been greatly enhanced by the work done by the lawyers for the victims in the U.S. They had provided evidence that gave us the means to go forward with a lawsuit and to bring Linda's case before the public.

In Canadian courts, we often use American cases as precedents. Given the narrow band of political options in the United States, in that country initiatives that would in Canada be taken in Parliament or by the provinces are often brought in the courts. In *Calder,* we relied on the great judgements of Chief Justice John Marshall written in the nineteenth century. In the early development of our Charter of Rights, Canadian courts often looked for guidance to the jurisprudence of the U.S. Supreme Court. It's true that on their part Americans are not much interested in our legal lore, but this fact is hardly surprising in a country of three hundred million that pays little or no attention to its well-behaved neighbour of thirty million.

I was, however, once mistaken for Chief Justice Warren Burger of the U.S. Supreme Court. My name is pronounced with a softer "g" than his, but I am used to answering to my name pronounced either way.

When I conducted the Alaska Native Review Commission, between 1983 and 1985, I had to travel regularly between Anchorage and Washington, D.C. The commission was not especially well funded, and I travelled economy. The flight made a stop at Seattle. I was dozing in the rear of the aircraft when two employees of United Airlines outfitted in blue blazers turned up at my seat and asked, "Are you Justice Burger?" I said yes, I was. I had left the bench, but in Alaska was often referred to as "Justice Berger" pronounced with a hard "g." In the U.S. judges keep their titles, at least on an informal basis, after they depart the bench. The folks from United told me they had a seat for me in the first-class cabin: "We didn't realize you were on this flight." A seat upfront was made available—they also made certain the seat next to mine was empty. Then the steward hastened to offer me a choice of wines. I commandeered a copy of the *New York Times,* settled back with a glass of wine and, as the aircraft headed down the runway again, realized that perhaps a mistake had been made. I thought, "What the hell." Such was my attenuated connection with the highest judicial office in the United States.

One American lawyer who does look to Canada is Ralph Nader. He made a name for himself as a champion of automobile safety, specifically of the use of seat belts. He has written admiringly of Canadian innovation in many fields. Once, after he had spoken at UBC to an audience including my daughter, Erin, who was a student there, he spent the evening at our home. When I drove Ralph to his hotel, Erin accompanied us. As we pulled out of the driveway, Erin, seated behind me, leaned forward and whispered, "Dad, fasten your seat belt."

In presenting Linda Macdonald's case, armed with the American evidence, we could show that Cameron had been guilty of medical malpractice. He had not obtained his patients' consent to his experiments, and the experiments were themselves a marked departure from the standards of the time. And, if they were not, they fell so far short of any reasonable standard as to be unjustifiable in law on any footing. They were not mere errors in judgement, which medical men and women can make, but represented an unconscionable failure to observe elementary standards of medical ethics.

Our strategy was to sue Canada in the Federal Court. In the Quebec courts, AMI's liability would be determined according to the Civil Code of Quebec. Linda had already been to two lawyers before she came to me. If she were to sue in Quebec, Linda would have to employ a Montreal law firm to take on the case. The whole idea seemed impractical.

Instead of going to Montreal, we would ask the Federal Court to try the case against the federal government in Vancouver. But how would we link the government of Canada to Cameron in such a way as to hold Canada liable for funding the experiments? What responsibility does an agency of government have when it funds a research project? We would point out the Department of National Health and Welfare was not simply a government agency with a bucket of money to hand out. Granting agencies had a responsibility to establish proper review procedures. Any review should have included an examination of Dr. Cameron's applications for funding as well as an examination of the relevant psychiatric literature. If there had been a review, it was obviously inadequate.

The evidence showed that the reviewers at the Department of National Health and Welfare, if they had read Dr. Cameron's applications for grants carefully against the background of psychiatric practice at the time, would have known or ought to have known about the experimental nature of the treatment at AMI, the breakdown in the distinction between research and healing, and the enormous risk to Dr. Cameron's patients.

The funds provided to Dr. Cameron and his associates under the National

Health Grants program should have been provided for the purpose of promoting and preserving the health and well-being of Canadians, including Linda Macdonald, but they were instead provided to serve the research interests of government agencies, both Canadian and foreign.

Cooper found it necessary to concede in his report: "To be sure, the institution [AMI] and the granting agency [Department of National Health and Welfare] always bore some measure of responsibility ... But this responsibility was vaguely defined at best until at least the 1960s and 1970s." Cooper argued that the federal government had no reason to suspect that Cameron's experiments were likely to injure his patients.

Yet Dr. Omond Solandt, chairman of Canada's Defence Research Board, who had been present at the meeting at the Ritz-Carlton in 1951, made it clear that he was skeptical of Cameron's methods to the point that he regarded him as a menace. In his deposition in the American proceedings, Dr. Solandt said that, after seeing the results of "depatterning" on one of Dr. Cameron's patients:

I knew that this kind of work was something the Defence Board would have no part in. It was my view at the time and continues to be that Cameron was not possessed of the necessary sense of humanity to be regarded as a good doctor ... Cameron never applied for Defence Research Board grants to fund [AMI's] psychiatric research and would never have received such support had he applied.

Perhaps the most renowned of the American psychiatrists who testified in the U.S. proceedings was Dr. Robert Jay Lifton, a professor of psychiatry and psychology at City University of New York and Lecturer in Psychiatry at Harvard University. He had conducted extensive research into "thought reform" or "brainwashing" during the 1950s and early 1960s and was widely published on the subject.

Referring to Cameron's 1957 grant application, Lifton stated, "In my opinion, it is clear from the Cameron application, itself, that these procedures were experimental and deviated from standard and customary psychiatric therapies in use during the 1950s. In my opinion, the purpose and design of the experimental procedures described in the Cameron application closely paralleled the techniques of 'thought reform' or 'brainwashing' used in Chinese prisons and elsewhere, and represent a mechanized extension of those 'brainwashing' methods." According to Dr. Lifton, the Cameron application was "a transparent proposal to conduct experiments in brainwashing extrapolated from methods documented in the academic literature *and would have been seen as such by anyone reviewing it during the 1950s*" [emphasis added].

There was a labyrinthine procedure for obtaining a grant in Cameron's day. The application went first of all to the provincial government. Once approved at the provincial level, the application would be forwarded to Ottawa where Health and Welfare officials would, according to Cooper, review it "to satisfy themselves generally as to the scientific and medical adequacy of the proposed research." Two outside experts then gave detailed, anonymous, written commentary to the department. Then the research subcommittee of the Mental Health Advisory Committee reviewed it "to ensure its scientific and medical adequacy." The subcommittee reported to the advisory committee. Employees of Health and Welfare sat as chairman of and secretary to the advisory committee to provide liaison between the government and its appointed peer-review group of experts in psychiatry, psychology and related fields. The advisory committee reported to officials of Health and Welfare, who would then recommend or decline to recommend the grant to the minister. If approval were given, the application was sent back to the provincial government, which would then confirm the approval.

This procedure might be thought of as fail-safe, with many layers of review designed to ensure that scientific and ethical standards were observed. It was also likely to ensure that no one could be held responsible for approving the suitability of any grant. Or it may be that the bureaucracy was occupied solely with moving the application along, and no one examined it because they thought those at the next level would do so.

But, however it was viewed, we could argue that this complicated set of procedures was an acknowledgement by the government of Canada of its responsibility to scrutinize grant applications thoroughly. Canada had to do so because it had a duty to ensure that the research projects it approved conformed to appropriate medical standards. Canada had what in law is called a duty of care—a duty to protect the patients who were the subjects of the experiments. Cameron's applications were, however, apparently granted without any scrutiny. The elaborate procedure was only that: an elaborate procedure with no substantive safeguards.

Cooper acknowledged in his report that government officials, external reviewers and government-appointed research advisory panels were expected to raise any ethical concerns to the funding body. They just didn't do it.

Officials within the civil service who reviewed the application, the external reviewers and the research advisory panels are to raise any concerns of an ethical nature that they might have in regard to the proposed research. While *this was also true in the 1950s and early 1960s*, the custom then was to place much greater reliance on the integrity and competence of the investigator [emphasis added].

Cooper also conceded that:

Dr. Cameron's pre-eminence in his field, added to his forceful and aggressive personality, may well have resulted in a *certain deference* being shown to his applications by those whose task it was to review them . . . What is suggested is that it is likely that some members of the reviewing groups may have been somewhat reluctant to express doubts, if indeed they had any, about the medical or scientific basis for the procedures under review in the proposal [emphasis added].

Well, of course, that was their job—to express their doubts if they had them and, if necessary, to act on them.

Grantees were required to submit an annual progress report to the Mental Health Division. Continuation of the grant for the subsequent year required approval from the Mental Health Advisory Committee based on the progress report and on-site visits by department personnel.

The department's practice was to send a representative on occasional visits to the institutions that received grants. There were, however, no surprise visits to AMI because the federal government's investigators always obtained permission from the institution before they were to visit. Cooper sought to justify the practice with this explanation: "In those days public servants and members of the advisory panels did not consider it to be their responsibility to be much concerned about the ethics of the proposed research, or about the quality of the consent that had been obtained from the patients and/or volunteers."

There existed what in law we call a causal connection between the wholly ineffectual review by the federal government of Cameron's grant applications, along with its equally ineffectual supervision of Cameron's experiments, and the dire consequences suffered by Cameron's victims. If the federal government had properly reviewed his grant applications and maintained any reasonable level of supervision, the government would have realized that the experiments had to be stopped. Canada's failure to do its duty had in that sense been one of the causes of Linda's condition, a contributing cause, and that is sufficient in law to establish liability. We felt, therefore, we had a sound basis for arguing that Canada ought to be held responsible for Dr. Cameron's experimentation on Linda Macdonald, for the damage she had suffered, and should be required to compensate her accordingly.

Moreover, we could show that in February 1963, Cameron had publicly admitted before the American Psychopathological Association in New York City that he had made "a wrong turning" and that he had "continued to walk without a glint of success for a long time." According to *In the Sleep Room*, Cameron also stated:

Let me say simply that we have vastly increased the number of repetitions to which the individual was exposed, that we continued driving while the individual was asleep, while he was in a chemical sleep, while he was awake but under hallucinogens, while he was under the influence of disinhibiting agents. We tried driving under hypnosis, immediately after electroshock, we tried innumerable combinations of voices, of timing and many other conditions, but were never able to stop the mechanisms [which the human brain sets up to protect itself].

This was a startling admission. It was made in February 1963. It was only one month later that Linda Macdonald entered AMI. Cameron apparently subjected Linda Macdonald to a more intensive regime of depatterning than any previous patient.

While we were preparing our case, events were moving forward in the United States. The American government, which had all along rejected the claim by the nine Canadians, had now agreed to settle rather than have the U.S. District Court rule on the case.

The U.S. had all along claimed that "Cameron may have received much more substantial financial support from Canadian sources than from [the CIA]." This surely was the point. The CIA, no more exposed to liability than Canada, had settled with the nine victims who sued in the U.S. Yet earlier the CIA had declined to acknowledge any responsibility. It was obviously the evidence taken in the American proceedings that made the CIA decide to settle.

We could argue that the Cooper Report should not stand because of its own internal conflicts, and because the new evidence that had become available in the U.S. since 1986 completely undermined its conclusions. Cooper's absolution of the government of Canada of any responsibility for the suffering of Dr. Cameron's patients could not now be justified.

We could, we believed, assemble a strong case of malpractice against AMI. But it would not be clear sailing. As we completed our preparations, the Quebec Court of Appeal handed down its judgement in Mary Morrow's case; they upheld the judgement at trial, absolving Cameron and AMI of liability. We would still have to prove that Canada was legally responsible.

Although we had launched our lawsuit against Canada in the Federal Court, we might still be faced with a claim by Canada that the trial should take place in Montreal. There would be examinations for discovery. On her examination for discovery, Linda could be examined at length and required to relive the catastrophe that unfolded following her stay at AMI. It might take five years to get to trial. Then she could be asked the same questions all over again at the trial.

Although Linda would be better able than most plaintiffs to withstand such an interrogation, this procedure is always a concern in such cases. In 1995, when as special counsel for the attorney general of B.C. I made recommendations for a compensation scheme for the victims of sexual abuse at B.C.'s residential school for deaf and blind children, I urged that it be structured so that claimants would not be put through a courtroom-like procedure, which for many of them might be an ordeal as damaging as the original trauma. A panel was set up to determine compensation in each case, but to proceed informally.

Much had been written about AMI. There had been earlier approaches to Ottawa, without success But we thought a thorough analysis of the Cooper Report and a complete exposure of the evidence that had come to light in the American proceedings might persuade Ottawa to change its attitude.

Contemplating, as I write about these experiments, almost four decades later, the indifference of Cameron to the condition of his patients, the unwillingness of his colleagues to dispute his ascendancy, the prolongation of suffering—the whole story is dismaying. But in 2000 I would be retained in a case with many of the same features. This time it would be mental patients, virtually all of them women, who decades before had been sterilized under B.C.'s Sexual Sterilization Act, passed in 1933. This statute was an outcome of the eugenics movement, whose followers believed that persons suffering from mental infirmity should not be permitted to have children. Statutes authorizing the sterilization of the mentally handicapped were passed in Europe and in North America.

In the U.S., the issue went to the Supreme Court. Could a state government carry out involuntary sterilization? Justice Oliver Wendell Holmes, who believed in allowing the states a free rein for legislative experiments, upheld the legislation, using the famous phrase "three generations of imbeciles is enough," a phrase sufficiently striking that it may have impeded legislators and the public from taking a hard look at the flaws in eugenics.

In Canada, Alberta was the pioneer, passing a eugenics statute in 1927. B.C. followed in 1933. In Alberta, perhaps five thousand men and women were sterilized. In B.C., the number was much smaller. The Roman Catholic Church was opposed, however, and forestalled legislation in the other provinces. None of them succumbed to the eugenics crusade. Alberta repealed its eugenics legislation in 1972, B.C. in 1973.

In Alberta, lawyer Jon Faulds brought a test case for a waitress named Leilani Muir, who had been sterilized. In the Alberta Court of Queen's Bench, Justice Joanne Veit decided that the sterilization had been unlawful. Muir, then a teenager, had been placed in the custody of the mental health authorities. So Alberta, in deciding how to provide for her, had to act in Muir's best interests. This obligation is called fiduciary duty. Justice Veit decided that the mental health authorities, by sterilizing Muir while she was in their custody, breached their fiduciary duty. Justice Veit awarded damages to Muir. As a result of Justice Veit's decision, Alberta set up a compensation scheme for all the men and women who had been sterilized.

Jay Chalke, B.C.'s public guardian and trustee, asked me to represent those of his clients in B.C., mostly women, who had been sterilized under the province's Sexual Sterilization Act. In B.C., we had a Board of Eugenics from 1933 until 1972. It had the authority to order sterilization, but only with consent of the patient, the patient's spouse, parents or guardian, or the provincial secretary. It was limited to cases where the board concluded that mental patients were likely, if they were to have children, to pass on their mental illness. Just as in Linda Macdonald's case we were able to build on the work done by American lawyers, so also in the case of these women, we would be able to build on the work done by Jon Faulds and Alberta lawyers.

A Supreme Court judge chaired B.C.'s Board of Eugenics. This would supposedly ensure a proper judicial approach to decisions about sterilization. The other members were to be a psychiatrist and a social worker. The chairman for many years was Justice A.M. Manson, our judge in 1959 in the Ironworkers' case. In 1944, Isobel Harvey, the superintendent of child welfare, a member of the board, wrote to the assistant deputy provincial secretary about the processing of the cases by the board. She complained about Justice Manson. Her letter reveals that fifteen years before my encounter with the judge in the ironworkers' case, his peremptory methods were already ingrained.

I have just returned this morning from a meeting of the Board, and both Dr. Minorgan [also a member of the Board] and I are so disturbed that we agreed that I should write you and tell you the way we feel about it . . .

Neither Dr. Minorgan nor I would like to have to go on a witness stand and give evidence that these hearings are held in the proper manner. In the first place, Judge Manson's mind is never on Eugenics, and I am telling you the literal truth when I say that I do not think he listened to me for more than half a minute consecutively this morning and, as I have to present the cases and give the medical evidence, I felt that he really did not know when the patient came in to be interviewed exactly what was the matter with him. He telephoned,—he went several times to the filing cabinets and hunted for files,—he made entries in a book,—he searched his law bag for things he wanted,— all the time while we were trying to discuss these cases. There were four cases seen, and

I do not suppose there was one minute's discussion of them aside from what Dr. Minorgan and I did privately while we waited for the Judge. I did manage to get a passing consent from him to have a study made of the cases we have done since the Board was organized in 1935, but I do not suppose he would remember about it again.

I have checked through and note that Judge Manson's appointment was made on March 6, 1936, which means that he has completed eight years. Judge Robertson held the position a little over a year. Would it not be possible in some diplomatic way to thank Judge Manson for his eight years' service, and point out that it is too much to expect of a man in his position to carry on any longer than that?

Justice Manson served as chairman of the Board of Eugenics until his departure from the bench in 1961. Isobel Harvey's appointment to the board was terminated soon after her letter complaining about the judge was written.

We would argue that these sexual sterilization procedures had not been carried out for the purposes of the statute, but rather for a variety of unlawful purposes, including the convenience of hospital administration; that there had been no valid consent; and that in the circumstances they constituted a sexual assault.

If we are to live by the rule of law, there must be lawful authority for sterilizing the mentally infirm; they must be accorded the same protection as those who have no disability, the same measure of bodily integrity and privacy as the rest of us enjoy.

I was struck by the difference, in terms of the public relations aspect, between Linda Macdonald's case and that of the women who had been sterilized. These elderly women, mentally infirm, some of them in group homes, some in mental hospitals, some living with family, could not speak for themselves. Linda, though she still had no recollection of her life before AMI, could talk about all that had happened to her since and about her struggle to recover. There is a public relations aspect to such cases. Governments are more likely to settle if there is a groundswell of public support for a particular cause.

Linda could speak for herself. She represented proof that, even if depatterning had worked, psychic driving had failed. The mind has its own defence mechanisms. The implanting of new ideas and attitudes did not succeed. Linda's life was proof of the indomitability of the human spirit. She was candid and confident. There was no one better—no lawyer, no politician—who could make the case for the victims of AMI.

We had to go public with Linda's case. Canadians were aware of the American proceedings. But they did not appreciate that it was their own government, not only the CIA, that had been responsible for funding the experiments in brainwashing at AMI that resulted in pain and suffering to perhaps hundreds of

Canadians. It was not something for which the faceless bureaucrats of the CIA were responsible, but our own faceless bureaucrats here in Canada.

Canada had a new minister of justice, Kim Campbell. We thought it would be worth taking the case up with her but in a public setting.

We prepared a lengthy submission to the federal government, which we sent on February 26, 1990, to Kim Campbell, and we made it public at the same time. We held a news conference in Ottawa at the National Press Building. Two MPS, Svend Robinson of the NDP and Mary Clancy of the Liberals, came to offer their support. We had obtained a resolution supporting our cause from the Canadian Psychological Association, but not, unhappily, from the Canadian Psychiatric Association. Linda and I did media interviews. Supportive members of parliament raised Linda's case in the House of Commons.

Linda's public appearances on TV and radio, I think, were enormously helpful to her cause. She was forthright, articulate and unforgiving, but not bitter. No one could help but be impressed with this woman who had succeeded in rebuilding her life.

One of the endearing features of the trip to Ottawa, where Linda had been raised, was that she was reunited with a high school girlfriend, both of them now past fifty. They still had common interests and spent much of the time together. The lost years had fallen away, even though Linda had lost all recollection of their earlier friendship.

Linda's claim gave the issue a public profile. But there were a lot of claims like hers. Compensating Linda would likely mean compensation for many others.

We didn't hear from Kim Campbell until December 1990, ten months later. Perhaps emboldened by the fact that on July 12, 1990, the Supreme Court of Canada had refused leave to appeal in *Morrow*, she turned us down, saying that:

I have come to the same conclusion as my predecessors who have reviewed this matter, namely, that the allegations of impropriety against the Canadian government are unfounded in light of the evidence when reviewed as a whole.

I replied in a letter to the minister:

I cannot believe you have read our submission. We did not make allegations of impropriety against the Canadian government. Certainly we made allegations against Dr. Cameron and others.

Against the Canadian government we made an allegation of negligence, that is, that the government funded these experiments with knowledge of what they were about, and undertook to supervise them, and therefore had a duty of care.

I pointed out, "Impropriety involves wilful misconduct. We do not have to meet such a standard in seeking to hold the federal government responsible." I then said: "The true impropriety, the true scandal is your failure to address the real issue in this case."

Campbell's rejection of Linda's claim, expressed as an answer to allegations of impropriety that were never made, had aroused a great deal of support in the media for Linda and concomitant criticism of Campbell. Allan Fotheringham wrote a withering column in the *Financial Post,* saying, "Someone in Campbell's department can't even read." Geoffrey Stevens of the *Globe and Mail,* that newspaper's national affairs columnist, urged that the claim be accepted. He wrote that Campbell's letter of rejection "must have been written for her by a committee of bureaucrats whose concept of public service does not encompass the realities of human need and human suffering." Or, I would have added, the disposition to discuss the claim on the grounds on which it was advanced in the first place. The *Vancouver Sun* ran an editorial urging there be compensation. Peter Calamai, writing in the *Ottawa Citizen,* urged Canada to accept liability. The *Toronto Star* had an editorial urging there be compensation.

On March 6, 1991, Kim Campbell said the government was now willing to discuss an out-of-court settlement in Linda's case. On April 10, when Campbell appeared before the House of Commons Justice Committee, she indicated that the government was having second thoughts about its rejection of Linda's claim. Under questioning by Liberal MP Russ McLennan, she continued to deny that Canada had any legal responsibility. She did say, however, that Linda's case was under "active consideration to see if we can be of some assistance." Outside the committee room, she said that any payment would have to be made on "humanitarian and compassionate grounds" without any admission of legal liability by Ottawa. "I'm asking my department to look creatively at how this might be approached . . . I am concerned about her plight and would like to find some way to respond."

At last, the minister of justice was signalling a breakthrough.

There were perhaps, besides Linda's, twenty other lawsuits filed. The Department of Justice estimated that eighty persons, perhaps many more, had been subjected to similar treatment. If Canada settled with Linda, the government would have to act on these other claims. The machinery in Ottawa moves slowly. But in November 1992, John Power, who had been our opponent in Dr. Jerilynn Prior's case, phoned me to say that he had wanted for a long time to make the call he was making. Canada was prepared to settle. Linda would receive $100,000. All of her legal fees would be taken care of by the federal government. Of course, it fell short of what we could expect if we were to go to trial, establish liability and obtain a verdict for all of Linda's damages. But we had no guarantee we would succeed at trial. At least one case, *Morrow*, had been tried and lost, and then appealed and lost, and the Supreme Court of Canada had refused leave. Under this settlement, there would be money for Linda now, not five years down the road.

On November 18, 1992, Kim Campbell announced that Canada had settled with Linda for $100,000. We had shaken loose the $100,000 that Cooper had proposed in the appendix to his report.

Linda said: "I accept the government's symbolic apology through compensation, but no amount of money can compensate me for the loss of memory of the first twenty-six years of my life and the enormous difficulties my family and I have suffered subsequently. My biggest concern has always been that the government acknowledge its role in funding the experiments so that we can hope that such a negligent act can never occur again in this country."

Ewan Cameron had victims all over the country. At Kim Campbell's initiative, Ottawa established a panel to provide compensation of $100,000 to every victim who could establish that they had been subjected to depatterning. The federal government agreed to make available records from AMI to all claimants who wished an opportunity to submit a claim. Seventy-seven of these claims were paid. The claimants owed their compensation in large measure to the courage and determination of Linda Macdonald.

In the letter she had written in 1987, Linda had said:

I knew I had a case, I was angry beyond words . . . I wanted to take my government to court . . . I wanted a public apology and compensation. I wanted justice for every one of Cameron's victims. I also believed that I was emotionally stable enough to launch an action against the Canadian Government and maintain my health and my life and job for however long it took to see it through.

She had seen it through.

Let one of the witnesses in the American proceedings, Dr. David J. Rothman of Columbia University, have the last word. He wrote, in the *New York Times*, on August 12, 2001:

There is a very clear sense that physicians and researchers could not be left alone to make decisions. In the research world they will minimize the risk and in the medical world they will simply allow their own perspective to trump the patient's perspective.

10   *The Montney Treasure*

THE NISGA'A CASE was a claim relating to Aboriginal title. The whole object was to *achieve* a treaty. But a hundred years before, across the prairies and the northern woodlands, Canada had made treaties with the Indian nations. These treaties are known as the numbered treaties, because they are numbered one to eleven.

Under these treaties, beginning with Treaty No. 1 in 1871, the Indians surrendered their Indian title. In return, reserves were set aside. All of this treaty-making was done under federal authority. In 1899 the Crown entered into Treaty No. 8 with the Indians. The treaty covered much of northern Alberta and, in an effort to encompass all the Athabaskan tribes, it included that part of B.C. east of the Rockies. The B.C. Indians living there, on the eastern side of the Rockies, were closely related to the Plains Indians and the Indians of the northern woodlands; they lived beyond the salmon rivers flowing to the Pacific, which sustained the Nisga'a and the other Native peoples of the coast. They lived in the Peace River valley, whose waters flowed, ultimately, to the Arctic Ocean.

On May 30, 1900, the Beaver band, located near Fort St. John, adhered to Treaty No. 8. In 1916, the Crown set aside a reserve, called Indian Reserve 172 (I.R. 172), comprising eighteen thousand acres of prime agricultural land, for the exclusive use and benefit of the Beaver. Almost, however, from the start, I.R. 172 was sought by the settlers who had already arrived in the region and by those who followed after the end of the First World War. They wanted I.R. 172 opened up for agriculture.

But this use meant a surrender had to be obtained from the band. Under the Indian Act, once a reserve was established, the federal government could not take away the reserve or any part of it without obtaining the consent of a majority of male adult members of the band. (Today, consent must be obtained from a majority of adult members of the band, both men and women.) The government's policy was, however, to maintain Indian reserves in Indian ownership.

Reserve land might be leased to local farmers. The mineral rights might also be leased. But the policy was not to sell Indian reserves. This policy made sense: the Indians had formerly been lords of the prairie. Under the treaties, they were giving up their title to a vast area. It was in their best interests to hold on to the reserves—that was all they had left. But even a lease of land or mineral rights required a formal surrender, signed by the band.

Traditionally part of a hunter-gatherer society, the members of the Beaver band had lived in the woodlands of northeastern British Columbia for centuries. At the time they signed Treaty No. 8 and at the time their reserve was set aside for them, Canada intended that they would one day have to give up their way of life in the bush and take up farming. This reasoning was behind the policy of the Department of Indian Affairs (DIA) of refusing to countenance the sale of reserve land.

When the treaty commissioners travelled from Ottawa to the West in 1871 and afterwards to make treaties with the Indians, the meetings were solemn conclaves, attended with a good deal of formality. The commissioners spoke for Queen Victoria (who reigned until 1901) and made pledges on her behalf. Indians came from miles around. They signed the treaties, which they believed established a special relationship between them and the Crown. Often the treaty commissioners made promises orally, promises not found in the treaties but recorded in their reports to Ottawa. After negotiating Treaty No. 8 in 1899, the treaty commissioners reported to Ottawa that they had given oral assurances to the Indians who signed Treaty No. 8 that reserves were to be set aside for their protection, to secure land for them to hold in perpetuity as settlement advanced.

When I.R. 172 was created in 1916, the people of the Beaver band were not engaged in farming. The reserve was set aside at the behest of officials of DIA who feared that, if a reserve were not soon set aside for the band, all of the best land would be taken up as a result of the entry of settlers into the area. DIA officials recognized the agricultural potential of I.R. 172. It had to be kept in Indian ownership against the day when the members of the Beaver band would settle down as farmers. From the band's point of view, the land, known as Montney, had always been important to them as their summer gathering place in their seasonal round of hunting, fishing and gathering.

As the area grew more settled and as the abundance of game diminished, the members of the band made less and less use of I.R. 172, but officials of DIA knew that the land would eventually be needed by the band.

After the First World War, pressure was exerted on DIA to make Indian reserves in Western Canada, including I.R. 172, available for settlement by veterans returning from the war. In 1920, DIA formally took the position that I.R. 172 could not be opened up for settlement as it would eventually be needed for agricultural purposes by the band. In the 1930s, DIA received more requests to open I.R. 172 for non-Indian settlement. DIA refused. In the 1940s, as the Second World War drew to a close, pressure to open I.R. 172 to returning veterans was renewed. In 1945, the federal government departed from its long-standing policy and had the Beaver band sign a surrender of the whole reserve, including the mineral rights. The Beaver band thereby gave up Montney; they no longer had any claim to the use and benefit of I.R. 172.

This is a story of loss and deprivation. The federal government was to blame. But the government was not a monolithic force dedicated to undermining Indian rights. There were many civil servants who sought to protect the interests of the Beaver band.

As a matter of policy, DIA had consistently held to the view that protection of reserves from alienation was fundamental to the survival of Indian peoples in the face of advancing settlement. The Crown considered itself trustee of the land held for Indian bands; all decisions were to be made in the best interests of the bands. Indeed, this obligation was mandated by the Indian Act. The Department of Indian Affairs was, as a matter of policy, unalterably opposed to the sale of reserve lands where there was any possibility that the Indians would need the land in the future. Mineral rights were not to be sold under *any* circumstances. However, leasing (both lands and mineral rights) was encouraged; it provided needed revenue for the Indians.

In 1945, the very year that DIA obtained the surrender from the Beaver band of the reserve, Thomas Crerar, the minister of Indian affairs, reiterated DIA's policy in his report to Parliament:

The Department has set its face solidly against alienation by sale of lands for which there is any likelihood of Indian need in future years. Lands surplus to immediate needs are administered under leasing arrangements and from such lands substantial revenues have accrued.

This was a prudent policy calculated to serve the long-term interests of the Indians. Until 1945, DIA had consistently refused all proposals for surrender of I.R. 172 for purposes of settlement.

There is a tendency to abuse the civil service, especially those members who have historically had charge of Indian affairs. On the Montney file, however, they consistently urged the need to keep I.R. 172 in Indian ownership, until they were overruled by their political masters. Two successive inspectors of Indian agencies advised in the strongest terms against transferring I.R. 172. In 1933, M. Christianson, inspector of Indian agencies, wrote:

The White people who have settled in that part of the country have driven the Indians away from the Fort St. John Reserve [I.R. 172] and it is necessary for them to go away up North for the purpose of hunting: Trap lines must be registered there and the whole country there has been taken up and registered by White trappers, the Indians having been more or less "left out in the cold." This evidently is not sufficient for them: They now want to take the land away from the Indians; in other words,—to crowd them off the face of the earth, and unless something is done by the Department to help these Indians, the White settlers will accomplish this in a very short time.

Strong language. Christianson continued:

The Indians up there are gradually dying off, and if left to shift for themselves as they have done in the past, they will certainly not last very long. My advice is that the Rose Prairie Board of Trade be told that the land in question belongs to the Indians and cannot be thrown open. Even if the Indians were willing to surrender the land, this is not the time to bring this about.

In 1940, an application for a permit to explore for oil and gas on I.R. 172 had been made to DIA. In accordance with DIA policy, officials sought and obtained from the band a surrender to the Crown of the mineral rights to I.R. 172, but only to lease. In other words, under the surrender signed by the members of the band, the Crown could *lease* the mineral rights to the oil and gas industry, but it couldn't *sell* them. Once the lease expired, the mineral rights would once again be held entirely for the use and benefit of the band. Exploration permits for I.R. 172 were issued by DIA, and the fees that were collected from the industry were credited to the band's account.

With the advent of the Second World War, the pressure to open up the reserve itself did not abate. C.P. Schmidt, inspector of Indian agencies, wrote in 1941:

There is some talk of asking the Indians to surrender this Reserve for sale. If this matter does come up, I cannot recommend it. This Fort St. John district will some day become a wonderful mixed-farming area, and our Indians could make a living on the Reserve. The new airport being built a few miles East of Fort St. John Village will boost the place . . .

I am told that trapping is not as good as it used to be, and that White trappers are crowding our Indians out of their trapping areas . . .

There is no doubt in my mind that the day is coming soon when [the Indians] will have to establish themselves and make permanent homes on their Reserve. Already the Province has built a highway through the Reserve, which is heading Northward;

this will no doubt be followed by a railway in this district, and all arable land for miles North and West will be taken up. To the East and South the land is already settled. Mixed farming will be the solution for these Indians.

In 1943, two years later, Inspector Schmidt wrote to Ottawa again. His report concluded: "May I close with a plea on behalf of our Indians. Please do not entertain or consider the matter of selling any Reserve, in part or in whole."

In the meantime, the Indians had been driven from the reserve. Ranchers used the reserve to graze their stock. The Indians didn't farm even an acre of it. But Inspector Schmidt said again in 1944: "The time will come when the younger people [in the band] will make use of their Reserve land."

In Ottawa, the Indians had an important ally. Dr. Harold McGill was the director of Indian affairs. In 1944, he recommended to the deputy minister that it was not in the interests of the band that the reserve be sold. He advised that it was the consistent policy of DIA to oppose the sale of I.R. 172. He gave his opinion that it "is quite possible and even probable" that the band would in the future have to alter its means of livelihood and would need to rely on the resources of the reserve. He realized that something might have to be done to deal with the demands by veterans for agricultural land. He suggested that, to contend with the pressure being exerted on their behalf, DIA should lease the best agricultural land on the reserve to local farmers. This leasing would not be an unalterable step. Once the lease came to an end, the band would still be able to have the use and benefit of the land in future.

McGill prevailed. On August 11, 1944, Charles Camsell, the deputy minister, wrote to the Canadian Legion and to Grey Turgeon, the local M P, to advise them that although I.R. 172 was admittedly not being used by the band for farming, "the property was set aside for their use for all time and we are not justified in reaching the conclusion now that all of this land will not be required for their descendants in the future. Experience has shown the wisdom of retaining all the lands which have been reserved for the Indians." This practice was, of course, exactly what was in the best interests of the Indians. By Treaty No. 8 they had surrendered their vast tribal territories. The Crown had promised them that their reserves—the small portion of their ancestral lands still held for their use and benefit—would be inviolate.

Canada's policy was at the time a policy of assimilation. But if the Indians were to be assimilated into the mainstream economy, they had to have agricultural land. DIA's people were insisting on the logic of the Crown's policy. But Dr. McGill, the band's highest-placed advocate in Ottawa, retired in December 1944. Once he was gone, events moved swiftly.

In 1945, Jack Grew, an employee of DIA, was sent from Ottawa to make treaty payments to Treaty No. 8 bands. Grew reported back that he had discussed with the Beaver band the idea of selling or leasing I.R. 172. He said the band was agreeable provided it was given alternative reserves. Grew said that I.R. 172 was not of much use to the band because encroachment by local settlers had destroyed pasturage and berry sites. R. A. Hoey, who had replaced Dr. McGill as director of Indian affairs, instructed Grew to return to Fort St. John and to hold a band meeting to vote on a surrender for sale or leasing purposes. Hoey wrote:

As you are probably aware, it is an extremely difficult and embarrassing situation and subject to much criticism of this Department to attempt to hold this land vacant for a group of Indians who are making no use of it, when it is in demand for ordinary settlement. On the other hand, the Reserve has a very substantial cash value and if it could be sold as appears probable from your report and from other information we have, for $150,000.00 or better, such a substantial capital asset would be for many years of more practical value to the Indians than a block of land of which they are making no use nor are likely to for some time.

The policy, to which DIA had held firm, had now been shredded. Dr. McGill had been willing to see I.R. 172 leased until the Indians were ready to become farmers, however many years that might be. But this new policy urged by Hoey entailed the abandonment by the Crown of its obligation to the Indians. They would have no future in farming.

From DIA files, it is difficult to tell precisely how the change in policy came about. I believe that Dr. McGill's retirement had much to do with it. A champion of a cause at a bureaucratic choke point can be effective in preventing action. And from the point of view of the Indians' interests, that was the soundest policy—to take no action to sell Montney.

On September 22, 1945, members of the Beaver band were summoned from their camps to two surrender meetings held near Fort St. John. DIA brought some of them to the meetings on the deck of a flatbed truck; others arrived on horseback.

The members of the band were still engaged in hunting and trapping, though some were becoming involved in the wage labour economy. None of the band members, however, had attended school and very few spoke English. In 1944, a year earlier, the inspector of Indian agencies had described the majority of band members in these terms: "timorous," "subjugated," "illiterate," "very backward" and in need of "strong sympathetic leadership and guidance." As late as 1944, DIA did not allow the band to elect its own chief and council.

At the meetings, the men of the band were persuaded to sign a surrender of I.R. 172 to the Crown "in trust to sell or lease the [reserve] to such person or persons, and upon such terms as the government of the Dominion of Canada may deem most conducive to our welfare and that of our people." DIA promised that it would find alternative reserves for the band.

The surrender signed by the band left it open to DIA to sell or to lease the reserve. DIA didn't have to sell it. If the Crown were to lease the reserve, when the Indians were ready to take up farming they would have good agricultural land.

Many weeks at trial were later spent determining whether DIA officials at the meetings had disclosed to the band members the consequences of a surrender. Did the members of the band comprehend the implications of signing the surrender: they were giving up immensely valuable reserve land for a doubtful and unspecific promise of "alternate reserves?" Did they understand that they would also be giving up mineral rights? True, the mineral rights had already been surrendered in 1940, but only for lease. If they were swallowed up in a surrender of the whole reserve, they, too, could be sold off. Given that the Indians were illiterate, and unwise in the implications of real estate transactions, it seems unlikely that they would have understood all these points.

The band had now lost the reserve, including the mineral rights. The longstanding policy of DIA had been overthrown. It is true that under the surrender it was open to DIA to lease the reserve, but now DIA also had the power to sell it. Which course they were to adopt was wholly a matter for DIA discretion. The band was at its mercy.

In fact, leasing the reserve was never considered by the minister or his officials at DIA. Immediately after the surrender was signed by the Indians, DIA stated publicly that the reserve would be made available to the Director of the Veterans Land Act (DVLA) for sale to returning veterans.

A price, however, had to be reached between DIA and DVLA. For this purpose, the reserve had to be appraised. On December 7, 1946, DIA accepted DVLA's offer of $70,000. Two years later, on January 20, 1948, DVLA completed the purchase of I.R. 172 for that amount.

This sale was from a government department (DIA) to a government agency (DVLA). A price was agreed. Money changed hands. It was a transaction within the confines of government, but it resembled outwardly an arm's-length deal. There had been three appraisals. The transaction was based on market value.

But, strangely, the mineral rights, surrendered in 1940 but only for lease, were not evaluated in DIA's appraisals of I.R. 172, and no payment was obtained by DIA from DVLA for them. Mineral rights were not discussed when the land was transferred to DVLA or when, after the purchase by DVLA was completed in 1948, DVLA began to enter into agreements for sale with veterans.

Since 1940, there had been exploration on I.R. 172. The oil and gas industry had shown an interest, if only slight, in the mineral potential of I.R. 172. The permit fees, such as they were, were paid into the band's account. But nothing was obtained by DIA in exchange for the mineral rights. In law, there was no consideration (that is, money) given for them. The $70,000 purchase price for the reserve was for the surface rights only. The mineral rights were simply passed along to DVLA, and then by DVLA to the veterans together with the land itself.

Meanwhile, in the Peace River country, game had become scarce. By 1947, members of the band were near starvation. Tuberculosis was widespread. The regional superintendent of DIA in charge of health services visited the band in the summer of 1947 and reported: "These Indians have a special claim on the sympathy of the Department as their complete extinction seems possible. I will not venture at this time to say what can be done."

What about the alternative reserves that were to replace Montney? In 1950, five years after the surrender of I.R. 172, three replacement reserves were acquired from the province of British Columbia for $4,962.50 and set aside for the Beaver band. During this period, the material condition of the band had greatly deteriorated.

The $70,000 from the sale of I.R. 172 had been placed in the band's account. Most of the money, however, had been spent trying to establish a farm for the Indians on one of the three replacement reserves, a task difficult to the point almost of impossibility because these new reserves consisted of land unsuitable for agriculture. It is paradoxical that DIA should have been willing to see the Indians give up prime agricultural land and then seek to train them as farmers once they had settled them on moose pasture.

The Indians remained as squatters on Crown land at a place called Peterson's Crossing for the next decade. They were kept there to be near the local school. The Indian agent withheld rations from those families with children who sought to return to live in the bush.

Now DVLA held the land, including the mineral rights, and were busily engaged in transferring to the veterans the land that once was the Montney Reserve—and they were also transferring the mineral rights. The veterans expected to acquire the land for farming; the mineral rights would unexpectedly make them wealthy. As soon as DVLA acquired the reserve, on January 20, 1948, it subdivided it and then began the process of transferring it to veterans under agreements for sale. The first of the agreements for sale was signed on

September 10, 1948; the last on April 3, 1956. When the veterans had completed their payments, DVLA gave them title deeds to their properties. But from the moment each of the veterans signed an agreement to pay in instalments and took possession of his farm, he was treated as the owner.

In the meantime, in 1949 and the years following, oil and gas exploration in the neighbourhood of Montney continued. On December 10, 1952, DVLA entered into a petroleum and natural gas pooling agreement with the veterans, who were described in the agreement as the "farmers of the Fort St. John Indian Reserve, number 172," to share equally among themselves in the exploration revenues from oil and gas found in the pools beneath the reserve. It was also agreed they would share royalties equally among themselves from the production of oil and gas. So the veterans, forty in number, who now owned the reserve, would enjoy all of the oil and gas revenue from the lands they now held. No discovery was made on I.R. 172 until 1977, but after that oil was produced in abundance.

In tracing this bureaucratic paper trail, the question arose, what had happened to the mineral rights? The surface rights (that is, the land itself) had been surrendered by the band. The mineral rights had been surrendered for lease in 1940. But when the surrender of I.R. 172—a surrender of the whole reserve—was signed in 1945, the band's entire interest in the mineral rights had been surrendered, the surrender for lease swallowed up in the surrender for sale.

As for DIA, it seemed not to know what had occurred. In 1949 a natural gas company wrote to DIA seeking an exploration permit for I.R. 172. Natural gas had been discovered forty miles southeast of the reserve. DIA immediately sent the local Indian agent out with instructions to obtain a surrender of mineral rights from the band. The sale to DVLA had been completed in 1948, and the first sale to a veteran made that same year. Yet DIA did not realize the mineral rights had already been transferred to DVLA and on to the veterans. The Indians did not own the mineral rights anymore. Nor did DIA.

In 1961, a solicitor in the Department of Veterans Affairs made a note in his file that it had "always been a mystery" to him how DVLA had acquired the mineral rights. As for the Department of Indian Affairs, the best theory that DIA could come up with was that the mineral rights had passed from DIA to DVLA because there was no specific reservation of mineral rights in the "sale" to DVLA.

However it had occurred, the loss of mineral rights was a breach of trust by DIA. It had decided, in a marked departure from policy, to sell the reserve for $70,000, the appraised value of the surface rights. But there was nothing to prevent DIA from continuing to hold the mineral rights and leasing them to the oil and gas industry, retaining the royalties for the Indians. This had always been the policy. Instead, it had passed the rights on without receiving any consideration in return. DIA had given them away, apparently in a state of absent-mindedness.

Now the Beaver band's patrimony had been lost entirely—the farmland had been sold, and the mineral rights apparently given away. And DIA did not seem to know how it had all come about.

The band was virtually powerless to act on its own behalf. A 1963 survey classified all adults in the band over thirty years of age as illiterate, and stated that very few under that age had more than a Grade 1 or 2 education. In those days, Indians and Indian bands did not have lawyers; they didn't sue. They left their affairs entirely in the hands of DIA. Besides, the Indians were unaware that they might have a claim. Indeed, it would not have occurred to anyone that they might have a claim at law.

Even if they had retained a lawyer, it is unlikely that at that time anything *could* have been done. The Crown, in the shape of DIA, was a trustee of I.R. 172. There was a trust, but it was understood to be merely a political trust. The department understood its duty was political; that is, if it did not act in the best interests of the Indians in disposing of their surrendered lands, DIA would have to explain to Parliament and the public. But it did not regard itself as legally accountable; that is, DIA was not accountable in the courts, nor did anyone think the Indians could take DIA to court seeking damages for any breach of trust.

In 1975, another civil servant dedicated to the best interests of the Indians entered the picture. In that year C.S. Johnson-Watson was appointed district manager of the Fort St. John Indian Agency. Johnson-Watson was to testify that the band's leaders relied on him to make their decisions "as if I were the boss," and he rated the band's capacity to manage their own affairs as being one on a scale of one to ten.

Johnson-Watson began to inquire how the band had lost the reserve. He was puzzled because he found that the band was trying to develop marginal land for farming on the alternative reserves, even though Montney, which had been held for the band from 1916 to 1945, seemed well suited to that purpose. At his urging, the band consulted a lawyer, Louise Mandell. In 1978, DIA divided the Beaver band into two bands: the Blueberry River and Doig River bands. When a lawsuit was commenced in September 1978, it was in the names of the chiefs of the Blueberry River band and the Doig River band. But this lawsuit was thirty years and eight months after the transfer of the Montney Reserve, including the mineral rights, to DVLA on January 20, 1948.

British Columbia had in 1975 in its statute of limitations adopted a thirty-year ultimate limitation period; that is, no lawsuit could be commenced more than thirty years after the event that gave rise to a right to sue. In any event, when the lawsuit was commenced, too late or not, there was in truth no realistic basis for a suit against the federal government. Everyone regarded DIA as accountable to Parliament, not to the courts.

In 1984, the Supreme Court of Canada changed all that in *Guerin v. The Queen*. The Musqueam band, which held lands adjacent to Vancouver, had surrendered part of its reserve. Under the surrender, DIA held that land in trust for leasing and granted a lease to the Shaughnessy Golf Club on terms contrary to the expressed wishes of the band. The band sued for breach of trust. The band argued, relying on American jurisprudence, that DIA was a trustee. The trial judge agreed and awarded $10 million. The Federal Court of Appeal, however, upheld DIA's view that there was no legal trust, merely a political trust. DIA was responsible to Parliament but not to the courts. There could be no legal remedy. But the Musqueam band and its redoubtable lawyer, Marvin Storrow, were not willing to give up. They obtained leave to appeal to the Supreme Court of Canada.

When the case went to the Supreme Court of Canada, the court rejected the argument that the Crown's obligation to the Indians was not legally enforceable. Though the court did not hold that the Crown was a trustee, it held that the Crown was a fiduciary. A fiduciary is someone who has been given a discretion to deal with or dispose of someone else's property, placing that other in a vulnerable position. The Supreme Court went back to the Royal Proclamation of 1763. In that year the Crown had undertaken a historic responsibility to protect the interests of the Indians in transactions with third parties. The Indian Act, said the court, confirms that responsibility, founding it on twin pillars: the first is that Indians cannot sell their reserves to anyone except the Crown; the second is the discretion given to the Crown to decide, when the Indians sign a surrender, what is in the best interests of the Indians. In *Guerin,* Justice Brian Dickson, for the majority, wrote:

The Royal Proclamation of 1763 provided that no private person could purchase from the Indians any lands that the Proclamation had reserved to them, and provided further that all purchases had to be by and in the name of the Crown, in a public assembly of the Indians held by the governor or commander-in-chief of the colony in which the lands in question lay ... This policy with respect to the sale or transfer of the Indians' interest in land has been continuously maintained by the British Crown, by the governments of the colonies when they became responsible for the administration of Indian affairs, and, after 1867, by the federal government of Canada. Successive federal statutes, predecessors to the present Indian act, have all provided for the general inalienability of Indian reserve land except upon surrender to the Crown.

He went on:

The purpose of this surrender requirement is clearly to interpose the Crown between the Indians and prospective purchasers or lessees of their land, so as to prevent the Indians from being exploited. This is made clear in the Royal Proclamation itself, which prefaces the provision making the Crown an intermediary with a declaration that "great Frauds and Abuses have been committed in purchasing Lands of the Indians, to the great Prejudice of our Interests and to the great Dissatisfaction of the said Indians . . .". Through the confirmation in the Indian Act of the historic responsibility which the Crown has undertaken, to act on behalf of the Indians so as to protect their interests in transactions with third parties, *Parliament has conferred upon the Crown a discretion to decide for itself where the Indians' best interests really lie* [emphasis added].

Justice Dickson held that the Crown was therefore a fiduciary. Once a band voted to surrender its reserve land or part of it, it was entirely up to the Crown to decide what to do with it. The Crown has a discretion, but it has to exercise its discretion in the best interests of the Indians. That is the touchstone. If the Crown fails to act in the best interests of the band, it will be guilty of a breach of fiduciary obligation and will have to pay damages.

By the time the lawsuit by the Blueberry River and Doig River bands got to trial, the law had changed. They could rely on *Guerin.* DIA could no longer claim that its accountability was strictly political; now it was plainly accountable legally.

The case went to trial in 1987. The trial judge was Justice George Addy. The trial took three months. Arthur Pape and Leslie Pinder represented the band.

Justice Addy rejected the bands' claims. He found that there had been "informed consent." The band members knew what they were doing in 1945 when they signed the surrender. They could not come forward forty years later and complain that they did not know. Moreover, he held that the thirty-year ultimate limitation period under B.C.'s statute of limitations began to run at the time of the transfer of I.R. 172 by the Crown to DVLA on January 20, 1948; therefore, the lawsuit, which was not filed until September 1978, eight months *after* the thirty-year period had expired, was statute-barred.

By now it was apparent that the mineral rights were the key to the lawsuit. Justice Addy made a finding that DIA had *not* told the bands when they signed the surrender of the reserve in 1945 that they were giving up the mineral rights, too. Nevertheless, he held:

I find that, taking into account the fiduciary relationship then existing between Her Majesty the Queen and the plaintiffs, none of her officers, servants or agents, exercising due care, consideration and attention in the discharge of those fiduciary duties, could reasonably be expected to have anticipated at any time during 1948 or previously that there would be any real value attached to potential mineral rights under I.R. 172 or that there would be any reasonably foreseeable advantage in retaining them.

The bands appealed to the Federal Court of Appeal. They asked me to argue their case on the appeal. Gary Nelson worked with me; Leslie Pinder and Arthur Pape stayed on to help us.

On October 26, 1992, I presented our opening argument in the Federal Court of Appeal. It was at the Federal Court of Appeal's courtrooms in the Pacific Centre, in downtown Vancouver. Though members of the court live in Ottawa, they travel around the country to hear appeals.

Why do I remember the date? It was the date of the Charlottetown Referendum, a nationwide ballot on a series of complicated amendments to the Constitution. Chief Justice Julius Isaac, Canada's first black chief justice, announced that the court would adjourn early if necessary to give us all time to cast our ballots. I had served on the "Yes" Committee, urging adoption of the Charlottetown Accord. I spoke at a number of meetings in support of the accord. "This time," I said, "the establishment has got it right!" The accord went down badly to defeat. I had not lost my political touch.

As I opened my argument, I thought about Justice Addy. We were appealing his judgement. We alleged that he had failed to fairly assess the evidence and to apply the law. Ten years had gone by since he had complained to the Judicial Council about my intervention in the constitutional debate. A man who thought that speaking out in defence of Aboriginal rights was worse than impaired driving or sleeping with a prostitute must have some peculiar ideas. Some had, we thought, bobbed up in his reasons for judgement. He had not applied a fiduciary standard, but had instead applied a test of informed consent. This distinction was not esoteric, but basic.

The law of fiduciary duty is that a fiduciary must look after a beneficiary's property with the same prudence he would use if it were his own property. A prudent owner would not have given away the mineral rights. A prudent owner would have done exactly what DVLA did on behalf of the veterans: *lease* the mineral rights to oil companies. The leasing of the mineral rights to Montney in 1940 was in the best interests of the Indians. The *sale* of the mineral rights in 1945 was not. It wasn't a question of whether the Indians had given their informed consent, but whether DIA had acted in their best interests.

Then there was a second issue: If there had been a breach of fiduciary duty, what was the extent of DIA's responsibility?

Justice Addy's judgement turned on a particular phrase he had used. He described the Crown's fiduciary duty as "a duty on the Crown to take reasonable care in offering the advice to or in taking any action on behalf of the Indians." Taking reasonable care is what we expect, for example, of persons driving their cars along the highways. They are liable for the consequences of their own negligence that they, as reasonable persons, can foresee. If they travel at a dangerous speed, and an accident happens, they are legally responsible. They should have foreseen it. But that's all. They are not responsible for what they cannot reasonably foresee. The same is true in cases of breach of contract.

So, applying this same test, the argument we had to meet was that in 1948, when I.R. 172 was sold and the mineral rights disposed of, no one thought there might be oil and gas in large volumes beneath the reserve. Justice Addy held that there was no reason to believe the Crown should have foreseen that the mineral rights might turn out to be valuable.

But this test does not apply to a fiduciary. If you are a fiduciary, you are liable for all the consequences, whether you could foresee them or not. A fiduciary has a higher duty than the driver of a car or a businessman entering into an ordinary commercial contract. A fiduciary has an obligation of honour.

We pointed out that the law had been established by the Supreme Court in *Canson Enterprises Ltd. v. Boughton & Co.* In that case, Justice Beverley McLachlin had written:

It does not lie in the mouth of a fiduciary who has assumed the special responsibility of trust to say the loss could not reasonably have been foreseen . . . In the case of breach of fiduciary duty . . . we do not have to look to the consequences to judge the reasonableness of the actions. A breach of fiduciary duty is wrong in itself, regardless of whether a loss can be foreseen [emphasis added].

The fiduciary is responsible for all the consequences, foreseen or unforeseen.

The hearing before the Court of Appeal went on for five days. On the fifth day, when the time came for my reply, I had arranged to meet Gary, Art and Leslie over coffee in the morning, before we went back into court.

I went over what I intended to say. They all approved. Then I said, "Why not use Othello's line, referring to his murder of Desdemona, that he had behaved 'Like the base Indian, who threw a pearl away richer than all his tribe.' " That's what had happened here. The Indians, trusting in DIA, had lost a fortune. Horrors. Don't say that, they said. Othello was black, and Chief Justice Isaac is black.

My idea was to capture the essence of the case, in a metaphor that would stay in the judges' minds. To quote Shakespeare or the Bible is not to display a spurious or meretricious learning—I've cited the poetry of F. R. Scott, too. It is because Shakespeare or the Bible is likely to have used an image in an unforgettable way, and because most judges and juries have some knowledge of Shakespeare and the Bible.

The telling phrase is not forgotten. As a law student in the 1950s, I had gone to the courthouse in Vancouver to hear John Diefenbaker (soon to be prime minister). He had come from his Saskatchewan fastness to defend Deane Finlayson, the leader of the B.C. Conservative Party, who had made public the allegations in a statement of claim filed in a civil case against Robert Sommers, a member of W. A. C. Bennett's cabinet. The claim alleged that Sommers had accepted bribes. (He was later convicted and sentenced.) Sommers had applied to have Finlayson found guilty of contempt, on the ground that the allegations should not have been made public, even though they appeared in a public document filed in the courthouse. John Diefenbaker, in his peroration on behalf of Finlayson, urging the fullest disclosure, had said, "A closed door on free speech is an open door to tyranny." Diefenbaker vibrated as he said it, but in my mind the phrase rumbles on to the present.

Why would the Indians have thrown away the Montney treasure if they had known what it was? The "base Indian" in Shakespeare didn't know the wealth he held in his hand. Well, when our clients had put their Xs to the surrender in 1945, did they know the extent of the wealth they were giving up? Of course not. Then again, perhaps the use of the phrase would have been a bad idea. What did it reveal about our case? It may be I hadn't thought it through. There is a tendency to become enamoured of these bits of filigree. Luckily, they are usually rejected when the moment comes to utter them. In any event, I succumbed to the protests of my colleagues. I was to have no opportunity to display my knowledge of *Othello*. They may have been right to urge me not to use it. The quotation evokes an image of feckless Indians. Our clients were Indians who had no choice but to trust DIA. It was DIA, not the Indians, who had fecklessly thrown away a fortune.

There is always the danger of lawyers lapsing into legal language so abstruse that it flies beyond the region of true meaning. Jury trials, civil and criminal, are a means for citizens with no training in the law to participate in the administration of justice; to sit in judgement, an exercise in citizenship fully as important as voting in elections. But jury trials are also a kind of discipline for lawyers and judges. Lawyers are obliged, if they expect to be understood, to cast their arguments in everyday language. Only in this way can they be effective with juries. There is nothing simple-minded about the use of everyday language. I have found that the most reliable experts in any field, whether law, economics or engineering, are those who can explain their approach in language that any intelligent person, taking the trouble to pay close attention, can understand. The most profound thoughts can usually be expressed in language that is understood at once or almost at once.

Although it is important to put legal propositions with clarity when addressing a jury, it is equally important to do so when addressing a judge sitting without a jury or in the appellate courts. And there is no reason why judges should not express themselves in plain language. Judges get used to talking to each other, and writing for each other—or for legal academics—in the law reports. But there is no reason why the law reports should be stuffed with legal arcana.

When the Federal Court of Appeal's decision came down, we had lost. Chief Justice Isaac, however, dissented in our favour. He would have restored the Montney treasure—or at least provided compensation for its loss.

Justice Louis Marceau, writing for the majority in the Federal Court of Appeal, affirmed Justice Addy's view that the Crown as fiduciary had no more than a duty to take reasonable care to use skill and competence in giving advice to the Indians. This was the language of negligence, not fiduciary obligation. It did not take into account the special elements of loyalty and trust that give rise to the fiduciary duty. Moreover, it did not take into account that no advice had been provided to the Indians regarding their best interests, and no attempt made by the Crown to protect their best interests.

Justice Marceau went on to shrink the Crown's obligation to the vanishing point. He resurrected the theory that the king can do no wrong, ruling that the Crown as fiduciary is not to be held to the same standard as an individual, because the Crown always has to deal with the perfectly legitimate needs of other constituencies. If the Crown sells Indian land to serve those other needs, even though it is not in the best interests of the Indians to do so, the needs of the Crown's other constituencies are a sufficient justification. On this view, the Crown's fiduciary obligation is dissolved in the Crown's willingness to acquiesce, at the expense of the Indians, in the needs of its other constituencies.

Of course, the Crown may have to deal with many claims, political and otherwise, to a parcel of land. But it does not owe a fiduciary obligation to these other claimants, not even to veterans who have fought for their country. If the Crown signs a contract to sell a parcel of land, it cannot ignore its obligation to the buyer. If it does, the sale will be in breach of contract. The courts will hold it accountable. In the same way, if the Crown has a fiduciary obligation and ignores that obligation, it will be guilty of a breach of fiduciary obligation and be liable in damages.

Justice Marceau also held that time began to run on the band's claim on January 20, 1948, when DIA transferred Montney to DVLA; as a result, he held, as Justice Addy had done, that the action was time-barred by the thirty-year ultimate limitation period.

Chief Justice Isaac, in his dissenting judgement, focussed on the mineral rights. He held that the Crown had acted in breach of its fiduciary duty in transferring the mineral rights. He also held that the Crown could not relinquish its fiduciary duty by a transfer of I.R. 172 from the Department of Indian Affairs to DVLA. The Crown's duty continued as long as DVLA held the land, because DVLA is an agent of the Crown. Accordingly, B.C.'s thirty-year ultimate limitation period did not apply. He would have allowed the band's claim for damages in respect of the loss of the mineral rights and sent the case back for a new trial.

The majority in the Federal Court of Appeal avoided the real question: Was it prudent for the Crown on behalf of the Indians to give up eighteen thousand acres of prime agricultural land? Was the Crown obliged to consider whether it was prudent? Was it consistent with the honour of the Crown to promote the surrender of Montney in violation of the Crown's declared policy of refusing to sell Indian lands? Since 1763, the idea of the Crown's role as guardian of Indian interests has been to see that the Crown is interposed to protect Indians against imprudent transactions. But here the Crown promoted the transaction. Most important of all, was it imprudent to transfer the mineral rights?

If the majority in the Federal Court of Appeal were right, the surrender provisions of the Indian Act were not a scheme to protect the Indians' land, but simply a means for obtaining the Indians' consent to the orderly disposal of their land. If, on the other hand, Chief Justice Isaac was right, the Crown had the same responsibility for a breach of duty as any other fiduciary.

With a strong dissent from Chief Justice Isaac on an important question of law, I thought the Supreme Court would grant leave to appeal. We applied, and on March 23, 1993, leave was granted.

The trial had taken three months. The appeal had lasted five days. The Supreme Court of Canada, however, had adopted a policy of giving each side one hour to present its case; the court expected a case to be fully argued before noon or, if it started after lunch, to be completed by the end of the day. I thought we needed more time. I asked Chief Justice Antonio Lamer for a three-day hearing. The lawyers for the Crown agreed. Chief Justice Lamer said that the patriation reference involving the challenge by the provinces to Pierre Trudeau's assertion of Parliament's power to bring home the Constitution had only taken two days. He didn't give us three days, but he did give us two days.

In *Calder*, the Supreme Court had opened up the issue of Aboriginal title: the Indians had lost a whole country to which they held Aboriginal title. Land claims were to be the means of achieving compensation for such an immeasurable deprivation. But land claims settlements had to be negotiated. Except in elaborating matters of principle, the courts have a restricted role; they are not engaged in determining what compensation there ought to be—again and again in such cases they have urged negotiations.

What the Indians had been left with, out of this limitless patrimony, were parcels of land reserved for them called Indian reserves. Under the Indian Act these reserves could be surrendered. A surrender could leave a band with little or no land. After the decision in *Guerin*, the Supreme Court took upon itself the task of determining the conditions under which such surrenders could be set aside and compensation awarded.

The Montney case required the court to deal with at least three major issues. What is the Crown's fiduciary duty in a case where DIA has obtained a surrender and then disposed of Indian reserve lands in a way contrary to its own long-standing policies? If there has been a breach of fiduciary duty, would the Crown be liable for the loss of the fortune discovered beneath Montney even if the Crown had no reason to foresee it was giving away a fortune? And there was the question of limitations: Would B.C.'s thirty-year limitation period be an insuperable obstacle to recovery? We would be arguing all three.

I keep saying "we argued." In a case like Montney, this is the only way consistently to acknowledge the role of other lawyers working with me. In the Supreme Court lengthy factums are filed. Hours of study and discussion go into these written submissions. Our factum in the Montney case was developed by Gary Nelson. We discussed it constantly as he worked on it. We reviewed it with Arthur Pape and Leslie Pinder. But it was largely Gary's work. My job was to present the oral argument. This presentation does not consist simply in reading the factum. It is fair to assume that the judges will have read the judgements given by the lower courts and will—or at least their law clerks will—have read the factums.

The record of the trial is usually too voluminous for easy reference. In the Montney case, thousands of pages of evidence had been assembled. As well, the earlier cases decided by the Supreme Court, many of them of considerable length, were all photocopied and placed before the court. In this welter of testimony, documents, exhibits and legal precedents, it is important to lead the court through the evidence by going to the key testimony, the critical findings, and reminding the judges of what they themselves have said in their own decisions.

In the appellate courts, the volume of written material—transcripts, briefs, precedents—threatens to overwhelm the courts with detail. It is impossible to believe that anyone reads it all, but still it grows. Even at the trial level, certainly as far as civil cases are concerned, the same tendency prevails.

To raise your head above this parapet of paper—more important still, to persuade the judges to consider the case without becoming buried in the avalanche of ring binders—is essential if your argument—your take on the case—is to be considered, let alone prevail.

But too many lawyers regard themselves as bound to the wheel of these tonnes of minutiae. They eschew the use of all but the most mundane language. Of course, you have to master your brief; make sure the court understands the key documents, the important testimony, the real issues in the case. But you have to break through the flurry of paper to help the court find its bearings.

In the Montney case, I spent a week determining exactly how I would present the case. There will be questions from the court; issues may be raised by the other side in a telling manner. But you must have confidence in your own judgement, in saying, in effect, to the court: "No, this is what is critical; this is where the law takes us."

It is a question of judgement—what line to take; the issues to emphasize. What is the best way—often it may be the only way—to persuade the court? This is so at trial and in the appellate courts. At trial there may be time to move away from an unpromising line of attack; in the appellate courts, you have plenty of time to prepare, but you may nevertheless in mid-appeal decide to make an alteration in course. In the Supreme Court, there is no time to do that. The whole case often must be compressed into a single hour's presentation.

In 1989, I was retained by John Laxton to argue the appeal in *Just v. The Queen*. Laxton had been unsuccessful at trial and an appeal to the Court of Appeal for British Columbia had been dismissed. John Laxton is probably British Columbia's leading lawyer in the field of torts and one of the leading lawyers in the country in the same field.

Why would John Laxton call on me to take the case to the Supreme Court of Canada? He had as much experience, indeed more, than I had in the field of tort law. The answer is that he had lost the case at trial, then lost again in the Court of Appeal. He still thought that his client had a case. But he felt he had grown stale on the case, that it needed a fresh look.

Laxton's client was named John Just. Just and his daughter were driving along the Squamish Highway, on their way to a day of skiing at Whistler. The Squamish Highway curves along, at sea level, between the waters of Howe Sound (to the left, when driving north) and a mountainside (to the right). The mountainside is treed, but the incline is steep. There had been a heavy snowfall, and traffic was stopped. A great boulder, weighing more than a tonne, worked loose from the wooded slopes above and crashed like a meteor onto Just's car. He and his daughter were severely injured.

Could John Just sue the provincial government? The province owned the highway. The province had a duty to maintain it. But how far did that duty extend? It was a highway built along a mountainside. There was a danger to motorists of falling rock. The province had taken precautions. It provided periodic inspections.

Should the government be responsible for everything that can go wrong *on a mountainside?* Must it have its employees patrol the mountainside to watch for falling rock? How could a government afford to do so? Somewhere out there the government's duty to take care of motorists travelling along the highway below the mountain peters out, like a dusty country road. But no one is exactly sure where that point is reached.

The case involved an argument about government policy and government operations. The courts will not review government policy. So if the government decided, as a matter of policy, not to inspect the mountainside to guard against falling rock, John Just would not have a case. But if the government did decide, as a matter of policy, to carry out inspections, that decision would bring us into the area of government operations. The courts might be persuaded that the government had thereby assumed a duty of care towards motorists and that the courts should consider whether the inspections were frequent and thorough enough to discharge the duty of care. At this point, the courts would be dealing not with policy but with operations.

In Just's case, the Supreme Court allowed us only one hour to make our case. The trial may have taken days or weeks or even months. The appeal may have taken days in the Court of Appeal. The volumes of materials filed with the court may be stacked almost to the ceiling. So what use do you make of your single hour?

Sometimes the choice is not altogether your own. The court may throw questions at you from the outset. You want to answer the questions. If you have determined exactly what the issue is, and how to frame it, the questions may provide an opening to discuss the issue plainly. Or not. If not, you must be prepared to indicate, as politely as you can, that neither the question nor its answer will get to the heart of the case.

John Laxton came with me to Ottawa. He was to appear at my side as I presented the argument. We were working in the library of the Supreme Court on the day before the hearing. I still had to decide how best to use that hour. John was writing furiously. He kept handing me notes across the table where we were working. I read them and carried on with my own preparation. When the flow of notes across the table threatened to overwhelm me, I took to scrunching them up and throwing them into the wastebasket. John was distinctly unhappy about this development. After breakfast the next morning, however, as we walked to the Supreme Court building for the hearing, he said, "You're right; it's your case today. You have to do it your way."

I decided to use a simple analogy. I said that, as I left the Four Seasons Hotel that morning, the sidewalk in front of the hotel was scraped free of ice and swept. But if the job had been done negligently, and someone had been injured, the hotel would have been liable.

The stairs to the Supreme Court building had also been scraped and swept. The government of Canada had, as a matter of policy, decided it should keep the stairs of public buildings in the capital scraped and swept. It had assumed a duty of care. If the government decided that it was not going to keep the stairs of public buildings in the capital free of snow and ice, that would be a policy decision. The government would not be liable if snow and ice accumulated. If, however, it adopted a policy of keeping the stairs to public buildings in Ottawa safe, it had to do the job properly. The same applied to inspections of the rock cliffs on the mountainside on the road to Whistler. Once you decided to inspect, you had to do it properly.

We won the case. The Supreme Court held there was a duty of care. It is, I think, regarded as the high-water mark for imposing liability on government for negligence while carrying out public duties. A new trial was ordered; Laxton persuaded the trial judge to award $1.5 million in damages.

In the Montney case, before the Supreme Court, I argued that the 1945 surrender was manifestly improvident and that the Crown was well aware that it was improvident. That is why DIA officials had consistently refused, until 1945, despite pressure from the white community, to ask the band to surrender I.R. 172. DIA had reversed course in 1945 when renewed political pressure to make the land available for "ordinary settlement" became "difficult and embarrassing" and resulted in "criticism and censure," to cite the words of R. A. Hoey, Dr. McGill's successor. Notwithstanding that, the surrender of I.R. 172 was contrary to departmental policy, which was "solidly against alienation by sale of lands for which there is any likelihood of Indian need in future years," as the minister of Indian affairs had advised Parliament that same year.

Even if the band made little use of Montney in 1945, there can be no doubt that the Crown as fiduciary was obliged to look ahead to consider what the best interests of the band might require in the future. There was no dispute about the fact that the band would need the land some day for farming, when the pressure of settlement on hunting and trapping put an end to its traditional way of life. The Crown's policy required (to use the language of the minister in his 1945 report to Parliament) that it "set its face" against any sale of Montney; instead, it promoted the surrender and sale of Montney.

We took the argument further. Here we had an illiterate band, unschooled in property values. Even if the Indians had, independently of the Crown's importuning, decided they wanted to sell Montney, the Crown should have refused to accept the surrender. A fiduciary cannot dispose of a beneficiary's land imprudently, even at the beneficiary's request.

We concentrated, however, on the mineral rights. Even if the band had consented to the sale of the reserve, how could it be said it had consented to the sale of the mineral rights? Here Justice Addy had made an important finding. He had found as a fact that "no mention of mineral rights were [sic] made at the [surrender] meeting." Our argument would be: The Indians had agreed in 1940 to surrender the mineral rights to the Crown for lease. They should have been told in 1945 that, by signing a complete surrender of I.R. 172, they would lose them altogether.

If the mineral rights *were* included in the 1945 surrender, it was a breach of fiduciary obligation for the Crown to obtain their surrender without disclosing to the Indians that the mineral rights would pass entirely out of the Indians' ownership as a result of the surrender, and a further breach to acquiesce in the mineral rights being taken over by DVLA and transferred to the veterans.

We adopted the reasoning of Chief Justice Isaac, who had said in his dissenting judgement:

If the Crown intended that the 1945 surrender was both to divest the Indians of their entire interest in the reserve and to relieve itself of the willingly assumed obligation to administer the mineral rights to the Reserve in the Indians' best interests, *it would have been under a positive duty to inform the Indians that this was the case* [emphasis added].

I emphasized how, through what the civil service itself described as inadvertence, the mineral rights had slipped away. In 1961, A.F. McWilliams, a lawyer in Veterans Affairs, wrote to the director of Veterans Affairs:

It has been known here The Director, The Veterans' Land Act is the owner of the mineral rights underlying the Fort St. John Indian Reserve. *It has always been a mystery to the writer how he acquired these mineral rights, and our file on the Fort St. John Indian Reserve does not disclose how this came about.* We would be interested to know therefore, under what arrangement did The Director, The Veterans' Land Act [DVLA] acquire the mineral rights under the Fort St. John Indian Reserve [emphasis added].

H.R. Holmes, the superintendent of the securities and property division of Veterans Affairs, replied:

1. I think the simple answer to your query of June 14th is that the reason we acquired the mineral rights when we acquired the surface rights is because the Letters Patent which issued did not reserve the mines and minerals.

2. The chief and principal men of the St. John Beaver Band of Indians executed a Surrender dated the 22nd of September, 1945, and the Governor in Council by Order in Council P.C. 6506 dated the 16th day of October, 1945, accepted the Surrender and authorized the Minister of Mines and Resources [under which ministry DIA came at the time] to sell or lease the said lands subject to the conditions of the Surrender and the provisions of the Indian Act. *During purchase negotiations with Indian affairs, there was no reference, to the best of my knowledge and belief, to the question of mineral rights. As I have already said, the mines and minerals, either deliberately or inadvertently, were not reserved with the result that we acquired them. I think possibly the failure to reserve the sub-surface rights was inadvertent* [emphasis added].

In the 1920s, 1930s and 1940s, members of the civil service had fought like tigers to prevent the Montney Reserve passing from Indian ownership. But in the transfer of the once-Indian land from DIA to DVLA and thence to the veterans, other members of the civil service had completely overlooked the mineral rights. They had not reserved them for the Indians when the land was transferred to DVLA; instead, they had allowed them to slip out of their hands for no consideration. Holmes's letter characterizes what occurred in understated language suitable to the argot of the civil service. But there could be no masking the fact that there had been a grim failure by DIA to protect the Indians' interests.

A few years earlier, Christianson, Schmidt and McGill had cogently urged the protection of the Indian interests. Now, nameless bureaucrats (nameless because it was never possible to identify them) in DIA had inadvertently given away a fortune in mineral rights belonging to the Indians.

This was the heart of our argument: DIA in 1949 took the position that the minerals had passed to DVLA by the transfer in 1948. DVLA then leased the rights to oil companies for the benefit of the veterans. Later, the lands were transferred to the veterans in fee simple. The Crown failed to take any steps to protect the band's interest in the mineral rights or to obtain any benefit for the band. How could it be said that this failure fulfilled the Crown's duty under the 1945 surrender to dispose of Montney upon such terms as would be, according to the language of the surrender signed by the Indians, "most conducive to our welfare and that of our people"?

As regards the extent of the Crown's liability, we argued that it was responsible for all the losses that followed. A fiduciary's liability, we argued, according to the Supreme Court's ruling in *Canson*, was not limited by foreseeability.

We still had to get around the thirty-year limitation period. Our main argument was that time did not start to run so long as the land that had once been I.R. 172 was still in federal hands. And there could be no doubt that DVLA was an agent of the federal government. Before I had finished my argument, Justice McLachlin asked about a little-known section of the 1927 Indian Act, which authorized DIA to cancel any sale made in error. I confess I had not appreciated the significance of this provision. We seized on it to argue that DIA was under a continuing obligation, even after the sale to DVLA, to cancel the sale and return the mineral rights to the band. That meant the limitations clock would not begin to run until DVLA had passed the rights on to the veterans.

We waited for the court's decision, which came in December. I arrived at the office before seven, to wait for news by the fax machine. Seven o'clock arrived. It would be ten in Ottawa. What was the outcome? Then the phone rang. It was a call from the office of Harry Slade, the band's solicitor. We had won. The court had allowed the appeal. But I wanted to see the reasons for judgement. When the reasons for judgement arrived, I realized the court had sawed the baby in half. But first of all, the court had laid out the ground rules for fiduciaries.

The court found that the 1945 surrender of the surface rights was not obtained in breach of the Crown's fiduciary duty: after all, the Crown intended that alternative reserves could be acquired for hunting and trapping; it was, Justice McLachlin held, a defensible decision. Moreover, the court was obviously reluctant, fifty years on, to engage in too close a review of what course of action might have best served the interests of the band. But as regards the loss of the mineral rights, the court had no such compunction.

Turning to the mineral rights, Justice McLachlin focussed on two aspects of the case:

First, at the time the mineral rights passed to the DVLA, and hence to the veterans, the Indians were unsophisticated and may not have fully understood the concept of different interests in land and how they might be lost. Second, they were never advised of the transfer of the mineral rights to the DVLA. They discovered it only in 1977, when an employee of the DIA brought to their attention that oil and gas had been discovered on their former lands and queried how the mineral rights had come to be transferred from the Band to the veterans.

The court decided, four to three, that the mineral rights had been included in the 1945 surrender. (Justice McLachlin and two others thought not, believing that the mineral rights were still held by the Crown under the 1940 surrender but only for lease.) That meant that the mineral rights had been lost as part of the 1945 surrender of the whole reserve, including subsurface as well as surface rights. But regardless of this dispute, all of the judges agreed with Justice McLachlin as to what followed.

Justice McLachlin wrote for a unanimous court. She held that the key was Justice Addy's finding that when the 1945 surrender was signed, the Crown had not disclosed to the band that by signing the surrender of the whole reserve the mineral rights would be irretrievably lost. The Indians knew that in 1940 they had surrendered the mineral rights but only to be *leased*. But they did not know that the 1945 surrender would mean that the mineral rights could be sold or given away by the Crown.

Justice McLachlin pointed out that selling the mineral rights was out of keeping with DIA's policy. How had it happened? She said:

Years later, wonderment persisted as to why the mineral rights had been passed to the DVLA. The wonderment was understandable given the well-known policy of the DIA to reserve out mineral rights and the fact that the only interest of the DVLA was to obtain land for agricultural purposes, not to enrich veterans through procuring mineral rights for them. The best explanation of how the mineral rights came to be transferred to the DVLA appears to lie in simple inadvertence.

Then Justice McLachlin turned to the question whether the inadvertence of DIA amounted to a breach of fiduciary duty. Justice Addy had found, as a matter of fact, that nobody at DIA had any reason to believe that the mineral rights were other than worthless. Justice McLachlin said:

The finding of the trial judge that the Crown could not have known in 1948 [when the mineral rights were transferred to DVLA] that the mineral rights might possess value flies in the face of the evidence on record. Accordingly, this is one of those rare cases where departure from a trial judge's finding may be warranted.

The Crown's own prior experience sufficed to establish that the mineral rights had actual and potential value. After taking the surrender in 1940, it issued a permit for prospecting for oil and gas on the property. The 1940 permit alone was worth $1,800, a not insignificant sum.

Justice McLachlin pointed out that the Crown, when its own interests were involved, always held on to the mineral rights when it conveyed property. This was the practice of the federal government and of the provinces. She went on:

If more were required, events close in time to 1948 reveal that these particular mineral rights might have considerable value, if only from the point of view of revenues from exploration rights. In 1949 interest in further exploration on the land for oil and gas gave rise to negotiations which resulted in a pooling agreement by the veterans in 1952. The Department of Mines and Minerals noted in its 1949 recommendation that gas had been discovered (in 1948) 40 miles south of the reserve and that detailed geological exploration of the reserve was in order.

But Justice Addy had found that there was no basis for treating the mineral rights as having any potential value. Justice McLachlin found that he had "confused potential with actual value."

She continued to dissect Justice Addy's judgement. He had held that because the mineral rights had no value, the Crown had no duty, as a fiduciary, to retain them for the Indians. This was, of course, contrary to common sense, perverse even. Judge McLachlin went on:

If indeed the mineral rights had minimal sale value in 1948, it does not follow that a prudent person would give them away. It is more logical to argue that since nothing could be obtained for them at the time, and since it would cost nothing to keep them, they should be kept against the chance, however remote, that they might acquire some value in the future. The wisdom of the latter course is demonstrated by the Crown's policy with respect to its own mineral rights; it reserved them to itself, regardless of actual value. It lies ill in the mouth of the Crown to argue that it should have done less with the property entrusted to it as fiduciary to lease for the welfare of the Band.

The value of the royalties might well be $300 million. There were about five hundred Indians belonging to the Blueberry River and Doig River bands. If successful, they would receive a lot of money. Justice McLachlin indicated that Justice Addy had a bias. She said:

The trial judge's emphasis on the apparent low value of the mineral rights suggests an underlying concern with the injustice of conferring an unexpected windfall on the Indians at the Crown's expense. This concern is misplaced. It amounts to bringing foreseeability into the fiduciary analysis through the back door. This constitutes an error of law. The beneficiary of a fiduciary duty is entitled to have his or her property restored or value in its place, even if the value of the property turns out to be much greater than could have been foreseen at the time of the breach.

She concluded:

The matter comes down to this. The duty on the Crown as fiduciary was "that of a man of ordinary prudence in managing his own affairs." A reasonable person does not inadvertently give away a potentially valuable asset which has already demonstrated earning potential. Nor does a reasonable person give away for no consideration what it will cost him nothing to keep and which may one day possess value, however remote the possibility. The Crown managing its own affairs reserved out its minerals. It should have done the same for the Band.

So we had won: there was a fiduciary duty, and the Crown had breached its duty; moreover, the Crown had to compensate the band for its losses, foreseeable and unforeseeable.

But there was still the thirty-year limitation period. If the court did not find a way around it, the bands would wind up with no recovery.

We argued that the transfer from DIA to DVLA was simply an interdepartmental transfer. The Crown still held the land. It could restore it at any time to the band. The Crown's fiduciary obligation still remained as long as the land was still owned by an agency of the government of Canada. If this were so, the thirty-year limitation period would not begin to run until the parcels of land were transferred to the veterans—even then, not until *title* had been transferred, and that process had not been completed until 1956, well within the thirty years. Chief Justice Isaac in his dissenting judgement in the Court of Appeal had supported this approach.

The court rejected our attempt to postpone the running of time. Justice McLachlin said that the clock had begun to run earlier than that. The transfer by DIA to DVLA on January 20, 1948, would be the starting point. The sale by DIA to DVLA should be treated as if it were a sale to a third party unconnected to the government. This was not helpful; in fact, it left us outside the thirty-year period.

Then Justice McLachlin returned to the little-known section of the 1927

Indian Act that she had raised at the hearing. That section provided that DIA could revoke any sale or lease made "in error or mistake."

Justice McLachlin said that because the transfer of the mineral rights to DVLA had been inadvertent, it constituted "error or mistake." DIA could have revoked the erroneous grant of mineral rights at any time before they were transferred to the veterans.

She concluded that DIA had a fiduciary duty to correct the error. "Reasonable diligence required that the DIA move to correct the erroneous transfer when it came into possession of facts suggesting error and the potential value of the minerals that it had erroneously transferred."

So where did that leave us? Justice McLachlin found that as of July 15, 1949, DIA was in possession of information that I.R. 172 had potential mineral value. And on August 9, 1949, DIA had been reminded that the mineral rights had been sold to DVLA.

So even though DIA had given away the mineral rights, it still retained the power to cancel the transfer to DVLA. When it came into possession of evidence that the mineral rights were potentially valuable, it had a duty to act—to cancel the transfer to DVLA and restore the mineral rights to the band.

The key question was: When did DIA come into possession of such evidence? We knew that all thirty-one sections of Montney had been transferred to DVLA on January 20, 1948. How many agreements for sale had been made by DVLA—how many sections were already transferred to the veterans by August 9, 1949, Justice McLachlin's cut-off date? Justice McLachlin found that 6.75 of the thirty-one sections of land still remained in DVLA hands at that date. So the Crown had a duty to restore to the band the mineral rights to those 6.75 sections. It wouldn't amount to three hundred million dollars. But it would, we hoped, be substantial.

A new trial was ordered to determine how much by way of compensation the bands should receive.

The question now arose: The bands were entitled to compensation for the revenue from the mineral rights to 6.75 sections out of thirty-one, but how much oil and gas had been produced from those sections?

Would the sections of land transferred by DVLA to the veterans *after* August 9, 1949, turn out to be oil-bearing? This question meant another tense week or two while we consulted oil and gas experts. The answer turned out to be yes; they were oil-bearing; in fact, two sections had been very big producers. All that remained was to determine the actual value of the oil produced from the 6.75 sections. That entailed two years of negotiations.

Harry Slade, the lawyer for the bands, acted as lead negotiator. The bands settled for $147 million. It wasn't the whole of the lost treasure. It was a compromise figure founded on a calculation of the revenue that would have been earned on the 6.75 sections, interest on the lost revenues, and the present value of the oil and gas still lying beneath those six sections. But it was very, very substantial.

Moreover, it represented a remarkable victory for the bands. Once poor, they were now wealthy.

Jerry Attachie, chief of the Doig River band, had for twenty years been the champion of the Montney cause. He had taken the file to a lawyer in the first instance. He had, after the trial judgement went against the Indians, urged an appeal. He had, together with Joe Apsassin, the chief of the Blueberry River band, and Harry Slade, come to see me to ask me to take the appeal to the Federal Court of Appeal. He had come to Ottawa for the hearing before the Supreme Court. No one had been associated for as long as he had been with the Montney claim. I think his band members must at times have wondered about his obsession with the pursuit of the Montney cause. But every cause needs someone who will not give up. Jerry was there at the finish. He was there when the settlement of $147 million was reached.

And then he was voted out of office. He was the man to win the war but not to administer the judgement obtained in the war. I told him that there was a precedent. In 1945, the year that the old Beaver band had signed the surrender of I.R. 172, Winston Churchill, Britain's leader in the Second World War, had been removed from office by the people of the United Kingdom just as the war came to a victorious end. Jerry thought it was an interesting comparison.

Jerry had always realized something was wrong. How had the band lost Montney? Why had others become wealthy from the riches beneath Montney while the Indians remained impoverished? To be sure, when you have observed the loss of your patrimony, when you are yourself a casualty of what seems a kind of arbitrary injustice, it often serves to sharpen the mind. It can, of course, utterly cloud the mind, obscuring and obstructing any kind of rational thought. Most lawyers have seen legions of complainants whose lives have been unhinged by calamity and who have long since given themselves over to a career of lamentation, whether through petitions, letters to the editor, carrying signboards on the street or simply turning up at lawyers' offices, carrying bundles of papers, to urge that they take up their forsaken cause.

Jerry was not one of these. He was not well educated in a formal sense; he did not know the law. But he kept asking a question that had never been answered until we had reached the Supreme Court of Canada: How could a people's patrimony have been lost? He believed there must be a remedy. It turned out that he was right.

II *Ximena and Her Family*

I N J A N U A R Y 1 9 9 4 , I had just returned to Vancouver from a vacation in Mexico, from the tropics to mid-winter in the city by the rain forest. Back at the office, I was gazing at the window, wondering if the rain would ever stop. I didn't feel at all like working. I thought nothing could stir me from my apathy except a fascinating case. In my law practice, that case often seemed to turn up.

As I was musing, a lawyer from Prince George turned up. His name was Charles Lugosi. He was a criminal lawyer, but he had taken on a medical malpractice case. He told me that his client was a little girl who had been born prematurely at Vancouver General Hospital (VGH). Lugosi had been working on the case for two years. He felt he was getting nowhere. He needed to retain senior counsel. He had already been to see two of the province's leading courtroom lawyers; both told Lugosi the case was desperate to the point of hopelessness.

Lugosi told me that the little girl was named Ximena Renaerts. She was eight years old. Her mother, a single woman, had not wanted a baby. She claimed that she had gone to Bellingham, just south of the Canada–U.S. border, in Washington, to have an abortion. Something had gone wrong during the procedure. She was still carrying the baby when she returned to Vancouver. In a few days, she had become ill, and had been admitted to the emergency ward at VGH.

At VGH, they did not deliver babies; they had closed down their maternity department. They do, however, carry out therapeutic abortions. Ximena's mother wanted an abortion. She told the admitting physician in the emergency ward that she had been carrying the baby for only three months. She disclosed that she was pregnant, but she did not tell the truth about the length of her pregnancy. In fact, she had been carrying the baby for seven months. Perhaps in Bellingham, perhaps somewhere else, a procedure of some kind had been done, but it had not succeeded. Now she had contracted a very severe infection. A second doctor, Dr. Kamal Jaroudi, examined her. His examination was not apparently a thorough one; it did not reveal that she was carrying a baby of seven months. He sent her up to the gynecological ward.

The records of Vancouver General Hospital revealed that at 3:20 A.M. on December 17, 1985, a baby had been born alive on the gynecological ward. Forty minutes later, at 4:00 A.M., a code blue had been called; that is, the hospital's resuscitation team had been sent for. The team must have arrived within minutes. But what had happened between 3:20 and 4:00 A.M.? The baby was by any standard premature. Because there was no maternity ward at VGH, the hospital was not equipped to care for a premature baby. Why didn't they send at once for the code blue team? What had happened on the ward?

Those in charge on the ward should obviously have sent for the Infant Transport Team at Children's Hospital. This team travels in an ambulance with an incubator and consists of a physician trained to treat infants at birth and two paramedics. The team members are on-call around the clock. They would, if summoned, have come at once to VGH and taken the baby to Children's, where she would have had the best of care. In fact, the records showed that VGH had called Children's, but not until 4:30 A.M., more than an hour after the baby had arrived. Why not earlier? Why not at 3:20 A.M. when the baby was delivered? Why not at 4:00 A.M. when the code blue was called? Why allow seventy minutes to pass before taking such an obvious step? Children's is no more than a mile and a half away. In the early hours of the morning, the Infant Transport Team would have reached VGH in less than five minutes.

I have said all of this information was apparent from the records. But to say that Vancouver General Hospital had anything like complete records would be an exaggeration.

None of the nurses' notes taken at the time of the delivery of the baby were available. The notes had been destroyed in 1992, the hospital's policy being to destroy nurses' notes after seven years. All we had to go on were some notes prepared by nursing staff for the assistance of the Infant Transport Team when it arrived; there had to be some information provided to travel with the baby to Children's. These notes had been made available by Children's Hospital.

The records at Children's showed that after the Infant Transport Team arrived at VGH, the team ministered to the baby and then removed her that same morning to Children's. At Children's, the baby was found to have suffered extensive brain injury. She had cerebral palsy, and she was a quadriplegic. Her mother didn't want to keep her, so she was taken into custody by the child welfare authorities. She remained at Children's Hospital for three months, where the medical staff undertook heroic measures to save her life.

When the baby left Children's, she was placed by the child welfare authorities in a series of foster homes. When she was five, she went to live with Bert and Margaret Renaerts in Chilliwack. It was they who gave her the name Ximena (pronounced "Shiména"). In due course, they adopted her.

What Charles Lugosi had unearthed was a remarkable event. A hospital that did abortions had found a live infant on its hands—an arrival from another planet. The records, such as they were, revealed little about what had occurred that night. What had the nursing staff done for the baby during that first forty minutes? Why was no call placed to Children's for over an hour?

There was no indication that vGH had carried out an investigation after the fact, no explanation anywhere of the silent passages in the first hour of Ximena's life. Were Ximena's cerebral palsy and quadriplegia an inevitable result of the failed abortion procedure that her mother had undergone before she was admitted to vGH? Or were they the result of a failure on the part of vGH to take reasonable steps to provide the care this newborn needed?

Something had happened to Ximena's mother before she got to vGH. Had she been to an abortion clinic in Washington as she claimed? It seemed unlikely that an abortion clinic would have failed to remove the fetus and sent her away in an infected state. Had she attempted a homemade abortion?

When Ximena came to stay with the Renaertses, the family understood Ximena had been a premature baby. When Margaret Renaerts took Ximena to the medical clinic at nearby Abbotsford, Ximena was seen by Dr. Lionel Traverse. He was pleased and amazed to see Ximena, because he had been the physician on the Infant Transport Team who had answered the belated call to vGH in the early morning hours of December 17, 1985. Dr. Traverse told Margaret that Ximena's condition arose out of an incomplete abortion procedure. When the Renaertses took steps to adopt Ximena, they were told by a social worker that the child welfare authorities had considered whether to commence legal action against vGH but had decided not to proceed.

In March 1992, Margaret Renaerts contacted Charles Lugosi to ask him to find out, if he could, about the origin of Ximena's condition—to find out what had happened. And, after two years of struggling with the file, Lugosi, having unearthed what documents he could and having commenced an action against vGH based on allegations of criminal misconduct, had arrived in my office. It is a compliment of sorts to be a court of last resort, but what were we to do?

The records, such as they were, did reveal one thing: between 3:20 A.M., when the baby was born, and 4:00 A.M., when a code blue was called, there was nothing to indicate that anything had been done for the baby. When a baby is born, three steps are called for: the baby must be suctioned to enable it to start breathing; it must be made warm; and in the case of a premature baby, oxygen must be provided. There was no sign—no record at least—that any of these steps had been taken. But how could that be? The baby had landed in the heart of the province's greatest health-care complex. Surely the best possible care had been provided? If a code blue had not been called until forty minutes following the birth, that could only have been because it did not appear until then to be necessary. If the Infant Transport Team had not been summoned until more than an hour had gone by, there must have been a good reason.

We had very little information. Whom to sue? The doctors? The nurses? The hospital? All of this had happened in December 1985. Now it was January 1994. The lawsuit was statute-barred. British Columbia's statute of limitations provided for an ultimate limitation period of six years for suing doctors, nurses and hospitals for medical malpractice. Ximena had been born on December 17, 1985. The time to sue anyone had run out for Ximena six years later, in 1991, a year before Margaret Renaerts consulted Charles Lugosi and three years before Charles Lugosi came to see me.

What about the clinic in Bellingham? Could we sue the clinic? We didn't know even the name of the clinic, or if it existed or ever had existed. Or what had happened at the clinic, if it did exist.

Could we make a claim against the child welfare authorities? Time had run out on Ximena's case while she had been in their custody. They must have known something had gone wrong. Did they investigate? Why had nothing been done? To sue them was to sue at one remove; that is, we would be bringing a suit against them because they had failed to bring a suit against VGH. We would still have to prove that if they had sued VGH on Ximena's behalf, they would have been successful. Whatever we did, we would still have to get to the bottom of the case.

This was a malpractice case (that is, a claim that VGH and its staff had been negligent), if it was a case at all. But there were only six years in which to bring a malpractice suit. And time had run out. Was there a way around the limitation period?

We had to find some basis for a lawsuit other than negligence. The key to the case was to establish a tort was committed that fell outside the scope of B.C.'s statute of limitations; that is, a wrongful act for which we could still sue—one that did not fall under the category of negligence.

All we knew was that the notes prepared by the staff at VGH for the Infant Transport Team did not indicate that any steps had been taken to care for the child in the first forty minutes of her life. We might be wrong; perhaps proper care had been provided. But the records provided nothing to indicate this to be the case.

I spent a week in the law library at UBC. I looked at the American cases. Each of the fifty states has its own legal system, and, of course, the U.S. has a federal legal system. And in the U.S., there are a lot of lawyers—more per capita than anywhere in the world—so it is fertile with legal precedents. In some U.S. jurisdictions, there were references to a tort of abandonment. It had been recognized by the courts in a few states. It was a long shot but worth a try. So we developed a claim for abandonment. Ximena, we would argue, was not the victim simply of negligence but of deliberate abandonment. According to the notes prepared at VGH for the Infant Transport Team, nothing appeared to have been done. If the failure to take proper care of the baby was deliberate, something that went beyond mere negligence, we could argue that it amounted to abandonment. What other explanation was there for the fact that from 3:20 A.M. until a code blue was called at 4:00 A.M. nothing was done for the baby?

We had been driven to our theory of abandonment because it offered a legal loophole. Now we would have to find the evidence.

We focussed on what had happened at VGH and concentrated, in particular, on the injury caused when the baby was apparently left without help for the first forty minutes of her life. We sued VGH and all the doctors and nurses who had any connection with the case, as well as the child welfare authorities. This tactic meant naming as defendants doctors and nurses who might turn out to be altogether innocent. But we had no choice.

We decided not to proceed with the claim against the unnamed Bellingham abortion clinic. We saw no evidence that an attempted abortion had been carried out at a clinic in Bellingham. The abortion procedure, if it had taken place, had been incomplete; Ximena's mother was still carrying the baby when she returned to Canada. The report prepared by the social worker who interviewed Ximena's mother before she left the hospital indicated that she had also interviewed the natural father of the baby following the baby's birth. He was American and claimed to be a Vietnam veteran. The boyfriend said that he was surprised by the result because the procedure had always worked in Vietnam. We concluded that the most likely thing was that Ximena's mother had attempted, with the help of her boyfriend, to perform some kind of homemade abortion. She was carrying a baby into the third trimester. She could not, therefore, at that time, obtain a legal therapeutic abortion in Canada. She had resorted to self-help.

Somewhere, somebody had attempted, in what appeared to be an amateurish way, to abort the fetus, and it might be that Ximena's condition had originated there. VGH could not be held responsible for that. We would surely have to deal with this question along the way.

Before long, we got our first break.

On June 2, 1994, B.C.'s statute of limitations was amended to remove the ultimate limitation period for personal injury claims by infants. Doctors, nurses and hospitals would still have the benefit of a six-year ultimate limitation period.

But in cases involving injury to infants, it would not apply. That is, the six-year clock would not start until a child turned nineteen, the age of majority in B.C. And the amendment was made retroactive, so it applied to all the cases involving injury to infants occurring before as well as after June 2, 1994. That would include Ximena. We could rely on a straightforward claim for malpractice. We would still bring forward our claim based on abandonment. But we were now on familiar turf.

We had, however, just begun. We had to retain experts to evaluate Ximena's present condition and to advise regarding the cause of her cerebral palsy and quadriplegia. Could her present condition be traced to what had gone on at the hospital? The burden of proof is on the plaintiff. We would have to prove that VGH was responsible—Ximena was our plaintiff and we had to prove that she had a case. This requirement brought us back to the question: What had taken place in the hospital during the crucial first forty minutes of the baby's life, before the code blue? And given that VGH must have realized the place to obtain the best care for the baby was Children's Hospital, why was no call made to Children's for more than an hour?

Most people do not have the resources to undertake a major lawsuit against a great institution, a lawsuit that may entail hundreds of thousands of dollars in legal fees. We had taken the case on a contingency basis. We would get a percentage of the damages if we succeeded. We had to be prepared to match the hospital and the doctors, expert for expert. This requirement for expert testimony would cost a lot of money. In the end, it took four years to bring the case to trial. In the meantime, our law firm would pay for the experts and bear all the expenses of the litigation. This practice is not at all unusual. The Renaerts family were in no position to bear the expenses. Our ordinary legal fees on an hourly basis would be far beyond their means.

Bert Renaerts was a logger. He and Margaret had adopted seven children with disabilities (one child was deceased), including Ximena. *Seven*—that is not a misprint. The Renaertses had three children of their own. Two of them were now young men and worked with their father in the woods. The first time Bev and I visited the Renaertses' home in Chilliwack to see Ximena, we were astonished to meet not only Ximena but also five other children with disabilities. Ximena had cerebral palsy. Karsten was physically disabled but very bright. Elshvah was a blind, disabled girl of Indo-Canadian descent. Myeisha was a microcephalic baby but bright-eyed and sparkling. Quirida was mentally disabled. Tara-lee had hearing and mental disabilities. The Renaerts had adopted all of them. The Renaertses' daughter Nicole helped Margaret to take care of these children. In fact, Nicole told us that her ambition was to adopt a disabled child of her own.

Ximena could crawl, though she could not get to her knees. Her speech was that of a two or three year old. But she was happy within this cheerful and loving family.

Margaret and Bert devoted their lives to these children; they regarded their lives not as an unforgiving labour but as an opportunity to be of use in the world.

We knew that VGH would defend its residents and its nurses. The Canadian Medical Protective Association would defend the doctors. Both VGH and the doctors would be represented by some of Vancouver's ablest lawyers, accustomed to waging a war of attrition against any plaintiff willing to sue their clients.

But once in, you can't turn back. We would spend the next four years on the case; not full-time, but giving the case as much of our time as was necessary. Not just myself. Charles Lugosi and my colleagues, Gary Nelson, Erin Berger and Margaret ("Margie") Vanderkruyk, were all needed.

At once we ran up against the difficulty of obtaining an expert to testify on behalf of Ximena, if need be. We needed a world-class expert on pediatric neurology. Finding this kind of expert is not easy at the best of times. But it can be extremely difficult if you want your expert to testify against colleagues in the medical profession. In this case, we found it necessary to go outside Canada. We were fortunate to find Dr. Harvey Sarnat, head of pediatric neurology at Children's Hospital in Seattle, whom we then retained to review the case.

After a preliminary review, Dr. Sarnat advised in December 1994 that in Ximena's case there had been negligence in the postpartum period, but that the child's brain damage might also have been the result of the attempted abortion. There was, in his opinion, a strong case that lack of care at VGH contributed to Ximena's condition, but it was not the only cause of injury. Not all of the neurological damage could be attributed to what had happened postpartum.

We had been afraid of this conclusion. VGH could say that the child's brain had been damaged during the attempted abortion. Any injury to Ximena, the hospital could contend, had already occurred before her mother entered VGH. Dr. Sarnat made it clear, however, that in substantial measure Ximena's condition was attributable to lack of care at VGH.

By this time we could put together the outlines of our case. We had to conduct examinations for discovery of each defendant. There would be thirteen of these examinations in all. The defendants' lawyers would be there, of course, and could object to any questions they might regard as inappropriate.

We had two names to start with. The nurse who had made the notes for the Infant Transport Team was Vera Wood. Dr. Kamal Jaroudi, a resident at Vancouver General Hospital, had examined Ximena's mother in the emergency room and sent her up to the gynecology ward. Dr. Jaroudi had completed his residency at VGH but had returned to his native Saudi Arabia.

First up was Vera Wood. She was the senior nurse on duty the night that Ximena was born. She had been a maternity ward nurse at VGH in the days when they still delivered babies. She had prepared the notes for the Infant Transport Team, the only documentary evidence that we had so far.

The baby, according to Vera Wood's notes, was born at 3:20 A.M. She testified that Nurse Judy McDonald, the nurse looking after Ximena's mother, ran to her saying, "Come quickly, it's alive." She accompanied Judy McDonald to see the baby. The baby had been delivered in a commode. Vera Wood took the commode, with the baby in it, into a small service room.

Vera Wood said that the baby was "moving, gasping, crying weakly." In fact, she had written in the notes she prepared for the Infant Transport Team: "Baby cried spontaneously after one minute following birth and had spontaneous gasping respirations and body movements." On further questioning, she admitted the baby was viable; that it was a premature baby and not, in her words, "a candidate for tagging, the plastic bag and the lab," which would have been the case if it had been the product of an ordinary abortion. This was a vital concession on her part. When abortions are carried out, they may in some cases result in the delivery of a fetus that is alive but not viable—it cannot be expected to live. This baby could be expected to live.

Then we moved on to the next issue: The baby being viable, what was done to care for her? I asked Wood, "Did you know what was to be done when a premature baby was delivered?" She answered, "Only insofar as to keep the baby warm, making sure an airway was clear and that it was receiving oxygen, if necessary, and to be transferred to medical care." These are precisely the steps that had to be taken. But had she taken them?

Our case had to be that Vera Wood had done none of these things; that she took the baby to the service room and left it there, in the commode, still gasping for air, and did nothing to care for it. We had to proceed on the assumption that she did not suction the baby; she did not provide warmth; she did not provide oxygen. As a result, the baby suffered severe brain damage. That had to be our case.

Vera Wood testified that when she took the baby to the service room, she placed it on a counter. She claimed that she had suctioned it, made it warm and put a mask beside the baby's face to provide oxygen. But notes that she had made for the Infant Transport Team, relating to "nursing care and observations," contained no indication opposite the entry for 3:20 A.M. (the time of the baby's birth) that she had taken any of these steps. Wouldn't a competent nurse have recorded these items? Wouldn't it be essential information for the Infant Transport Team to have? Then she wrote that the baby was "moved to service room for observation. Supervisor and Dr. Jaroudi notified re: condition. Dr. Jaroudi coming.

V. Wood, R.N." Nothing more. Her notes didn't make sense. Why would she take a viable baby into the service room "for observation?" Why not take steps to help the baby?

I questioned her about these omissions. She swore that she took these steps, but her notes didn't back her up, and her answers to my questions were evasive.

Q Had you ever failed to make out complete nurses' notes before this occasion?
A I can't recall or can't answer that question for you.
Q Can you tell me if you recollect any other occasion in your career when you had prepared nurses' notes which were incomplete in this way?
A I can't answer that for you.
Q Can you tell me if you can remember any occasion when you prepared nurses' notes you knew did not record every step taken in nursing care for the patient?
A No, I do not remember that.

Vera Wood also told us that she gave workshops for the nurses at VGH on the importance of recording these steps when preparing their nurses' notes.

The inference had to be that she had not taken these elementary steps. If she had, she would have recorded them. She knew the baby was going to Children's Hospital. She was writing up a history—brief as it was—for Children's. Why wouldn't she record that these vital steps had been taken?

Vera Wood's notes said that at 3:46 she called the nursing supervisor and the obstetrical resident. But this call for assistance should have been made as soon as the child was born.

I continued with the questioning: "Why hadn't there been an incident report?" Vera Wood conceded that an incident report should be made at VGH whenever there is an "unusual occurrence." She gave as an example a medication error. I carried on:

Q This foetus, born December 17, 1985, was living and viable, wasn't it?
A Yes.
Q Had that ever happened before, in your experience?
A Not in my experience.
Q Wasn't it then an unusual occurrence calling for an incident report?
A No.

I asked her, "Did it ever occur to you—even if you decided at the end of the day that it didn't require an incident report, did it ever occur to you that you ought to consider filing an incident report?" She replied, "No." I'd had enough.

"Just another day at the office?" I asked, at which point VGH's lawyer intervened: "Just a moment, Mr. Berger. That's argumentative. Save it for the jury."

Then Vera Wood disclaimed any responsibility for the care of the baby. She said that she was not responsible for the baby, that it was not her patient. Whose patient was it? She said, "It was the result of the baby of Judy McDonald—Judy McDonald's patient." I asked her, "It wasn't anybody's patient, then, was it?" She said, "It had not been assigned."

This was a pathetic attempt to take refuge in the interstices of the VGH bureaucracy.

Vera Wood conceded that what the child needed was to be sent at once to an infant intensive care unit; that there was no such unit at VGH; that there was such a unit at Children's Hospital; and that she knew the Infant Transport Team at Children's could be called at once. Yet she did not call the Infant Transport Team when the baby was born. She said that she could not herself remember making a call to Children's; that she may have "suggested" to Dr. Jaroudi that Children's be called; but this suggestion would have been at least forty minutes after the child's birth.

We thought Vera Wood was lying to cover up not only neglect but deliberate abandonment of the baby.

Then we examined the night nursing supervisor—Nurse Joyce Hatherall— who had answered Vera Wood's belated call for assistance. Nurse Hatherall testified that she was paged at around 3:49 A.M., twenty-nine minutes after the birth of the child. She went at once to the ward. She described what happened after she was called:

Q   How far did you have to go?
A   From Heather Pavilion through the tunnel to Centennial Pavilion.
Q   How long does that take?
A   Well I ran, so it couldn't have taken me more than three or four minutes.
Q   You arrived within three or four minutes of the call from Vera Wood?
A   Yes.
Q   When you arrived there where did you go?
A   I went to West 7 from the elevator and I saw Vera Wood at the desk and I said, "Where is it?" and she said, "In the service room," and I went into the service room.

Vera Wood had testified that she had taken the baby to the service room, suctioned it, made it warm and put a mask beside the baby's face to give it oxygen. Nurse Hatherall testified:

Q   What did you see?

A   In the hat there was this little, pink baby.

Q   In the hat?

A   In the hat, yes. The hat—we call it the hat, it is the plastic potty that fits into the commode, into which the baby was aborted.

Q   And the baby was in the hat?

A   Yes.

Q   Tell me what else you observed about the baby.

A   It was pink and I picked it up and took it to the counter. Somebody brought a towel or blanket or something to place on the counter, it was a stainless steel counter. I popped the baby on and I called to Vera Wood to call a code.

Q   To call code blue?

A   Yes.

Q   The resuscitation team?

A   Yes.

Q   Did you keep any record of the times when these events occurred?

A   No. I was more interested in doing something with the baby. It had to be resuscitated.

Q   It was necessary to call code blue at once, as far as you were concerned, when you saw the baby?

A   That's right.

Q   When you found the baby in the hat or the potty, it was not covered?

A   No.

Q   When you held it in your arms and you spoke to Vera Wood again, where was she?

A   She was at the desk.

Q   What did you say to her?

A   "Call a code".

Q   Do you know whether she did call?

A   Oh, she called a code right away.

The call to code blue, we knew, had been made at 4:00 A.M. I continued:

Q   What did you do with the baby then?

A   I placed the baby on the towel or blanket or whatever it was and when I called a code of course the nurses who were in the room—there's a little cart in the unit which comes with resuscitation airways and bags and we tried to pass an airway into this baby and it was too big.

Q   Was the mask too big?

A   The mask was too big and the airway would have been too big. The mask would fit over an adult face, not over a baby's face. One of the nurses ran upstairs to the 9th floor to get a baby airway, which would be the only floor that would have it. Because we were an adult unit we were not equipped to deal with live babies.

Sometimes it is important to seek out the obvious, to have it on the record. I asked Nurse Hatherall:

Q   You told Vera to call a code. I know this must sound elementary, but can you tell me why you thought she should call a code? Why was it necessary? What was wrong with the child?
A   It was early, or rather, it appeared to me to be a baby that was about two pounds and, as Vera had said on the phone, it was alive, it was pink. You should make some attempt to save this life.

Nurse Hatherall went on to discuss the steps that she had to take. Vera Wood had said she had placed an oxygen mask beside the baby. But there was no mask.

Q   When you arrived there was no mask in the room that you could see?
A   No.

Vera Wood had testified that she had suctioned the baby. I asked Nurse Hatherall, "Was there any indication the baby had been suctioned?" She answered, "No." She also said that there were two or three nurses standing around the service room, but there was no indication that anyone had given assistance to the baby. "I couldn't see anything being done."

I turned again to the obvious, and asked Nurse Hatherall about a nurse's responsibility.

Q   This child was just a few minutes old and it was vulnerable. Any nurse who was in the vicinity and saw that the child was in distress would have had an obligation to assist it, isn't that right?
A   Yes, I suppose so.
Q   That's what you did when you arrived?
A   That's right.
Q   And that is your obligation as a nurse, isn't it?
A   Yes.
Q   As well as an employee of the hospital?
A   Yes.

Nurse Hatherall had refuted virtually everything Vera Wood had said about suctioning the baby, providing warmth and giving oxygen. Moreover, when Nurse Hatherall arrived, Vera Wood was *not* in the service room but at the nursing station. And the baby was still in the commode.

Nothing had been done to care for the baby. The baby had not been suctioned. There was no oxygen mask and no cart in the service room. The baby had no covering of towels or blankets. Instead, she had been left marooned in the "hat."

It was not only Nurse Hatherall whose evidence showed that the child had been left in the commode. We examined Judy McDonald. It was her first night on duty as a nurse. She had arrived at Ximena's mother's room when the baby was delivered into the commode. It was she who had sought out Vera Wood, crying, "Come quickly, it's alive." Judy McDonald testified that the baby *remained in the commode,* and every thirty seconds made a gasping motion.

Judy McDonald was also able to tell us what happened when help began to arrive. After Vera Wood belatedly called for assistance, Dr. Jaroudi arrived at the ward. This would have been at around 4:00 A.M. It was Dr. Jaroudi, as the resident gynecological intern, who had examined Ximena's mother in the emergency ward and sent her up to the gynecological ward. He had examined her but had not discovered that she was carrying a baby close to term.

Judy McDonald said that when Dr. Jaroudi came up to the ward, "He instructed us not to resuscitate." By that time there were a sufficient number of responsible persons present that Dr. Jaroudi's direction was ignored. It was, however, indicative of Dr. Jaroudi's attitude; it might also have been the result of a realization on his part of his misdiagnosis in the emergency room.

When he examined Ximena's mother in emergency, Dr. Jaroudi had obviously failed to realize that she was carrying a fetus with a gestational age of twenty-six to twenty-nine weeks, not merely the remains of a failed abortion. If he had conducted a proper examination in emergency, he would have discovered otherwise; he would not have sent her to the gynecological ward to complete the abortion but would have treated the case as a delivery, and all necessary care would have been provided, including immediate transfer to Children's Hospital. If Dr. Jaroudi had discovered the fetus and taken such measures, the neglect of the baby post-delivery would have been avoided. It is true that Ximena's mother had misled him; she claimed that she had been carrying the baby for only three months. But would this excuse his failure to discover that she was carrying a baby close to term when he conducted his examination?

We had to examine Dr. Jaroudi. He agreed to travel from his home in Saudi Arabia to Spain for us to question him there.

Dr. Jaroudi said on his examination for discovery that when he saw Ximena's mother in the emergency room, he had palpated her abdomen and done a vaginal examination. But he did not detect the fetus. The admitting physician at VGH emergency made a note indicating that Ximena's mother told Dr. Jaroudi that she had been advised by the clinic in Bellingham that "the foetus was left inside." Dr. Jaroudi's own notes show that she told him "that the Embryo is still inside her uterus."

There had not been a call for the Infant Transport Team promptly made to Children's. But there had been a call. Not by Vera Wood. But somebody had called. It turned out it was Dr. Jaroudi; when he arrived at the gynecological ward at about 4:00 A.M., he phoned the on-call specialist at home, who told him to call the Infant Transport Team at once. Had Dr. Jaroudi called Children's? It appeared he had. But the call had been as badly managed as his diagnosis of Ximena's mother.

We had interviewed at Children's Hospital Dr. Michael Whitfield, the physician who received the call. He had authority to dispatch the Infant Transport Team to any hospital within the local area. Dr. Whitfield said that a doctor called in the early-morning hours of December 17, 1985, saying, "Come quickly, you need to get the baby." But the doctor who made the call hung up without saying who he was or where he was calling from. Dr. Whitfield said the voice was a foreign or accented voice.

Could Dr. Whitfield have guessed the call came from VGH? Hardly. VGH had no maternity ward; the hospital only did abortions, so the call would not have been expected from VGH.

Dr. Whitfield said it was not until some time later that a second call came, he believed from a nurse, requesting Dr. Whitfield to dispatch the Infant Transport Team to VGH. The Infant Transport Team did not depart Children's until 4:34 A.M., according to Children's records, and did not arrive at VGH until 4:37.

There was therefore an additional thirty-minute delay, for which Dr. Jaroudi appeared to be responsible, in placing a call that should have been made immediately after the delivery. Obviously, Dr. Jaroudi simply forgot, in the crisis, to advise Dr. Whitfield that he was calling from VGH. This was negligence. Or, having made the initial misdiagnosis in the emergency ward, he was doing his best to bring the baby's life—and his involvement—to an end. This would explain his "do not resuscitate" order.

Our case proceeded on the footing that hospital staff, except for Nurse Hatherall, had behaved in a way that was almost impossible to believe. They were all professionals dedicated to helping and healing those in their care. Dr. Jaroudi had denied on his examination for discovery Judy McDonald's claim that he had said "do not resuscitate." If he had said it, could it be that he was concerned chiefly about covering up his misdiagnosis? Was it wholly uncharitable to make such assumptions?

These things do happen. In the case of a young woman who came to our office in 1998, a doctor had operated on our client at Lions Gate Hospital in North Vancouver, then had closed up her abdomen but inadvertently failed to remove a four-foot-long abdominal roll. When she complained of excruciating abdominal pain three months later, he decided to do an exploratory procedure. He discovered the roll, removed it and then pledged the nurses in the operating room to secrecy, saying, "There will be nothing in writing about this." Only when, two months later, the nurses decided that they could not conscientiously live any longer with knowledge of the concealment of what had occurred, and they told the doctor that he would have to report what he had done to the hospital authorities, did his altogether flagrant treatment of his patient come to light. He was ordered to pay damages. The College of Physicians and Surgeons suspended him for three months.

We would argue that something similar had happened in the case of Dr. Jaroudi—an initial act of negligence snowballed into an act of the grossest misconduct.

We were claiming on Ximena's behalf damages to compensate her for her pain and suffering, for her loss of earning capacity and for the cost of care for the remainder of her life.

But the story as it unfolded showed that this situation was a case for punitive damages. The courts award punitive damages (that is, damages beyond what is required to *compensate* the plaintiff) to punish a defendant for high-handed behaviour. Certainly, Vera Wood's behaviour and that of Dr. Jaroudi were deserving of an award of punitive damages. In fact, punitive damages are sometimes called exemplary damages: they are intended to make an example of the defendant to deter others from such conduct. What Vera Wood had done was not merely a regrettable lapse from the ordinary standard of care. The evidence indicated that she had abandoned Ximena. As for Dr. Jaroudi, the evidence was that he had directed no resuscitation. Wood's conduct and that of Dr. Jaroudi were unconscionable; moreover, VGH itself had never disclosed what occurred; indeed, VGH appeared to have covered it up.

Vera Wood testified on her examination for discovery that there had been no incident report in the case. But a whole cluster of VGH employees knew about the incident. VGH's management must have known.

Dr. Jaroudi had told us on his examination for discovery that he fully expected, given this unprecedented event, that there would be many questions asked. As a result, he went to another physician at VGH the following day to explain his role in these events. He was surprised when no further steps were taken by VGH to find out what had occurred. Dr. Edward Welsh, who led the VGH resuscitation team that answered the code blue at 4:00 A.M., said on his examination for discovery that he was appalled by the failure to call the resuscitation team as soon as the child was born. He asked questions of those present but did not receive any satisfactory answers.

Andrea Bisaillon, a vice-president of VGH, was examined for discovery; she was asked whether VGH had ever investigated what had happened in Ximena's case. This was on September 17, 1997. She did not have an answer. We finally received, on April 30, 1998, only a month before the trial was to commence, a series of answers, including this one: "There was no investigation by the hospital into this incident."

There was no attempt by VGH to determine what had happened; no attempt to uncover the truth; no attempt to make redress. Our claim on Ximena's behalf therefore included a claim against VGH for punitive damages on the ground that VGH was complicit in these dismaying events.

We had obtained a trial date, June 2, 1998. Even though juries are rarely allowed by the courts to determine malpractice cases, we had given notice to the defendants in June 1996 that we wanted a trial by jury.

Plaintiffs often ask for juries in malpractice cases. But defendant physicians and defendant hospitals invariably ask the courts to proceed without a jury, and in almost every case the courts agree. The lawyers for VGH and the doctors applied to the court to set aside the jury. This was a case, they argued, that could only be properly tried by a judge sitting alone.

Usually in malpractice cases, medical experts—specialists in a particular field—are called on either side to give their opinion whether diagnosis, surgery or nursing care came up to an acceptable standard. The evidence can be extraordinarily complicated. Judges believe juries can become lost in a welter of medical and scientific detail. So they routinely set aside juries.

On April 20, 1998, the defence's motion was heard. Justice Mark McEwan heard the motion. We argued that to pass judgement on the evidence in Ximena's case did not require medical expertise but common sense. The failure by Vera Wood and the other VGH nurses, except Joyce Hatherall, the night nurse supervisor, to take any reasonable measures to care for the baby was so deplorable that it could only lead to the conclusion that they had treated this living baby as if it were merely a fetus that could not or should not survive.

I told Justice McEwan that we intended to argue that Vera Wood's testimony was a series of deliberate lies. She had experience as an obstetrical nurse. She was the senior nurse on the ward. There was here a stunning departure from ordinary nursing standards. You hardly needed an expert to state that it is negligence for a nurse deliberately to abandon a newborn in a commode. We would argue that Dr. Jaroudi, despite his denials, had said "don't resuscitate" and in his call to Dr. Whitfield at Children's Hospital had failed to tell him to send the Infant Transport Team to VGH.

We had the transcripts of the examinations for discovery. The case, we argued, would come down to a simple question: Whom do you believe? Vera Wood or Joyce Hatherall? Whom do you believe? Dr. Jaroudi or Judy McDonald? Dr. Jaroudi or Dr. Whitfield? These were, we claimed, questions of credibility, pre-eminently for a jury to decide. They did not entail comprehending complicated medical theories and choosing between experts.

We submitted that a jury would be perfectly capable of determining whether the misdiagnosis in the emergency room, the initial failure to call the Infant Transport Team, the decision to abandon the baby in the service room, the failure by Dr. Jaroudi to inform Dr. Whitfield of the location of the emergency— whether all of these things amounted to malpractice; whether they fell below the standard of care required of health professionals. The whole misshapen course of events was best left to a jury.

On April 28, Justice McEwan handed down his decision. He refused to strike the jury notice. We still had our jury trial.

An application for leave to appeal was made by VGH to the Court of Appeal. Such applications are heard by a single judge, in this case, Justice David Hinds of the Court of Appeal, on May 15, 1998. He refused to allow leave to appeal. Then the defendants made an application for a three-member panel of the Court of Appeal to review Justice Hinds's decision refusing leave to appeal, but by this time the trial date, June 2, was imminent, and the appeal to the three-judge panel could not take place before the trial date.

We were able to hold our jury.

Now we had our case. Dr. Jaroudi, if he had conducted a competent examination in the emergency room, would have discovered that Ximena's mother was carrying a baby close to term. There was Vera Wood's failure to call Children's at the moment the child was delivered. Then, of course, Vera Wood's deliberate neglect of the child, and Dr. Jaroudi's failure to tell Dr. Whitfield that the Infant Transport Team should be sent to VGH. As a result, Ximena had been left mentally retarded, a victim of cerebral palsy and quadriplegic, requiring lifetime care. VGH would have to pay.

Or would it? The evidence of malpractice was compelling. I believed we would prove our case against VGH. But even though VGH might have been guilty of the grossest kind of neglect, had its wrongdoing caused Ximena's condition? We still had another cause, perhaps *the* cause, out there. What about the botched abortion procedure that had brought Ximena's mother to the hospital in the first place? Jury or no jury, we were still left with the issue of causation: Was the cause of Ximena's condition the attempted abortion or the failure to provide proper care at VGH?

Would the defence bring in a string of experts to say that the damage to the child's brain—all of it—had already occurred when Ximena's mother was admitted to VGH? The onus would be on Ximena, as the plaintiff, and on us. We had to prove that neglect at VGH had *caused* Ximena's brain injury. If the defence could show that Ximena's brain had already been irrevocably damaged when she entered VGH, it could be argued that the blunders at VGH, though deplorable, had not contributed to Ximena's condition. If that were so, Ximena would receive no compensation.

Dr. Sarnat had prepared a report for us in which he addressed the issue of possible injury from the attempted abortion. He explained why he believed that the medical evidence did not point to the attempted abortion as the cause.

The attempted abortion before delivery is not likely to have caused the brain damage, though it did induce premature labour. Imaging of the brain by ultrasound and CT in the neonatal period demonstrated no lesions that could have occurred prenatally, such as hemorrhages or infarcts. The lack of meconium staining of the infant or the amniotic membranes or fluid is additional evidence against severe fetal distress. I believe that this infant was viable and potentially normal at birth without irreversible brain damage; many prematurely born infants delivered at 26–27 weeks gestation do very well with good neonatal care and develop into neurologically normal children, though the complications of prematurity in the weeks after birth are certainly a high risk.

He was firm in his view that the principal cause of the damage had occurred at VGH:

The brain damage occurred in the period immediately following delivery, during which she experienced prolonged hypoxia and acidosis [deficiency of oxygen and consequent over-acidity] for at least 40 minutes, a sufficiently long interval to produce permanent brain injury. This hypoxia and acidosis could have been prevented or at least corrected soon enough to avoid this brain damage if the infant had been resuscitated promptly at birth and provided with standard care under the circumstances, rather than neglected. The conclusion that the infant could not survive was obviously wrong at the time of delivery, and did not give the infant the benefit of the doubt.

But the defence had now come up with someone who disputed Dr. Sarnat's conclusion: Dr. Alfonso Solimano, a neonatologist at Children's Hospital. Dr. Solimano provided an expert opinion in which he wrote:

In my opinion, the most critical determinant of Ximena's neurodevelopmental outcome was the attempt to terminate pregnancy at such an advanced gestational age. Independent of judging the legality of such an act in 1985, the method used for that purpose was medically inappropriate.

All subsequent events after the termination attempt, contributed incrementally to Ximena's neurodevelopmental outcome. *However, it is probable that by the time of . . . arrival at the hospital brain damage had already occurred and Ximena would probably have had some neurodevelopmental sequelae in the form of cerebral palsy.* It is also likely that even had she been adequately resuscitated immediately after birth she would have such sequelae in the form of cerebral palsy [emphasis added].

Solimano was supported by two other experts, Dr. Jerome Dansereau and Dr. Paul Thiessen. Both of them ascribed the damage mainly to the attempted abortion.

All of this came as a shock to us.

We held a council of war: Gary, Erin, Margie, Charles Lugosi and me. We were for a time uncertain where this testimony left our case. But, I reminded our team, Solimano's report would not by itself be sufficient for VGH to succeed. Two years earlier, in 1996, I had gone to the Supreme Court of Canada, in *Athey v. Leonati,* to argue that if a wrongdoer contributed in any way to a plaintiff's injury, the wrongdoer was to be treated as just as responsible as if he or she had caused one hundred per cent of the injury. I had always thought this to be the law. But there had been some backsliding. The Supreme Court of Canada, in *Athey,* reaffirmed the law in the plainest language.

Jon Athey was struck by a car driven by Leonati and injured his back. Later at his fitness club, he strained his back, aggravating the original injury. The trial judge held that he should receive only twenty-five per cent of his damages, because the car accident had caused only twenty-five per cent of his injuries, the accident at the fitness club being the cause of the remaining seventy-five per cent. This view was upheld by the Court of Appeal for British Columbia. Frits Verhoeven, who represented Athey, asked me whether we should ask the Court of Appeal to reconsider its judgement. I thought it was worth a try. Gary Nelson prepared a written submission to the court, asking it to reconsider, but the court would not hear the appeal.

We applied to the Supreme Court of Canada for leave to appeal, which was granted. In argument before the Supreme Court, I relied on first principles: if you have, through your own negligence, materially contributed to someone else's injury, you are responsible for the whole of the damage. It may seem like a hard rule, but it has always been fundamental to the law of torts. Justice John Major, who wrote the judgement for the Supreme Court of Canada, said: "It is not now necessary, nor has it ever been, for the plaintiff to establish that the defendant's negligence was the sole cause of the injury." He continued: "As long as a defendant is *part* of the cause of the injury, the defendant is liable, even though his act alone was not enough to create the injury . . . The law does not excuse a defendant from liability merely because other causal factors for which he is not responsible also helped produce the harm . . . It is sufficient if the defendant's negligence was *a* cause of the harm." Justice Major went on to say, however, that if a defendant's negligence was *de minimis* (that is, did not contribute to the injury in any significant way), no liability would follow. *Athey v. Leonati* has become the Canadian case most often cited in our law reports.

In Ximena's case, even on the basis of the testimony of the defendants' experts, the attempted abortion had not been the *sole* cause of damage to her brain. Perhaps, as the defendants claimed (though it seemed doubtful), it had been the dominant cause, but it had not been the sole cause. The injury had undoubtedly been *partly* caused by neglect at VGH. Even on Dr. Solimano's testimony, the events at VGH, though not the dominant cause, were *a* cause. The judge would have to tell Ximena's jury that this was the law to apply; Ximena would be entitled to one hundred per cent of her damages.

Then the defence played still another card. They had obtained a report from Dr. Michael Sargent, a pediatric neuroradiologist. Dr. Sargent was engaged to review the ultrasound and CT-scan films taken at Children's Hospital. He was at the time one of only two specialists in pediatric neuroradiology in B.C. His reading of the films led him to say:

It is my opinion that in-utero hypoxic-ischaemic injury [deficiency of oxygen and consequent reduction of blood supply] was initiated by attempted abortion performed three to four days before birth. From the radiological evidence, it is not possible to determine whether the subsequent events which occurred during and after birth affected the extent or severity of periventricular leukomalacia.

This carried the Solimano thesis even further. Sargent's report was intended to show not only that the attempted abortion was the "dominant" cause of the injury (Solimano's thesis) but that it was possible to reduce the significance of the events at VGH to the *de minimis* level.

All along we felt that we had to match the defence—expert for expert, resource for resource. This we did throughout the lawsuit. The process reached its apogee when we received the Sargent report. We turned again to Dr. Sarnat. He stood by his original opinion. Dr. Sarnat felt that Dr. Sargent's reading of the films—films taken six hours after Ximena's birth—was deficient. He pointed out:

In the first place, the cranial ultrasound is the least precise and has the lowest resolution of any of the commonly used imaging studies . . . In the second place, the particular examination upon which Dr. Sargent is basing his conclusions is of poor technical quality for even an ultrasound examination, and details are not as clear as they might be . . . Thirdly, and perhaps of greatest importance of all, is the fact that six hours is not a long enough period to transpire to detect significant changes in cerebral tissue to provide any basis for saying whether there has been or not an additional hypoxic insult in the postnatal period. Even microscopic examination of brain tissue at autopsy rarely demonstrates any but the most subtle changes in cells or surrounding tissue; if it cannot even be seen with a microscope, it surely cannot be detected by crude imaging techniques such as cranial ultrasound.

Dr. Sarnat then turned to Dr. Sargent's almost exclusive reliance on the radiology.

Radiological examinations should be considered in their clinical context and not as isolated findings . . . I maintain that the major clinical manifestation now exhibited by Ximena is *irreversible brain damage occurring during that first hour and not prenatally* . . . Even from a radiological viewpoint, the more extensive damage later demonstrated in subsequent imaging studies of various types during the course of the first year of life reflected the damage that was inflicted upon her during the first hour of life, superimposed upon a less extensive prenatal insult.

But the defence's army of medical experts was growing. We needed reinforcements. We felt it was imperative to obtain the opinion of a pediatric neuroradiologist (Dr. Sargent's specialty). It is, however, a new specialty; the only other physician in B.C. practising in that specialty had already been retained by the defence. They had cornered the market.

We needed to canvass physicians outside B.C. engaged in this new specialty, to persuade one of them to look at the ultrasound images and to let us have an opinion. We recruited Don Rosenbloom, a colleague with many years' experience in personal injury cases. He was soon on the telephone to many of these experts to obtain an opinion we could use.

His efforts to obtain a report from a pediatric neuroradiologist entailed calls to San Francisco, Seattle, Montreal, Boston, Pittsburgh, Los Angeles, Toronto and Calgary. Finally, he was able to persuade Dr. Richard Boyer, chair of pediatric medical imaging at the Primary Children's Medical Centre, University of Utah School of Medicine, in Salt Lake City, to examine the films. Within two days, Dr. Boyer advised by telephone that he disagreed with Dr. Sargent. His written report arrived soon afterwards. He said: "Review of the clinical record suggests that *the most likely cause of this insult relates to the period of significant stress experienced by the neonate [baby] in the period immediately following birth. This* . . . indicates an added insult, not explained by prematurity alone [emphasis added]." He concluded: "I believe that the most significant injury to this child's brain occurred during the first hour of the neonate's life."

We lined up two other neonatologists, Dr. Reg Sauve of Edmonton and Dr. Dennis Mayock of Seattle, to answer Dr. Solimano's opinion. Though the lawsuit was settled before their reports were drafted, they were prepared to testify that they agreed with Dr. Sarnat and Dr. Boyer. And we had also obtained a report from Dr. Michael Whitfield (who had taken Dr. Jaroudi's call on the night of Ximena's birth) in his capacity as a neonatologist at Children's Hospital. He had led the team that kept Ximena alive at Children's. He expressed the firm opinion that the post-delivery lack of care at VGH had caused injury to the deep structures of Ximena's brain. Her mental retardation as well as her quadriplegia, he said, was mainly attributable to lack of care at VGH.

We had conducted thirteen examinations for discovery, travelling as far as Spain for one of them. We had cast our net across the continent of North America in search of experts.

We were ready for trial. But now VGH wanted to adjourn.

On Wednesday, May 27, VGH applied to adjourn the trial, which was scheduled to start five days later, on Monday, June 2. The hospital wanted to bring what are called third party proceedings against four doctors in Bellingham, Washington, as well as the Bellingham clinic (which they claimed to have located) where the abortion procedure had allegedly been done. The hospital also sought an adjournment of the trial so that the third party proceedings could be tried at the same time as the trial of Ximena's case against VGH. Moreover, Dr. Jaroudi had advised VGH's lawyers that he refused to attend the trial. VGH's lawyers said it was no fault of theirs that Dr. Jaroudi would not come to Vancouver for the trial; they needed an adjournment on this ground as well. Finally, VGH alleged that there should be an adjournment because it was now apparent, owing to the very large number of expert witnesses, that the case could not be tried in the twenty days allotted.

The application by VGH was heard on May 27 and May 28 before Justice Donald Clancy. In the meantime, in early May, VGH had made an offer of settlement. We had rejected it. The hospital had countered. As the trial date bore down on us, both sides agreed to mediation. Mediation was scheduled to take place on Friday, May 29, and Saturday, May 30, and the trial was scheduled to begin Monday morning, June 1.

We were successful in persuading Justice Clancy to dismiss the application to adjourn.

This was a pivotal moment. If we had lost the application to adjourn, and VGH had brought the American defendants into the case, the litigation could have gone on for another four or five years. The complications entailed in VGH's bringing into the lawsuit four physicians and a clinic from another country, together with the questions of jurisdiction, limitations, liability and causation that would have arisen, would have entailed still more examinations for discovery and a constellation of other proceedings. We might not have been able to continue to hold the order for a jury trial, on the ground that the proliferation of defendants and the swelling chorus of experts would make the case too complicated for a jury. And it would have meant that Ximena, now twelve, would likely have been sixteen or seventeen years old before her case would finally come to trial.

The dismissal of the hospital's application to adjourn meant that serious negotiations could take place. VGH now faced a jury trial with a large potential claim, including punitive damages.

I asked Don Rosenbloom to take the lead in negotiations that weekend. By this time I was entirely focussed on getting the case ready for trial. Ximena's cause was consuming all my time and all my emotional energy. I had ceased to be detached. I recognized that I was not prepared to lead our negotiations. But I sat in on the negotiations. Gary Nelson and Charles Lugosi worked with Don in formulating and reformulating our demands. Erin and Margie worked and reworked the figures.

At the same time, I had to put the finishing touches on my opening speech for the jury. Charles and Erin were preparing Margaret Renaerts and other members of the Renaerts family to testify, going through the matters I would canvass with them when they were on the stand and the questions they would likely be asked in cross-examination.

On the eve of trial, you are in a state of high readiness, casting your mind over the whole scene, reviewing the evidence, making sure that every detail has been considered—you are keyed up and remain in more or less that same condition until the trial is over.

In a jury trial, the tension remains unbroken until the verdict is in. A year or two before the denouement in Ximena's case, I had been addressing the jury on behalf of a boy who broke his neck in a rugby game during a physical education class at school. My task was to show that the physical education teacher was negligent. No doubt the jury sympathizes with my client. But they pay school taxes. Accidents will happen. Can we compensate everyone? I have to demonstrate that the teacher in giving his testimony did not tell the truth. It's a gamble, but unless I go for it, there's simply a jumble of recollections: the boys trying to recall what happened on the school ground seven years ago at the time of the accident; the teacher saying that he was doing his best, that he can't guarantee no one will ever be hurt. But if the jury members believe he deliberately lied about what happened, they'll have something on which to hang a verdict. The defence makes a more than plausible argument on the other side. Aware of how well it is done, I affect indifference: well, not indifference, the jury would see through such nonsense, but indicating by my steady expression and demeanour that nothing the defence says has altered my conviction in the soundness of my case.

The jury's out. They're back soon. They can't agree on a verdict. The judge tells them to keep trying. They go out again, then they go home to sleep. (In civil trials in B.C., a judge can allow a jury to disperse for the night, with a warning not to discuss the case.) While the jury is out, the boy's mother speaks to me, "Mr. Berger, whether we win or lose, we think you've done a magnificent job, and we're grateful." Well, we certainly haven't won yet. I'm awfully nervous. Yet the boy's mother is sufficiently composed to offer a generous remark when she knows it could all turn out badly. Ordinary people—she is the boy's principal caregiver—can be extraordinarily classy.

It's the waiting that is worst. When you're cross-examining a witness, when you're arguing a point of law, even if it's uphill, you're engaged; you're functioning, not simply left to wait and to consider the worst. I start developing in my head the grounds of appeal in case we lose: Where did the judge go wrong in summing up the case? Did he make a mistake in his analysis of the law?

After a few hours the following day, the clerk of the court runs into the law library, where I'm hiding out with the family's lawyer, to tell us the jury has reached a verdict. We walk stiff-legged back to the courtroom. Afraid to say a word, holding our breath, so much depending on the verdict: Will the boy have adequate care? Will his parents be relieved of the burden—one they won't be able to bear much longer—of looking after the boy?

When the jury returns, filing into the jury box, in the moments that pass before the judge takes his seat, and the jury members are asked if they have reached a verdict, and their verdict is announced, the tension is excruciating.

Quite awful for the client—in a few moments his life, her life, will be changed forever. Quite awful for the lawyers, too—the outcome of months, perhaps years of work, will be known in all too short a time. It is as if all that has gone before is compressed into an instant.

The foreman stands. He is asked, "Was there negligence by the teacher that caused or contributed to the boy's accident?" "Yes."

The relief throughout the room is palpable. I can hear the exhalation of breath. There is a cry of happiness from the members of the family.

The formal procedures are observed. The judge thanks the jury members for their verdict and discharges them. They glance towards the boy and the members of his family, fully aware of the difference their verdict has made. The school board will settle now; damages will be agreed.

Congratulations all around. The whole saga is recapitulated. My God, what a dismal scene it would have been if we had lost. How much more could this family take? Contemplating these ghastly alternatives makes victory all the sweeter.

There would be no jury trial, no verdict, in Ximena's case. We settled with VGH two days before the trial was to commence. The litigation, the negotiations left our team absolutely drained. The Renaertses rejoiced; we did, too. We were all immensely relieved. But the joy felt by the clients at the settlement and the relief felt by the lawyers was not very different. And the lawyers had reason to be pleased. I was proud of our legal team.

I had, apart from five years at Shulman, Tupper, Southin and Gray, practised on my own during my early years at the bar. A small group of congenial, compatible and dedicated colleagues suited me. Doug Sanders had worked for me, then Don Rosenbloom and Harry Boyle. Doug had become a law teacher, specializing in the field of indigenous peoples' rights around the world. After I left to go on the bench, Don had become one of Vancouver's ablest practitioners in the field of personal injuries. Harry Boyle became a judge.

After I returned to practice in 1985 and commenced a second career in law, Gary Nelson joined me and we became partners. Ron Shulman joined us, then Erin, then Margie Vanderkruyk. We worked with Don Rosenbloom and his colleagues, Jim Aldridge and Marcus Bartley. Together we formed a single practice group. Each could call on the expertise of the others. We had the resources we needed. But we weren't bogged down in firm meetings. Any collective decisions that had to be made were made over coffee or during a stroll down the corridor. I was able to take on major cases by enlisting one or more members of our group, depending on the nature of the case and the resources and expertise required. In Ximena's case, all of us working on the case believed passionately in the cause.

Throughout Ximena's case, lurking in the background, was the issue of abortion. Well-meaning people in the pro-life movement wanted this case to be about the evils of abortion. We received news from them of other babies at VGH who had been aborted, were viable and had been left to die. But any evidence of such cases seemed always to turn to dust. On the other hand, the pro-choice forces seemed to wish for nothing more than that the case would go away.

After the facts came out, I thought the pro-life movement would use the occasion to urge that we should consider how a constant stream of abortion procedures can lead doctors and nurses to develop an attitude of indifference towards human life, or, to be more precise, the life of human beings. Vera Wood had delivered many babies when she had worked in VGH's now-closed maternity ward, yet it was arguable the evidence showed that she had left Ximena to die. Other nurses apparently stood around the service room while the baby gasped for air in the commode. Why? Had duty on the ward altered their mindset? The case raised all kinds of questions about the consequences of carrying out abortions on a large scale. But the pro-life movement managed to shoot itself in the foot. Betty Green, president of the Vancouver Right to Life Society, said, according to the Vancouver *Province*, "that the lesson from the settlement is 'to make sure you finish the job and kill them' or there will be malpractice suits."

Our job was to advance the claim of a child who had been delivered into the world. Ximena, as soon as she left her mother's body, became a human being under Canadian law and entitled to every protection that would have been accorded a viable baby who entered the world in a normal delivery. Both sides, pro-choice and pro-life, presumably could agree as to that.

As the gruesome nature of the evidence unfolded, as the dereliction of duty by VGH became more and more striking, including VGH's failure to conduct any internal investigation, Bert and Margaret Renaerts, in my office one day, asked, "Isn't there going to be an investigation, an inquiry?" I said, "This lawsuit is the inquiry." And it was; the only one.

Ordinarily, a settlement is a private affair, with both sides required to maintain confidentiality. But where the plaintiff is an infant (in B.C. under the age of nineteen), the settlement must be approved by the court. In Ximena's case, Justice Paul Williamson held that the hearing to approve the settlement should be open to the public. The judge approved the settlement:

$8,000,000 plus $500,000 for costs, plus disbursements. $3,000,000 has taken the form of a structured settlement which will provide the infant plaintiff with a monthly income of just under $10,000. As well, payments of $100,000 will be made upon each of six specified days occurring every five years from December 2003, to December 2028.

The judge reviewed what the settlement would bring to our clients:

I am told it is the highest personal injury settlement to date in this province. It includes the maximum recovery for non-pecuniary loss, substantial awards for future wage loss, and some 84% of the costs set out in the plaintiff's expert report on future care requirements. It provides funds for appropriate housing and for insurance on the lives of the parents to the benefit of the infant plaintiff. It also includes a large award ($500,000) for costs.

The result, he said, is "excellent."

That was in 1998. How are Ximena and her family faring today?

Bev, Erin and I visited them in Chilliwack in August 2001. The Renaertses now have, altogether, adopted fifteen children, ten with disabilities, eight of whom are still living. They have bought a large home, along the lines of a good-sized country hotel, and built a new wing with a wheel-in shower, washing facilities, and rooms for all the children, some of them children delivered from the civil war and ensuing famine in Ethiopia—children who lost their childhood. They have a bus for holiday trips and a trailer. Ximena is a girl of fifteen now, always smiling. She can't walk, mostly crawls, but is obviously happy.

Margaret Renaerts runs the household. She and her daughter Nicole provide care for the children. Nicole has adopted two children herself, one from Ethiopia and one a Ladino child from Guatemala. Bert looks after the farm. There are chickens, pigs, horses.

The Renaertses have demonstrated that even the most unfortunate of children can thrive in a warm, caring and secure environment. One of the joys of law practice is the chance, which comes along more often than you think, to set the world right.

12　*Duelling Charter Rights*

I N   M A Y   1 9 9 7, I was in the Chilliwack courthouse, in the heart of B.C.'s Bible belt, to challenge Trinity Western University's admissions policy towards homosexuals. I was representing the B.C. College of Teachers, the governing body of the province's teaching profession. The college had rejected an application by Trinity Western University (TWU), a private university, for approval of a five-year teacher education program. If TWU's five-year program were approved by the college, TWU's graduates would be eligible to teach in the public schools of the province. The college had rejected TWU's application because faculty hired by and students entering TWU had to sign a contract subscribing to a code of conduct that, on Biblical authority, denounced homosexual behaviour as a sin.

The college took the position that TWU, as a private university, could set up whatever teacher education program it wanted. But the college also held that, in determining whether to approve TWU's program, it ought to consider the university's attitude towards homosexuality. The college felt that graduates of a teacher education program should be professionally prepared to teach amid the diversity that prevails in the public schools, which by law are secular; that is, no religious denomination runs them, and no religious dogma is taught there.

Canada's Charter of Rights came into force in 1982. Section 2(a) of the Charter guarantees freedom of conscience and religion. TWU asked: What use is such a guarantee if TWU, a private university, cannot teach the doctrines it believes in?

The College of Teachers also relied on the Charter. Section 15, the so-called equality provision, which had come into force in 1985, prohibits discrimination on a series of enumerated grounds: race, national or ethnic origin, colour, religion, sex, age or physical or mental disability. In 1995, the Supreme Court of Canada ruled that under section 15 discrimination on grounds of sexual orientation was also prohibited. The college believed that TWU's faculty and student contract discriminated against homosexuals. Would students subscribing to such beliefs be professionally prepared as teachers in the public school classroom where all students, no matter what their sexual orientation, are welcome?

Both sides relied on the Charter, the one on freedom of religion, the other on the principle of equality.

The trial took place in the courthouse in Chilliwack. (TWU's campus is in nearby Langley.) The gallery was occupied by TWU faculty and students. Much of the argument by TWU's lawyer, Robert Kuhn, seemed to be pitched to the occupants of the gallery. From the beginning, there was much disparagement of secular values, many references to "re-education." No doubt many of the faculty and students in the gallery thought we were there on behalf of the college to challenge beliefs that formed the religious core of their lives.

Erin was working with me on the case. We were staying at the local Holiday Inn. At dinner, we talked about *Inherit the Wind*. In that film, Spencer Tracy played Clarence Darrow, who represented the accused teacher Thomas Scopes in the "monkey trial" held in Tennessee in 1925, in which Scopes had been charged for teaching Darwin's theory of evolution in a state where such teaching was prohibited by law. The rustics, in the movie, were out in force. But it wasn't like that in Chilliwack. The faculty and students of TWU were not rustics whose education was limited to Biblical truths unfolded to them by rampaging fundamentalist preachers. They had, however, formally subscribed to beliefs that the college viewed as inconsistent with the secular values espoused generally by Canadians and expressed in the Charter of Rights.

As the hearing proceeded, we got to know the TWU people. Professor Haro Van Brummelen, prospective dean of TWU's Faculty of Education, told me that required readings at TWU included passages from my own books. A year later, in the same case, when Erin and I appeared on behalf of the College of Teachers in the Court of Appeal, in Vancouver, faculty and students from TWU were once again the main occupants of the gallery. Erin was pregnant with her third child. Everyone was happy to see her. Pregnant women, gowned in legal regalia, vest, tabs and gown, are no longer a rarity in the courts, but they do attract a certain notice.

On the third day of the hearing, I arrived in court without Erin. The gallery occupants were curious: "Where's Erin this morning?" I said, "She's checked into St. Paul's Hospital to have her baby." Murmurs and exclamations of sympathy, including some hand-clapping. TWU students were normal youngsters. But were they ready to become teachers in the public schools?

Would TWU graduates be professionally prepared to offer a supportive environment to all students in the public schools? Would they be able to relate to students of homosexual orientation? Fellow teachers of homosexual orientation? Children who come from homes with two mothers or two fathers? Freedom of religion is all very well. But if the values of an institution preparing graduates to teach in the public schools are inconsistent with contemporary ideas about equality, it is something for the college to consider.

For most Canadians, religious beliefs inform their moral values. The predominant religion in our country is Christianity. But Canada is a secular society. We have no established state religion. And though our laws converge at many points with Christian belief (and with the beliefs of other religions), the values to which Canadians subscribe represent a diversity of belief that in some respects is at odds with the dogmas of some Christian denominations.

All Christians do not agree on attitudes towards homosexuality. Jesus had nothing to say about homosexuality. But Paul the Apostle did, and for fundamentalist believers Paul's strictures, condemning homosexuality in the most graphic language, are compelling.

The question of homosexual rights is only the latest controversy over the legitimacy of discriminatory practices. In fact, prejudicial attitudes towards minorities are woven into the history of B.C. In the nineteenth and early twentieth centuries, the province enacted laws that expressly discriminated against Aboriginal peoples, as well as persons of Chinese and Japanese descent and other racial minorities. A similar tale could be told of other provinces. There has been in Canada, however, since the Second World War, an evolving recognition that certain categories of persons are to be protected from discrimination. The pervasiveness of racial, ethnic and religious discrimination has abated. In 1960, John Diefenbaker's government introduced the Canadian Bill of Rights. In 1982, Pierre Trudeau's government brought in the Canadian Charter of Rights and Freedoms. These were milestones on the way to building what Trudeau called the just society. They provide specific protection from discrimination that the framers of the Charter understood Canadians believed had no place in Canadian life.

Section 15 of the Charter enshrines the idea of equality:

Every individual is equal before and under the law and has the right to the equal protection and equal benefit of the law without discrimination and, in particular, without discrimination based on race, national or ethnic origin, colour, religion, sex, age or mental or physical disability.

Thus the Charter of Rights enumerates the categories of persons to be spared discrimination. At the time, the list seemed complete, though today we would say "gender" instead of "sex." But there was one item missing: sexual orientation.

We had learned that racism is evil. We had learned that discrimination on grounds of race, national origin, ethnicity or religion is evil. Discrimination on such grounds is prohibited by the Charter. But the Charter, like the Canadian Bill of Rights before it, said nothing about protecting homosexuals from discrimination. Yet we have, in a remarkably short time, begun to realize that discrimination on the ground of sexual orientation is evil, too.

In fact, the most salient issue in recent years relating to the condition of minorities is that relating to the rights of gays and lesbians. The Supreme Court of Canada has held that discrimination on the basis of sexual orientation is discrimination on a ground analogous to those enumerated in section 15, and therefore homosexual persons are entitled to the same measure of protection as if they were victims of discrimination on the ground of race, religion or any of the other grounds enumerated in section 15. In 1995, in *Egan v. Canada,* Justice Gerald LaForest wrote:

I have no difficulty accepting the appellants' contention that whether or not sexual orientation is based on biological or physiological factors, which may be a matter of some controversy, *it is a deeply personal characteristic that is either unchangeable or changeable only at unacceptable personal costs, and so falls within the ambit of s. 15 protection as being analogous to the enumerated grounds* [emphasis added].

In the same case, Justice Peter Cory wrote: "The *Charter* seeks to reinforce the concept that all human beings, however different they may appear to be to the majority, are all equally deserving of concern, respect and consideration." Canadian critics of the court, whose views were recently summed up by American jurist Robert J. Bork, in delivering the 2000 Barbara Frum Lecture, believe the court had no warrant, in light of the Charter's silence, to add sexual orientation to the list of prohibited grounds of discrimination in section 15. Bork denounced the decision, describing it as "extraordinary." In 1996, however, Parliament amended the Canadian Human Rights Act to include sexual orientation as a prohibited ground of discrimination. (B.C. had already done so in a 1993 amendment to its Human Rights Act.)

These are secular values held by Canadians generally. But they are not shared by all Canadians, particularly not by those who cleave to a literal interpretation of certain Biblical passages. A literal reading of the letters of St. Paul condemns homosexuals and homosexual behaviour. There is nothing muffled about his Biblical teachings. In I Corinthians 6.9–10, Paul said:

Do you not know that the wicked will not inherit the Kingdom of God? Do not be deceived: Neither the sexually immoral nor idolaters nor adulterers nor male prostitutes nor homosexual offenders nor thieves nor the greedy nor drunkards nor slanderers will inherit the Kingdom of God.

This is uncompromising. Paul's beliefs are held by many sincere Christians. They regard homosexual acts as unnatural, as contrary to God's law. To be sure, at TWU these exhortations were leavened by a firm belief that Christians should treat all persons with dignity and respect: "Love the sinner, hate the sin." There was, however, a contradiction within that phrase that lay at the heart of the dispute between TWU and the College of Teachers.

TWU claimed that propagating its Biblical views on its own campus is entirely within its rights. So it is. Under section 2(a) of the Charter, "freedom of conscience and religion" is guaranteed. What faculty and students at TWU believe is their business. But does it become the public's business when institutions such as TWU wish to send their graduates into the public schools? In 1996, when representatives from the B.C. College of Teachers came to see me, that was the question they had before them.

The College of Teachers had been established in 1988 under B.C.'s Teaching Profession Act. As the governing body for teachers in the province, the college determines whether teaching graduates are qualified to teach in the public schools. The council of the college consists of twenty persons: fifteen members elected by teachers, two appointed by the provincial cabinet, two by the minister of education and one nominated by the deans of the faculties of education of the province's public universities.

British Columbia has four public universities, all required by law to conduct themselves as secular institutions. But TWU is a private university. Moreover, TWU operates under the aegis of the Evangelical Free Church. Two-thirds of TWU's Board of Governors must be members of the Evangelical Free Church.

The contract that each student and faculty member at TWU was required to sign was entitled "Responsibilities of Membership in the [TWU] Community." With the contract, each student and faculty member agreed, among other things, to:

REFRAIN FROM *PRACTICES THAT ARE BIBLICALLY CONDEMNED*. These include but are not limited to drunkenness (Eph. 5:18), swearing or use of profane language (Eph. 4:29, 5:4, Jas 3:1–12), harassment (Jn 13:34–35; Rom. 12:9–21; Eph. 4:31), all forms of dishonesty including cheating and stealing (Prov. 12:22; Col. 3:9; Eph. 4:28), abortion (Ex. 20:13; Ps. 139:13–16), involvement in the occult (Acts 19:19; Gal. 5:19), *and sexual*

sins including premarital sex, adultery, homosexual behaviour, and viewing of pornog-
raphy (I Cor. 6:12–20; Eph. 4:17–24: I Thess. 4:3–8; Rom. 2:26–27; I Tim. 1:9–10).
Furthermore married members of the community agree to maintain the sanctity of
marriage and to take every positive step possible to avoid divorce [emphasis added].

TWU filed evidence to show that the Evangelical Free Church believes the Old
and New Testaments are "the inspired word of God, without error in the original writings, the complete revelation of His will for the salvation of men, and the
divine and final authority for all Christian faith and life." According to the teachings of Paul, the man who organized the Christian Church, homosexuals are
destined for the flames of hell. Paul's is by no means a view held by all those who
believe in the Christian faith. It is a belief, however, fervently held by the Evangelical Free Church.

TWU relied on the testimony contained in an affidavit made by Dr. David
Milne, a theologian of the Free Church, who quoted from what Paul said in
Romans 2.26–27:

26: Because of this, God gave them over to shameful lusts. Even their women exchanged natural relations for unnatural ones.
27: In the same way the men also abandoned natural relations with women and were
inflamed with lust for one another. Men committed indecent acts with other men,
and received in themselves the due penalty for their perversion.

This passage, denouncing homosexuality as unnatural and a perversion, is,
according to Dr. Milne, the principal basis for the Evangelical Free Church's
belief that homosexual behaviour is Biblically condemned.

TWU has had a teacher education program since 1985. Their teacher education students have graduated and gone on to teach in the public schools.
Although they have taken four years at TWU, they have taken their fifth year of
teacher education, the professional development year, under the aegis of Simon
Fraser University (SFU), a public university. As a result, there is a joint TWU-SFU
program in the fifth year: the students take some classes at SFU, the remainder
at TWU's campus. SFU faculty teach some of the classes at SFU, and the student
practicums are supervised by SFU.

Now TWU had applied to the college to have its teacher education students do
all five years of their studies exclusively at TWU. There would be no joint SFU-TWU
program for fifth-year students. The college, however, had said, "No, we think it
best that your teacher education students should continue to do their fifth year
under the aegis of SFU."

The college had one question for me: Could they, in deciding whether to approve TWU's teacher education program, take into account TWU's beliefs about homosexuality, in particular, the language relating to homosexuality found in the contract that students and faculty were required to sign?

The council of the college had already declined TWU's application on that very ground. Now the council had before it an application by TWU for reconsideration. It was not too late to change the decision.

The approval process had been painstaking. After TWU applied to the college in 1995 for approval of its five-year teacher education program, the college had appointed a program approval team. The team provided a thorough analysis of TWU's proposal. The team recommended approval of Trinity Western University's program for a five-year interim period subject to certain conditions. The college's teacher education programs committee carried the recommendation of the program approval team, including many of the conditions for approval, to the council of the college.

When the recommendation reached the council, TWU's program was rejected on the ground that, according to the resolution passed by the council, "it is contrary to the public interest to approve a teacher education program offered by a private institution which appears to follow discriminatory practices that public institutions are, by law, not allowed to follow." The council's focus was on the contract that students and faculty had to sign.

The contract stated that "students who cannot with integrity support those standards [set out in the contract] should seek a living-learning situation more acceptable to them." In other words, a potential student or faculty member whose sexual orientation was not heterosexual had to accept that homosexual behaviour is a sin—that it falls generally into the category of "dishonest or dishonourable practices such as cheating or stealing" or at least is comparable to "viewing pornography"—or go elsewhere to teach or to study. The Biblical references in the contract categorized homosexuality as unnatural, perverted and an abomination. It was reasonable to assume that neither faculty nor students of homosexual orientation could in good faith sign the contract and study or teach at TWU.

This was not a case of overweening sensitivity on the part of the college. It was not a question of fearing that TWU graduates would go out into the classroom to proselytize for their faith. No one thought that TWU graduates in the classroom would be taking aside students with homosexual proclivities and scolding them as sinners. But there was an issue of professional preparedness.

TWU claimed that, on the ground of freedom of conscience and religion, its teacher education program was immunized from scrutiny by the college. TWU asserted it was free to inculcate what doctrines it wished; it would not be open to the college to consider those doctrines in determining whether graduates of such a program would be professionally prepared to enter the public school classroom.

TWU claimed its beliefs are sacrosanct: religious belief is not subject to secular examination by the college. The college, on the other hand, believed it had a mandate to inquire into the effect of certain beliefs, even if they were religious beliefs conscientiously held, on professional preparedness for the classroom environment.

This question involved, on the one hand, ideas of morality derived from Biblical injunction and, on the other, a widespread, modern belief in a morality that affirms equality, founded on a broader view of our common humanity than Paul's teachings permit fundamentalist Christians to observe. It involved a weighing of values. Because the values held do differ.

I gave the college my opinion. I said the council could determine whether the beliefs of TWU would have an effect on professional preparedness. The Supreme Court had decided *Egan* the year before. Canada had in the following year amended its Human Rights Act to protect homosexuals. I thought consideration of the vulnerability of homosexuals ought to be the next logical development in Canada's passage to a more tolerant society founded on principles of equality. TWU required faculty and students to sign the contract, a contract that entailed subscribing to a view of homosexuality at odds with the Charter's insistence on equality. That was a matter the college could consider.

The college had not been established as a human rights tribunal. It didn't exist to hand down judgements on discriminatory practices. But it could, in my opinion, take such practices into account in deciding whether graduates of TWU's teacher education program would be ready to teach in the public school system.

The college relied on section 4 of the Teaching Profession Act, which reads:

It is the object of the college to establish, *having regard to the public interest*, standards for the *education, professional responsibility* and *competence* of its members, persons who hold certificates of qualification and applicants for membership and, consistent with that object, to encourage the professional interest of its members in those matters [emphasis added].

The council, I felt, in exercising its discretion under section 4 of the Teaching Profession Act, had to have regard to the public interest as expressed in the Charter of Rights and our human rights statutes. The public had an interest in seeing that teachers were professionally prepared to deal with homosexuality and its ramifications in the classroom. Suppose a student approaches a teacher on the subject. Suppose a homosexual student is being tormented by other students. Or suppose a colleague on the teaching staff is gay or lesbian. Would graduates of TWU be ready to cope with these situations? These were in my opinion issues of professional competence, to be determined by the college.

TWU's request for reconsideration of its proposed five-year all-TWU program was heard by the council on June 14, 1996. The request was rejected, on the same grounds as before.

Trinity Western University filed a petition in the Supreme Court of B.C., alleging that the college had exceeded its powers under the Teaching Profession Act. This was the proceeding that had brought us to the hearing in Chilliwack.

Robert Kuhn, for TWU, claimed that the college had added a new dimension to political correctness, a phrase from which all meaning has been drained. It is too often used to turn away real injustice and to sanctify discriminatory attitudes and behaviour that cannot be defended except on the ground that the world used to uphold them ("Call me old-fashioned but . . ."). I argued that under section 4 of the Teaching Profession Act, the college could not ignore that TWU's beliefs regarding homosexuality might have an effect on the professional prepared-ness of its graduates. The joint TWU-SFU program for the fifth year should be maintained.

Justice William Davies upheld TWU's claim to immunity. He ruled that sec-tion 4 of the Teaching Profession Act did not allow the council to scrutinize TWU's religious beliefs. He made an order setting aside the decision of the coun-cil and requiring the council to approve the proposed five-year all-TWU teacher education program.

The B.C. Court of Appeal upheld Justice Davies, two to one. The court said that TWU's religious beliefs were none of the council's business. Justice Michael Goldie, for the majority, held:

In my view the object stated in section 4 relates primarily to the establishment of teaching standards, that is to say, to a policy-making role. There is no reference in s. 4 to the regulatory role of Council which was invoked in the examination of TWU's application. Nothing expressly required Council to employ its views of Charter values and human rights legislation in the case at bar.

Charter values as such, according to Justice Goldie, including the Supreme Court of Canada's attribution to the Charter of a condemnation of discrimina-tion against homosexuals, were irrelevant.

In the Court of Appeal, Justice Ann Rowles dissented. She held that the public did have an interest in upholding "discriminatory-free values in the pub-lic classroom."

It is clear from the terms "professional responsibility and competence of its members" [in section 4] that the College can consider the effect of public school teacher education programs on the competence and professional responsibility of their graduates. On that view of the matter, the College does have jurisdiction over the requirements for graduation and it is open to the Council to concern itself with whether graduates from an applicant program will be perceived as upholding discriminatory-free values in the public classroom.

Justice Rowles considered that TWU was engaged in discrimination against homosexuals. She referred to a recent case in which the Supreme Court had held that Alberta's human rights statute violated the Charter in that it contained no protection for gays and lesbians.

In *Vriend* [the earlier case], the Supreme Court found that the government was sending a "message" that gay men and lesbian women were not equal in dignity and rights through its omission to include sexual orientation as a prohibited ground of discrimination . . . In my respectful view, TWU's "message" is much more explicit in terms of its condemnation than the one found to be discriminatory in *Vriend*.

TWU had argued that, though it condemned homosexual behaviour as a sin, it taught that believers should nevertheless be supportive of the sinner: "Hate the sin, but love the sinner." Justice Rowles wrote:

Human rights law states that certain practices cannot be separated from identity, such that condemnation of the practice is a condemnation of the person. For example, condemnation of someone's religious practice central to his or her religious faith would be discrimination against the person on the grounds of religion. Human rights jurisprudence accepts that homosexual behaviour is as central to the personal identity of gays and lesbians as religious practices are to the religious identity of the faithful . . .

Even if the Community Standards are understood only to condemn homosexual behaviour and not people, the condemnation is still a harmful one. It is an insidious type of harm because it requires people to deny, condemn, or conceal a part of their own identity.

I had given my opinion to the college. Now the courts had twice rejected my view. But our argument had attracted a powerful dissent. I advised an appeal to the Supreme Court of Canada.

We had to obtain leave to appeal to the Supreme Court of Canada. Since 1975, in virtually all civil cases, it is necessary to obtain leave to bring an appeal to the

Supreme Court of Canada. This used to be done by filing a motion, going to Ottawa and arguing the case for leave before a panel of three judges. But since 1988 that, too, has changed. Now you have to file a written submission. Of course, the other side files one, too. But you don't get to look the judges in the eye. You don't have any idea how they are reacting to the words on the page. Your brief simply goes to a panel of three judges, who, with the assistance of their law clerks, read it over and decide whether the Supreme Court should hear the appeal.

Happily, in the TWU case, we did get leave. Now we had to prepare our appeal.

We were supported throughout by our clients. Doug Smart, the registrar of the College of Teachers, and Marie Kerchum, the deputy registrar, understood from the beginning we were setting out on a journey that would likely take us to the Supreme Court of Canada. Doug and Marie were informed, articulate and engaged. Their chief concern throughout, and that of the council, was the welfare of the students in the public school classroom. We discussed the case with Doug and Marie at every stage, sent them drafts of our written submissions, then sat down with them to discuss the drafts. It was an ideal situation for an advocate: having a client who understood the issues and could make sure that the facts of the case, presented against the background of B.C.'s teacher education system (about which they knew a lot more than we did), were accurately portrayed. There is nothing worse than going into court and being confronted by the bench with a question about the factual background and being unable to answer it. "I'll check that out and advise the court after the mid-morning break." Or cycling backwards, keeping your end of the colloquy going, while trying desperately to remember what, if anything, your clients had told you about the matter.

Clients like Doug and Marie are a great asset. We could analyze the court's reasons for judgement for them, discuss the law and give our views about appeal. They could then go to the council of the college for a decision.

Gary Nelson and I prepared our written submission to the Supreme Court. We had to consider, at the outset, what are the public schools for? Are they to pass on academic learning, or are students expected to learn about values that as citizens we share? The Supreme Court had once before considered this issue. In 1992, in *Ross v. New Brunswick School District No. 15*, a teacher had, strictly outside the classroom and on his own time, promoted anti-Semitic views. There was a complaint to the Human Rights Commission of New Brunswick. A board of inquiry established under the province's Human Rights Act found that, by retaining the teacher as a classroom teacher, the school board was guilty of discrimination against Jewish students on the ground of religion. The board of inquiry ordered the school board to remove the teacher from the classroom and to find him a non-teaching position, on the ground that his out-of-classroom activities had poisoned the educational atmosphere. The board of inquiry's decision was upheld by the Supreme Court of Canada. Justice Gerald LaForest, for the Supreme Court of Canada, discussed the role of the teacher in Canada's public schools. He wrote:

A school is a communication centre for a whole range of values and aspirations of a society. In large part, it defines the values that transcend society through the educational medium. The school is an arena for the exchange of ideas and must, therefore, be premised upon principles of tolerance and impartiality so that all persons within the school environment feel equally free to participate. As the board of inquiry stated, a school board has a duty to maintain a positive school environment for all persons served by it.

Teachers are inextricably linked to the integrity of the school system. Teachers occupy positions of trust and confidence, and exert considerable influence over their students as a result of their positions. The conduct of a teacher bears directly upon the community's perception of the ability of the teacher to fulfil such a position of trust and influence, and upon the community's confidence in the public school system as a whole . . .

By their conduct, teachers as "medium" must be perceived to uphold the values, beliefs and knowledge sought to be transmitted by the school systems.

We reminded the Supreme Court that the college was not dealing with an application by a graduate to be certified as a teacher. No religious test was being imposed. The college had never taken the stand that it could refuse to allow a graduate to teach on the ground of religious belief. The college had never taken the stand that believers in the dogmas of the Evangelical Free Church are disabled by their beliefs, or ineligible because of their beliefs, from teaching in the public school system.

The decision of the college, we argued, simply proceeded on the footing that exposure to Canadian secular values is a necessary element in the education of teachers who are to be considered qualified to teach in the public schools or, put another way, that they should not be considered qualified to teach when their only training has been at an institution that discriminates against homosexual persons and requires them, if they are to teach or study there, to subscribe to the view that homosexual persons are sinners.

The college's solution, designed to uphold the public interest and at the same time to respect the right of a private institution to instill its denominational beliefs, was to continue the current practice, allowing TWU to grant degrees, but requiring the fifth year of teacher education to be completed in the joint TWU-SFU program.

The vital issue of principle was whether TWU could claim for its beliefs a zone of immunity. In Canada, since the Second World War, ideas of equality have been extended. In our own time, discrimination on the ground of sexual orientation has come to be considered as opprobrious as discrimination on the ground of race or religion. How did we—a great many of us—come to generally accept this? One reason is because these ideas are enshrined in our Charter and in our human rights legislation. Did they stop at TWU? Did freedom of religion, protected by section 2(a) of the Charter, constitute an impermeable barrier to the ideas of equality exemplified in section 15 of the Charter?

Suppose, we suggested, a university was founded on a belief, said to be Biblically inspired, in the racial inferiority of blacks. Should that be countenanced in the name of pluralism and tolerance? Would such an institution's proposed program of teacher education be entitled to approval by the college without any consideration of such a discriminatory policy? This was not fanciful. In 1983, the Supreme Court of the United States upheld a ruling of the Internal Revenue Service denying parents who sent their children to Bob Jones University in South Carolina the right to deduct school fees from taxable income on the ground that the university's belief in segregation, based on its reading of the Bible, was inimical to the values enshrined in congressional legislation and presidential orders.

Here we had discrimination against homosexual persons. In what way, for purposes of the public interest, was this different from discrimination against blacks? Both are inconsistent with the Charter, which, since *Egan,* prohibits equally discrimination on the ground of race or sexual orientation. The Supreme Court refused to treat sexual orientation as a matter of individual choice; it is to be considered on the same footing as other prohibited grounds of discrimination.

In the public schools all children are welcome. So students whose sexual orientation is homosexual should be welcomed to the community of learning as warmly as students whose orientation is heterosexual. As Justice LaForest said in *Ross,* it is essential that a public school "maintain a positive environment" for all students.

If the particular definition of Christianity that inspires the Evangelical Free Church compels it to regard homosexual behaviour as a sin, and thus effectively to deprive homosexual persons or anyone who does not share that belief of the opportunity to study or teach at TWU, that is the business of the church. But the matter ceased to be altogether a private matter and acquired a public dimension when TWU applied for approval by a public regulatory body of its teacher education program. TWU, a private institution, sought the college's approval to present itself to the world as a private institution whose programs for teacher education stand on the same footing, and have received the same approbation, as those of public universities in the province.

It might be argued that TWU's discriminatory practices, even if opposed to the fundamental values of Canadian society, ought not to be considered; that ignoring them is consistent with the idea of a healthy pluralism in education. This argument would weigh on one side of the scale. But the council, having regard to the public interest, came down on the other side. We argued that this position was the council's prerogative, the job given to it by the legislature.

At least three-quarters of the council's members are by statute members of the teaching profession; they know teachers, teaching, the classroom and the school system. Our argument was that it was up to the council of the college to decide.

But TWU had a second argument. There is no proof, TWU's counsel said, that our graduates are likely to discriminate, that they will behave intolerantly towards homosexuals in the classroom. Indeed, none of TWU's graduates—and the university had been graduating teachers since 1985—had been shown to have behaved in such a manner. If any of them were to behave in that way, they argued, that would be the time to consider the impact of TWU's religious teaching on its graduates.

This argument found favour with Justice Davies and the Court of Appeal. The court held that there was no evidence that signing the contract had affected the behaviour of TWU graduates. Well, of course, it hadn't. All TWU graduates had done their fifth year in the joint TWU-SFU program. The question the college had to face was: If these graduates were to spend the whole five years at TWU, if the fifth year would no longer be under the joint TWU-SFU program, would they be ready to enter the public schools? That was, in the nature of things, unknowable. The college had to anticipate what might occur. Or it could wait to see how the proposed all-TWU five-year program turned out. But, we submitted, that was a decision for the college to make.

Should the college wait for evidence that graduates of a five-year TWU program might not be ready to deal with the classroom? We argued that the protection of children had to come first. The college could not simply be reactive. This argument entailed a judgement based on the evidence before the council, the public interest in a discrimination-free environment in the public schools, and the council's own knowledge and experience as teachers. In the result, the council decided that it would be best to continue to require that TWU students do the fifth year, the professional development year, under the joint TWU-SFU program.

We had lost in the Supreme Court of B.C. and in the Court of Appeal. Both courts had held that the college had no authority to consider the impact of TWU's religious dogma on the suitability of its graduates to teach in the public schools. The Supreme Court of Canada had given us leave to appeal. I had now to prepare to deliver oral argument.

When *Calder* went to the Supreme Court of Canada in 1971, the argument lasted five days. A hearing at the Supreme Court of Canada was then a set-piece presentation. You were given virtually all the time you thought you needed. All that has changed. Moreover, the members of the court regard the hour set aside for your argument as belonging to them as much as to you. They and their fleets of law clerks have already worked over the case. They have questions that they want answered. Sometimes virtually the whole hour may be used up in questions and answers.

Your planned presentation, no matter how concise, how elegant, how meticulous and yet touching upon the main themes, may never find its way out of the starting gate.

Instead of relying on a measured oration, you now have to be ready for a barrage of questions. Is this change a good thing? I am not sure, but I suppose it is inevitable. In the U.S. Supreme Court, each side is given half an hour. As a result, in the U.S. the hearing before the court is nothing more than a pro forma occasion for the judges to state their positions.

In Canada, the judges of the Supreme Court know that their station is at the end of the line. They know there is no further appeal. No higher court will scrutinize their work. They have to get it right. Not that there is always a right answer to the cases that reach them. But they have to discover the closest thing there is to a right answer. They have read the judgements of the lower courts. The issues have been defined. Now they have to come up with answers. Their answers are usually found in lengthy reasons for judgement. These swatches of prose may sometimes be difficult to get through. But the judges have to be exact. They have to get the law right as it applies to the case before them. Because other, similar cases may be pending and yet raise issues not so far addressed, they may have to keep an important thought open-ended. They don't always have the freedom to write in a way that can be understood with a swift glance across the page. In searching for a pithy phrase, they may go too far.

At the hearing, therefore, the judges can be forgiven if, instead of settling back to enjoy the eloquence of counsel, they use the hearing to obtain answers to questions that are troubling them.

The court set aside a day for the college's appeal. I had an hour. Mr. Kuhn had an hour. The rest of the time was given over to interveners, organizations allowed to participate to bring to the argument distinct perspectives that might otherwise not be considered. They are like skirmishers riding in to aid the cause of one side or the other. The college had, on its side, EGALE, an organization representing gays and lesbians, and the Ontario Secondary School Teachers Federation. The Roman Catholic Church and the fundamentalist churches had made common cause against us. Catholic teaching on homosexuality is founded, like that of the Evangelical Free Church, on the teachings of St. Paul. They had obtained leave to intervene and they turned out in force, a heavenly host of interveners.

When we obtained leave to appeal to the Supreme Court of Canada, I was confident, despite the judgements of the B.C. courts, that we would win on the main issue; that is, the Supreme Court would hold that the college was entitled to scrutinize the religious beliefs held at TWU; that the Charter guarantee of freedom of religion did not establish a zone of immunity for religious beliefs. If we were successful on this issue, we could then argue that it was for the college to decide whether the evidence was sufficient to establish discriminatory practices at TWU, the ground on which the college had declined to approve the five-year all-TWU program.

It is true the council was relying on the contract signed by students and faculty. Was that sufficient evidence? We based our argument on the rule laid down by the Supreme Court of Canada: Was the decision of the council patently unreasonable? In *Canada (A.G.) v. Public Service Alliance,* the Supreme Court held that "it must be shown that the impugned decision is irrational, that is, evidently not in accordance with reason." This is a very high standard for anyone challenging a decision of a tribunal to meet. We would argue that by such a standard any challenge to the decision of the college must fail.

Gary and Erin came with me to Ottawa. At the hearing on November 9, 2000, the court peppered us with questions. These show how the court approaches these policy issues.

Justice Ian Binnie raised the question: Since TWU urged tolerance and understanding of all sinners, could it really be said that there was discrimination against homosexuals?

MR. JUSTICE BINNIE: Dr. Milne, when he testified, said:
"The Bible is very clear that while Christians must not condone or participate in homosexual behaviour, they must maintain an environment of love, understanding and acceptance of all people, including those in the homosexual community. Fear, prejudice, discrimination and hatred are also Biblically condemned."
The distinction between the behaviour and the sinners you put into your factum is certainly supported by the witnesses called on behalf of TWU.
MR. BERGER: Yes, and it is for the Council to say, because they are charged with the

responsibility of considering whether graduates of this program will be prepared as professionals in the public schools to deal adequately with attitudes towards homosexuality and homophobia. Will they be able to offer a supportive learning environment to all children? Will they know the appropriate way of dealing with situations where homosexuals are bullied by their peers, and so on? That's the responsibility of the Council, and we can—

MR. JUSTICE BINNIE: Yes, but when you're dealing with what is biblically condemned, they do—Dr. Milne goes on to state that it condemns intolerance as well.

MR. BERGER: Oh yes. "Love the sinner, hate the sin." But this court has said, in the case of homosexuals, that homosexual behaviour is something that bears on their identity. It is at odds with everything this court has said under the *Charter* and under human rights legislation about separating personal characteristics that are virtually unchangeable from the identity of the person in question.

Then Justice Louis LeBel raised the issue of a religious test in the case of individual teachers.

MR. JUSTICE LEBEL: But, Mr. Berger, I'm trying to ascertain what's really the position of the College, at least perhaps in respect, let's say, of individual certification of teachers. Would the position mean that if the College finds out that a teacher or someone applying to become a teacher believes that homosexuality is a sin, that he cannot be certified as a teacher?

MR. BERGER: No. What the College is saying is, we have a university that says it is an arm of a church, a church that holds certain views about homosexuality and homosexual behaviour. We are obliged to take that into account because we live in a society where there is concern expressed in the *Charter*, the *Human Rights* statutes, by this court, by society generally, for homosexuals as a vulnerable minority, and deserving of protection. They took that into account and they said, are these young people in this program, we don't have anything to say in the sense of repudiating their religious beliefs, that's for Trinity Western. That's for the people who hold these beliefs. We simply want to make sure that when they enter the public schools, they're equipped to deal with the diversity they find there.

Justice Michel Bastarache, too, raised the question of whether the college had imposed a religious test.

MR. JUSTICE BASTARACHE: I'd like to ask you, what of someone who doesn't go to that university, goes to a public university, but is part of that church? And what of all the other people who graduate in the public faculties but they're members of various faiths that espouse the same principles? Does the College verify whether they're fit to teach?

MR. BERGER: No, it doesn't.

MR. JUSTICE BASTARACHE: And why is that?

MR. BERGER: It doesn't conduct a religious test of any graduate. Why is that? It is because if they have taken their teacher education program at a public university, it is to be expected that they have been taking their practica under the mentorship of teachers from SFU or UBC or UVIC [B.C.'s public universities].

MR. JUSTICE BASTARACHE: How does that 5th year eliminate their religious convictions?

This, of course, was what we had faced all along from TWU—a claim that in counsel's more excited moments alleged the fifth, joint TWU-SFU year constituted a kind of Maoist re-education. Justice Bastarache had raised it squarely: Was the Council seeking to "eliminate their religious convictions"?

MR. BERGER: No one's trying to eliminate their religious convictions. Let me give you this example. Suppose you had a university in the Fraser Valley of British Columbia that was an arm of a church that said, it is our belief—because we derive this from the Bible—it is our belief that Jews are the Antichrist; or it is our belief that blacks are inferior to whites and must be segregated; or it is our belief—and there is a university, a well-known one in the United States, Bob Jones University, that believes virtually all of these things—that Catholics are a cult falsely called Christian.

Now, we say, a body charged with the responsibility of determining whether a teacher education program at such an institution should be allowed to give the five-year program and then its graduates should go out into the public schools, would be derelict in its duty if it did not say, no, we have to look at that. And it might say, as the Council has in this case, we think the attitude towards homosexuals at this institution is one that is not in conformity with broad Canadian values and attitudes.

Then Justice Bastarache went on to another subject.

MR. JUSTICE BASTARACHE: What bothers me is that here you're saying, this university obtained a charter from the Province which knew very well what its standards were. And in the examples you're giving, it seems to me that those people would not obtain a charter and that's where the control would be. But if you're going to give a charter and then say, but we won't give effect to the diplomas they give, it seems to be pretty inconsistent.

MR. BERGER: Well then what you're saying, Judge, is that once a university gets a charter from the Province, once there is an Act establishing the university, that university can teach anything it wishes, any dogma deleterious to Canadian values, and yet its graduates must be accepted in the public schools—

MR. JUSTICE BASTARACHE: That's not at all what I said and I think—

MR. BERGER: Then, forgive me.

MR. JUSTICE BASTARACHE: What I'm saying is, if the Government gives a charter, having taken into account the very policy of that church and that university, it seems inconsistent, I said, that the same government through another authority would take away the benefit of that accreditation on the basis of that very same document. That's what I said.

Perhaps the judge had a point. Presumably no charter would be granted in the first place to an institution espousing dogma inconsistent with Canadian attitudes towards minorities. How could another agency of government step in later and curb its activities on the basis of beliefs that must earlier have passed muster? I thought we had an answer.

MR. BERGER: But the mere fact that a university is chartered, and is chartered as an arm of a particular church, does not, with respect, lead to the conclusion that all of the programs they may teach over a period of many years have received the imprimatur of the Legislature and cannot be reviewed by a public body which the Legislature has charged with the duty of considering whether a program is likely to produce graduates fit to enter the public schools.

Justice Frank Iacobucci then came back to the question that Justice Bastarache had first raised, putting it another way.

MR. JUSTICE IACOBUCCI: Let me just ask you the follow-up question on this. Because someone has beliefs—has a religious belief, why is there an immediate assumption by the College that, that person who's been exposed to that religious belief cannot perform a teaching role but does not proselytize that does not advance or communicate those religious beliefs in carrying out the functions of a teacher?

MR. BERGER: It's not an assumption. The College doesn't assume that any of these students are going to go into the public schools to proselytize for their faith. No one is suggesting that. But you have in the public schools a diverse society, you have students who may be struggling with their sexual identity. You may have bullying by their peers, you may have other staff members who are homosexual. You may have children in the school who have two mothers, a not uncommon situation nowadays. This is the milieu which they're entering. The College says to them, you are entitled to your faith but we think that if you're going to go into the public schools, you should be exposed to the great panorama of Canadian life, you should know more about what Canadian values expect of you.

Justice Charles Gonthier returned to "Love the sinner, hate the sin."

MR. JUSTICE GONTHIER: In dealing with that, Mr. Berger, the various standards of Trinity Western also insist on such things as—and I'm reading from Exhibit 3: "Compliance with these standards is simply one aspect of a larger commitment by students, staff, and faculty to live together as responsible citizens, to pursue biblical holiness, and to follow an ethic of mutual support, Christian love in relationships, and to serve the best interests of each other and the entire community."
   And one finds this sort of thing repeated in many instances. This would seem on its face to call for, not just tolerance but positive respect for other people, including, of course, homosexuals.
MR. BERGER: Yes, it would. And if you, Judge, were sitting as a member of the Council of the college, with experience as a teacher—because the majority are teachers and have been such in public schools—you might say, I don't think there's a problem here. We don't need to require this SFU-TWU joint program anymore. On the other hand, you might say, I think there is something here that is troubling and I think that given the fact that it is an arm of the church, given the deep roots in the faith of the teaching of St. Paul which I've read to you, given the—
MR. JUSTICE GONTHIER: Both teachings did not condemn the persons.
MR. BERGER: They condemned homosexual offenders.

Justice John Major wished to focus on what he obviously regarded as a weakness in our case. What evidence did the college have that TWU dogma would have any effect on the capacity of TWU graduates to function adequately as teachers?

MR. JUSTICE MAJOR: What is the discriminatory practice?
MR. BERGER: The discriminatory practice is one that discourages homosexual students from entering that institution and makes it clear that their homosexual behaviour, if it occurs, is offensive to God, that it is . . . in the same category as activities which are described as dishonest and as sinful. There is an atmosphere that does anything but encourage homosexual persons from attending or being at all comfortable there.

I had to confront the court with its own test. It wasn't a question whether the Supreme Court would have reached the same decision on the evidence. Was the decision of the college patently unreasonable? I felt that, even if the court was doubtful about the sufficiency of the evidence that as a result of TWU's discriminatory practices, TWU graduates would not be professionally prepared to enter the public schools, the court could not reach the conclusion that the council's decision was irrational. If, therefore, we won on the main issue, we were home and dry.

I argued:

We had evidence. Members of this court might say, well, I don't think that I would have acted on that evidence. It was the function of the College, not of the Courts. If you say, they acted irrationally, you have met your own test. But I say it is not possible to fulfill that test in this case. They looked at the Mission Statement. They looked at the Community Standards Code. They looked at the Statement of Faith. They looked at the commitment faculty had to sign. They looked at the fact that all the students subscribed . . . And they said, on the merits, we think that this program does not equip you to enter the public schools, and we believe that you should do your fifth year under the aegis of a public university.

When Robert Kuhn, counsel for TWU, got up, he had to face Justice Claire L'Heureux-Dubé, the court's greatest champion of minority rights.

Justice L'Heureux-Dubé made it clear at once she thought there was no zone of immunity for religious belief. She raised with Kuhn my example of a university espousing, on the basis of Biblical authority, the inferiority of blacks.

Justice L'Heureux-Dubé was often acclaimed or condemned as a liberal. But it was difficult to pigeonhole her views. In criminal cases, she was not often inclined to uphold the defence. She broke out of the liberal-conservative frame and engaged in cross-voting. In *Chambers,* where the court had affirmed the right to silence, she dissented; in fact, she was the sole dissenter. I suspect she believed that defence arguments in criminal cases are often woven from gossamer. Her inclination was to side with victims of crime, and with victims of discrimination. She said:

May I just interrupt you for a second? Using the example that Mr. Berger has given us, for example, there would be all this love stuff [she had not been impressed by "love the sinner, hate the sin"] and they would be saying, 'but blacks are out', would you say that it is unreasonable for a board to focus on that particular thing, or would you say, because there is love there, let's forget it?

Justice L'Heureux-Dubé is fluent in both official languages, but sometimes she prefers to be colloquial to get to the point. Mr. Kuhn answered:

Justice, it's a very good question and the analogy's been posed at each level in the Court. Great care must be taken with the facts in any analogy, and the facts of that analogy have not been specified with any degree of particularity, but let me address it in a couple of points. I will address the issue of whether or not Charter values themselves can be imported into the discretion, into the jurisdiction of the [college] at this juncture on the basis of this wording, and we'll address that separately. Those apply equally to my comments.

Is there a need to import *Charter* values?

MADAM JUSTICE L'HEUREUX-DUBÉ: You may answer that later but I was just asking you a very specific question that related to what exactly you are saying to us. So we have all this . . . I say "black", you say "homosexual". I said, would the college be entitled to take that into account? . . . I just put it in the extreme to use the example of your colleague to say, if it were "but no blacks". Would the College be entitled to take into account that phrase? . . .

MR. KUHN: On the basis of that policy, that would be a human rights issue, my suspicion is that, as a human rights question, it would be answered in the negative in any event; taking it into consideration as a question of law, may be an issue, taking it into consideration as a question of value is a different consideration that I will address specifically. It is on the basis of the analogy stated that [it] is discrimination against blacks purely and simply not admission of blacks, the answer is yes, that would be taken into consideration. It will be taken into consideration because on most readings, it would be illegal.

Justice L'Heureux-Dubé continued to press:

So, the argument that you develop that the College is not entitled to use *Charter* values is contradicted here. If they would object to [discrimination against blacks], and they would object rightly to that, then they would take *Charter* values into consideration. So how can they do that here, and couldn't do that in [the] other— according to your proposition?

MR. KUHN: With respect, the difference between *Charter* rights and human rights and *Charter* values and human rights values must be borne in mind. If it is illegal to have discriminated in the manner in which a university, college of education or any application for a public benefit, then that is a question of legality. What is admitted in this case is that Trinity Western is not guilty of any illegality in respect of its *Charter* position, in respect to its human rights position. And that is a clear and necessary distinction. I would go on to say, Justice, that in this case, it's extremely different. In this case, there is no attempt to disparage the individual, and I will address that specifically.

Despite the evidence, the [college] refused to approve Trinity Western's otherwise acceptable educational program because of what [the college] called "discriminatory practices". In drawing its conclusion, it relied on the document we've referred to.

Justice Binnie had raised with me at the outset TWU's belief in tolerance for all persons. Now he confronted Mr. Kuhn:

MR. JUSTICE BINNIE: I don't understand this proposition. I mean it's all very well to say, "Love the sinner, hate the sin," but if I say, well, I dearly love "X", but I totally and utterly condemn what is a very important part of the character and personality of "X". Is it not a contradiction in terms? What you're loving is a sort of idealized version of "X", but the reality is condemnation; religion may preach tolerance, but religion has often been an engine of intolerance.

MR. KUHN: I can't argue that from time to time, religion has not been an engine of intolerance. History would bear that out.

MR. JUSTICE BINNIE: Isn't that what's put against you here?

Mr. Kuhn wisely used the question as an opportunity to answer in a way that shifted the ground.

MR. KUHN: In this case, if history is put against us rather than specific facts of this specific case, there is no evidence of intolerance by any graduate at Trinity Western despite 35 years of producing graduates.

Chief Justice Beverley McLachlin weighed in on the same question as Justice Binnie had.

CHIEF JUSTICE MCLACHLIN: Well, it's put against you that you're in a dilemma. Either the teaching is against homosexuality, or it's a teaching that suppresses the identity of the person . . . In other words, we should be encouraging these teachers to allow people to fulfill all their human attributes and characteristics . . . Even if you're going to love these people, you're loving them while you're suppressing their true human flowering.

MR. KUHN: Chief Justice, in the context of the public school classrooms, the evidence before this court on the record is that Trinity Western advocates the very respect, honour, and dignity afforded, and should be afforded, to people of different cultures, of sexual orientation, or for that matter, any particular behaviour as not disqualifying them from the deserved tolerance, deserved respect. And in fact, the Christian principle will take it more broadly and higher than that.

MADAM JUSTICE L'HEUREUX-DUBÉ: With that philosophy, would that, as your colleagues have pointed out, eliminate every person who is homosexual from applying and to sign that code of conduct?

MR. KUHN: There's no evidence—

MADAM JUSTICE L'HEUREUX-DUBÉ: The effect—the effect.

MR. KUHN: There's no evidence to that effect, but the effect may be to discourage, and I think I have to acknowledge that. The effect may be to discourage a homosexual from applying because of the behavioural context of the Code. And I don't think that has ever been denied. There's certainly no evidence of that having occurred, anymore than there's evidence of this translating into some sort of inappropriate conduct. There simply isn't any evidence in this case of many of the aspects of what the Appellants are arguing. But in the case of, "would it have that effect?", it may have that effect, we don't know, but it may have that effect.

This was a key admission. TWU had all along claimed there was no discrimination. Justice Davies and the Court of Appeal had found there was no discrimination. Now TWU's own lawyer was driven to admit that requiring the signing of the contract "may have that effect"; that is, to discourage homosexuals from applying to TWU.

Then Justice L'Heureux-Dubé turned to the principal issue on the appeal. Could the college actually take into account Charter values, or was that a consideration lying beyond its authority?

Are you saying that they are not entitled to take account of the law of Canada which is the *Charter* and [its] values? I think we [the court] have said that everyone is subject to the *Charter*, everybody knows that, but also, adjudicators, tribunals, whatever, are obliged to take it into account. So are you saying the contrary, or what?

MR. KUHN: ... The effect of encouraging or requiring administrative tribunals to embark upon a consideration of *Charter* and human rights values in weighing the public interest, however, in our submission, will result in setting a precedent that would inevitably lead to a confusing gridlock of administrative process . . .

MADAM JUSTICE L'HEUREUX-DUBÉ: Were they saying, the program is not satisfactory?

MR. KUHN: If that is what the [college] said, it would be a different question. In my submission, firstly, that is not what the [college] said. It found discriminatory practices. That is the extent of its decision.

This was Mr. Kuhn's strongest ground. He went on:

The discriminatory practices can only be translated back to one phrase in one document. It is not a question of the program itself, the program itself is not under any cloud of disapproval.

Chief Justice McLachlin, pursuing the same issue, then put the matter squarely, combining the two issues on which leave had been granted.

CHIEF JUSTICE MCLACHLIN: What would you say if, to this hypothetical situation, you have a university that teaches and sets out as part of its credo, to bring us within the *Ross* analogy, the Jewish people have been responsible for many evils visited on the western world—let's put it that way, that's part of their credo. If that university applied [for approval of its teacher education program], would you say that [the college] would have to wait for evidence?—the council would have to wait for evidence, or would you say, they could just say there's such a danger here that . . . we should step in preemptively?

Justice L'Heureux-Dubé had taken on board the issue of blacks. Now the chief justice had put the very question, relating to anti-Semitism, that we had urged. It would be very difficult in such a case for the council simply to be reactive. In the case of TWU, wouldn't the same reasoning apply?

MR. KUHN: The first way to respond to the question, clearly, that's not the case here. But in any event, the appropriate response beyond that is, does it affect their ability to teach? Is it part of the curriculum? Is it part of what is actively taught that, in the case of *Ross*, people of Jewish descent, people of Jewish heritage, people of Jewish culture, people of Jewish religion, are in fact to be hated, or there's to be a promotion of [the] negative? If that's part of the curriculum, they don't need the *Charter* value to do that. They can look at the curriculum and say, this curriculum isn't preparing you to teach in a public school setting. It's not what is done.

CHIEF JUSTICE MCLACHLIN: My example suggested it's not part of the curriculum but it's part of the code of ethics, or values, to which students subscribe.

William Sammon, who appeared for the Roman Catholic Bishops of Canada, emphasized the intrusive nature of the council's decision, what he described as the undermining of freedom of religion. Justice Louise Arbour, in close questioning of Sammon, indicated what lay at the heart of the dispute.

MR. SAMMON: The position the College has is based on the assumption that people who hold certain views on morality, sexual morality, are going to be intolerant. And therefore, those people need this further education.

MADAM JUSTICE ARBOUR: I think the assumption is that some elements of breadth of exposure to ideas and views and differences is a prerequisite. Some may be in moderate amount but it is a legitimate prerequisite for the council to be worried about when it validates a program that will then qualify people to teach in a very pluralistic environment.

I was startled by the fact that the Roman Catholic bishops, in none of their written submissions, and in nothing that was said on their behalf in court, included a word, a line or a sentence evincing the slightest understanding of the evolution of Canadian attitudes towards homosexuality, nor any hint of compassion for those belonging to that group. To be sure, their lawyers no doubt composed the bishops' written submissions, but didn't at least some of the bishops examine it before it was filed? Did their instructions to their lawyers not allow for some indication that Catholic teaching might amount to more than a reiteration of St. Paul?

The chief justice gave me an opportunity for an extended reply.

MR. BERGER: Now, my learned friends have said that what has been required here by the College is cleansing and de-programming and reeducation. Senator McCarthy's name has been used. This is inflammatory. I ask the Court to remember that nobody said that the graduates of this program are intolerant or would behave in an intolerant way. The sole question is their professional preparedness for going into a public school classroom.

Mr. Sammon said, for the Roman Catholic Bishops, that we have branded them as intolerant. Well, it's important to remember the resolution that was passed by the Council. They said, it appears that there are discriminatory practices at Trinity Western. They didn't say that anybody was intolerant, they didn't brand the students, they simply reached a conclusion they were entitled to reach about the institution itself. Everyone concedes that Trinity Western as a private institution, an arm of the Evangelical Free Church, is entitled to teach what it wishes to teach, to inculcate the beliefs it wishes to inculcate. But that doesn't mean that the beliefs that they teach are immune from scrutiny by a public body which has to determine whether their graduates are ready to enter the public schools . . .

It has been said that these young persons are being prejudged on the basis of their beliefs. Mr. Sammon said that they are being stigmatized as intolerant. Well, you can do anything with words I suppose that you want to, but if you look at this case, you will see that the Council is concerned whether in light of their beliefs they are professionally prepared to go into the diverse environment that we have in the British Columbia public schools.

Is there a risk that they will treat students of homosexual orientation, or students struggling with their sexual identity in such a way as to discount their worth or to impair their self-esteem? Will they be equipped to deal with students who are bullying students thought by their peers to be homosexual? Will they be able to offer comfort and support to the students who are the object of such bullying? Even if there are no students of homosexual orientation in the classroom, will the attitude of the graduates cause students to think of homosexuals in the same way that their teachers do? What of children in the classroom being raised by same sex parents, or who have homosexual siblings? What attitude will TWU graduates have to these family situations? To what extent will they be adequately equipped to deal with them?

That was the Council's concern, and TWU cannot simply say that the College's concern relates to our religious beliefs so you can't scrutinize them.

It had been a hectic day. Now we would wait for the decision. It would come six months later.

On Tuesday, May 15, 2001, at a sixteenth-century hotel in Arles (Bev and I were travelling in southern France), I received a fax from my secretary, Marci Rose: the Supreme Court of Canada would be handing down its judgement two days later.

Five years of study and advocacy had gone into the TWU case. In forty-eight hours we would know. But then I realized our flight home from France would be crossing the Atlantic on Thursday, 10:00 A.M., when the decision came down. Everyone else would know, but I'd be somewhere over the mid-Atlantic.

Bev reminded me that there are telephones on aircraft now. But when we boarded, I didn't see any telephones. "Why not ask the flight attendant?" she said. I wasn't sure I wanted to know. I'd wait until we reached Vancouver. But then the flight attendant pointed out that there was a phone lodged in the back of the seat in front of me. So I had to phone.

Marci answered the phone. She said, "We lost, eight to one." She didn't have to tell me that Justice L'Heureux-Dubé had dissented in our favour.

I was stunned. It doesn't matter how long you've practised law. You live and die with your clients. But before the flight had reached North America, the thought did occur to me that perhaps we had won on the main issue but lost on the issue of whether there was sufficient evidence for the college to conclude that graduates of an all-TWU five-year program would not be ready to enter the classroom. Most everyone had forgotten that, in fact, we had actually lost *Calder*, yet we had in that case won the battle for recognition of a place in Canadian law for Aboriginal title.

When we did see the judgement, we were comforted. Justice Iacobucci and Justice Bastarache wrote a joint opinion for the majority.

It came down to the meaning of two words in section 4 of B.C.'s Teaching Profession Act: public interest. Writing a judgement in a case like this one is not the same thing as deciding the meaning of two words in a commercial contract or in a will. In such cases, detachment comes more easily. In a case like TWU, the values of your fellow citizens, the beliefs of your co-religionists, the priority that you give to equality on the one hand or freedom of religion on the other must be weighed. In the end, what is likely to tip the scales are your own convictions.

The judges' deepest convictions, the conditioning of a lifetime, undoubtedly played a part. As Benjamin Cardozo said, "We may try to see things as objectively as we please. Nonetheless, we can never see them with any eyes except our own." The judges in many cases, certainly in TWU, are making policy choices, value judgements. The advocate's job is to persuade them that the value their client is championing should prevail.

Justice Iacobucci and Justice Bastarache referred to the first question we had posed to the court: "Did the Council exceed its jurisdiction, when it denied approval to TWU's five-year B.Ed. program, by taking into account TWU's discriminatory practices? Was this an extraneous consideration?"

This was the question on which I had been consulted five years before. This was the question whether section 2 of the Charter, enshrining freedom of religion, established a zone of immunity for TWU. The Supreme Court upheld the council's power to consider the discriminatory practices of a private institution in determining whether to approve its teacher education program. This assessment, the court said, may entail an explicit consideration of Charter values and human rights values. Private institutions cannot, on the ground of freedom of conscience or religion, claim that the beliefs held at such an institution are immune from scrutiny. Specifically, the court ruled that the college had jurisdiction to consider discriminatory practices at TWU and to determine whether it would be in the public interest to allow public school teachers to be trained at an all-TWU five-year program.

As for section 4 of the Teaching Profession Act, which provided the college was to have regard to the public interest, the court concluded, citing *Ross*:

It is obvious that the pluralistic nature of society and the extent of diversity in Canada are important elements that must be understood by future teachers because they are the fabric of the society within which teachers operate and the reason why there is a need to respect and promote minority rights. The suitability for entrance into the profession of teaching must therefore take into account all features of the education program at TWU.

This was the main issue in the case: Had the college overstepped its jurisdiction in considering the attitude at TWU towards homosexuality? We had persuaded the court that Justice Davies and the Court of Appeal had been wrong in their interpretation of section 4 of the Teaching Profession Act. The judges said:

Schools are meant to develop civic virtue and responsible citizenship, to educate in an environment free of bias, prejudice and intolerance. It would not be correct, in this context, to limit the scope of s. 4 to a determination of skills and knowledge.

The court held that "concerns about equality were appropriately considered by the [college] under the public interest component of the *Teaching Profession Act.*" The court went on to say: "While the BCCT was not directly applying either the *Charter* or the province's human rights legislation when making its decision, it was entitled to look at these instruments to determine whether it would be in the public interest to allow public school teachers to be trained at TWU."

We had won on this fundamental point. There would be no zone of immunity for religious beliefs if they were inconsistent with the values enshrined in the Charter. The court then turned to the question of evidence: "If the Council was entitled to consider 'discriminatory practices' was there evidence of such practices and of discriminatory ramifications?"

The court considered to what extent the courts ought to defer to the council of the college as a specialized tribunal. In our case, there was in fact a contract subscribed to by faculty and students, which condemned homosexuality as sinful. That was evidence. It might or might not be sufficient in the view of the court, but we had argued that the Supreme Court itself had held that, provided there was evidence, it was for administrative tribunals such as the college to weigh it up and decide.

The court held, however, that "the existence of discriminatory practices is based on the interpretation of the TWU documents and human rights values and principles. This is a question of law that is concerned with human rights and not essentially educational matters." With this statement, they had moved the goalposts. It could not be said that the college had proceeded without evidence. Nevertheless, the court would intervene. The question whether the religious beliefs taught at TWU would have an impact on the professional preparedness of

TWU graduates was now a question of law, which depended on striking a balance between conflicting Charter rights. The court said: "The Council [of the college] is not particularly well equipped to determine the scope of freedom of religion and conscience and to weigh these rights against the right to equality in the context of a pluralistic society . . . The accommodation of beliefs is a legal question."

The issue being one of law, it followed that the standard of review was a simple one: does the court agree with the actual decision of the council based on the evidence it had before it?

The court held that the college, in weighing the matter up, had not allowed for the impact of its decision on freedom of religion at TWU.

The [college] did not weigh the various rights involved in its assessment of the alleged discriminatory practices of TWU by not taking into account the impact of its decision on the right to freedom of religion of the members of TWU. Accordingly, this Court must.

The court then undertook itself to review the evidence of discriminatory practices. It said:

Although the Community Standards are expressed in terms of a code of conduct rather than an article of faith, we conclude that a homosexual student would not be tempted to apply for admission, and could only sign the so-called student contract at a considerable personal cost. TWU is not for everybody; it is designed to address the needs of people who share a number of religious convictions. That said, the admissions policy of TWU alone is not in itself sufficient to establish discrimination as it is understood in our s. 15 jurisprudence. It is important to note that this is a private institution that is exempted, in part, from the British Columbia human rights legislation and to which the *Charter* does not apply. To state that the voluntary adoption of a code of conduct based on a person's own religious beliefs, in a private institution, is sufficient to engage s. 15 [of the Charter] would be inconsistent with freedom of conscience and religion, which co-exist with the right to equality.

The court then dealt with the issue of equality under section 15 of the Charter, and freedom of conscience and religion under section 2(a). The court said: "The issue at the heart of this appeal is how to reconcile the religious freedoms of individuals wishing to attend TWU with the equality concerns of students in B.C.'s public school system, concerns that may be shared with their parents and society generally."

Duelling Charter rights. Then the court said: "Neither freedom of religion nor the guarantee against discrimination based on sexual orientation is absolute . . . What the [college] was required to do was to determine whether the rights were in conflict in reality."

The court provided some guidance for the determination of such issues, saying that the college could not, on the strength of the contract, pre-empt the issue.

TWU's Community Standards, which are limited to prescribing conduct of members while at TWU, are not sufficient to support the conclusion that the BCCT should anticipate intolerant behaviour in the public schools.

The court had referred to "intolerant behaviour." We had never argued that such behaviour would occur. The court then put it this way:

Clearly, the restriction on freedom of religion must be justified by evidence that the exercise of this freedom of religion will, in the circumstances of this case, have a detrimental impact on the school system [emphasis added].

This statement was closer to the mark.

The court concluded:

The proper place to draw the line in cases like the one at bar is generally between belief and conduct. The freedom to hold beliefs is broader than the freedom to act on them. Absent concrete evidence that training teachers at TWU fosters discrimination in the public schools of B.C., the freedom of individuals to adhere to certain religious beliefs while at TWU should be respected. The [college], rightfully, does not require public universities with teacher education programs to screen out applicants who hold sexist, racist or homophobic beliefs. For better or for worse, tolerance of divergent beliefs is a hallmark of a democratic society.

Acting on those beliefs, however, is a very different matter. If a teacher in the public school system engages in discriminatory conduct, that teacher can be subject to disciplinary proceedings before the [college]. Discriminatory conduct by a public school teacher when on duty should always be subject to disciplinary proceedings [emphasis added].

Once again, the court was speaking as if the college's concern had been "discriminatory conduct" by teachers rather than a concern about their professional preparation.

The court turned to the evidence required.

For the [college] to have properly denied accreditation to TWU, it should have based its concerns on specific evidence. It could have asked for reports on student teachers, or opinions of school principals and superintendents. It could have examined discipline files involving TWU graduates and other teachers affiliated with a Christian school of that nature. Any concerns should go to risk, not general perceptions.

But evidence of what? Of intolerant behaviour? We had all along maintained that the college was concerned about professional preparedness. Could TWU graduates be expected to be supportive of all students? *That* was the college's concern.

The judgement of the majority of the court appeared to be a pastiche. In seeking to justify its determination that the council must wait and see, rather than acting on the basis of avoiding risk, it lapsed into language bearing no resemblance to the arguments advanced.

But in the end the ship appeared to right itself.

The Supreme Court upheld the conditions earlier recommended by the college's program approval team and its teacher education program committee, before TWU's application was rejected by the council. These provided for close monitoring by the college of the five-year all-TWU program for a five-year period. This decision was an affirmation of the college's argument that its concern related to the teaching environment itself. The judges affirmed the college's jurisdiction to monitor TWU's program "to ensure that a proper teaching environment, in particular one that is free of discrimination, is provided by TWU graduates." I think this statement best expresses the view of the court. The judgement may be uneven; at any rate, it does qualify as open-ended.

Justice L'Heureux-Dubé dissented. She agreed that the line was to be drawn somewhere between belief and conduct. On Justice L'Heureux-Dubé's reckoning, the line had been crossed: Faculty and students had *signed* the contract requiring them to adhere to community standards; this act was properly classified as conduct; it went beyond belief or affirmation of belief. She said:

Signing the Community Standards contract . . . makes the student or employee complicit in an overt, but not illegal act of discrimination against homosexuals and bisexuals.

She rejected the idea of converting a question of fact into one of law. She went on:

Whether or not TWU students' signatures on the Community Standards contract reflect their true beliefs, it is not patently unreasonable for the BCCT to treat their public expressions of discrimination as potentially affecting the public school communities in which TWU graduates wish to teach.

We had lost the battle but won the war. In a free society all people have the right to religious belief, to pray, to preach and to proselytize. But if their values are at odds with the values of Canadian society, they cannot expect that—where these values collide—there will be no scrutiny of the beliefs they hold sacred, no weighing of them in the balance. TWU, the Evangelical Free Church and the Roman Catholic Bishops had failed in the attempt to carve out of section 15 a zone of immunity for their religious beliefs. In their own churches, in their own institutions of learning, they can teach what they will. But the college is entitled to scrutinize those teachings and, on proper evidence, to act on them. If those beliefs bear on secular interests—and there can be no more compelling secular interest than the education of children and adolescents—they must be weighed in the balance. In such a case, the secular may trump the sacred.

Of all the cases discussed in this book, TWU is the most recent, and I have found it the most difficult to view in perspective. Yes, we had won on the main issue. Nevertheless, in reflecting on the case, I think the judgement of the majority on the question of proof is flawed.

As Chief Justice McLachlin asked Mr. Kuhn: If you had a university that taught anti-Semitism as part of its credo, would the council have to wait for evidence, or could it step in pre-emptively?

Would the proclamation of a belief by a church in the malign nature of the Jews, the inferior nature of blacks or the corrupted character of the Roman Catholic Church cross the line? These are beliefs antithetical to our hard-won ideas of racial, ethnic and religious tolerance. No doubt a proclamation of belief by an institution seeking to establish a teacher education program that the disabled have brought their own illnesses upon themselves, or that women do not have the mental capacity of men, would be sufficient without evidence of impairment of the classroom environment, to justify a fifth year under the aegis of a public university. All of these are minorities protected by the Charter. But so are homosexuals. Why did the court require that the council must have proof that TWU graduates had already entered the public schools and been found to be unready? Would the court have required that the college must approve a program at an institution built on a belief in anti-Semitism or the inferiority of blacks?

We have not been able to get our minds around the idea of homosexuals as a minority. We think of minorities as based on race, ethnicity or religion. Homosexuality may easily be reduced merely to a question of sexual preference. But it is in reality a question of sexual orientation; that is the way you are.

The belief held by the Catholics and the Christian fundamentalists in the possibility of reformation—indeed, categorizing homosexuality as a sin—is derived from the idea that you can—and ought—to change your life. But if you would thereby be required to change an essential part of your nature, you might as well ask a Jew to change religion or a black person to change skin colour.

In February 2002, I spent an afternoon with the civil liberties class at the law school at the University of Victoria. We discussed the TWU case. The students had already reviewed the judgement of the Supreme Court. Their comments were illuminating on the question of whether the college should have been required to wait and see. One of them put it this way: "If the case was reframed in the context of race, gender or a non-Christian religion, what is the likelihood that the Supreme Court would reach the same conclusion?" Another cited the Kingdom Identity Ministries, which propagates the view that the "White, Anglo-Saxon Germanic" people are the only true Christian nations, superior to other races, and excoriates the Jews as evil. If such an institution sought to establish a teacher education program, "does anyone actually believe the Supreme Court would have required the college to approve the overtly discriminatory teaching program?"

Aren't the students right? Didn't the Supreme Court in TWU stop short of affording the same measure of protection to homosexuals that we can reliably predict the court would have extended to other groups protected by the Charter?

The Charter offers minorities a place to stand, ground to defend. And the Supreme Court has the job of securing that place and marking out that ground. Having determined that homosexual persons are entitled to the protection of section 15, shouldn't the court have followed the logic of its decision in *Egan*?

In TWU, the court was only grudgingly prepared to acknowledge the rights of homosexuals, and it gave up ground that ought to have been defended. Justice L'Heureux-Dubé, however, would not yield any of that ground. She described the struggle taking place there in these terms:

The principal metaphor for the homosexual and bisexual experience of discrimination has been that of the closet, an isolated refuge of invisibility often enveloped in fear. Indeed, the history of struggles against sexual orientation discrimination has been described as a battle against "the apartheid of the closet."

Primordial fears and ancient stereotypes still inform our attitudes. Religious institutions continue to denounce homosexuality as perverse and unnatural. The place of homosexuals as a vulnerable minority entitled to the protection of the Charter has not yet been fully accommodated in our consciousness.

The path of the just is as the shining light, that shineth more and more unto the perfect day. Proverbs 4.18

Acknowledgements

I MUST ACKNOWLEDGE the willingness of my colleagues to read chapters in draft form: Gary Nelson, Jim Aldridge, Erin Berger, Ron Shulman, Margaret Vanderkruyk and especially Marcus Bartley. Other friends at the bar, Cec Branson, David Martin, Dan Webster and Dean Andrew Petter, looked over various chapters.

I wrote the book during my spare time. I would bring chapters to the office to be typed and retyped. The work began when Becky Trewella was my secretary. But it is her successor, Marci Rose, who did the lion's share of the typing. She worked on draft after draft; without her able assistance, the book would never have been completed.

I must also thank my editor, Brian Scrivener, who helped to give the book its present shape, and whose advice was invaluable throughout.

Margaret Renaerts, Richard Price, Linda Macdonald, Bruce Abbey, Dr. Terence Anderson, Dr. Jerilynn Prior, Doug Smart, Marie Kerchum and Justice Harry Slade were kind enough to review the chapters in which they had played a part. My sister Susan Brooks read over the chapters touching on family history. I am grateful to them all.

My wife, Beverley, and I talked about the book as it progressed; then she read the manuscript while we were on vacation. She was a source of common sense advice throughout.

Finally, I must thank Scott McIntyre for persuading me to undertake the project.

Chapter Notes

In writing this book, I have gone back to the files and the notes I made at the time. Of course, the book also contains extracts from transcripts, the actual record of what was said at the time. Then there are the written briefs or factums filed in court. I have also included excerpts from the written reasons for judgement by the judges in many cases.

What about the passages containing conversations, exchanges in court, where I have nothing to go on but my memory? In some instances, such as Monday, October 30, 1992, the opening day of the Montney case in the Federal Court of Appeal (chapter 10), I recall the day vividly, because Goldie, my first grandchild, was born, and the country voted on the Charlottetown Accord. A great many days in the courtroom are invested with that glow of remembrance. I do not remember word for word the conversations that are related here. But I do recall the substance of each. And particular words used, for example, Prime Minister Trudeau's use of the word "patsy" at lunch at Sussex Drive (chapter 6), remain lodged in recollection.

Many of the lawyers mentioned in this book are Queen's Counsel, a mark of distinction conferred by the federal and provincial governments. But I have not indicated that any of them hold a QC. To do so would clutter up the pages with initials.

I have referred to all judges of the superior courts as "Justice." We used to say "Mr. Justice such and such" or "Madam Justice such and such." That usage is coming to an end.

In the Ironworkers' case, Chapter 2, I addressed Justice Manson as "My Lord." That was in 1959. By the time we get to Chapter 12, the Trinity Western case, in 2000, I simply addressed the judges of the Supreme Court of Canada as "Justice" or "Judge." They had not long before issued a statement that they did not wish to be addressed as "My Lord" or "My Lady."

Carolyn Swayze wrote about my early career in *Hard Choices: A Life of Tom Berger* (Vancouver: Douglas & McIntyre, 1987). I am relying here on what I recollect today, what seems important now, though I trust it is consistent with what I may have told Carolyn then.

Chapter 1: "The Bitch"

The *Coffin* case is reported in the Supreme Court of Canada as *R. v. Coffin*, [1956] S.C.R. 191.

When I started out, drug prosecutions were brought under the Opium and Narcotic Drug Act, in force at the time of the prosecution against Margaret Hall. Her case is cited as *R. v. Hall* (1959), 124 C.C.C. 238 (B.C.C.A.). It was replaced by the Narcotic Control Act, S.C. 1960–1961, c. 35, which was in force at the time of the prosecution against Bruce Abbey.

R. v. Gonzales is reported at (1962), 132 C.C.C. 237. In *R. v. Drybones*, [1970] S.C.R. 282, the Supreme Court reversed *Gonzales*, holding that there had been a breach of the equality provision of the Canadian Bill of Rights. This was the only case prior to the Charter in which the Supreme Court gave life to the Canadian Bill of Rights. In *A.G. Canada v. Lavell*, [1974] S.C.R. 1349, and *A.G. v. Canard*, [1976] 1 S.C.R. 170, the Supreme Court backed away from the view expressed in *Drybones*. See also *Andrews v. Law Society*, [1989] 1 S.C.R. 143, after the advent of the Charter, in which the Supreme Court got it right. The equality section of the Charter does not simply mean administrative equality: if burdens are imposed on a group that are not imposed on others, section 15 may apply.

R. v. Paton is reported at [1968] S.C.R. 341. *R. v. Haddon* is reported at [1968] S.C.R. 258.

The old "vag.(c)" provision under which prostitutes were prosecuted was replaced in 1972 by the offence of soliciting (S.C. 1972, c. 13, s. 12(1)).

Professor Michael Jackson of the law school at the University of British Columbia did a definitive study of the subject of habitual criminals, for the B.C. Corrections Association, in a 1982 report entitled "Sentences That Never End."

In this chapter I have referred to accused persons as "he" or "him," except in the case of Margaret McNeill, since the vast majority of crimes are committed by male persons.

Chapter 2: A Bridge Too Far

The Ironworkers' case is reported as *Dominion Bridge v. International Union of Bridge, Structural and Ornamental Ironworkers, Local 97 and AGBC* (1959), 20 D.L.R. (2d) 621 (B.C.C.A.).

Louis Battaglia's case is reported in the B.C. Court of Appeal as *Re Battaglia and the Work - men's Compensation Board* (1960), 32 W.W.R. 1; 24 D.L.R. (2d) 21. The widow's case against the WCB that Justice Manson heard is reported in the Supreme Court of Canada as *Farrell v. Workmen's Compensation Board*, [1962] S.C.R. 48.

Justice McIntyre's judgement in *Canadian Pacific Railway v. United Transportation Union* is reported at (1970), 14 D.L.R. (3d) 497. The Oilworkers' case is reported as *Imperial Oil v. Oil, Chemical and Atomic Workers Union*, [1963] S.C.R. 584. The sedition case is reported as *British Columbia (Attorney General) v. Georgetti* at (1987), 14 B.C.L.R. (2d) 119.

Chapter 3: The Jones Boy

In Jones's case, the judgement of Justice McInnes is reported at (1966), 55 w.w.r. 143; the first judgement of the Court of Appeal at (1966), 57 w.w.r. 56. The judgement of Justice Ruttan is reported at (1967), 59 w.w.r. 449; the second decision of the Court of Appeal at (1968), 66 d.l.r. (2d) 497. The decision of the Supreme Court of Canada is reported as *Jones v. Bennett*, [1969] s.c.r. 277.

Wells v. Newfoundland is reported at [1999] 3 s.c.r. 199.

Re Gonzalez-Davi and Legal Services Society of B.C. is reported at (1989), 66 d.l.r. (4th) 362 (b.c.s.c.), and at (1991), 81 d.l.r. (4th) 12 (b.c.c.a.). In *Winters v. B.C.*, [1999] 3 s.c.r. 160, Justice Binnie, writing for the Supreme Court of Canada, said it has been estimated that the *Gonzalez-Davi* decision has cost the Legal Services Society $3.5 million a year.

I confess I am not certain whether Premier Bennett's reference to fifteen thousand telegrams supporting his stand was in connection with the Jones case or some other controversy. It exemplifies the good-naturedly facetious and yet exasperating quality of his political pronouncements.

Chapter 4: Resurrecting a Treaty

R. v. White and Bob is reported in the Court of Appeal for British Columbia at (1964), 52 w.w.r. 193; 50 d.l.r. (2d) 193, and in the Supreme Court of Canada at [1965] s.c.r. vi.

The Delgamuukw case is cited as *Delgamuukw v. B.C.*, [1997] 3 s.c.r. 101.

Justice Norris's definition of a treaty in *R. v. White and Bob* has been adopted by the Supreme Court of Canada in *Simon v. The Queen*, [1985] 2 s.c.r. 387 and *R. v. Sioui*, [1990] 1 s.c.r. 1025.

Wilson Duff's *Indian History of British Columbia: The Impact of the White Man*, vol. 1 (Victoria: Queen's Printer, 1965), was intended to be the first of a series, but the series was never completed, owing to Duff's untimely death.

In *R. v. Corbett*, [1988] 1 s.c.r. 670 the Supreme Court of Canada took the same view as Justice Norris, upholding the constitutionality of section 12 of the Evidence Act (Canada), which allows previous convictions to be put to witnesses, but ruling that trial judges have discretion to exclude previous convictions where it would be unfair to bring them up in cross-examination.

Chapter 5: The Nisga'a Odyssey

I have written about the Calder case in *Fragile Freedoms: Human Rights and Dissent in Canada* (Toronto: Clarke, Irwin, 1980) and in *A Long and Terrible Shadow: White Values, Native Rights in the Americas, 1492–1992* (Vancouver: Douglas & McIntyre; Seattle: University of Washington Press, 1991). As the Nisga'a saga continues to unfold, I have here brought it up-to-date. In this book, I can as well look back over the vista of three decades and gauge more accurately, with the signing of the Nisga'a Treaty in 2000, how far the Nisga'a cause has been advanced.

Calder v. Attorney General of B.C. is reported in (1969), 8 d.l.r. (3d) 59 (b.c.s.c.); (1970), 13 d.l.r. (3d) 64 (b.c.c.a.); and [1973] s.c.r. 313. The impact of *Calder* on federal government land claims policy is discussed by the Supreme Court in *R. v. Sparrow*, [1990] 1 S.C.R. 1075 at 1103–1104.

The judgements of Chief Justice Marshall of the United States may be cited thus: *Johnson v. McIntosh*, 21 U.S. (8 Wheat.) 543 (1823); *Cherokee Nation v. Georgia*, 30 U.S. (5 Pet.) 1 (1831); *Worcester v. Georgia*, 31 U.S. (6 Pet.) 515 (1832).

The figures for Indian populations in British Columbia are taken from Duff's *Indian History of B.C.: The Impact of the White Man*.

Duff's "bright tile" piece appeared in *The World Is as Sharp as a Knife* (Victoria: B.C. Provincial Museum, 1981).

R. v. Van Der Peet may be cited as [1996] 2 S.C.R. 507.

Justice Williamson's judgement upholding the constitutionality of the Nisga'a Treaty is reported at (2000), 79 B.C.L.R. (3d) 122; [2000] 8 W.W.R. 600. His judgement awarding costs against Premier Campbell and others is reported at (2001), 11 C.P.C. (5th) 384.

The Supreme Court of Canada indicated the limits of Aboriginal and treaty rights, in *R. v. Sparrow* [1990] 1 S.C.R. 1075, and *R. v. Badger*, [1996] 1 S.C.R. 771.

Alexander Morris's book, *The Treaties of Canada with the Indians*, was published in 1880 (Toronto: Bedford's Clarke & Co.).

Chapter 6: To the Bench and Back

My commission reports include: Reports of the B.C. Commission on Family and Children's Law, 1973 to 1975, vols. 1 through 13 (Victoria: Queen's Printer); *Northern Frontier, Northern Homeland: Report of the Mackenzie Valley Pipeline Inquiry* (Ottawa: Queen's Printer, 1977; rev. ed., Douglas & McIntyre, 1988); *Report of Advisory Commission on Indian and Inuit Health Consultation* (Ottawa: Department of Supply and Services, 1980). The report of the Alaska Native Review Commission was published as *Village Journey* (New York: Hill and Wang, 1985). *Sardar Sarovar: The Report of the Independent Review* was published for the Independent Review by Resources Future International (RFI) Inc., Ottawa, 1992.

Chapter 7: Questions of Conscience

In the *New Statesman* (August 31, 1984), political editor Peter Kellner wrote "Churchill, Mountbatten and the Noble Art of Leaking." See also Roy Jenkins, *Churchill* (New York: Farrar, Straus & Giroux, 2002).

In *R. v. Smith and Thompson* (1993), 84 C.C.C. (3d) 221, the Nova Scotia Court of Appeal dealt with a claim of selective prosecution on grounds of race. The claim was rejected on the basis that there had not been a selective prosecution: in that case both whites and blacks had been investigated and prosecuted.

Dr. Prior's case, *Prior v. Canada (Minister of National Revenue)*, is cited in the Federal Court Trial Division at (1988), 18 F.T.R. 227, and in the Federal Court of Appeal at 89 D.T.C. 5503; (1989), 28 F.T.R. 240.

R. v. Big M Drug Mart is reported at [1985] 1 S.C.R. 295.

Andrews v. Law Society of B.C. is reported at [1989] 1 s.c.r. 143.

The quotes from John Woolman appear in *The Journal of John Woolman,* ed. Janet Whitney (Chicago: Henry Regnery, 1950), 66–68.

The quotation from William Penn appears in the *Journal of George Fox,* 8th edition, 1891.

William Stringfellow, *An Ethic for Christians and Other Aliens in a Strange Land,* 1973, 72–73.

The Upper Canadian provision for diverting taxes to roads and bridges is found at *Upper Canada Statutes,* Victoria, cap. 2, 1841.

R. v. Morgentaler (No. 2) is reported at [1988] 1 s.c.r. 30.

The quotations from John Keegan are from *A History of Warfare* (New York: Alfred A. Knopf, 1994) and *War and Our World* (London: Hutchinson, 1998).

Chapter 8: A Fair Trial

R. v. Chambers is reported in the B.C. Court of Appeal at (1986), 26 c.c.c. (3d) 353 (s.c.c.), and in the Supreme Court of Canada at [1990] 2 s.c.r. 1293.

R. v. O'Brien is reported at [1954] s.c.r. 666.

R. v. Noble is reported at [1997] 1 s.c.r. 874.

The judgement of the Court of Appeal for British Columbia in *R. v. Dersch* is reported at (1989), 47 c.c.c. (3d) 503. *R. v. Playford* is reported at (1987), 40 c.c.c. (3d) 142 (Ont. c.a.). The judgement of the Supreme Court of Canada in *R. v. Dersch* is reported at [1990] 2 s.c.r. 1505.

The amendments to the wiretap provisions of the Criminal Code to provide that unlawfully made interceptions were no longer absolutely inadmissible are in s.c. 1993, c. 40.

A.G.N.S. v. MacIntyre is reported at [1982] 1 s.c.r. 175.

Justice William Esson, one of B.C.'s finest judges, and who provided moral support during the controversy discussed in chapter 6, turns up as the champion of the "law and order" argument (with the emphasis on order) in this chapter. That point of view could not have had a more eloquent champion, even if his arguments did not prevail.

Bob Lundy's case is reported in the B.C. Court of Appeal as *337965 British Columbia Ltd. v. Tackama Forest Products Ltd.* (1992), 67 b.c.l.r. (2d) 1.

In this chapter I have referred to accused persons generally as "he" or "him" for the same reason as in chapter 1.

Chapter 9: Linda Macdonald

The passage quoted is from *In the Sleep Room: The Story of the CIA Brainwashing Experiments in Canada* (Toronto: Lester & Orpen Dennys, 1988).

Nurse Peggy Edwards's statement is found in *In the Sleep Room,* 165.

Dr. Cleghorn's statement about "therapy gone wild" is found in the Cooper Report, App. 36, Part III, 88.

The reports of Dr. Grunberg, Dr. McDonald and Dr. Lowy appear in the Cooper Report as appendices.

Orlikow v. U.S.A. is cited as United States District Court for the District of Columbia, Civil

Action No. 80-3163. The evidence of the physicians, Canadian and American, who testified in the American proceedings is found in their depositions in *Orlikow v. U.S.A.* Dr. Omond Solandt, chairman of Canada's Defence Research Board, who had been present at the meeting at the Ritz-Carlton in 1951, made a deposition in the American proceedings.

The procedure for obtaining grants in Cameron's day is set out in the Cooper Report.

Cameron's statement to the American Psychopathological Association in New York City in 1963 is found in *In the Sleep Room*, 189.

The statement that the U.S. had all along claimed that "Cameron may have received much more substantial financial support from Canadian sources than from the [CIA]" is based on a U.S. Embassy Statement dated April 12, 1984.

Morrow v. Royal Victoria Hospital and the Estate of Ewan Cameron was decided at trial on September 18, 1978, in the Quebec Superior Court and in the Quebec Court of Appeal on December 12, 1989, Docket No. 500-09-001247-782 (Quebec C.A.). The Supreme Court of Canada refused leave on July 12, 1990; see [1990] S.C.C.A. No. 54.

It wasn't until amendments to the Federal Court Act came into force in 1992 that Linda Macdonald could have sued both Canada and AMI in the same court, whether in Quebec or B.C.

B.C.'s eugenics legislation was known as the Sexual Sterilization Act, S.B.C. 1933, c. 59, in force from 1933 until 1973; repealed by S.B.C. 1973, c. 79. *Muir v. Alberta* is reported at (1996), 132 D.L.R. (4th) 695.

I have not indicated the outcome of the proceedings brought on behalf of the clients of the Public Guardian and Trustee who are suing B.C. because, at the time of writing, their cases have not yet been heard.

Chapter 10: The Montney Treasure

The case brought by the Beaver band and continued by its successor bands is now known as *Blueberry River Indian Band and Doig River Indian Band v. Canada*, cited as [1995] 4 S.C.R. 344. In the lower courts, it is cited as *Apsassin v. Canada*, [1988] 3 F.C. 20 (Federal Court Trial Division), and [1993] 2 C.N.L.R. 20 (Federal Court of Appeal).

Guerin v. The Queen is cited as [1984] 2 S.C.R. 335.

Canson Enterprises Ltd. v. Boughton & Co. is cited as [1991] 3 S.C.R. 534.

Just v. The Queen is reported at [1989] 2 S.C.R. 1228.

Chapter 11: Ximena and Her Family

The transcripts of the examinations for discovery, from which excerpts are taken, were filed in the B.C. Supreme Court on Vancouver General Hospital's motion to strike the jury, and they were reprinted in the appeal books filed on VGH's application for leave to appeal the jury verdict. The same materials were before Justice Williamson on the application to approve the settlement. When VGH applied to seal the file before Justice Williamson, no request was made to include the transcripts; in any event, the motion was rejected, and all of these materials are public documents.

Athey v. Leonati is reported at [1996] 3 s.c.r. 458.

Justice Williamson's judgement approving the settlement and fees is reported at *Renaerts (Guardian ad litem of) v. Korn* (1998), 64 b.c.l.r. (3d) 131.

Shannon Shobridge's case is reported as *Shobridge v. Thomas* at (1999), 47 c.c.l.t. (2d) 73.

Chapter 12: Duelling Charter Rights

The Supreme Court of Canada's judgement in *BCCT v. TWU* is reported at [2001] 1 s.c.r. 772.

Egan v. Canada is cited as [1995] 2 s.c.r. 513. *Ross v. New Brunswick School District No. 15* is cited as [1996] 1 s.c.r. 825. *Canada v. PSA* is cited as [1993] 1 s.c.r. 941.

Robert H. Bork's book is *Coercing Virtue: The Worldwide Rule of Judges* (Toronto: Vintage Canada, 2002.)

In the excellent legal thriller *Protect and Defend* (New York: A.A. Knopf, 2000), Richard North Patterson, to highlight the intricacies of the law relating to abortion, invented a lengthy question and answer session between appellate judges and lawyers on each side. I thought, why not look at the real thing? Hence, the use in this chapter of the transcript of questions and answers in the Supreme Court.

The discriminatory policies of Bob Jones University, which I referred to in my reply, were considered by the U.S. Supreme Court in *Bob Jones University v. United States* 461 U.S. 574 (1983).

Index